BY ERNEST K. GANN

FATE IS

✵ ✵ ✵

Ernest K. Gann

THE HUNTER

A Touchstone Book
Published by SIMON & SCHUSTER, Inc.
NEW YORK

Copyright © 1961 by Ernest K. Gann
All rights reserved
including the right of reproduction
in whole or in part in any form
First Touchstone Edition, 1986
Published by Simon & Schuster, Inc.
Simon & Schuster Building
Rockefeller Center
1230 Avenue of the Americas
New York, New York 10020
TOUCHSTONE and colophon are
registered trademarks of Simon & Schuster, Inc.
Manufactured in the United States of America

10   9   8   7   6   5   4   3   2   1   Pbk.

Library of Congress Cataloging in Publication Data

Gann, Ernest Kellogg, date.
  Fate is the hunter.

  1. Gann, Ernest Kellogg, 1910-   —Bibliography—
Careers.   2. Novelists, American—20th century—
Biography.   3. Air pilots—United States—
Biography.   I. Title.
PS3513.A56Z465   1984
ISBN 0-671-63603-0 Pbk.

✧

To these old comrades with wings . . .
forever folded.

DeWitt, Albert AA	Sanborn, R. B. EAL
Courtell, F. L. CPT	Jakle, F. C. PAA
Henderson, E. A. CAP	Disoway, J. S. DAL
Meyer, P. F. CAP	Ice, J. R. Inland
Hull, W. J. CAP	Greisbach, G. G. UAL
King, R. H. BNF	Bryan, T. E. AAA
Armstrong, R. P. TWA	Willingham, K. EAL
Bass, W. E. DAL	Porter, G. H. AAA
Sweetland, R. W. NEA	McMains, W. W. TWA
Fortenberry, W. H. PAA	Burnham, J. T. NEA
Burke, C. R. CAP	Ferrier, J. T. UAL
Carmichael, J. G. CAP	Ward, D. M. UAL
Ritner, J. H. TWA	Showman, D. H. BNF
Gandy, J. S. TWA	Hogan, G. W. BNF
Lohr, G. A. RAL	Barron, H. C. AA
Cooke, C. C. UAL	Bliven, L. H. NWA
Gates, W. G. AA	Pitts, V. L. NEA
Tobin, A. R. BNF	Brown, G. H. PAA
Spong, I. R. TWA	Currie, L. F. ASA
Pickering, W. A. BNF	Shirley, R. F. UAL
Cawley, M. R. WAL	McBrien, T. F. EAL
Schanken, W. J. AA	White, D. A. UAL
Jacobson, R. C. WAL	Salisbury, R. D.
Swallow, E. K. UAL	Gahan, M. F. AA
Dowd, J. H. Pioneer	Quinn, J. W. TWA
Penn, L. A. PAA	Wacha, F. F. ASA
Wolderhoff, J. L. US	Wilde, W. B. BNF
Foster, W. G. NAL	Stewart, J. P., Jr. D-C&S
Jewett, G. A. UAL	Stentz, J. W. AA
Tower, H. G. UAL	Springer, E. NAL
Havlena, G. PAA	Graham, J. H. MCA
Podgurski, H. A. CAP	Gander, E. J. NWA
Carter, H. L. Robinson	Powell, J. T. PAA
Wolfe, V. F. NWA	Crockett, W. B., Jr. US
Jones, D. B. NWA	Reid, T. J. AA
Porter, L. L. CAP	Hedden, M. W. UAL
Davis. W J. CAP	Appleby, J. R. UAL

DETWILER, R. F.
LAMPMAN, L. G.   NWA
HAMMITT, H. J.   TWA
LIND, R. C.   NWA
SIMMONS, JULIEN   EAL
MATTHEWS, L. R.   EAL
HUFF, J. A.   NWA
SALTONIS, P. J.   EAL
HOLLOWAY, G. L.   DAL
BRENNER, D. F.   NWA
HASKEW, H. M.   EAL
FOSTER, L. A.   PAA
WARNER, GEORGE   UAL
STARK, HORACE   PCA
POE, K. N.   Avianca
MONSEN, ALF   PAA
PALAU, E. M.   TACA
LEHR, R. B.   AOA
HAM, F. M., JR.   AA
BROWN, F. L.   UAL
EITNER, R. G.   AA
WEBER, R. J.   WAL
MILLER, G. J.   WAL
REPACK, W. T.   PCA
KELLY, R. A.   FAL
FRANCIS, D. B.   AA
CLOUD, C. C.   CPT
BRADY, K. J.   CAP
LEAKE, D. F.   BNF
BASS, L. M.   Ellis
WYGANT, W. P.   PAA
LUNN, W. M.   PAA
HARMS, R. W.   UAL
HALL, L. H.   UAL
ROSSOW, S. T.   UAL
NASH, G. J.   ASA
VOLK, D. P.   D-C&S
GREBER, C. E.   FTL
RICKMAN, L. M.   NWA
ST. CLAIR, C. E.   NAL
DEBLAUW, J., JR.   LAA
CRAWFORD, F. J.   PAA
WEBB, W. B.   TWA
RAY, GEORGE   EAL
SCHEMBER, R. C.   UAL

HENSON, C. M.   PAA
HART, J. H.   PAA
WALLACE, EVERETT   PAA
PITMAN, C. B.   Avianca
KNIGHT, R. S.   EAL
BANEGAS, ANTONIO   TACA
PAULIS, RAYMOND   PCA
KING, J. O.   EAL
BETHEL, A. T.   TWA
BRAND, W. J.   AA
SMITH, G. E.   TWA
JUDD, O. K.   PAA
ELZEY, R. M.   PAA
BROWN, W. C.   PNG
TURBYNE, R. W.   PNG
O'BRIEN, W. E.   PCA
LOEFFER, E. J.   WAL
WILLIAMS, W. C.   TWA
PEDLEY, C. F.   AA
KUSER, R. E.   EAL
FIFE, M. L.   AA
BRIGGS, W. P.   UAL
BRIGMAN, R. M.   AA
STONER, S. E.   AA
BAMBERGER, T. L.   TWA
McCAULEY, J. R.   AA
JONES, H. H.   PCA
BURTON, R. L.   Inland
HODGSON, W. B.   UAL
SOMMERS, A. E.   UAL
ALCOCK, G. A.   PAA
EDWARDS, L. O.   ASA
ALEXANDER, R. S.   PAA
BETTLE, D. O.   EAL
GLENDON, R. J.   RAL
GIN, W. F.   FTL
CREASON, J. J., JR.   TWA
CROTHER, R. F.   WAL
CLARK, R. E.   WAL
TOLER, P. K.   MCA
GROSSARTH, ALBERT   PAA
CREW, C. D.   LAA
BOWNE, F. S.   AOA
LLEWELLYN, F. A.   Robinson
McGINN, W. T.   NWA

HAZELWOOD, C. R. EAL	BUCHER, C. L. CA
JOHNSON, R. L. NWA	BONTRAGER, C. M. UAL
McCOY, R. S. PAA	ANDERSON, L. A. UAL
CONEY, W. E. EAL	RIGGS, R. S. AA
SANDS, R. E. UAL	MONTIJO, J. G. VAT
McMILLEN, E. UAL	LYNN, J. B. C&S
CARSON, S. A. PCA	LUCAS, H. Wyoming Air
WESTERFIELD, W. R. AOA	ZEIER, C. F. C&S
STROUD, JAMES AA	NOE, E. TWA
HOLSTROM, A. E. AAA	MORGAN, H. R. TWA
CARPENTER, B. A. AA	FULLER, R. AA
SNOWDEN, J. P. TWA	DAVIS, A. W. UAL
MAJORS, R. R. AA	WALDRON, J. AA
GARDNER, G. W. PNG	HALLGREN, W. A. AA
DRYER, D. F. AA	SHARPNACK, J. W. UAL
BROWN, D. W. UAL	ROUSCH, C. W. NWA
STILLER, H. A. AA	POTTER, N. W. UAL
MARTIN, K. R. NWA	LUCAS, V. Ludington
GILLETTE, M. A. TWA	HILL, G. W. AA
SHANK, F. S. NWA	BRIGGS, F. W. AA
MINER, W. H. UAL	ANDERT, P. A. UAL
SCOTT, P. T. TWA	BIGELOW, E. UAL
THOMAS, R. E. CAP	WEBB, V. N. UAL
PERRY, J. A., JR. EAL	GALT, J. R. NWA
COOPER, D. I. AA	ONSGARD, ALDEN NWA
BRUNCK, P. S. PAA	JONES, L. E. UAL
PERSON, A. G. PAA	BRANDON, J. L. UAL
KING, G. B. PAA	NORBY, R. B. NWA
CHAMBERLAIN, C. NWA	COPE, ALONZA Marine Airways
SANDGREN, T. UAL	SCROGGINS, L. PCA
DIETZ, S. G. EAL	FEY, HOWARD UAL
DeCESARE, F. PNG	DeCESARO, J. G. UAL
BOGEN, W. L. WAE	BOHNET, F. TWA
ADAMS, J. B. UAL	BICKFORD, L. A. PNG
WALLACE, C. W. TWA	WEST, F., JR. NWA
TERLETZKY, L. PAA	WALKER, M. A. PAA
SHEETS, D. K. PNG	SUPPLE, R. E. PNG
MERRIFIELD, A. S. UAL	SAUCEDA, J. M. PAA
PASCHAL, A. PAA	MAMER, N. B. NWA
UNDERWOOD, S. L. AA	WOLF, J. E. WAF
MARSHALL, G. AA	MOSSMAN, R. C. C&S
LEWIS, H. C. TWA	LIVERMORE, J. T. NWA
HAID, A. A. NWA	KINCANNON, T. N. AA
BLOM, E. W. UAL	BORCHERS, A. PAA
PURSLEY, C. H. PNG	THOMPSON, A. R. UAL

Owens, C. P.   WAE
Bowen, L. L.   BNF
Barron, J. M.   AA
Sherwood, G. C.   WAL
Noyes, D. L.   AA
McMickle, H.   PNG
Dixon, A., Jr.   DAL
Bolton, H. F.   TWA
Tarrant, H. R.   UAL
Neff, H. L.   UAL
Jamieson, W. L.   EAL
Fields, G. T.   AA
Weatherdon, E.   AA
Holbrook, C. M.   AA
Vance, C. K.   UAL
Sandblom, J. V.   CP
Robbins, W. J.   AA
Malick, F. E.   UAL
Kelsey, H. J.   AA
George, H.   TWA
Bowen, J. E.   TWA
Odell, M. T.   AA
Dozier, H.   UAL
Kocher, J. D.   UAL
Render, R. F.   NWA
Kennedy, V. G.   TWA
Christian, B. W.   NWA
Davidson, W. A.   AA
Zundell, W. R.   AA
Weeks, R. E.   TWA
Fidroeff, W. M.   WAL
Amthor, W. E.   TWA
Schwartzback, M. D.   WAL
Wilson, W. C.   AA
Fischer, J. F.   NWA
Barrett, J. C., Jr.   PAA
Cohn, H. G.   WAS
Komdat, A.   EAL
Wieselmayer, O.   PAA
Sederberg, R. S.   RID
Johnson, D. M.   PAA
Gay, R. A.   AA
Hall, S. H.   EAL
Salisbury, H. M.   TWA
O'Connor, J.   TWA

Swander, L. D.   NAL
Witt, P.   NWA
Jameiller, S .E.   CAL
Harker, R. K.   TTA
King, D. J.   NWA
Petry, R.   NWA
Van Cleef, J. G.   NWA
Antonia, S. B.   PCA
Kuhn, K. H.   NWA
Bucklin, F.   NEA
Christian, F. L., Jr.   NWA
Funkhouser, R. W.   TWA
Golden, G.   AA
Josselyn, J.   PCA
Morgan, H. W.   PAA
Shelton, G. E.   TWA
Sumrall, M. B.   PAA
Burks, J. A.   UAL
Clark, F. M.   Continental
Dietze, R. H.   AA
Hunt, E.   AA
Ireland, B. L.   CAL
Mitchell, J. W.   EAL
Vanderbusch, R. E.   NWA
Whidden, R. G.   NEA
Clayton, R. C.   C&S
Cole, D. C.   UAL
Christensen, E. L.   TWA
Winkler, F. X.   TWA
McKiernan, P. S.   TWA
Elder, McLemore   AA
Stehle, W. C.   AA
Nilsen, N. A.   TWA
McLaughlin, J. J.   AA
Holland, G. A.   BNF
Walbridge, D. C.   BNF
Radoll, R. W.   UAL
Grover, R. B.   UAL
Montee, R.   TWA
Zeh, R. W., Jr.   EAL
Williams, B. R.   Ozark
McAfee, W.   PAA
Holsenbeck, W. M.   PAA
Williamson, P. B.   EAL
Venderley, P. W.   AA

STULTZ, H. L.   TWA

JONES, W. H.   UAL

BROUGHTON, D. E.   UAL

BASS, W. E.   DC&S

RYAN, C. W.   NWA

STICKEL, J. J.   NWA

WORTHEN, J. A.   WW

PFAFFINGER, J. J.   NWA

MILLER, G. D.   NWA

BULLIS, R. L.   PAA

DYJAK, R. J.   NWA

GILL, D. N.   TWA

INMAN, R. R.   TWA

KROEGER, J. H.   PAA

OBRI, N. F.   PAA

SMOOT, C. H.   BNF

WATKINS, E. C.   AA

CHARLETON, H. T.   AA

DALEY, B. H.   TWA

HART, J. F.   NWA

INMAN, W. B.   EAL

LAMB, C. S.   UAL

PICKUP, C. V.   EAL

WASIL, N. A.   TWA

BATES, C. F.   NWA

CHILDRESS, R. K.   TWA

DACE, F. E.   WAL

THOMAS, L. E.   EAL

FORTNER, W. F.   EAL

OLSON, K. S.   NWA

RHEW, J. N.   C&S

PROEBSTLE, R.   NWA

HENDRICK, A. G., JR.   PAA

POPE, F.   TWA

SPRINGER, E.   NAL

HAMMOND, R. G.   BNF

JONES, H. H.   PCA

RAY, G.   EAL

SCOTT, P. C.   UAL

SWAIN, W.   AA

JEBERJAHN, F.   AA

MILLER, B. D.   AA

RALEY, R. J.   NWA

WAGAR, G. K.   UAL

FLETCHER, D. B.   TWA

NASH, G. J.   ASA

RINYU, J. J.   EAL

WARD, D. M.   UAL

COX, F.   Ludington

DAVIS, D.   EAL

ROUSCH, C. W.   NWA

WARNER, G.   UAL

JOB, H.   AA

Their fortune was not so good as mine.

E.K.G.

✻

CONTENTS

✷

"I'll teach you how to escape death.

. . . there is a raven in the eastern sea which is called Yitai ("dull-head"). This dull-head cannot fly very high and seems very stupid. It hops only a short distance and nestles close with others of its kind. In going forward, it dare not lead, and in going back, it dare not lag behind. At the time of feeding, it takes what is left over by the other birds. Therefore, the ranks of this bird are never depleted and nobody can do them any harm. A tree with a straight trunk is the first to be chopped down. A well with sweet water is the first to be drawn dry."

—TAIKUNG JEN, in a conversation with Confucius

✾

PREFACE

THIS IS NOT *a war story—and yet it is. Any tale in which the protagonists are so seriously threatened they may lose their lives demands an enemy capable of destruction.*

The difference between what is told here and familiar war is that the designated adversary always remains inhuman, frequently marches in mystery, and rarely takes prisoners. Furthermore, armistice is inconceivable and so is complete victory for either side.

This war continues as you read these words and must prevail so long as man insists on striving for progress.

None of the warriors here involved were forced into battle, a circumstance which removes a certain amount of ugliness and the saddening, hopeless sense of futility normally created when the soldiery is impressed. Here the human combatants have engaged themselves willingly, knowing full well that their blood might stain the field.

Therefore this is the only kind of war which might be considered inspiring.

With new fronts constantly exposed, it becomes increasingly doubtful that this war will become any less adamant. Like other wars, it began in a small way and in the very beginning there were few casualties.

As it would be with any war, the entire conflict cannot be covered in a single book. Therefore, only a single front is described here and a mere fragment of that front presented. This is not a matter of choice but of knowledge, since the author's engagements occurred as a member of a single unit, and it would be presumptuous to include the complicated and equally sanguinary activities of other groups. I know little of military aviation, and even less of experimental flying, which is perhaps the most inspiring and yet fateful of all. These divisions deserve their own written testimony.

Whether living or dead, most of the men in this book are called by their true names. Their characters and activities are also as truly re-created as my abilities allow. A very few individuals have been labeled with false names in a deliberate effort to confuse any reader who might be so misguided as to accept my occasional opinions for indisputable truths simply because they are set down on a printed page. No one save the author will ever know which names serve as a disguise.

Insofar as one mind can reveal a vast and extraordinarily complex endeavor, all the facts and events described are true. I have attempted to tone down rather than color, realizing that time has a way of exaggerating both the good and evil in our memories.

I regret that portions of this book appear as a personal memoir. Yet a completely objective viewpoint is impossible in anything except purely documentary history, especially when the teller happened to be an active participant. On this faltering excuse I ask forgiveness of those who might have seen the same men and events through different eyes.

Any one of a number of men could have told of this same era. Sloniger and Boyd, McCabe, Bledsoe, Robinson, Nelson and Smith, and many of the others are sensitive, articulate men. Yet they were, and some of them still are, too busy making war and history to write of it—a curious relation since all of them were exactly so engaged long before I came upon the scene.

Fortunately, I was not obliged to rely entirely upon the tricky concoctions of memory to prepare this book. No span of time is so carefully documented as the working hours and minutes of a professional pilot. The facts are firmly recorded in fine-lined logbooks, and to the initiated, the bald, uninspiring figures can easily be revived into actuality.

It must appear from following these pages that the pilots were solely responsible for the near miracle we know as air transportation. They would be the first to deny this distortion of the truth. But quantitative analysis of credit belongs in formal history and not in a fleeting series of observations which merely intend to create a sensation of being there. The men who drove the spikes on the transcontinental railroad were just as important to the final effort as the Indian scout who preceded them. It is simply human that we prefer to read and write about the Indian scout. And any examination of fate's nefarious or beneficial doings is better seen through those constantly exposed to both forces.

Many airline people, both as individuals and in groups, find no place in this book. Mechanics who have alternately broiled in equatorial suns and frozen their skins in the arctic are woefully neglected. Engineers who have schemed and wrought pure wonders of ingenuity are even slandered on occasion. Radio men, meteorologists, dispatchers, navigators, and a multitude of associated craftsmen receive little or no attention.

I apologize. The large majority of these people are as devoted to their work as any pilot. On several occasions they contributed to the saving of my own life, which only compounds my miserable ingratitude.

Yet their mental and spiritual habitat is the earth. The physical adventure of this particular war and the individualistic temper of the Indian scout are more likely to be found in the air—which is why this book, in the main, remains aloft.

E.K.G.

FATE IS THE HUNTER

THE TIP OF
THE ARROW

✸

**AN UNDESIRED RENDEZVOUS
IN THE NIGHT**

THE NIGHT is sinister. There are no stars to enliven it. This air mass has not changed its shape or moved so much as fifty miles in a week, and so there is only stagnation and staleness—near suffocation when we pass through occasional dank tendrils of cloud. This sky is exhausted, having given to the earth below nearly all that it can. It should be shoved along by younger air and pushed out over the Atlantic Ocean so that the process of rejuvenation can begin.

As we pass between layers of cloud the sensation of flight, even the notion of purposeful existence, is lost. We are suspended, yet to all appearances we are without motion. We lie inert within the mass, only a trifle larger than one of its perished molecules.

Here aloft, there is a distinct odor to this summer night, a fetid, musty smell which often precedes or accompanies lightning and which the ignorant sometimes call ozone. There does not seem to be any better designation.

Yet there is not even a hint of lightning. There is a dead void and that is all. It would be better if there were something to relate to something else and so provide a focus for the mind.

Beattie, who sits on my right, is aware of my dissatisfaction. I know that he shares it because of the tentative, almost exploratory way he fingers the control wheel. There are other indications of his sympathy. His tie is pulled away from his collar, the collar is unbuttoned, and even in the faint light from the instruments I can see that his uniform shirt is soaked beneath the arms. His rather prominent lips are held slightly apart, as if to form a question, but he has been silent a long time. Minute rivulets of perspiration glisten along the side of his forehead. The rivulets meet where the earphones press against his flesh and form larger tributaries which finally join along the line of his chin and slide downward to his collar. Even his dim reflection in the window beyond him looks frowsy, a condition which heat alone could never bring about, for Beattie is an extraordinarily fastidious man.

Yet now I can smell him and I am quite certain he can smell me.

I reach into that special cupboard of the mind where airmen store potential troubles and find it empty. Then how, without a word passing between us, should Beattie also sense that all is not as it might be? We are, by long test and tradition, not given to imaginary fears.

I lean forward until my face is against the windshield, actually depressing the end of my nose like a child peering into an aquarium. My cupped hands shield off the cockpit lights. I stare into the night, now ahead where there is nothing, now above where there is nothing, and finally down where I search almost wistfully for a familiar light. We are quite in the clear, yet there is no visible feature in the night from which I can obtain the slightest satisfaction.

I retreat slowly from my deserted aquarium, still vaguely disturbed. Why should I have bothered to investigate beyond the windshield? With an overcast above and below I could not honestly have expected anything but disappointment.

For a time I stare at the ceiling of the cockpit which curves only a foot or so above my head. There, at least, everything is familiar. I know the printed figures on the placards by heart. I can, without fumbling, reach surely for each switch, button, and knob. I can do it with my eyes closed. I know the diamond design sewn into the green leather which is supposed to insulate the ceiling against cold and noise and which does neither. If you spend over two thousand hours in the same little room, a room smaller than a prisoner in solitary confinement could tolerate, and if in spite of its cramped area you like the room and devote your entire career to mastering its peculiarities, then you must know that room and everything within it as certainly as a miser knows his hoard. For two thousand hours is a long time.

Although I realize there is no logic in the movement, I reach upward and flip the landing-light switches. The gesture is involuntary, as if in my childish restlessness I must toy with something —or perhaps it is a more basic urge, a longing for more light. Instantly, two illuminated spears stab forward into the night.

Beattie turns his head slowly, with owl-like deliberation. He stares at me and then squints resentfully at the sudden brilliance beyond the windshield. In cockpits very few things are done without reason. If you wish to ascertain the proper functioning of a reciprocating engine you do not, under ordinary circumstances, turn on the landing lights and regard the engine as you might a wounded beast of burden. At best the lights could reveal little more than the outline of the nacelle, the engine cowling, and the great translucent medallion of the whirling propeller. The place to inquire after the health of an engine is on the panel ahead of our knees. There, instruments connected with its vitals report exactly on its sickness or well-being. They rarely lie.

Beattie is waiting for an explanation. Now his lips are compressed and the ends forced downward in disapproval. His large brown eyes are eloquent with censure, as if he were saying, "Now, Captain, those lights are for spotting the earth on landing, or observing the formation of wing ice in the wintertime, or for signaling other aircraft. The designers did not place them in this ship for your amusement or as a convenient diversion for your idle hands."

Beattie, who is much the better educated of us, can say such things in that way. His dignity is innate. Without any apparent intent, he can sometimes make you feel the fool. Now he contains himself, which is another proof of his intelligence, for he is still flying below the salt. He is not exactly mortal. Existing in a sort of purgatory, he waits with all the patience he can muster for the day when he will no longer be a co-pilot. Until then he must mind his manners, ever balancing the obedient against the obsequious, salving his pride and temper only in his most hidden thoughts. For a number of reasons, not the least of which is his eventual promotion to a captaincy, he must observe the code of master and apprentice. The rules are fixed and catholic. I am, in *all* eventualities, supposed to know more than he does, a theory we both secretly recognize as preposterous.

Now, still blinking at the light, his eyes accuse me of being thirty, of being already encrusted with aerial verdigris, and therefore on the verge of senility. Encased in the new and still shining armor of his eagerness, he has not yet known a sufficiency of weariness and fear to fake boredom successfully.

So he merely smiles, and in my opinion there is too much understanding in his eyes.

"Pyrotechnics," I say, and rather sheepishly flick off the lights. A pause while his lips work thoughtfully. "Ah, yes. . . ."

Then a long silence except for the monotonous snoring of the engines. During this silence I am convinced that Beattie's façade of confidence also has a new crack in it. Somewhere, somehow, *something* in this night is askew.

Thus, wrapped in suspicion for which there is no apparent cause, we proceed through the darkness. Our speed, in comparison with modern aircraft, is that of oxen. The indicator, quivering slightly, reads one hundred and seventy miles an hour. We can achieve this only because we happen to be flying a new ship not yet subjected to the inevitable series of rough landings, each one of which will ever so slightly destroy its aerodynamic efficiency. Nor has our company enjoyed either the time or the money to add various technical contrivances which protrude from the fuselage and contribute their minute share to speed reduction. Our load is also light, which is normal rather than otherwise. Behind us, in the dimly lighted cabin, there are eleven passengers and one stewardess to attend them. In our estimation some conspirator on the ground has been wonderfully cunning and persuasive. For it must have required a touch of witchery to lure eleven people on the same airplane bound from Buffalo toward the complex of New York City. The vast majority of the public shares our understanding that one hundred and seventy miles per hour is sufficient to terminate the life span instantly.

We are being paid to avoid hazard, but there are still many unexplored crevasses in our reservoir of knowledge. Our zeal for air transport is always soured when we so easily reflect on failures involving certain late comrades, who proved in the final analysis to be, like ourselves, only the tip of the arrow. We are obliged to recognize our possible epitaph—His end was abrupt.

These thoughts of actual disaster are, paradoxically, the prime favorite conversational meat in any cockpit. Each, as it occurs, is analyzed, argued, disputed, and distorted with such lugubrious fascination that it is some wonder any of us continue to venture aloft. We become businessmen discussing the bankruptcy of a recognized firm, and the only factor which rescues these conversations from outrageous morbidity is the purely clinical nature of the dialogue. Consequently those who so recently flew without fortune are characterized as symbols even though they may have been well known to us. They, as symbols, did this or that or failed to do this or that, or this almost incredible difficulty arose unavoidably, and they were not able to combat it. Charity in such conversations is standard form. Only very rarely will a pilot expose his own bowl of fortune cookies to the possibility of air decay and be tempted into blurting out what is sometimes the undeniable truth. It is a brave man who would conclude such a conversation with the opinion that the subject calamity was entirely old Joe's fault and if he had placed more faith in his head and less in the seat of his pants, he would be alive today.

Over Wilkes-Barre there is a break in the lower cloud deck. A small cluster of lights sparkles on a ragged oblong of black velvet. Staring down at this penurious collection of jewels, I become content. At least they are something. And my headphones provide additional relief to the monotony. Now the soprano whine sent out from the range station below changes in character. The volume increases very suddenly. There is an even quicker fading away as we pass through the cone of silence, and then the tone begins once more. Beattie, who has actually been adjusting the volume on our radio, turns his hand over and points at the floor with his thumb. I nod sagaciously, for I must always maintain the illusion —that I know what must happen and when it must happen. I cannot admit that a good commander is one who is lucky enough to have his intuitions coincide with the sequence of events.

By grasping a wire at my side in just the right fashion, I contrive to whip the microphone from its leather holster. It flies across my chest and I catch it neatly in mid-air. The gesture is sheer display, the cheap trick-tossing of an acrobat's handkerchief before he stands on tiptoe and dives from his perch. There are many ways of reaching for a microphone, all of them individualistic and expressive of the man. Certain pilots employ a calculated series of marionettelike jerks which is intended to demonstrate the apex of efficiency; others, even more pompous, favor a deliberate, diamond-in-the rough style which must be followed by a matching solemnity of voice. There are even those who make a bold pretense of fumbling for the instrument, as if they were uncertain of its precise location. They are quite capable of abandoning this fancy when in trouble and are seeking comfort from the ground. My affectation is of the hoyden variety, followed by a self-conscious clearing of the throat.

"New York from Flight Five . . ."

I recognize the answering voice in my earphones although I have never seen the man. For some obscure reason I have always pictured him as bald-headed and unloved by his wife.

"Over Wilkes-Barre at seventeen. Seven thousand . . . between layers. Estimating La Guardia at fifty."

The neglected husband repeats my words and, without pausing, recites our clearance to proceed and land. His intonations are unusually sad and I wonder if perhaps he has a stomach-ache. When the ritual is done and I have repeated our flight number, I deposit the microphone in its socket without histrionics. They return again when I flex my fingers and place them on the control wheel. I wiggle it ever so slightly, the signal for Beattie that now I, the captain, will take over physically as well as spiritually, and from the abundance of my knowledge and the almost superhuman quality of my skill will safely bring this flight to earth.

There is, in my being, a familiar anticipation of a task well completed. I am no longer at odds with the night. I am the craftsman cleaning up his bench, the proprietor storing his wares. Soon I shall put on my coat with its brass buttons and gold-plated wings over the left breast, and the two somewhat tarnished gold stripes on each sleeve, and become the workman returning home. I am, in this peculiarly delicious moment before descent, complete as only a skilled artisan can be when he is able to stand back from his work and regard its near-end happily. We are not lost, the engines are functioning perfectly, the air is smooth, and though here the clouds still obscure the earth, the weather in New York is good. I am filled with the strutting honesty of usefulness and I am young enough to be proud.

My thinking is almost entirely mechanical. I am only vaguely aware that in spite of unctuous advertising claims, the element about me is not natural to mankind. Like the depths of the sea, the atmosphere allows us minor degrees of penetration and easily reveals its basic structure. But there are certain secrets both elements hold in reserve, and it is not too farfetched to suppose that only the dead have ever truly discovered them.

Even so, these obscurities are frequently glimpsed by living intruders. It is then that a man may quickly discover his mental reliability and learn, to his chagrin, that when caught out of his natural boundaries, his mind may become as tricky as a gambler's involved in a dice game operated by strangers. There is a point, ever varying and always frivolous in appearance, when diligently acquired scientific understanding is suddenly blinded and the medieval mind returns to dominate. This mixture of the mystical and factual produces quick confusion followed by a needling sense of peril. This moment of realization and discovery is verbally identified as luck, or fate to the more elegant. Whatever the label, it presupposes a firm belief in powers supernatural. Therefore, partly in shame and partly in hopeless lack of understanding, the factor of luck is officially ignored among those engaged in any endeavor dependent upon science and machinery. Those charged with the success of the enterprise *must* ignore luck—or they will soon go crazy.

Unfortunately, pilots of any experience whatever are forced to bear with this painful division in their thinking and develop a tolerance for it—or *they* would go crazy. It is a considerable tribute to their general stability that so few of them have.

An airplane crashes. There is a most thorough investigation. Experts analyze every particle, every torn remnant of the machine and what is left of those within it. Every pertinent device of science is employed in reconstructing the incident and searching for the cause. Sometimes the investigators wait for weeks until the weather is exactly the same as it was during the crash. They fly exactly the same route in exactly the same kind of airplane and they go to elaborate trouble trying to duplicate the thinking of the pilot, who can no longer communicate his thinking. Often at considerable risk to themselves, the investigators attempt what have been reported as the final tragic maneuvers of the crashed airplane. And sometimes they discover a truth which they can explain in the hard, clear terms of mechanical science. They must never, regardless of their discoveries, write off a crash as simply a case of bad luck. They must never, for fear of official ridicule, admit other than to themselves, which they all do, that some totally unrecognizable genie has once again unbuttoned his pants and urinated on the pillar of science.

As on this summer night at precisely nine-twenty-six, at precisely five thousand and fifty feet, at precisely one hundred and seventy-one miles per hour. The chief participants are easily identified as Beattie and myself. Both airmen possess Airline Transport ratings numbered 42453 and 36631 respectively. Both men are fully qualified on the equipment and route—see chief pilot's report of recent date. Company and government physical examinations, also of recent date. Eyes 20-20 or better; pulse before and after reclining, satisfactory. Schneider test of both men, 18, the highest possible. Outside influences which might lead to emotional disturbances—none. Condition of aircraft and engine satisfactory. Records show no history of major mechanical or structural deficiencies or repairs. Last routine check, date of incident. Signed off in logbook by company crew chief Buffalo with confirming signature attached thereto. Weather good. Visibility approximately twenty miles. Position reports checked against flight plan and found routine. Proper Air Traffic Control clearance received from New York shortly after reporting over Wilkes-Barre. Witnesses. Farmer located approximately on airway claims he observed subject flight first blink landing lights and then . . .

Beattie reaches to the floor beside his seat and takes up the logbook. It is two pieces of metal hinged together and painted a dark blue, with the number of the aircraft stenciled on the outside. The forms are inside. It is the uninspiring duty of every co-pilot to complete these forms. Some do so begrudgingly; others approach the task with the grubby exactitude of postal clerks writing a money order. Our pay is calculated from the times recorded in these logbooks, and the formula for computation is so absurdly involved that a mistake of only a few minutes can result in the loss of several dollars. Therefore all pilots take an inordinate interest in the time figures, whereas if the flight is routine they hardly notice those recording engine temperatures, pressures, and fuel consumed.

Beattie turns up the small spotlight behind his head and focuses it on the logbook. He sighs audibly and begins to fill in the vacant squares with symbols and numerals.

I can feel the passengers moving about in the cabin, almost count their individual trips to the washroom in the tail. They have been looking at their watches and know we must soon be on the ground. Their movements come to me through the adjustments required on the stabilizer. I am obliged to move the wheel, controlling it frequently, and thus counterbalancing their weight. The stewardess will come forward in a few minutes. Her name is Katherine and she will smell better than we do and she will ask how soon we are going to land. When she is told, she will stand for a moment in the darkness between the baggage and mail bins and adjust her girdle. Then she will return to the cabin. Or because Beattie is a bachelor, she may linger without explanation.

I reach into my left-hand shirt pocket and take out a celluloid disk about the size of a small saucer. Actually it is a slide rule by means of which I can quickly calculate the time required to descend from five thousand feet to approach altitude at New York. I can easily compute the time in my head. The slide rule is merely habit, and a good one, for it is always a reminder that the days of happy guesswork are gone.

Our altitude is still five thousand and fifty feet. The time now: nine-twenty-eight.

Two things displease me. The extra fifty feet above five thousand is sloppy flying and there is too much light in the cockpit.

I glance at Beattie, then ask him to turn down his light. As he complies, my eyes return to the flight instruments and my hand caresses the stabilizer wheel. I rotate it forward an inch or so, then pull back the two red-topped throttles a like amount. At once a subtle change occurs within the cockpit. The constant muffled roar of our slip stream takes on a more urgent tone. The rate-of-climb needle sags. The air speed increases to one hundred and eighty and the altimeter starts its slow unwinding. For the moment both Beattie and myself are entirely absorbed in the instruments, for their silent passing of information has a remarkable, nearly hypnotic way of capturing any pilot's eyes. The momentary result is an unblinking stare, as if we would question their honesty for the ten-thousandth time. This is as it should be. When things are going well, as now, our faces are those of men in harmony with the exactness of machinery. We are attentive, yet lulled by the security so gently transmitted from the luminous dials and needles. We are the masters in sure command of all those mechanical contrivances which comprise the unit of this one flying machine. We do not trouble our sense of authority in brooding on those rare enough occasions when we were more the frightened servants than the masters; when the machine rebelled with the instruments to rob us of all dignity and make us feel like the sorcerer's apprentice.

The altimeter needle indicates precisely five thousand feet. We have lost only the sloppy fifty feet, and I hold the exact five thousand for perhaps thirty seconds while my eyes travel upward to the windshield glass. This trifling hesitation before continuing the descent is not to rest my eyes. It is only because my seat is somewhat too far back. Now my sole desire is to adjust it according to long-established personal taste, thereby innocently deceiving myself that from such a particular position of the seat, and from no other, can I make a good and proper landing.

I bend down, seeking the lever which controls the fore and aft movements of the seat. I ease the seat forward one notch and hear the lever click. As I straighten, Beattie snaps the metal logbook closed with a gesture of finality.

My hand seeks the stabilizer wheel again. My eyes alternate between the rate-of-climb needle and the black windshield. A few seconds pass. Beattie is preoccupied with stuffing a pencil into his shirt pocket. He also looks ahead, but not in anticipation of seeing anything—facing the windshield is simply the most easy and natural position. There is just enough light within the cockpit to reflect faintly Beattie's image in the glass. Compelled only by his scrupulous regard for personal appearance, he bends forward and starts to adjust his tie. This humble gesture is almost the very last the human body identified as Beattie will ever be called upon to make.

For his next movement is a parting of the lips, followed by a horrible, inarticulate sucking sound, audible even above the engines. His actual cry of instantaneous shock is still unfinished when my own attention is drawn to the windshield. My every sense is appalled. There is not time-space for true fear to build, but the primeval urges are instantly uncovered. My stunned brain demands a challenging scream yet I am unable to make any sound. My body, along with my soul, has stopped dead, severed of all vitality within.

My hands freeze on the control wheel. In the blackness ahead there is a sudden, hideous apparition; the mass is no more than a thickening of the night, but it supports a green wing-tip light and, just below it, two flickering tongues of engine exhaust flame.

The whole frightful assembly slides swiftly across our field of vision. It is so close it seems I could reach out and touch it. It is too late for any reaction. Almost before our minds can appreciate its significance, the spectacle is gone from ahead. Beattie, his face pressed against the glass, follows its disappearance off to our right. His whole body swivels quickly with its ghostly progress.

The entire drama begins and ends in two seconds. Beattie and I are sole members of the audience, for it is obvious that those in the other airplane never saw us. Yet, except for a miraculous separation of no more than fifty feet, they would also be quite dead. Only a new audience on the ground would have heard the explosion. And watched the descent of two bundles of flaming metal.

It is over. The peril was instantly there and then almost as instantly not there. We peeped behind the curtain, saw what some dead men have seen, and survived with it engraved forever on our memories.

Now we are not even afraid. That will come when there is time for contemplation. I have not moved, nor is there even a quickening in my breathing.

Slowly Beattie turns in his seat and our eyes meet. A smile touches the corner of his mouth, but it is a melancholy smile and for the moment it seems the perfect comment on what had been our utter helplessness. Those fifty additional sloppy feet held only a few minutes previously—so insignificant then—are now revealed as the pinion of our lives. To have maintained those fifty feet one second more would have matched our altitude exactly with the stranger's. Then who chose the moment to descend? Why just then? It was certainly not our own premeditated decision.

I pick up the microphone slowly, my movements now devoid of flourish.

"New York from Flight Five . . ."

"Go ahead Flight Five."

"Have you any reported traffic?" I want desperately to accuse him—any handy victim will do until I can vent my fury on Air Traffic Control. Yet even as I wait I realize they cannot be aware of every outlaw ship in the sky. The reply is a foregone conclusion or we would have been warned.

"No reported traffic. . . . Five."

"Okay. Five."

I replace the microphone carefully and fumble in my pants pocket for a cigarette. When I bring it out, the package is squashed. They are always squashed, which they would not be if I ever learned to carry them elsewhere. In such poor thoughts my mind seeks momentary refuge, convincing itself, or trying to, that what I have just seen really was not seen. I should much prefer the innocence of our passengers, who almost performed the interesting feat of instantly perishing while in the act of combing their hair or dabbing a drop of perfume behind an ear.

Since the choked, half-born sounds which were more plaintive than defiant, Beattie and I have not had any audible exchange. Lighting my cigarette with a hand that has no good reason to be so steady, I prospect through several things I might say to my companion in fortune.

Tradition calls for me to be outwardly calm and collected, which is not overly difficult, doubtless because the actual exposure to imminent death was of such short duration. Peace within is not so easily re-established. That one second's difference, its selection, the reason for it, must haunt the rest of my living days whatever their number. Years may pass before I shall relive that instant, but it must come to me again and again, always jeering at logic, always mysterious and incomprehensible. Why should that second of time have been given to Beattie and myself and to our eleven passengers, whoever they might be, and to Katherine the stewardess? I can only assume that the occupants of the outlaw plane were not deliberately bent upon a combination of suicide and mass murder. They too were spared by a particle of time.

And then, what of the uneasiness Beattie and I had both known before the near catastrophe? There had been no basis for it, yet it would not be denied. Strangely, now that the moment has passed, the feeling no longer persists.

To my personal God I mutter two words of gratitude. My thank you is given almost begrudgingly, for it is still extremely difficult to appreciate our salvation. I can only think that the moment was an evil one, and so long as the issue does not constitute a mere reprieve, I am content to believe it must be good.

After a decent time, as if he is reluctant to break the silence between us, Beattie asks for a cigarette.

"I didn't know you smoked."

"I don't. I just think I might like to try one . . . now."

☼

I

THE INNOCENTS

☼

AND OF THE FACTS OF AERIAL LIFE

IN THE beginning many of us were scientific bar-
barians. We had neither the need nor the opportunity
for technical culture. The interior of a cloud was a muggy and
unpleasant place. We knew only that to penetrate cloud for any
extended period of time was inviting trouble we were ill equipped
to meet. Though we had long delighted in playing about the edges
of cumulous battlements, we stayed on the ground when we could
not see. Night flying was also a limited indulgence, if only because

the fields from which we operated were the most humble in every respect and nothing about them, including the inevitable high-tension wires, was ever illuminated.

Thus, unlearned, credulous, and bewildered, certain of us emerged from the lower strata of aerial society. We had not been trained by the army or the navy and consequently occupied a social position roughly equivalent to that of a Hindu untouchable. Many of us still had that unremovable grime beneath our fingernails which could only have come from working on our own engines.

Our chief item of costume in this strange new world was the familiar, much-faded and much-loved leather jacket. We clung to them pathetically, for they were the last tangible evidence of a more carefree life. Our natural pride did not cover the fact that we were the most uncouth neophytes. Many of us still moved our lips as we plowed through the books and brochures designed to raise us higher in our chosen profession.

We are in a cheerless classroom. In the adjoining hangar a mechanic is pounding on a piece of metal. A man named Lester frowns upon our bumpkin manners. His open disapproval is repeated in the dour face of McIntosh, who serves as his assistant inquisitor.

Lester is a man whose face is not his own but a hodgepodge repair job which at least complements his patched-up body. Only a few years before, he was taking off from Rochester in a Stinson "A," a ship which had three engines, one in the center. Somehow he caught a wing tip on the snowbank which paralleled the runway. The Stinson cartwheeled. When the debris was finally torn away Lester was an integral part of it; so much so that it was nearly impossible to separate his vitals from the still-smoking center engine. It was said that every major bone in his body was fractured in one fashion or another and that his chances for survival in any form more interesting than a vegetable were nil.

The experts did not count upon Lester's magnificent courage and determination. He survived, if not truly to fly again, then to teach others the refinements demanded of an airline pilot.

We stand huddled together as Lester appraises us with his soul-chilling blue eyes. To please him is important, for it means eventual confirmation in our new positions. To fail means a certain return to the wilderness and the semistarvation of itinerant flying. Hence we are nearly terrified of this man who appears so frail as to seem almost translucent. And he soon proves not of the sort to soothe our fears.

Staring at us one by one, he paces the classroom like a great long-legged bird, wounded in body and grievously offended in spirit. His long thin hands pinch frequently at his broken nose. His voice is high pitched, almost a whine, as he calls the roll. He pronounces each name with open distaste, as if he has just bitten into a rotten persimmon.

"Gay, Lippincott, Sisto, Watkins, Mood, McGuire, Owen, Charleton, Carter . . ."

We confirm our presence solemnly, each of us unable to resist imitating the nervous monotone of the man before. McIntosh, gloomy-eyed, his thoughts impenetrable, lurks near the large aerial map on the wall. He puffs gently on an enormous pipe and, ignoring us completely, seems rapt in a streak of mud along one of his shoes.

Lester moves into the pale January light from the window, and the collection of freckles spotting his face and neck suddenly takes on a brilliant hue, emphasizing the parchmentlike texture of his skin. He begins by setting us very firmly in our places.

"You are supposed to know how to fly or you would not be here. You will now learn to fly all over again. *Our* way. I have examined your logbooks. They contain some interesting and clever lies. If you are lucky and work a good solid eighteen hours a day in this school, it is barely possible that a few of you may succeed in actually going out on the line—that is, if the company is still in such desperate need of pilots that it will hire anybody who wears wings in his lapel and walks slowly past the front door.

"However—" he sighs—"mine is not to reason why. Just remember, you were hired on a ninety-day probation clause. To begin with, you are going to know every damn . . ."

The lecture on our shortcomings and the penances to be assigned continues for the better part of the morning. The requirements seem overwhelming. In six weeks we must pass severe examinations in air mass analysis, instrument flight, radio, hydraulics, maintenance, company procedures, routes, manuals, forms, flight planning, and air traffic control. Not only the company but a government inspector will check our final grades.

Lester drones on, pausing only occasionally to crack the knuckles of his talonlike fingers. I study the others, curious about my fellow unwashed who have come from flying fields all over the land. They are strangers still, and I wonder if their natural cocksureness, without which they could never have survived to reach this room, is being as thoroughly squashed as my own.

With Gay I am the most familiar. We share a room in the cheap, musty hotel where we are supposed to live and study during the period of our incubation. He is younger than I am, of dark complexion, very handsome, and most generous with his magical smile. He has come from a small field in Tennessee where he instructed and on Sundays flew passengers for a dollar a ride.

Lippincott is immensely eager. His alertness is almost offensive, and it is already apparent that he will have little difficulty in mastering the engineering aspects which Lester has emphasized so much, to my own despair.

Sisto, a hoarse-voiced *enfant terrible* from somewhere in California, seems defiant, even bold enough to prod Lester with questions.

I have spoken to Owen only as we gathered, and I was then astounded at the basso-profundo voice emerging from so slight a young man.

Mood and McGuire have also come up from the South, and the contrast between them is a measure of the group. For absolutely no reason, I have already taken a dislike to Mood and I am certain he regards me with equal antipathy. McGuire, however, endeared himself at once by confessing both homesickness for the sight of a Carolina mule and claiming his head is composed almost entirely of bone and therefore a poor receptacle for all that Lester demands. His face now, as he listens to Lester, is so chiseled in honest planes of concentration it would please the most finicky sculptor. I have learned only that hitherto he was mostly engaged in crop dusting—a chancy way to earn a living with wings.

Carter, large and red-faced, is propped audaciously and yet aloof against the back wall of the classroom. I do not know where he calls home, if indeed he has any in the usual sense. He must be a much-traveled man, for just beneath his shirt cuffs, encircling both wrists with intricate design, are the beginnings of what must be vast and elaborate tattoos. I am very impressed with anyone who can so absolutely disregard convention.

Charleton is a silent enigma, not having spoken so much as a word to any of us since first meeting. His face is kindly, although his eyes lack sparkle. His hair is prematurely gray and he seems very tired.

Peterson is a thin and hungry-looking man, slow-spoken and droll, and thus already much valued as a companion. Now straddling a bench, he looks like the reincarnation of Ichabod Crane.

Watkins is near him, sprawling in his seat as if even Lester could never alert him. He is very tall and in his debonair manner seems to patronize the gaunt figure pacing before him. He drums softly on a large silver belt buckle. He has a fine head of hair, blond, curly, and carefully groomed. Were his teeth better he would be an exceptionally beautiful man.

It is not in my power to know the ultimate destinies of these new companions. Certainly I cannot perceive or even imagine that three of them will be totally abandoned by fortune, six will several times experience incredible fondling and protection by whatever fates dispense them, and even the indestructible Lester will one day succumb in such a prosaic affair that it would seem his doom had been merely postponed.

Within a week it becomes obvious that our path to advancement will be strewn with thorns. Lester proves to be a devil, with a genius for probing his pitchfork into our most tender regions. His remarks are scalding as he becomes better acquainted with our individual faults. They become the more wounding because they are so frequently true.

I am a favorite target since I am an idiot at hydraulics. I cannot seem to comprehend the innumerable relief valves or the exact function of each pump and line, much less draw the whole intricate labyrinth from memory as I am supposed to do. My private excuse is that the hydraulic system of an airplane is a mechanic's business and that if the landing gear or the flaps—which the hydraulic system controls—refuse to go up or down, then there is nothing I can do to effect repairs while actually flying.

I am equally thickheaded in the matter of engine theory and maintenance, perhaps because those engines previously responsible for supporting me aloft were of extremely simple design. They either ran or did not run; there was no compromise. In the latter situation you landed in the nearest corn patch. In spite of Lester's insistence that a pilot should be thoroughly acquainted with the complexity of a Wright engine, I have difficulty visualizing myself climbing out on the wing and performing any beneficial repairs while still in flight. There were to come certain times when I devoutly wished it were possible.

Lester's caustic and brutally frank dictum becomes for us a standard flowing in the wind. "I do not care if you kill yourselves, but the company will care very much if you kill any of our passengers. We need their business. Since once you are in the air there is no practical way of separating you from our customers, you will completely master the meaning of flight safety or you will never go near the line."

Such businesslike thinking is not too easily assimilated by some of us who have been more inclined to regard an airplane as a basically joyous instrument. When skillfully rolled, slipped, spun, and dived, a plane could provide endless delight if not a bountiful income. For us there was still enough glamour left in flying to relegate all monetary considerations far to the background. We did not begin to fly because we might make more money with an airplane than we might have if otherwise employed.

We are, almost without exception, in love. It is more than love at this stage; we are each bewitched, gripped solidly in a passion few other callings could generate. Unconsciously or consciously, depending upon our individual courage for acknowledgment, we are slaves to the art of flying.

There is already ample proof that this love is not a passing infatuation or merely a steppingstone to be endured until time brings another opportunity. The wedding is permanent. Many of us are barely able to afford shelter and three full meals a day; indeed, some are existing on borrowed money, or have sold their planes or whatever they possessed in order to manage through this training period. Yet we should each have been completely uninterested if the company had offered other employment.

Separation of the dedicated from the merely hopeful has been a crafty affair performed mostly by the line's chief pilots. They are braced with a fixed set of standards from which, in self-protection, they rarely deviate. They are hard, suspicious men, navigating uncomfortably between what is a frankly commercial enterprise and a group of fractious, often temperamental zealots. And since it is also their lot to be the first to inform a pilot's wife that she is now a widow, they do what they can to see within an applicant. They try to picture him a few years hence, when he may find himself beset with troubles aloft. How will he behave in sole command, when a quick decision or even a sudden movement can make the difference between safety and tragedy? Yet the chief pilots do not look for heroes. They much prefer a certain intangible stability, which in moments of crisis is often found among the more irascible and reckless.

While Lester berates and McIntosh humiliates, we are separated into groups of three and allowed occasional relief from their porcupine society. Four times a week we are permitted to lie with our bride and actually fly an airplane. It is mostly a serious reunion, although when unobserved we still manage minor caprices such as vertical banks, sideslip approaches, and so-called cowboy take-offs. These energetics are not accomplished in an airliner, for we have thus far only been allowed to stroll through one. Instead, we are provided with a single-engine cabin plane in which we are supposed to perform, in actuality, lessons learned in the classroom. As medical students work over a cadaver, we have assigned problems to complete, each pilot taking over in rotation.

Though accompanied by others who impatiently await their turn, a student pilot striving to master the technique of instrument flight and radio orientation may well be the loneliest man in the world. If his problem is ill performed the results are so painfully obvious that no combination of excuses can serve to forgive him.

"God may forgive you," Lester is fond of snarling, "but I won't."

In practice flights a single mistake is allowed to breed further mistakes, as it must do in reality. All but the final sum is realized. Even so, the notion of disaster, what would or could have happened, lingers; and the chastened pilot will not be so lonely again until some dreadful time a few years hence when the scenery and the situation are real and he may learn to pray hurriedly.

For weeks we follow the same routine. In the mornings we struggle with hydraulics, weather analysis, and paper problems flown in the Link Trainer. To the uninitiated this machine can rival the Chinese water torture. It is a box set on a pedestal and cleverly designed to resemble a real airplane. On the inside the deception is quite complete, even to the sound of slip stream and engines. All of the usual controls and instruments are duplicated within the cockpit, and once under way the sensation of actual flight becomes so genuine that it is often a surprise to open the top of the box and discover you are in the same locality.

The device is master-minded by an instructor who sits at a special control table. He can make the student's flight an ordeal. Godlike, he can create head winds, tail winds, cross winds, rough air, fire, engine, and radio failure. He can, if he is feeling sadistic, combine several of these curses at the same time. McIntosh, our usual instructor, is ever partial to such fiendish manipulations. When the flight is done and the student emerges sweating and utterly shaken in confidence, he will blandly point out that reality may one day treat him with even less consideration.

Some of us soon learn to hate McIntosh. Only much later will we recognize that his persecution is well intended and thoughtfully designed to harden us for what is true and inevitable.

While McIntosh appears easy enough with Lippincott and Watkins, who are more inclined toward engineering and mathematics, he is near despair with Gay, McGuire, and myself. His views on our potentialities as airline pilots are merciless and without subtlety. We are charlatans, flying clods, vastly overreaching our native capabilities. We belong back in some converted pasture, our empty heads adorned with helmet and goggles, our thoughts untroubled with the complications of bisectors, time-turns, localizer beams, and power graphs. Our temperaments are better suited to pure barnstorming or the happy-go-lucky, pseudo-romantic existence of a flying circus.

McIntosh does not know how he tempts us. For a return to such a familiar environment would now be so comforting. Still awkward and unconvinced when we cannot see, we reflect all too often upon the peculiarly sensual delight found only in open-cockpit flight. We remember summer evenings when the air was smooth, the deep satisfaction in a steep sideslip down to a field of soft green grass, the wings of a biplane slow-rolling around the dawn horizon, the thrumming of flying wires in a dive through a break in the clouds, and the strangely pleasant odor of wood and shellacked fabric, of which our airplanes were made. All that is gone now. Like sailing-ship men, what we have left has already begun to disappear forever.

A shrewd observer would know that our troubles in the school are circumstantial and therefore meaningless. We are students, but not boys. We already know what it is like to be responsible for the lives of others; indeed, few men suffer and fret like an itinerant instructor watching a student make his first solo flight. We simply cannot, as yet, conceive of the heavy responsibility to which we pretend. McIntosh's efforts to sober our thinking only expose our tempers and reveal a shameful lack of discipline.

Even so, a change falls gradually upon all of us. The early anxieties and raw-edged nerves have disappeared by the time our afternoon flights are flown over an earth which is also changing. The snow of the winter, which always makes the fields and villages below appear like perfectly executed scale models, is gone. Now from aloft the fields seem dead and unyielding, yet every patch of forest and the lands bordering the muddy streams are gently touched with a seemingly weightless powder of green.

In the beginning of spring we are more certain of ourselves, and even Lester occasionally manages to maneuver his broken features into what could pass for a smile. Gay talks of marrying a girl from his home town once he is firmly established on the line. Lippincott, more effervescent than ever, waits impatiently for his actual assignment to one of the several possible bases. He is the star of our group and will doubtless be first to leave. Watkins still plays the clown occasionally, but his trickery is more intricate and assured. He delights in baiting the funereal McIntosh with such welcome diversions as pretending to have a fire in the Link Trainer. He reminds us that there is such a thing as laughter. McGuire seldom mentions his mythical, though much-loved mule.

Sisto, as incorrigible as ever, his roguish mind constantly alert to every possible advantage, has discovered the factor of seniority. He is distressed that so few of us seem to appreciate its importance. We are uncomplicated innocents in love with our work and totally preoccupied with finding a place on the line. It never enters our heads that a simple number can send us flying over lands we have never heard of, leave us to languish in boredom, or even chop off our lives just as they have truly begun to flourish.

All airline pilots are subject to the high cock-o-lorum of seniority, whether they like it or not. The system was established to banish favoritism and to provide some basis for assignment of bases, routes, flights, and pay. Its great fault, as in any seniority system, is the absolutely necessary premise that all men are equal in ability. The dullard and the genius must both live with the ostrich philosophy that one man can fly as skillfully as another. No one, of course, maintains this to be a truth. But the seniority system must ever persist if only because it is a protection of the weak, who are everywhere in the greatest number.

The ambush of evils crying seniority is always lurking near any man who must live with the system. It can make little, half-fearful automatons of men who, in their own milieu, might have the fire for greatness.

We are not yet aware of this. In our eyes the line pilots stand very close to heroes. Sloniger flew with Lindbergh. Coates won a medal for bringing a blazing ship to earth without harm to any of his passengers or crew. Cutrell was a pioneer in blind-landing experiments. Vine and McCabe flew the mail in open cockpits, as did DeWitt, Kent, and Hughen. Bittner was a part of Gates's famous flying circus. We cannot wait to serve such men as co-pilots.

By the time the green froth of the trees below has become a solid coverlet and the hardness is gone from the sky, we are considered ready for assignment to the line.

"Now that you are about out of my hair," Lester says, to his usual accompaniment of cracking knuckles, "I wish you luck. So much for sentiment." He purses his lips together until they are nearly invisible, and there follows another series of cracklings which sounds like a man building a small fire.

"Just do what your captains say in the air and stay out of trouble on the ground. This combination will keep you alive and also eating."

We do not depart from the school in a body. We dribble away singly and in pairs as the various bases express need of new pilots. Gay is sent to Memphis, which delights him. We will not see each other for over two years and then under the most peculiar circumstances. And after that meeting—never again. Mood is sent to Nashville, and I am happy for him since our original antagonism has suddenly reversed itself and we have become fast friends. I will one day hear his voice aloft very far from this place, plaintive but still courageous under the most frightening conditions. Watkins, handsomer than ever in his new uniform, is sent off to Boston. We are destined to survive several adventures together—except his very last.

McGuire remains in Chicago. In the curiously shy handshake of our parting there is no suggestion that our fortunes will be intertwined and lead to a situation in which McGuire's luck will very nearly collapse entirely.

Owen is assigned to Newark, and Carter to one of the southern bases. He growls a farewell and, with his new uniform cap tilted rakishly, lumbers off, already thumbing his nose at petty interference with his aims. He will one day prove himself a very brave man, hugely sentimental if not always discreet. Charleton, sadeyed and quiet as ever, is sent to Cleveland, a prosaic enough beginning for his heroic end.

I am also sent to Newark. Shortly after arrival, I am given the seniority number 267. Mood in Nashville is given 268, and Gay in Memphis captures 260. The differences we consider inconsequential, for our positions are so far down the list that we feel we could never achieve a captaincy in our lifetimes.

Thus we separate, our spirits as bright and untarnished as the one and one half stripes of gold braid on our uniforms. We are too old to have formed the youthful friendships of schoolboys, yet we are bound forever by the unbreakable numbers.

☼

II

A NOVITIATE

☼

**TANGLED AND STUMBLING IN THE ROBES
OF HIS ORDER**

O NE OF the special crosses borne by chief pilots is the
introduction of new co-pilots to the equipment
they will be assigned to fly. The process is uneasy labor for both
men and occasionally takes on the character of an unrehearsed
wrestling match.

On the unlikely theory that his future captain will suffer a heart
attack, be struck blind or otherwise incapacitated, the co-pilot is
required to perform three landings and three take-offs before he

actually flies the line. There are, of course, no passengers aboard during this always interesting experiment.

The chief pilot at Newark is the legendary McCabe, noted for his ability to handle rotten weather and recalcitrant men. He regards my spurious air of confidence with a pair of disenchanted eyes set in a face which should be surrounded by the helmet of a Roman centurion. Even his heavy jowls fail to conceal a remarkably determined chin, and his body construction is brother to a block of cement.

I am not prepared for the gorilla growl in his voice, nor can I as yet understand that his forbidding manner is deliberately assumed to protect a vast, butter-soft kindness of heart. Exhaling cigarette smoke through his nostrils with the force of an angry dragon, he announces that he will personally check me on the DC-2 type airplane while he will leave the DC-3 to Boyd, his assistant.

I follow him meekly through the operations office with its clicking teletypes, down the stairs to the hangar, and out to the cinder ramp where a ship is waiting.

It is a radiant, gusty morning, and while McCabe hefts his bulk through the cabin door I stand looking at the aircraft, trying in vain to remember all the theoretical lore which I was supposed to have absorbed in school. The effort is discouraging. I am like a fumbling groom who has lost the ring. Not having the wit to imitate McCabe's easy entry through the door, I clamber after him, winding up inside, quite significantly, on my hands and knees.

The only characteristic all airliners share is that upon proper urging they are normally capable of leaving the earth's surface. Otherwise, the various types, regardless of their natural origin, are as individual as breeds of animals. The Stinson A, which so abused poor Lester, is thought of as wanting a firm hand or it can quickly prove more treacherous than an unfanged cobra. The type is being retired and no one is sorry to see them molting behind the hangar. In contrast, the DC-3 is an amiable cow, grazing placidly in the higher pasture lands, marvelously forgiving of the most clumsy pilot. Its immediate predecessor, the DC-2, is not such a docile

beast although from a distance the unknowing can easily mistake
one for the other. It is the professional pilot's bounden duty to
know the idiosyncrasies of each type, for he must spend a large
proportion of his active career exploiting its qualities and compensating for its faults. These secrets cannot be discovered in a
ground school.

Dropping into the left-hand cockpit seat with a satisfied grunt,
McCabe says, "You'll learn to love this airplane . . . and you'll
also learn to hate it."

I am really not listening. I am just trying to settle in my own
seat and fasten my safety belt with as little fumbling as possible.
Accustomed to much smaller ships, I cannot imagine how I am
ever going to manage a decent landing when, even in a stationary
position, we are so far from the ground.

McCabe has either not noticed my inattention, or, by continuing
his monologue, hopes to set me at ease.

"You'll freeze up here in the wintertime, but you'll also find her
the greatest ice carrier ever built. . . ."

As I have never seen real ice on an airplane, this compliment
fails to arouse any special enthusiasm in me. I am entirely preoccupied with trying to sort out a hopeless tangle of seat belt, headphone wires, and seat adjustment levers.

"Ever drive a three-horse team that wants to go back to the
barn?" McCabe shakes his jowls in appreciation of his homily,
which he must have pronounced a hundred times before.

"No, sir."

I instantly regret the "sir." It has succeeded only in arching one
of McCabe's eyebrows suspiciously. I sense he would be considerably more impressed if I would only stop squirming and fiddling
nervously with everything about me and announce myself ready
for business.

"You won't have any trouble in the air. She flies sweetly enough.
But a DC-2 on the ground has ideas of her own. The braking
system is a left-over from the Wright brothers and you'll find them
hell to taxi in a strong cross wind. Such as we have this morning."

He snorts defiantly at the instrument panel, as if he dares the ship to come alive and misbehave.

"Never get the idea you know how to land a DC-2. You may make fifty perfect landings and the fifty-first will humble you for weeks afterward. These are stiff-legged brutes and once they start bounding you'd better shove the nose down hard or you'll continue the gallop until you fall off on a wing or run clear out of field. When we start bouncing this morning, *don't* let's try to see who's the strongest. I already have enough twisted vertebrae in my back."

I assure McCabe of my devout wish to co-operate. I find it hard to believe that my instinct for self-preservation could become so numbed that I would struggle for control against such a man.

It is said that many pilots undergo a marked transformation once they are aloft. This is partly fancy, but it is also true that certain changes are open and easily seen. Others are more subtle. Hence it is never safe to judge a professional pilot when he is on the ground. Whether it is the noise, the sense of power and purpose, the hint of risk, or the exalting view cannot be ascertained. But somehow the total environment does unbare hidden truths in men. There is no set rule, yet it always occurs, and the nature of the alteration is, strangely enough, often in the reverse. The loud-mouthed vulgarian slips into shyness. The carefree become moody and meditative; the introspective and taciturn, as if suddenly released, can become garrulous bores.

McCabe, with so many thousands of hours aloft that each flight is like a return to his personal hearth, is now readable evidence of the theory. We are above a deck of broken cloud and he is allowing me a few minutes to feel out the airplane. As I bank and turn, delighted in the belief that, thus far at least, I have done exceedingly well, McCabe sits utterly relaxed, with his hands folded in his lap. He seems to have forgotten me and even the reason for this flight. He is watching a high bank of cirrus clouds spread over Philadelphia to the south, and his expression is that of a man contemplating a favorite painting. The very deep blue of the sky is exactly repeated in his eyes, and in reverie his face has lost all of its hardness. Yet I am certain that if anyone were rash enough to accuse him of some emotion faintly resembling love he would, in wild embarrassment, cut such fancy thinking to pieces with the most stringent and profane denials. His protest must only prove his self-deception, for now it is obvious that this man who reacts like a bear disturbed in hibernation is content and wonderfully at peace. I am grateful for the change in his condition. He may not snap off my arm when I shortly must ruin his serenity.

By some miracle my first landing is a passable success. And I am, with only occasional assistance from McCabe, able to taxi the DC-2 in a fairly straight line. My confidence mounts rapidly and I murmur a word of gratitude to a clubfooted pilot whose true name was, of all names, Goodspeed. He had long ago, in the course of a barnstorming tour, allowed me a full day of take-offs and landings in his tri-motored Ford. Now McCabe is visibly pleased, and as we prepare for the second take-off I even venture to whistle in what I believe to be a most nonchalant manner.

Yet McCabe's smile is sad and weary. He suggests I beware of easy and casual acquaintances.

"A whore is easy to meet."

The second landing has the men in the control tower reaching for their alarm buttons. In fact, it is not a single landing but an endless series of angry collisions between the airplane and earth, each separated by spasms of engine roar as McCabe tries grimly to terminate the steeplechase. The entire exhibition is a resounding tribute to the plane's manufacturers. Incredibly, the plane is still in one piece when we eventually traverse the entire airport and execute a final, deliriously drunken bounce into the air again.

McCabe is sweating profusely from his repeated efforts to save us from actual calamity. As we climb toward safety he mutters something about his back and the possible depths of the new dents in Newark Airport. I am terribly cold inside, blushing hot in the face, and nearly helpless with chagrin and remorse. The palms of my hands are so wet I cannot manage a good grip on either throttles or control wheel. In a few stunning moments all of the pride and assurance I had mustered and so carefully nurtured for this occasion have been destroyed. I am certain that no other co-pilot anywhere has ever made so many errors in so short a time, and it must certainly follow that McCabe will insist I take up another line of work. I cannot believe that he will thrice suffer me to endanger his life and reputation.

I underestimate the man. As if my wretched performance were the most normal thing in his day, he indicates that I should circle back to the field for another attempt. His only plea, repeated while flexing his arms, is that I will kindly remember this is not a contest of strength between us.

Somehow I manage to wheel the DC-2 around and at least aim it at the field with reasonable accuracy. My feet are actually shuddering on the rudder pedals as I ease back on the throttles and begin the descent. McCabe frequently calls off the air speed, which is, maddeningly, always too fast or too slow. When he drops the flaps, I shove the nose down so violently that our attitude becomes nearly a straight dive. McCabe moans in protest. I haul back on the control wheel. We instantly balloon upward and hang ridiculously in a half stall. I shove the nose down again and repeat the entire sequence of ugly gyrations until we swoop over some telephone wires and wobble down toward the black cinder field.

This time I am determined there will be no more bouncing. I will astonish McCabe with the featherlike touch of our wheels.

As the edge of the field slides beneath the nose, I pull back on the throttles. The engines sputter and backfire. I wait, holding the glide nicely. I do not see McCabe's hands creep forward along his legs until they are only a few inches from the control wheel. He *must* allow me actually to make the landing or the whole session is meaningless—but he too has a strong sense of self-preservation.

I have not reckoned with the powerful psychological aftereffect of the previous landings. Now, suddenly, fear of repeating the debacle dominates my reactions. Earth-shy, I level off a good thirty feet above the swiftly passing cinders. Even McCabe is robbed of time to avert the crisis. The DC-2 hesitates as if bewildered by this giddy height and, abandoning all hope, stops flying instantly. Luckily I have kept the wings level, for the descent is as direct as an elevator's. There is no energy left for bouncing. We hit on all three points with a soul-shattering thump.

I am quite defeated. The sound of the landing is still echoing in my ears as I struggle at least to keep the ship rolling in a straight line. The sound was like a very bad accident in a large hotel kitchen.

"That," says McCabe, massaging his back, "was not a landing. It was an arrival."

My dark thoughts are devoid of excuses. I will save McCabe the trouble of firing me. For the first time since I began flying I resolve to abandon the profession forever.

As we taxi toward the hangar McCabe's only further comment is "Boyd will take you on this afternoon."

Later, obsessed with my failure, I mope about the hangar. I regard the mechanics with envy. They move so surely through their work. They know what they are doing. After a time their cheerful badinage becomes too much for my miserable spirit, and I feel compelled to seek some place where the atmosphere can better match my gloom. They all know each other and I am an unknown. The occasional pairs of pilots passing to their planes nod distantly. I am alone, the new boy in the neighborhood.

A refuge suitable to my bitterness proves impossible to find on a wind-swept airport in spring, even though its black cinder surface is anything but inspiring and the surrounding landscape of marsh and grimy factories is far from beautiful. So I stand for a long time slewing one foot across the cinders, my vicious self-censure relieved only by watching an occasional plane land or take off. Here, refreshed in the wind, I rediscover what I had previously held to be certain truths. I again become aware that no pilot alive can resist watching a plane take off or land. He may pass a motionless airplane without noticing it, but the moment his ears detect the first burst of power from a plane, however distant, he will turn his head regardless of everything else around him and watch it.

He will also rudely break off in the middle of a conversation to watch a plane landing, though there may be a constant flow of them. From observance of such activity he enjoys an abiding satisfaction, as basic and everlasting as that found by a deep-sea sailor on his obligatory pilgrimage to the nearest harbor. Is it not so, then, that if there is fascination there must be devotion and joy? Both ingredients are surely vital to men who would live fully and join any enterprise of great expectation. Therefore it must follow that the power of accomplishment is found in dedication, whether it be in the man who runs a small grocery store or in the scientist who flies to the moon.

Standing on the airfield, sensing the planes still over the horizon and watching others become specks against the sky and eventually vanish, I know that however small and unpromising my own part, I am a part of this and cannot forsake it. The morning's rebuff was temporary. I will do better in the afternoon.

The contrast between Boyd and McCabe proves to be as distinct as the difference in planes.

Boyd is a brisk young man, charged with boundless energy. He is short in stature yet neatly and powerfully put together, as if his body were specifically designed to match the quick facility of his mind. An overlarge pipe, which he nervously lights and relights, seems a fixture in his Irish face. His eyes, set wide apart and wonderfully alive with interest in everything which comes before him, appear genuinely sympathetic when I confess the morning's defeats.

"Don't worry yourself. McCabe doesn't. Now this is an an old lady's airplane."

As if he were actually enjoying himself, Boyd proceeds with my DC-3 education. Laughing, he places a folded blanket on his seat so that his head will be high enough to see beyond the nose. And even before we take off I cannot put down the notion that we have known each other a long time.

The DC-3 is kind to me. Neither my landings nor take-offs are entirely sure, yet the tolerant qualities of the plane itself allow them to be at least safely executed.

My confidence is thus renewed and I am enormously content.

When we are done Boyd informs me that I have been assigned to AM-21, the air-mail designation of the route between Newark and Cleveland. I will fly west in the morning. My captain will be Ross.

I express my pleasure to Boyd and enthuse over the flying characteristics of the DC-3. Then, suddenly wary of his smile, I ask the type of airplane flown on AM-21. Boyd chuckles, then shakes his head so solemnly my worries return.

"All I can say is, poor you."

I manage somehow to control my curiosity and conceal any flagrant display of apprehension until Boyd has left me. Then I make a pilgrimage to the young man I have already learned is soothsayer, sage, and confidant in all affairs pertaining to pilots at Newark. This is Robbins, and his haunt is a paper-laden desk behind the long operations counter. I have been told that he is sympathetic even to the new and humble.

Robbins' job has no counterpart in the operations of an airline. It is his function to schedule the flights of all the pilots based at Newark, which would ordinarily seem a routine accomplishment. Actually, it is an incredibly complicated task requiring a deep appreciation of human nature, oriental patience, discretion and tact, the sharp nose of a super-detective, and, at times, the shrewdness of a Syrian merchant. For all of these virtues, which he possesses in abundance, Robbins is cruelly underpaid.

Even so he is always cheerful, and his pale, melonlike face is unlined in spite of constant harassment.

Robbins knows every pilot on the airline by name, face, and reputation. Those flying out of Newark are his only family. Hence the most intimate details of their lives are seldom secret to him. As an offshoot of his pilot scheduling, Robbins frequently inherits the flight assignment of stewardesses. This is an even more complex affair, yet he carries it off with such care and vigilance that he is often accused of studying the phase of the moon before he sends one of the girls on a strenuous flight.

While the lines cannot do much about nagging wives or financial vexations, they recognize the insidious damage that overflying can do to any pilot's fitness. They insist on a safety margin and limit each man to eighty-five hours per month. It is one of Robbins' responsibilities to see that they fly no more than that. His trials begin with the devious business of seeing that the men on his list fly no *less,* and since even his remarkable clairvoyance cannot predict the weather for a month ahead, he must juggle men, minutes, and hours as if the slightest miscalculation might fuse an explosion.

Now Robbins listens to my own concerns as if they were new to him. Of Boyd's admonition, what of that? Of AM-21? And of Ross? What kind of a man is he?

Robbins stuffs his pencil in its customary place behind his ear and, staring at the ceiling, begins to speak in the vernacular of deepest Flatbush. His recitative, so pat as to sound rehearsed, is gilded with phrases discovered during his attendance at New York University.

"I will cue you," he begins. "You have done well to get yourself up here because I want no trouble from the likes of you. Should you fail to mark down your flight time on that there chart on the wall when you come in from a trip, and so make it easy for me to know what the hell is going on, which is not an easy thing to do, mind you, with a bunch of temperamental, forgetful prima donnas who are so damned anxious to get home to their wives or mistresses they rush out of here without marking their time down so I got to dig up the logbook and find out what really happened —well, just don't forget, that's all. Not unless you want nothing but ugly stewardesses and cold coffee on your flights. Not unless your heartfelt desire is to wind up flying every damn test hop we have so you're going back and forth to the airport like the shuttle in a loom. Remember. That there chart on the wall. Every minute and every hour you fly. And don't put down something different from what your captain puts down because you know as well as I do that's impossible unless you saw the airplane in half. Understood?"

I acknowledge my understanding and express a desire to please everyone. I also point out that thus far he has not had much to say about my original questions.

"As for AM-21, you fly two and a half trips a week, not counting cancellations, and you overnight in Cleveland at a hotel I'm told is a cross between the Garden of Allah and the Salvation Army."

I press him gently for something on Ross.

"A true gentleman, if somewhat difficult to handle. For example, he frequently forgets to record his time on that there sheet on the wall. If he weren't Ross, I would never let him get away with it."

I ask patiently what there is about Ross to so excuse his carelessness.

"I often like to think of Ross as a child of nature. He is a throwback and occasionally a trial to his mother, who is seventy-three years old and bakes the best cakes in the world—a few crumbs of which Ross may toss your way, if he is feeling especially mellow. One thing you can count on. Ross can fly a DC-2 as no other man."

It is customary for pilots to report at the operations office one hour before their scheduled time of flight. In actual practice, only a small proportion of the hour is consumed in work. If the weather is fine the captain spends perhaps five minutes examining the swirls, numerals, and arrows drawn by the meteorologist on his daily map. The presence of a well-regarded and experienced co-pilot is tolerated during these brief sessions, although he is expected to hold his tongue. Except for signing his name to the flight plan when it is done, and the clearance, the captain is then free to grumble at Robbins or dispense charm among the office groundlings, as may suit his mood. He may also employ his self-arranged leisure by greeting other captains bound in or out, and this he may do either affectionately or distantly, according to their respective histories. He will, except in the most unusual circumstance, utterly ignore the co-pilot of the captain to whom he has addressed himself even though the two may be standing side by side. In most captains the technique is so highly developed, so completely without malice or affectation, that only the rare co-pilot suffering from hypersensitivity will take offense. He is, and expects to be, quite invisible. If, by some irregularity, the co-pilot is directly addressed, then he is expected to answer briefly and not pursue the conversation. In time he realizes that whatever he might say goes unheard anyway and the original recognition was merely proof that his superior is not above greeting peasants who know their place. Thus, if a co-pilot desires conversation he speaks to one of his own kind, or sometimes, if the captain has not pre-empted him, to the stewardess.

At best, the co-pilot's time is limited. The captain almost always delegates the preparation of the flight plan to his assistant, a task which requires from fifteen to thirty minutes, according to route, destination, and weather. Once this is accomplished the co-pilot is expected to pick up his kit and go to the airplane itself, where he is supposed to examine its readiness for flight. There he encounters a separate aristocracy and once again is more than likely to be ignored. A group of expert mechanics, who invariably hold any pilot's opinion on matters mechanical in low esteem, have spent considerable energy and time making certain the plane is airworthy. They sign their names and reputation to the logbook and do not appreciate suspicion of their efforts, particularly in the wintertime when their hands are very cold. Therefore, as far as the airplane is concerned, the co-pilot can do little more than check the radio gear and make sure both wings are firmly attached to the fuselage. The remaining part of the hour he spends loading mail and baggage. These duties keep him busy and breathless until his captain arrives, which is rarely more than a few minutes before the passengers.

My first impression of Ross in the operations office was so clouded by external factors that I wondered if I had somehow encountered a Graustarkian officer. I would not have been surprised if he had spread his long arms and burst into song, for it seemed to me that he possessed every characteristic of a musical-comedy hero. About thirty-five years old, he was tall and magnificently proportioned. His complexion was dark, almost swarthy. His manner was alternately gay and seriously intent. I found his solemn mood produced a rather frightening quality in his searching black eyes. When he took my hand on meeting, there was a flicker of a smile, a wince on my part as his powerful grip tightened, and then no further personal contact. He tossed me a pad of flight-plan forms with a gesture better suited to casting alms to the poor and retired to the opposite end of the office, where he engaged in hearty conversation with a captain from Dallas.

And now that I have loaded the luggage and mail aboard, I have only to wait for Ross to join me in the cockpit. Wiping the sweat from my eyes, I lean over the control pedestal and watch for his appearance along the ramp. I can see several pilots moving about in the spring sunlight, and then, unmistakably, Ross. He walks very straight, covering the ground in great strides, yet there is not the slightest suggestion of stiffness in his movements. He is more like a released panther, gliding, very light of foot, each movement, down to the very swing of his arms, beautifully co-ordinated.

Watching his approach, I suddenly realize why it is that even in the office there had been a vague aura of the military about him. And yet he must create his own army, for now it is apparent that his uniform cap is not only worn with a certain distinctive tilt but is of a different cut from the standard. The bill is much shorter, set at a steeper angle, and instead of being the regulation dull leather, it is made of glistening patent leather.[1]

The morning is warm and he carries his uniform coat draped carefully over his heavy flight kit. As he passes beneath me, greeting the mechanics with what almost amounts to a slight bow, I cannot envision him as anything but an anachronism, a swashbuckler complete except for a sword.

I settle at once into the right-hand seat, concerned lest there be a repetition of the crazy entanglement witnessed by McCabe. Therefore I am quite ready when I hear Ross enter the narrow passageway behind me. I turn to watch him hang up his coat in so precise and careful a manner that it is easy to understand how his other articles of apparel present such an immaculate picture. His heavily starched shirt fits his powerful torso as if it were tailored by a master. The crease in his pants is knife sharp. His black ankle boots, of the type preferred by most line pilots, match the sheen of his cap bill.

He removes two pencils and a celluloid computer from his briefcase. These he places in the breast pocket of his shirt and afterward carefully buttons down the flaps. It is as if he were going on parade, though I am the only spectator. Finally he takes a clean pair of leather gloves from the briefcase and snaps the cover shut. Every movement he makes is economical and seems predetermined.

He comes forward, flips the gloves at some imaginary dust on his seat, and then, in spite of his long legs, glides into it with easy grace. Without looking at me, he asks if this is my first flight on the line. I reluctantly admit that such is the case.

"Then we shall see what we shall see. Where did you learn to fly?"

I have been anticipating the question, so invariably the first asked of every co-pilot as to be a ritual. From Ross's entire demeanor I have concluded that he must be army or navy trained and I am distressed at this, for then there is likely to be a haughtiness which can only contribute to my sense of not belonging.

In a suitably modest voice I admit that I learned to fly the hard way. To the knowing, this phrase is rich with implications. It means that while the speaker does not necessarily deserve a bar sinister, he must have been forced to scratch for his aerial skill and consequently may be suspect.

"Good! Your corn pasture was bigger than the one where I learned."

I am immensely cheered. The chances are now excellent that Ross and I will get along, for he too must have once been a simpleton. I will serve him well, not wishing to offend the good fortune which has brought us together.

III

HUMILITY
LEARNED

IN WHICH A MASTER IS TOLERANT

AM-21 is a puny and miserable couplet for the expanse of America it is supposed to designate. It fails utterly to suggest the easygoing beauty of the route in all seasons, its pleasures or its discomforts. Nor can such an insipid formula embrace the remarkable variety of the route, which is enough, without the need of spectacle.

The eastern terminus of the route is now Newark, an unsightly beginning to such a mixture of tranquillity and beauty. Just west of Newark, even before the climb to cruising altitude is completed, the threshold of the Alleghenies rises gently against the horizon.

The first specified landing for any flight embarking on the route is Wilkes-Barre. The airport is laid out upon a flat which stretches between two steep ridges. As a result, the location becomes a drafty tunnel where even a mild wind multiplies upon itself and, contrary to all the laws of nature, moves unpredictably back and forth across the draw rather than flowing with its contour. The strength of any wind is as fickle as its direction, and in the near vicinity of the field itself the downdrafts are notoriously treacherous. Hence the landing at Wilkes-Barre is often passed over by the more conservative pilots. Ross, however, rarely refuses the challenge, though the wind may blow thirty miles an hour directly across the single runway. On this first landing I am too preoccupied with my own simple duties to appreciate his skill and supreme self-confidence.

Once away from Wilkes-Barre, the route, which is actually an ever-changing combination of air space and terrain, veers northward toward upper New York State and Syracuse, the next point of landing. As the Alleghenies drop into minor ridges of the earth and the scars of mining along the hill flanks become obscure, all the land below begins to roll like a gentle sea. The ruggedness vanishes as quickly as it commenced in the east. In the vicinity of Binghamton the strange enchantment and quietly lush beauty of AM-21 begin.

In spring the land below is charged with life. The fields are a soothing green to match the easy configuration of the valleys, and the hillsides are speckled with fat brown cattle. The newly tilled soil in the flats and minor depressions along streams is a rich, warm umber. It blends delicately with the near black-green outlining the shaded roads, which are so pleasantly few and almost deserted.

The light at noon, which is customarily the time of flight transit over this region, is always of a peculiarly mellow quality, as soft and agreeable as the land below. In spring the air is tranquil. The heat of the earth is not yet sufficiently retained, so that as day progresses it will rise from the brown and sink into the green, thus transforming the lower air mass into a rocking ocean of discomfort.

Now, in spring, everything below is sharply etched, and from six thousand feet a farmer sitting on his tractor is as clear-cut as the furrows dribbling out behind him.

The stewardess brings two box lunches to the cockpit. She opens one for Ross and sets it upon his lap. With the same solicitude she might show a wayward dog, she places the other box on the floor for me.

There is no automatic pilot on a DC-2 so I am obliged to fly the ship until Ross has eaten. This is a task I am more than willing to perform since, by maintaining near perfect course and altitude, I may possibly redeem faults which have already created a certain coolness between us. First of all, my arithmetic talent became dulled with excitement, and I made an eleven-minute error in recording our flight time between Newark and Wilkes-Barre. Such an error could represent only stupidity or unforgivable carelessness. Ross's strong sense of exactitude was so insulted that he chose to erase and make the correction himself while I labored to overcome a second mistake.

On arrival in Wilkes-Barre I could not find either the mail or baggage destined for that city. Somehow I became convinced it was stowed near the bottom of the bin instead of on top, where it should have been. There followed an embarrassing delay while I heaved bags and suitcases about the passageway and, sprawling across them, sought in the ill-lighted bin for what should have been so handy. The items were eventually discovered by the ground agent, who had the imagination to look in the tail compartment. Neither he nor Ross took this casually, since the ensuing delay of eight minutes would require them to write explanatory letters to the company.

I did not witness our take-off from Wilkes-Barre in its entirety. Ross, as if bound to demonstrate my true usefulness aboard, nicely managed without my assistance. I was still reloading the baggage bin as we left the ground.

I had just resumed my seat when further trouble occurred. Ross shivered and said he was cold. The drop in temperature was confirmed almost immediately by the stewardess, who came forward long enough to complain of a chill in the cabin. I knew at once that my trials were just beginning, for co-pilots are the janitors of the sky, and it would now become my duty to nurse the heater of a DC-2 back to life.

This contraption is located in the passageway between the cockpit and the cabin. It has brought many co-pilots almost to tears. Others, more combative, have been forcibly restrained from smashing it to bits with the crash ax. The heater consists of a cylindrical-shaped boiler which is somewhat larger than a football. It obtains its heat from the exhaust of the right engine and is festooned with valves, the majority of which are usually stuck fast. The entire assembly has a certain human quality—recalcitrant, self-indulgent, and capricious. Everyone is agreed that it was designed by a maniac barely thwarted in his attempt to create an infernal machine. Captains have been known to cherish co-pilots who can keep a DC-2 heater operating, and others have made life aloft very unhappy for those who cannot.

The diagrams drawn in Lester's school could never illustrate the fiendish personality now knocking and sputtering complaints loud enough to be heard above the sound of the engines. I gingerly turn one of the valves, which, according to my memory, is supposed to lock off the system and permit the addition of water. I wait a moment, dubious, and quite resigned to the possibility of an explosion. The boiler becomes ominously silent. Ross calls from the cockpit, urging me to hurry. He claims he is freezing.

In desperation I bend down until it is possible to examine the glass sight gauge on the boiler. There seems to be an adequate supply of water. Perhaps there is too much? I smack the boiler with my fist; then, after a brief struggle, I resolutely turn a valve near the top of the boiler. The results are instantaneous and spectacular. A jet of steam hisses from some unseen outlet and at once obscures everything within the passageway. Now, thoroughly alarmed, I reach frantically into the seething cloud of vapor and manage to close the valve. Nothing has worked according to the book.

Ross calls me back to the cockpit in a voice vibrant with authority. He waves his hand as a sign for me to sit down and take over the controls. Then, with a great and all-enduring sigh, he strides back to the heater. He is gone only a few minutes before I feel a telltale draft of heat across my ankles.

Ross returns to eat his lunch in silence, although as he munches on his sandwiches I am well aware that he is examining me without enthusiasm. I am therefore astonished when he fails to take over the flying as we approach Syracuse airport. Certainly I must have misunderstood his casual hand wave. It would normally indicate the landing would be mine.

My eyes question, yet he nods his head affirmatively. This, then, will certainly be the end. My past performance with a DC-2 was anything but heartening, and I have never seen Syracuse airport in my life. Ross is either joking or has mistaken me for a more experienced man, which, in view of the morning thus far, is unlikely.

There is no rule or custom to dictate a captain's generosity. He may, if he pleases, never give away a landing or a take-off, both of which are as sweetmeats to any co-pilot. Many co-pilots go for months without touching the controls except when safely at cruising altitude. To refuse Ross's offer now would be unthinkable.

Trying not to dwell upon my adventure with McCabe, I ease the ship down through a thin deck of broken clouds. Ross has apparently lost all interest in our progress. He is thoughtfully chewing on a cooky, cupping his hand beneath it to prevent any possibility of a crumb falling on his trousers.

As we break out beneath the clouds, the airport is just over the nose. My former flying sense returns and I am alert to a multitude of signs and revelations, each important to a good approach and proper landing. An experienced barnstormer desiring to remain whole and also solvent must discipline himself to observe and evaluate considerable information before he attempts a landing on any strange field. He must do this without help from the ground, depending entirely on the lore accumulated by the very early birds. Handed down from veteran to neophyte, it becomes an integral part of his professional stock.

Though we are still three miles away, I instinctively compare the cloud shadows moving across the field with the wind sock on top of the hangar and find that the wind aloft is different from that on the ground. I must allow and compensate for this difference, executing the final turn somewhat sooner and thus permitting the plane to be carried on the invisible wind until it is aligned with the western runway.

The wind is gusting, according to the sock. By the manner in which the tree leaves are whipped and laid back until they glitter in the sunlight, I judge that its force is now close to thirty miles an hour. I must concern myself with those trees. They border the end of the runway, and their cool shade is certain to create vertically descending air, a downdraft not necessarily dangerous if the trees are given sufficient clearance, but a smooth and regular approach is the prelude to a good landing. A good pilot thinks far ahead of his airplane, knowing that his mind may become instantly and terribly crowded if things go wrong.

We descend. A glance at Ross finds him at ease, although I know that he has seen all that I have seen and added to it his familiarity with the field itself.

We pass over the trees at exactly ninety miles an hour. I chop off the power to the engines. The approach has been so proper and satisfying that Ross cannot fail to appreciate my careful planning. And now the final glide is right, a good angle, neither too fast nor too slow, just enough reserve of speed to handle the gusts.

We swoop over the edge of the field and sink gracefully to the runway. I spin the stabilizer crank and ease back on the control yoke. It must be a perfect landing.

My self-satisfaction dies before it is truly born. For once again I have literally flown this airplane straight into the ground. Its resentment is immediate and dramatic. The stiff-legged brute leaps crazily back into its element and proceeds down the runway in a series of ludicrous vaultings. Ross is quick and his hands powerful. He tames the ship in an instant. We roll on smoothly and I wallow in vileness, waiting for Ross to heap ashes on my head.

I am almost disappointed to discover him smiling. And his measured comment only increases my despondency.

"There are two kinds of airplanes—those you fly and those that fly you. With a DC-2 you must have a distinct understanding at the very start as to who is the boss."

My spirit revives slightly during the fifteen minutes required for refueling, unloading, and loading. We again prepare for take-off. The next landing will be Rochester, a mere ninety miles. Reviewing the events of the morning and hopefully applying the law of averages, I cannot imagine how I can commit any more misdemeanors this day.

Ross taxis to the end of the runway, handling the DC-2 as if it were an obedient quarterhorse, despite the increasingly gusting wind.

The landing gear of a DC-2 is retracted and lowered by hydraulic power. Once the landing gear is down a steel pin is inserted just above the retraction lever so that it cannot be moved inadvertently once the ship rests on its wheels. This pin is normally removed just before actual take-off unless both pilots forget about it, in which event there is an embarrassing delay in raising the landing gear. And though the pause may be only a few seconds it can be a very important interval because take-off is a critical time for a DC-2. If one engine should fail just after breaking from the ground, a twin-engined airplane can proceed with relative safety provided it is free of landing-gear drag. If not, there is trouble—very sudden and very serious.

For this reason the landing gear is always retracted soon after safe flying speed is attained. On no account must this moment be anticipated lest, faltering in a semi-stall, the ship sink back to earth. Then, at the very least, the whirling propeller tips will be smashed, which, in turn, must almost certainly result in a crash belly landing, with an excellent possibility of fire.[2]

The signal for pulling the lever and so raising the landing gear is made by the captain, who will smartly raise his hand, palm upward. At the same time he is supposed to command "Gear Up!" in a voice clearly audible above the engines.

Now, as Ross runs up the engines, I remove the safety pin from the gear lever. I watch Ross anxiously. I am pathetically eager to perform my co-pilot's duties quickly and efficiently. As he shoves the throttles forward and we start down the runway, I place my hand ready on the gear lever. I feel the tail lift. I bend down and slightly forward, my eyes fixed on Ross's hand, waiting for the signal. I believe that we already have good speed, but I am watching his hand, not the indicator. His hand moves as if to leave the throttles. Take-off noise level in a DC-2 cockpit is terrific. I am certain Ross has called "Gear Up!" I yank up the gear lever.

"Jesus! Man!"

Ross fights the control wheel, jockeying it desperately.

I glance at the air speed, then out the window. We are hanging in the air, sinking, then hanging again. Ross did *not* give a signal. Anxiety has duped me. I have deliberately pulled the gear out from under him!

The entire ship shudders in agony, a sensation which is transmitted directly to my bowels.

Then, just as suddenly, we are in smooth flight, and the ground falls away. In a magnificent display of flying skill, Ross has safely completed an abortive take-off.

I cannot look at him—yet I must. This has been no minor error which can be erased with the end of a pencil. I have, with my foolish hand, endangered the lives of every soul on this airplane. No matter how innocent in intent, the deed is unforgivable. Sick to the depths of my being, utterly demoralized, I cannot find the simplest words of apology. I would not be displeased if Ross pulled out his mail gun and put a bullet through my offending hand. He would be more than justified. His pride is never to put a scratch on an airplane and I, in one accursed moment, have brought him perilously close to ruin.

As we climb safely over the western hill the tautness leaves Ross's body. He raises a finger to his brow and flicks away invisible sweat. Then he meets my eyes, and the hard muscles about his jaw relax. I can see no anger in his face, not even accusation. Only his breathing, which is still quick, betrays the passing of a crisis. Fear is no stranger to him, and through much involuntary practice he has learned to extinguish it quickly once the torch is removed. He speaks slowly, enunciating each word with such care that the effect is comical, as he intends.

"If you ever do that again, I'll cut you out of my will."

No abuse. No recounting of my crime or its so obvious potentialities. Not the slightest show of resentment. My near despair, brought on by the series of blameworthy incidents ever since I entered Lester's school, somehow melts away. I keep my silence, thinking only that Ross is one of the great persons of the air.

In a moment he waves for me to take over the controls. Then he snatches up the logbook and methodically writes down our time of take off as if nothing unusual had occurred. I envy the steadiness of his hand and am vastly grateful for his sensitivity. Surely he knows that my only self-redemption is in actually flying.

I have yet so very much to learn.

Ross is but one of the captains holding a bid on AM-21. The others thus engaged are Dunn, who can barely squeeze his enormous bulk into a cockpit; Hunt, who is equally big although not so ponderous; Shoff, slight and already somewhat wrinkled in the face despite his youth; and Lewis, habitually stooped and somehow always a trifle forlorn. There is Konz, who was once an oboe player in the Rochester Symphony. There is also Brooks, who is handsomely gray and ever loquacious; Mitchell, paper-thin and as alert as a sandpiper; and Keim, the growling maverick of the lot. All of these men are forthright individuals of much flying experience, and they are thoroughly versed in the special features of the route as well as the idiosyncrasies of the DC-2.

Beyond Syracuse, AM-21 proceeds almost directly west, leaving the lovely Finger Lakes and their higher encompassing hills several miles to the south. The route parallels the Erie Canal as far as Rochester. Here the terrain becomes flatter, permitting flight all the way to Buffalo as low as two thousand feet. The land between

Syracuse and Buffalo is like a gay and harmoniously colored mosaic, and the villages, long ago established to receive the bounty of the canal, are settled in sophisticated peace.

In summer the prevailing westerly winds brush across the yellow grain in the fields, the hedgerows, and the tops of the trees in such a playful manner that the whole region appears to be alive and in rippling motion. In autumn, when the colors turn and become even more jolly, the welcome of the land is almost audible.

West of Buffalo the route follows the gently swerving south shore of Lake Erie. Here too the terrain is remarkably flat, although the oriental splendor of colors is replaced by a nearly solid green. The lake, so like a sea, stretches to the horizon from any altitude less than fifteen thousand feet, and only on the clearest days may the shore of Canada be seen.

AM-21 calls for a landing at Erie, which stands upon the lake shore and which is such a peculiarly uninspiring city from the air that few pilots pay it even the compliment of a downward glance. The route then continues west along the lake shore to Cleveland.

The captains flying AM-21 know much more of the route than its geographical pleasantries. And they are concerned with the sky as well as the land. They know that an east wind flowing across Syracuse in summertime is likely to carry fog along with it and may quickly seal off the airport. They know a way to approach Syracuse from the west without using the radio range leg. In haze or heavy summer rain, they know that in spite of poor visibility it is quite safe to drop down as low as seven hundred feet and follow the eastbound railway tracks until they make a junction with a certain sharp twist in the canal. Then, banking away to the southwest as the hill of Syracuse looms darkly upon their left wing, they follow this mass until it melts away. Now they execute a one-minute left turn, reversing their course to the northwest. Continuing, they descend cautiously until the hill reappears once more on their left. They are now in a flat and narrow valley which leads directly to the end of the northeast runway.

These men know that, in wintertime, icing of consequence is rare along AM-21, and that if it should come they may safely descend to a low cruising altitude and so carry the burden in better style. They know too that radio reception is freakish in all seasons and the eastern leg of the Rochester range should always be regarded with suspicion.

At Rochester they are mindful of ground fog, which is prone to collect very quickly on still summer nights and quite surprise the unwary. Though only a few feet thick and nearly invisible from aloft, it hangs just above the surface and can completely blind a pilot during the last and most important moment of flare-out for landing. And, like Syracuse, Rochester has a special approach most useful in poor visibility when the landing must be accomplished to the north. Then the railroad track is picked up just west of the field and held until a certain marshaling yard is intersected by a parade of high-tension towers. With this combination below, easily visible in snow or rain, the key is in the lock. A turn is made to the north, and the descent begins. By the time the landing gear is put down and final approach speed attained, the end of the desired north runway will appear just over the nose.

Even on fine days Rochester demands alertness because clear weather brings out the small training planes of which Rochester has an uncommon share. They must be watched with the greatest solicitude, for if there is one solid, deep-rooted, ever-present fear known to all airline pilots, it is the hanging sword of midair collision. No other prospect except structural failure, which is so rare as to be virtually ignored, can render a pilot so entirely helpless.[3]

A true route pilot is no more to be surprised by the geographical eccentricities found in his daily work than a mailman plodding his customary rounds. The AM-21 captains know that in wintertime Buffalo can become one of the coldest airports in the world and that reports of blowing snow, which can instantly hide or as suddenly reveal a runway, are almost standard for the season. If radio reception is poor, as it so often is in snow, even the best route captains will sometimes miss lining up with the proper runway and must at the last moment up-gear, shy away, and circle for another try.

AM-21 captains know that farther west Erie can be easily found in the worst visibility and radio conditions, simply by following the lake shore. And they may fly as low as their individual natures permit the disregard of regulations, without fear of hitting anything. AM-21 is not for the automation pilot whose route manual is an ironbound scripture from which even the slightest deviation is sinful. Such pilots do not like the route and its frequent demands for resourceful improvisation; nor does it seem that the route likes them, if the performance record of such occasional experiments is honestly evaluated. The rule sticklers pass over too many fields on AM-21. They cancel too frequently when a safe landing could be made.

Due in part to its special terrain and freakish weather, a certain maxim of flying becomes more apparent on AM-21 than on most other routes. The timid, super-cautious pilot is not necessarily the safest. Coupled with knowledge, a touch of boldness is required, and thus it is that captains on AM-21 have long established both a special pride and a tradition. No one envies their environment and the attendant extremes of heat and cold. The frequent landings and comparatively little night flying mean lower pay and much more work to achieve the same number of hours by the end of the month. Yet, as perverse and contrary as the route itself, the pilots of AM-21 are not easily persuaded to fly any other.

When Gay, Carter, Mood, and the others learn of my assignment, they express pity in various degrees. To them, flying fast and high on longer routes between greater cities, I have been sent into exile. I am a mere grasshopper. The planes are antiques, soon to be retired, the captains notorious taskmasters, and the weather always distressing. They do concede the route offers superb training.

✷

IV

A CAPTAIN

✷

AT WORK

So BEGAN my true apprenticeship. My contemporaries, with whom I might naturally share the trials
of progress, were rarely seen, although occasionally I recognized
their voices reporting position on the radio. They became lost in
the vastness of the line which sprawled across the width of North
America. Their voices echoing from a distant sky reported events
and conditions totally different from what I observed, and it soon
became difficult to remember any of us as we were.

Life aloft was not easy, for Ross proved to be a fierce and dedicated tyrant. His rebukes echoed even in my sleep.

It took Ross nearly a week to decide that something might be done with his clumsy and erring assistant. So prideful a man could not bear the thought of even a minor defeat. A word to McCabe or Boyd and he could easily have traded me in for a better man. That Ross failed to request a change was not due to any relaxation of standards on his part or sudden discovery of a soft spot in his heart. I could not have escaped Ross had I wished. I was a challenge to him. The authorities or the fates—it made no difference who was to blame—had given him a glove in the face. They would presently see, by God, that Ross would triumph as always.

Since his true love was flight, I must first of all learn to imitate and, if possible, equal the master. In Ross's personal world there was no compromise. I began to call him Svengali, a character with whom he was fortunately not acquainted.

Such tenderness as lurked in Ross's being was strictly reserved for his delightful little cake-baking mother. He never again displayed the sensitivity which meant so much to me on the awful occasion of the landing gear. Instead, as the weeks turned into months, he became continuously harder and less forgiving, until the man I thought I had known was at times a stranger. While he was always reticent about his past, he sometimes repeated a litany which was obviously based on truth. He said that he came from the toughest coal-mining town in the United States, which would be Massilon, Ohio. And in that town there was a street which was known to be tougher than any other. "And I," Ross would explain without a trace of modesty, "lived in the last house on that street."

Ross never relented in his instruction, which had the quality of ceaseless pounding, so that frequently at the end of a flight my brain seemed to hang limp between my ears, twisted and bruised. My percentage of mistakes fell away rapidly, a condition which caused those few remaining to stand out even more sharply. Punishment was always quick and sure. An acid tongue-lashing, at which Ross was wonderfully adept, would be followed by a hard blow on my shoulder or whatever other part of my anatomy was convenient. The free-swinging blow served as a sort of punctuation mark to his verbal acrimony. It was always delivered in such a way, however, that it was impossible to take offense although the region might throb for minutes afterward. To return such a blow, even in jest, was out of the question. You did not strike captains—especially Ross.

It was possible for co-pilots to make a discreet request for a change of captain. I would not have done so even if Ross had tormented me far more than he actually did.

These were the reasons:

His absolute trust in himself somehow spread to the man who was his co-pilot. From the beginning his rule and custom remained unvarying. He was one of the few who split landings and take-offs exactly fifty-fifty. This he did regardless of weather conditions or mechanical difficulties. If it was your leg to fly between two cities, and the weather worsened until the final approach at destination was obviously going to be a matter of maybe or maybe not, he did not rob you of opportunity or confidence by suggesting that it would be much better all around if he did the job. You "flew" it. And if an engine ceased to function en route, it was up to you to follow the proper procedure and see that the airplane arrived with a minimum of fuss.

He would, if the situation became obscure, sometimes give advice, but the actual execution was up to the co-pilot. And so, of necessity, the co-pilot who flew with Ross learned. And when each flight was ended, such fortunates walked with a dignity not easily achieved by those who merely kept the books and "rode."

As the spring sky clouded and became muggy and indefinite with haze, Ross's demand for perfection remained a match for the remarkable stiffness of his shirts. He was not satisfied with the allowable fifty feet of difference between chosen cruising altitude and that actually flown. If the flight plan called for five thousand feet, then the needle of the altimeter must stand at precisely five thousand. A variation of even twenty feet either above or below brought forth a searing admonition to sit up and fly right. Rough air was no excuse. Though the needle might flicker back and forth, it must average exactly five thousand. "How else," he would demand, "are you going to be in the habit when some day or some night a few feet *really* count?"

He was equally particular as to the compass course flown. Once the course was established with regard to the wind, three degrees' variation was characterized as "wandering all over the sky."

Ross was even more insistent, although a trifle more forgiving of error, in the physical handling of the airplane when on the ground or near to it. Here the innocent passengers provided a convenient platform from which to launch his best in raillery and humiliation. He reminded you that their nerves were sensitive, their faith in air transport most fragile, and under no circumstances should they know any sensation other than the smoothest movement from boarding to destination.

Although at times his treatment of a DC-2 in the air approached the brutal, Ross had developed a technique of handling the airplane during take-off, landing, and taxiing which was in a class by itself. This was even begrudgingly admitted by other captains. He often chose a triangular patch of grass between the forks of runways, sideslipping smoothly down with the engines cut full back, and setting the wheels precisely on the very tip of the triangle's apex. This he did so expertly that it was frequently impossible to be sure the DC-2 had actually touched earth. Nor would there be any further commotion of thumps and blasting engines. He would allow the landing roll to continue without application of either power or brakes until the final, sensuous result was that the twelve-ton airplane eased to a halt exactly in line with the waiting ramp. Throughout the entire show—and it was nothing other than sheer display—a passenger could have held a brimming cup of coffee in his lap without spilling a drop. There was never any indication of effort or special concentration on Ross's face. At these moments he was the true virtuoso, performing for his own joy, lost in it, and thus quite unaware of his audience.

The rub came in expecting me to match his skill. He teased, bullied, inspired, threatened, and connived until by the full heat of summer it came to pass that I could occasionally please him. He taught me to glide a DC-2 without touching the power from a point one thousand feet above the surface until the wheels softly kissed the grass, and he insisted that such union occur exactly on a preselected spot.

"You may need to land one of these things without engines someday—in a cabbage patch. We'll make sure you can." In true monarchial fashion he frequently used the term *we*.

Ross taught me to taxi this particularly unwieldy airplane at good speed in strong cross winds without uncertain wandering or mighty heaves on the brake system. We had no windshield wipers. So he taught me how to land in heavy rain, how to split my attention between what little could be seen of a runway over the nose, and, leaning back somewhat to avoid a complete drenching, see and adjudge much more through the open window at my side. He delighted in all such situations and managed to pass on his lack of trepidation until I too began to relish the difficult rather than the easy.

Now, in August, the route and particularly the sky above it have begun a change. The etched clarity of vision is gone and the mustard-colored fields are often nearly obliterated by haze. The winds are stagnant and sullen, yet the air is annoyingly potted with a multitude of minor vertical disturbances which sicken the passengers and keep us captives of our seat belts. We sweat in the cockpit, though much of the time we fly with the side windows wide open. The airplanes smell of hot oil and simmering aluminum, disinfectant, feces, leather, and puke. The earphones, dripping with our own moisture, produce a nearly unbearable cacophony of crashes, sounds of frying bacon, whines, wheezes, and crazy explosions, until it is torture to wear them. The stewardesses, short-tempered and reeking of vomit, come forward as often as they can for what is a breath of comparatively fresh air. Pinching their shirt collars to lift and flutter them, they blow down between their bosoms and pray for transfer to another route where the flying will be higher and the air presumably smoother.

When the planes are on the ground they bake in the sunlight

until the heat waves rising from their skin make them wriggle as if alive. To enter them even quietly is an ordeal, and to wrestle baggage and mail around in the narrow compartments is a bit of hell. On take-off we must watch head temperatures carefully for fear of blowing a cylinder. The soft, superheated air rising from the runways offers so little body for our wings that we ascend reluctantly, seeming actually to sag when the wheels break ground and sometimes barely surmounting the oncoming trees. Newark is a stinking vat, staved in smoke and coopered in swamp gas. Even Robbins is morose and out of sorts. Wilkes-Barre bubbles in the same tired air that has lain imprisoned between the ridges for weeks. Syracuse alone is tolerable, but it can only provide momentary and tantalizing relief after the rough flight from either east or west. Rochester is haze-laden, and the control tower difficult to raise because of its feebleness against the abominable radio conditions. Buffalo is noxious with smoke, and the bald location of the airport leaves it smoldering with heat even after night has fallen. Erie should have some relief from the nearby lake, but our landing is always in midafternoon when the irresolute breezes are least effective. Cleveland is one vast plate of parched concrete. These are the dog days of AM-21.

It is also the beginning of the thunderstorm season, and here in the region between the eastern seacoast and Cleveland the storms are surpassed in ferocity only by those truly evil monsters whose lair is farther to the south, between Washington and Memphis. Others of like pugnacity lurk about in the midwestern states; but a thunderstorm is a thunderstorm no matter where encountered, and all of them have the disposition of a Caligula.

Any pilot of sound mind avoids flying through a thunderstorm if he can possibly find a tunnel of escape. Unfortunately, there are times when the fray is unavoidable, and this is particularly so on AM-21, where climbing to a very high altitude is usually out of the question. On certain midsummer afternoons and nights, the route becomes a jungle roaring with resentment at all intruders.

And now, an airport long abandoned for inadequacy has been re-established along the route. This is Albany, and between it and

Newark is to be found an area of thunderstorm activity unmatched anywhere on earth, including the ill-famed west coast of Africa. For here the route follows the Hudson River southward, passing over the Catskill Mountains, where the legendary ghosts of Dutchmen bowl with such abandon. In this region a special combination of terrain, summer heat, and humidity serves to produce spectacular monuments of clouds. Pilots who would much prefer admiring this grandeur from afar frequently refer to such formations as sons-of-bitches. The pilots know they are not to be trifled with, for they can, on occasion, turn the boldest man into a little boy trembling beneath his bed.

It is here, with Ross, that I first witness the anger of God in new dimensions.

We are southbound for Newark at eight thousand feet. The sun is gone, but enough light lingers in the sky to illuminate the purple valley below which embraces the Hudson. In the east the sky is fast losing the violent hue of twilight, and ahead, lying at right angles to our course, is visible confirmation of the weather report received in Albany. From horizon to horizon the southern sky appears supported by a series of castles, battlements, and walls. Through the various indentations a few jagged gashes of the lower sky may still be seen. These are a sickly yellow, and above the highest escarpments the sky fades away rapidly toward the zenith until it becomes a pale blue tinged with black. The very summits of the highest cloud towers, of which there are two most prominent, still catch the escape of the sun and are golden.

I have completed the necessary entries in the logbook and, in spite of the insane crackling in my headphones, believe that I can recognize the easy voice of McGuire reporting the position of his plane over South Bend, westbound for Chicago. I am intrigued with the idea that the sun is doubtless still in his eyes and that he might soon be sipping a beer in a place near the Chicago Airport called "the Snakepit."

I sit far back in my seat, my right foot braced comfortably against the instrument panel, listening to the steady thrumming of the engines, content to reflect that I have at least come a long way since my barnstorming days. Not so long ago, in a rock-fenced field nearby, a young man named Blauvelt stepped away from a sputtering biplane and first sent me into the sky alone.

It is pleasant to think that now my ninety-day probation is safely past and I might reasonably invest in a pair of jodhpur boots like Ross's, and so keep my ankles warm during the coming winter. With concentration I might also acquire that certain swagger which must go with the wearing of such boots. I will break them in very carefully since they are extremely expensive for a co-pilot's purse, and I will try to keep them as well shined as Ross's.

As I stare at the gigantic panorama ahead, my mood attempts to match it and soon becomes so expansive as to ignore all reality. I fancy that I can handle a DC-2 in the air and on the ground as well as, perhaps better than, most men. I am being paid for moments like this as well as for the lesser times, and though my station is humble no man commands me for whom I do not hold the deepest respect. This in itself is certainly a most unusual and agreeable situation.

As we draw closer to the array of clouds ahead and even the minor patches of sky are obscured by overreaching claws of vapor, my musings take a truly heady turn. There is a new rumor that the line is about to purchase ten more airplanes. Applying an airline rule-of-thumb, ten new airplanes will require three crews each. That will be thirty new captains promoted from co-pilot. There are approximately one hundred co-pilots with a number lower than my own. Therefore, assuming the line continues to expand at the rate of ten airplanes per year, why shouldn't I make captain in about three years? What a prospect! Magnanimous in my daydreams, I resolve to treat my co-pilot with the utmost consideration, thus remembering my own uneven days of servitude.

These rich speculations are suddenly interrupted by a new and heavy surging from the engines. Ross has shoved the propeller controls into low pitch and is advancing the throttles. I see that he has put on his gloves and we are climbing to the best ability of the DC-2. He flips the switch which illuminates the seat belt sign and nods his head toward the cabin door.

"Go back. Tell the stewardess to make sure the passengers are really strapped in and haven't just got the belts lying across their legs."

There are only nine passengers. I move down the line of their inquiring eyes in a terrible parade of self-consciousness. Like most pilots, I have already learned to shy away from contact with passengers; their queries are often so penetrating that a straight-forward answer is only reasonable. The results are sometimes more embarrassing than reassuring.

When my message is delivered I start back to the cockpit. A young woman sits near the door. She is peacefully breast-feeding a baby, and, like most men, I am somehow astonished at the dis-covery. I look instantly away. The scene makes me strangely un-comfortable, yet as I resume my seat beside Ross, I cannot put it out of my mind. The young mother was far from beautiful, and still, in her absolute trust, she *was* beautiful. And the trust was in Ross and, to a degree, myself. I discover that it is the kind of faith I would just as soon not think too much about.

Now, looking at Ross, I see him in a new light. The difference is in his face, which has taken on a sternness I have never before ob-served. His entire body seems to gather itself as he squirms down slightly in his seat. He hunches his broad shoulders, holding and then releasing them, a flex of body much like a boxer's stepping from his corner. He lights a cigarette, takes a few puffs, then smashes it into the ash tray at his side.

His eyes are also new to me. Because he is constantly moving his head, searching all about the sky, it is difficult to appraise his thoughts, but his eyes are unusually alert and seeking, as if some-where in the gathering gloom ahead he has detected a physical threat to his well-being. Ross does not bear the spokelike glare wrinkles about his eyes common to so many pilots, but now the flesh there becomes pinched in a half-mischievous smile.

"Call Newark. Get us a clearance for twelve thousand. Ask for their weather while you're at it."

I comply, breathing more frequently than normal between my

requests because we are already at ten thousand feet, an altitude to which my AM-21 service has ill-accustomed me.

The voice from Newark is barely intelligible through the barrage of static in my headphones. It is gibberish orated from the bottom of a barrel, and I can only be certain that the clearance for altitude is granted. Fragments of the Newark weather gurgle through, sounding like the saliva-laden mouthings of an imbecile. "Thunderstorm over . . . heavy rain . . . visi . . . lightning to the . . . wind. . . ."

Nothing more.

Ross nods his head. He has apparently understood where I could not. And he has more important matters on his mind. His entire attention is devoted to the slowly floating scenery beyond the windshield, and his prediction is simple enough. "I think we're going to take a pasting."

We are still some three or four miles from the immense barricade, yet even at this distance the appalling energy contained within the dominant sections of cloud is all too apparent. There is nothing static about these pillars so hugely piled on top of one another. They are in constant motion, not horizontally, as wind might activate them, but appearing to roll about on a series of central axes, each pillar enlarging and twisting upon itself.

As we approach closer, the vaporous appearance proves a complete deception and each roiling protuberance takes on a solid look, like tremendous pus-laden pustules in the moment before eruption. Yet the air is still remarkably smooth, as if the barrier were spreading a carpet of invitation.

Quite suddenly, when we are barely a mile from the nearest tower, all sense of established proportion is reduced to the truth. The effect on my ego is stunning. For it is a value of normal flight that human beings carry aloft their usual visionary sense of relation between themselves and those extraneous objects familiar to their eyes. In an airplane cockpit, whether it be on the ground or in the air, the instrument panel remains the same size, as do the throttle, the controls, the windows, and the wings. Likewise, the accompanying human beings hold their stature. It is a cramped world in itself, but everything within it is quite standard and therefore bearable. All else, beyond the windshield, is so far away as to appear itself diminutive rather than the other way around.

Now, approaching this thunderstorm front, which is neither larger nor smaller than any other common to the season, our comfortable world is lost and no effort can bring it back again until we are either in the clear or cannot see at all. We are suddenly so puny we belong on glass, beneath a powerful microscope. The sensation is shocking, the escape of conceit from our being, instantaneous. How can such infinitesimal creatures presume to trouble the heavens with our mewling hopes and complaints? For here, alongside mightiness, we are nothing.

Our altitude of more than two miles above the earth is less than half that of the most prominent thunderheads. The phalanx forms a solid precipice which tumbles straight down from the edge of our wing tip, gray-black and green in the last light. Great blossoming fists of dirty white churn against each other all the way to its gloomy foundations. Inside the darker areas there are frequent explosions of light, marked simultaneously by savage crashes in our earphones.

Ross sighs heavily and regards the clouds with deep suspicion. He shakes his head sadly in the manner of a man affronted by a sidewalk bully. Here is work, unpleasant work, perhaps even dangerous if the bully gets out of hand, but the struggle is unavoidable.

The more realistic line pilots freely admit that most of the time they are overpaid. It takes a while to discover that this life is somewhat short of paradise. For there is, as in all pursuits of mankind, no true ideal or even near perfection. In airline flying the hitch always comes, and it follows an apparently unshakable cycle of once a year. A pilot may earn his full pay for that year in less than two minutes. At the time of incident he would gladly return the entire amount for the privilege of being elsewhere.

Now it appears that Ross may more than earn his wages this August evening.

He banks the ship steeply and for a time we fly along parallel to the unbroken cliff. And though we are proceeding at normal cruising speed we seem to hang dreamlike and nearly still in the air.

At last a gaping crevasse appears. It is guarded on both sides by vaporous gargoyles projecting from Byzantine towers. Though tortuous, it seems to offer good entrance, yet Ross dismisses it with a glance.

He carries on perhaps a mile until a second chasm appears. This one is darker, though not so confined. He switches on the cockpit lights, turns them up to full bright, and lowers his seat all the way to the floor. I wonder if he knows this is my first encounter with a thunderstorm.

He points to the position of his seat. "I recommend you do the same."

"Why?"

"You will see."

So hunched, our faces below the bottom edge of the windshield and thus somewhat protected, we enter the division.

I am not afraid, but reason that it is perhaps just as well I am not yet a captain.

For a few minutes our flight remains quite peaceful although there are minor bumps which are scattered and uneven, like rocks strewn before the entrance of a cavern. Looking upward from my side window, I can still see the formations which compose this entrance into the mass, and by twisting against my seat belt I can observe a patch of clear sky some ten thousand feet above everything. The fragment is now the color of slate.

Ross's attention remains entirely within the cockpit. He is flying on instruments and has taken up an approximate course for Newark. He is not tense, but very alert. He seems still to be waiting. I wish Ross would stop exploring the sky and get this airplane on the ground in Newark. I need a cool shower to draw away the heat and work of the day, and I am also very hungry.

I almost resent it when Ross suddenly reaches for the throttles and pulls them back. Our speed slows to one hundred and forty miles an hour.

Light rain hisses along the windshield, sounding for a moment like a disturbed nest of snakes. Ross calls for heat to the engine carburetors. I pull back the two red-knobbed levers on the side of the control pedestal and adjust them so that the temperature gauges read properly.

I am so engaged when our small world goes insane. Some preposterous genie turns a fire hose full on the windshield. We are suddenly not in an airplane but a submarine—one that leaks very badly. Water spews through the nose, the windshield scarfing, my side window, the roof. It dribbles down the instrument panel, sopping our pants. But it is the sound that chokes off my half-spoken curse of protest. It is a roaring of water, an angry, bewildering, sense-shattering cascade that completely obliterates every other noise. It is inconceivable that the engines can swallow so much liquid and continue to function. Or that we can maintain flight through the depths of an ocean.

I glance at Ross. He has both hands firmly on the control wheel, but he still seems to be waiting. I have a new and strangely sour taste in my mouth. I am wondering about it when the bottom falls out of everything.

We seem to smash against a solid obstruction. I am instantly weightless, jerked hard against my seat belt. The instrument panel shivers so beneath the shock that for a moment not a dial is readable. My confused eyes seek some reassurance in the turmoil. Ross, please! Bring back stability and reason!

When the instruments settle I am appalled at the altimeter and rate of climb. In spite of Ross's strenuous efforts at the controls, we are going down fifteen hundred feet per minute! The altimeter continues to unwind. Ross! This is not good. I am not afraid, of course, but certain of my glands are misbehaving. And the noise. My brain is pressing down on my eyes. It is difficult to think, see, or hear anything that is reliable.

Ross calls for more power and shoves the propeller controls to full low pitch. There is no familiar howl from the engines. This puny sound cannot dominate the roar of water. Only the instruments show they have responded.

Ross wrestles with the control wheel. He seems unperturbed

though defiant. He rolls the stabilizer wheel back a few turns trying to ease the ship into a climbing attitude. According to our power, we should be ascending at least six hundred feet per minute.

We do not rise an inch. Our descent continues as if the ship were actually in a dive. We are within the grasp of a power far more formidable than the Wright engine company can ever produce.

We continue down, sickeningly, to nearly ten thousand feet.

Then a second collision occurs. Once more the instrument panel dances in its rubber mountings. The dials blur, then shake themselves back into readability. To my amazement we are now going up at fifteen hundred feet per minute. Reversing itself, the altimeter winds back and passes eleven thousand in spite of Ross's shoving the nose down hard. He raises one hand and makes a deliberate gesture toward the cockpit floor. He yells above the pandemonium. "Gear down!"

Has he completely lost his wits? You can't, not even you, Ross, land in mid-air. He repeats the command. Since he obviously means it, I oblige.

Now he literally stands the ship on its nose. We are gear down in a steep dive. It becomes a ludicrous flight attitude when the instruments relay the very definite information that regardless of all efforts, we are still going up.

I soon appreciate the fact that were it not for the gear down and our consequent steeper angle of attack, we would be going up much faster.

As we pass through twelve thousand feet again my uneasy nerves are jolted by a new display. The roar of rain diminishes as suddenly as it came and I am momentarily blinded by an explosion of white fire which seems to occur directly within the cockpit. If Ross had not turned the lights up full bright, the blinding would last much longer. And we receive some protection from the lowered seats. I silently thank him for his foresight and store the trick in my memory.

The lightning continues in a series of flashings each accompanied by a blasting cannonade. I discover very quickly that thunder at the source is not in the least like thunder heard on the ground. There is nothing to provide an echo; hence the detonation is utterly flat in tone. Every salvo pierces straight to the soul. It is a hellish timpano and you wish you were deaf.

I am cold and there is a strange ache in my belly when we approach thirteen thousand feet with the ship still pointed down. Our lateral gyrations now become extremely violent. Tossed beyond its limits, the artificial-horizon instrument "tumbles" and becomes therefore useless. Ross is forced to fly on only turn indicator and air speed, an arduous commitment in such rough air. I prefer not to look back at the wings, even if I could see them. Some things are better unknown.

Our ascent slows and I breathe a sigh of relief which is cut short by a head-on collision with an express train. All previous noise is now insignificant. We are in hail.

I see Ross's lips move in malediction, but I cannot hear his voice. A thousand machine guns are directed upon us and we are in a tin can.

The hail is of short duration—perhaps one minute, or two at the most. The stones are not big enough to dent the ship's skin—by no means an unusual development—but they are sufficiently concentrated to remove the paint from the nose.

The unpleasantness continues for ten minutes. Then, as if the elements had wearied of playing with us, all action ceases. The air smooths as suddenly as it stormed up. We are in heavy cloud, but there are only occasional short spasms of rain. We glide down to proper altitude easily, in seeming silence. After so much noise the engines merely purr.

In my headphones there is still an uncomfortable crashing, but the Newark beam is easily detectable. A voice from our company radio is superimposed upon its reassuring whine, and the words spoken are quite intelligible. The voice is reciting the Newark weather to a plane in the vicinity. "Ceiling four hundred feet, light rain, visibility two miles . . . altimeter twenty-nine ninety."

We set our altimeters accordingly, and Ross calls for a clearance to six thousand feet. When it is received he waves the controls over to me. This is a mild shock, for it is his leg and therefore the instrument approach which the Newark weather demands should be his. I had thought to coast the rest of the way.

"We will now learn what it's like to make a real approach without an artificial horizon—" he points at the offending instrument which swims uselessly behind its glass face—"and a few other things which may someday be worth our knowing."

I cannot understand Ross. He is obliged to give nothing away—much less an instrument approach which could be difficult. He is not paid to be a mentor and can, in the doing, only risk his peace of mind.

"Now concentrate. Forget I'm here."

Forgetting Ross is like a slave forgetting the galley master even when he tips back his head, closes his eyes, and seems to be napping. Yet in no other way can he appear to set me on my own.

A radio range is simply a broadcasting station which transmits a monotonous though valuable program. The signals form four spokes, each narrowing and intersecting at the hub, like an ancient wheel. The spoke selected depends, of course, upon the direction from which the plane approaches the station. I pick up and begin to bracket the north spoke of the Newark range.

Basking in Ross's confidence, I move the controls gently. I am only too aware that his closed eyes are a sham. He is also listening and, like a temporarily relaxed conductor, waiting for a sour note.

When I have at length settled down to a steady course, Ross opens his eyes and presses a button on the instrument panel three times. In a moment the stewardess appears in the shadows behind us. He asks her about the passengers and how they fared through the storm.

"One man was sick. But they're laughing about it now."

Without turning from my work, I ask about the baby. I don't really care, but somehow I must know if it bawled.

"No. It slept all the way through. Anyone you know?"

"No. I was just curious."

But I brood on this for several minutes and can not decide why it seems so wonderful.

We pass over the cone of silence at Newark with very little meandering, once I have pinned down the leg. The initial descent is pleasing too—steady and nicely timed—and I can reasonably hope the rest of the performance will go as smoothly.

Then as we start the turn for the final descent, which is always the most complicated and demanding in accuracy, Ross takes a box of matches from his pocket and lights them one after another just under my nose. I gasp a protest. I am heavily engaged in trying to hold course and altitude exactly according to the book. This is the real thing. It counts.

"What the hell are you doing?"

I am bewildered. If I were not so extremely busy I would brush the flame away. It is difficult to see the instruments beyond the flame, and Ross holds it just close enough to make breathing difficult.

I blow out the match. Ross at once lights another. I am fifty feet too low, the compass is swinging in a direction it should not, and my speed is falling off.

"Steady . . ."

Ross's voice is calm and without malice or mischief. Then what in God's name is he up to? The performance, on which I was just about to congratulate myself, is rapidly going to pieces.

I fight to keep things in order, not because we are in the slightest danger at this altitude, but only because Ross has deliberately ruined what might have been a technically perfect approach. For this I cannot forgive him.

As one match after another flares before my eyes I become infuriated with Ross. He is a sadist, sick with weird complexities. He is afraid I *will* do a good job. To hell with him! I will keep everything as it should be regardless of his jealous interference.

Sweating profusely, inwardly cursing Ross's twisted sense of humor, I resolve to fly this ship safely and surely to earth in spite of any harassment. I force myself to ignore Ross's match, to see beyond it to the instruments.

As we turn in for the final descent I shove the propeller controls to full low pitch. We are exactly at required altitude, the speed is right, and also the course.

Ross shakes out his match and sits back in his seat. I glance at him, my resentment doubling when I discover him smiling. We will have this out on the ground!

In less than a minute, at six hundred feet, the faint glow in the clouds becomes an iridescent bloom. I hold the descent. Tatters appear in the cloud base, then the runway lights, and finally the guiding ladder of red neon tubes dead over the nose. I call for full flaps, chop off the power, and we swoop down through light rain until the wheels brush the cinders. I believe that even McCabe would class the landing as better than a bare "arrival," although so short a time ago I strained his back on almost the identical spot.

As for Ross, he can take his comic-opera cap and fly in other directions. I intend to ask for a transfer.

When the engines are stopped I complete the logbook in wounded silence. Ross leaves his seat and puts on his coat. It is raining harder outside. Maybe his ridiculous cap will shrink to the size of his brain.

I snap the logbook shut and am about to stand up when I feel his heavy hand on my shoulder. My grip on the metal logbook tightens. If he tries one of his playful swings—

But his voice is surprisingly tired and so is his smile. "Anyone can do the job when things are going right. In this business we play for keeps."

When he has left the cockpit I remain in my seat listening to the rain peckle on the aluminum above my head. The matches. Why would he light matches? He could more easily have created other distractions if that had been his only intent.

I walk slowly through the rain to the operations office, not really caring if my uniform is further soaked. I decide against asking for a transfer. Ross, in his peculiar way, is making a line pilot of me. And I suppose it is a good way.

Nearly four years would pass before I would again see Ross's matches flaming before me. Then, even though distracted by the drumming of my heart, I would know their incalculable worth.

THE SEASONING

WHERE THE MIND IS HONED AND SWEAT
IS FOUND TO MIX WITH ICE

F ROM spring until the beginning of winter there were
remarkably few variations in the pattern of our
flying. Occasionally I was assigned to captains other than Ross, but
seldom for more than a single trip. These men were solid veterans
of the line, even senior to Ross. They were Apitz, Dodson, Moore,
and Cutrell, all of whom held regular bids on the Newark to
Chicago route. The flights were mostly nonstop in DC-3's, thus
tending toward dullness for a co-pilot familiar with the constant

diversions of AM-21. I was treated with easy consideration and by direct inquiry picked up a few titbits of knowledge, yet no deliberate effort was made to increase my paltry store of wisdom.

The reason was simple. I was not their regular co-pilot whom they might indulge as a son. I was Ross's boy. To interfere with his teachings would be crude and impolitic. I was expected to operate the landing gear and flaps on command, keep the log, the flight plan, and my mouth shut. All of this I endeavored to do efficiently, for it was certain that if I erred, Ross would hear about it.

In late November when the red and gold AM-21 faded and the first snow flurries dusted the northern stretches of the route, there came a general shuffling of crews and I was dispossessed of my now comfortable seat beside Ross.

The ever-watchful McCabe, believing that variety had in itself a special educational value, assigned me to a captain named Keim. This selection could not have provided greater contrast.

I had seen Keim a few times when the landings of our ships coincided along the route. According to custom, he had ignored my existence and reserved only a grudging salutation for Ross. Thus he was an unknown quantity and once again I went to Robbins for background. Though we were now friends, I received the same obtuse answers I had on Ross. I came away quite innocent of the startling differences to be found in two men who flew identical airplanes over the same route. My only salvation was in the fact that this time I knew my duties well.

Or so I believed.

Keim was of medium height and stocky. There were evidences of corpulence about his waistline emphasized by the manner in which he wore his belt—so low his pants seemed to remain in place without reason. His neck and shoulders were powerful, perfectly suited for the support of his rather massive head, which was topped with an array of curly red hair. It matched exactly a fine brush of mustache.

Keim's face was so constantly expressive and quick changing that it was difficult to leave its colorful collection of wrinkles and freckles to concentrate upon his eyes, which were the key to his complicated self. For here was a man at war with the world yet always loving it. He could be, in successive moments, a hilarious comedian and a sage. He could be outrageously dogmatic, stubborn, and raucous, until he chose to transform himself into a reasonable, very straight-thinking individual whose modesty often approached complete retreat.

His eyes were utterly fascinating and he had a trick of waggling the brows above them which contributed marvelously to their versatility of expression. Neither his eyes nor brows were ever entirely still, as if they were in continuous rebellion against the natural lethargy which normally held his body nearly immobile. Except for hunting, which Keim pursued avidly, he seemed to hate all forms of physical exertion. When he sat down he remained rooted in place, as fixed as a statue. When he stood up he floundered to the nearest supporting object, where he remained until absolute necessity compelled him to move again. Yet his eyes were always restless, darting mischievously and sometimes in high disapproval over all that passed before him.

Keim's wit flashed with electric speed and was most frequently voiced in a cutting snarl. It was always original, at times droll, occasionally whimsical, and often bawdy. When it pleased him to turn the same growl upon himself, the result was a sharp dagger of deprecation.

Keim was army trained, a fact which no longer worried me. He was more typically a line pilot than Ross and ever so much more inclined to observe regulations. He held an abiding faith in seniority and was enormously proud of his own length of service with the line. He thoroughly believed that seniority guaranteed security, a prejudice from which he could never be dissuaded. Numbers were his righteous sanctuary. It was terrible when they could not protect him against the incredible turn of fate which brought an end to his active flying career.

As a captain, Keim was the embodiment of caution and cunning. He had an inner sense about weather analysis, predicting its whims so truly that there seemed to be a secret pact between himself and the elements. He could stare at the swirling lines on a map designed to illustrate an air mass or a front and, muttering dark incantations to himself, come away with a detailed prognostication which invariably proved to be of astonishing accuracy. He never regarded bad weather as a potential physical challenge. Instead, he schemed and plotted, winning a mental victory before he ever left the ground.

In flight he was venturesome only to the minimum needs of the moment, and under no circumstances would he experiment or tempt his fortune. His creed, torn as always from the side of his mouth, was steadfast. "One thing I'm sure about. If my ass gets there, so will the passengers'."

Now, while the skies above AM-21 became sullen and heavier winds swept down from Canada laden with snow, other transformations occurred which were not so easy to comprehend.

Though we still flew many trips without enough passengers to pay for the fuel consumed, there were times when nearly every seat was taken. In a flurry of optimism the company ordered new airplanes, which meant hiring new co-pilots to replace those eventually promoted. I learned with pleasure that there were now more than thirty pilots with numbers higher than my embarrassing 267.

Almost overnight the airline business seemed to gain vastly in respectability. Agents even urged line pilots to buy insurance, and since we had hitherto been pointedly ignored, some were so carried away with the flattery they actually did so.

The entire atmosphere, from the mechanics working in the hangars to the exuberant poets charged with the advertisements, was infectious, and everywhere there seemed to be exhilaration and desire for doing. No one could explain the exact reasons for this new energy or pinpoint the exact time when the surge began. Some said it was sparked by the faltering, still phony war in Europe. Others credited the general safety record which had never been matched before. The enthusiasm and anticipation was not confined to one line; all of them fell in with the quickening rhythm of their teletypes and, like children long neglected, emerged cheering into the light.

Some substance was given to the rumors by the opening of La

Guardia Field. All of the lines previously serving the New York area from Newark, except Eastern, moved at once into breathtaking grandeur. There were speeches loaded with touching phraseology about the dawn of a new age. There were people who said the entire project was a mad dream and someone should be investigated for stealing the City of New York's good money.

La Guardia Field became a symbol for the entire country, and other cities from Los Angeles to Washington and Boston were inspired at least to consider improvements on their own airports. A few of them haltingly turned their promises into action.

In truth, all the circumstances of American air transport were disgraceful. Except for the actual construction of good airplanes, we were so far behind the rest of the world that there was simply no comparison to be made. Imperial Airways had long been flying passengers in cocktail and full dinner service luxury. Their routes not only extended from England all over Europe but continued on all the way to India. Air France also sprawled over Europe and offered fairly reliable service across the Sahara to remotest Africa. Royal Dutch Airlines flew half around the world to the East Indies. Lufthansa was everywhere, and through shadow operations was firmly entrenched in South America. Even the confused Italians operated a regular service across the South Atlantic with Alor Littoria.

So air transport was accepted everywhere except in the United States. Unfortunately, our recent wave of enterprise and conviction stopped short at the hangar doors. We were still held in such distrust that many large firms forbade their executives to fly. And the price of the newly offered insurance for pilots was outrageous.

There was some reason for this rejection. Technically, we had barely emerged from strapping a parachute on our passengers and seating them on mail sacks. Flights across the continent were a slow ordeal, frequently hours late, and sometimes canceled altogether. Pilots were required to carry special form booklets which would enable them to put their passengers on a train.

Yet there were some tokens of progress. For example, we were suddenly authorized to carry our mail guns in our flight kits instead of strapping them, sheriff-wise, to our belts.

My first flight with Keim over AM-21 was not a success as far as I was concerned. He nursed a bitter hatred of the DC-2 heating system, to which, having at last learned its weird eccentricities, I had finally become attached. As if to ease his fury, Keim demanded the utmost from the boiler and kept the cockpit like a Finnish Sauna. Complaint of the temperature, voiced but once, met with the singular lack of enthusiasm I would soon learn to expect from Keim.

"Look. *I* happen to like it this way. You see that white stuff out there? It's called snow. I've shivered a million miles in these airplanes and I don't intend to do so any longer. If you feel yourself in a financial position to hire this airplane and employ me as pilot, then we might discuss the matter of heat. Until then I happen to be the captain, unless I've read our name platters on the door backward, and you're the co-pilot. So the temperature will stay the way I want it, which is the way it is now, period."

I glanced ruefully down at my still-new jodhpur boots in which my feet were slowly stewing. I had yet to learn that honest winter would soon come to AM-21 and all of Keim's heat plus my boots would do little to make cockpit life comfortable.

Keim also smoked cigars, which have an especially nauseating effect in an airplane. When he had made certain I disliked them his enjoyment of every puff increased immensely. In gasping self-defense I left the cockpit frequently and went back to the cabin. My absence did not disturb him in the slightest since he rarely relinquished the controls all the way to Cleveland. He did not even suggest giving me a landing or a take-off, a denial of confidence sorely felt after my months with Ross. He even did his own reporting on the radio, cupping the microphone tightly in his hand and growling our altitude and position from the side of his mouth as if daring the ground to answer. His every action marked my presence in the cockpit as nonessential.

Keim did not employ the rod in the manner of Ross. Since I could now handle the physical chores well enough, although not always to his entire satisfaction, it is doubtful that he would have troubled himself to punish me in any event. On the return flight he gave me a take-off at Buffalo which he observed without comment.

On our next flight he moved the quota up to two and added a landing, which, thanks to a soft bed of snow at Syracuse, proved to be what was known as a "greaser." Ordinarily such landings provoke some obligatory comment from the other pilot—"Are we down?" or, sarcastically, "Of course you do that every time."

Not from Keim. He chose to remain silent, but as the one eye I could see swam around to fix upon me, the attendant eyebrow climbed, and then descended slowly. There was no other evidence that he had even seen the landing, but such signs from him were enough to give me hope of his approval.

I could not know that while Ross concentrated upon perfecting my actual flying technique, Keim was equally determined to do something about my thinking. To him my flying brain was still woefully immature in flight planning, almost devoid of caution in maneuver, and altogether lacking in weather wisdom. He proceeded, in embittered patience, to set these matters right. After three trips his occasional grunts of approval held for me the thrill of a trumpet flourish.

Now winter came to AM-21 in all seriousness, and the land below was dead beneath a white shroud. Only the sky remained active, interchanging moods of bluster and stealthy cold silence.

The sun was timid and rarely visible from the ground. When we climbed through the nearly permanent cloud deck and emerged to fly on top, the sun came as a complete surprise, for its existence was nearly forgotten. Wrapped in his overcoat, Keim would alternately frown menacingly over his shoulder at the heater and then sit in resigned misery, blinking owlishly at the sun. Unlike other captains, he never left the cockpit. The very thought of appearing before what few passengers we carried seemed to terrify him.

My growing confidence irritated him beyond measure. When I ventured an opinion, which in the joy of baiting I sometimes deliberately made as wild as possible, his reaction inevitably began with an angry semaphoring of eyebrows. Then his voice would rise into a high-pitched complaining whine, tragic in forbearance, mightily abused. His eyes, darting from the instruments to the sky and finally fixing balefully upon me, spoke of a man asked to endure a crushing burden.

"Of course! Why *not* go down and have a look at Syracuse? Why should we pass it over? They're *only* reporting a ceiling of three hundred feet and half a mile visibility with blowing snow. Why not, indeed? What are we fooling around up here in the sun for? Obviously I have been completely wasting my time trying to learn a few things about this route the last five years! I should have consulted you much sooner! *Indeed!* I've never met a co-pilot who knew so very much. I should inform the payroll department they've made a serious mistake. *You* are the one who should be paid for doing the thinking around here! Obviously my stupidity can never be overcome by what very *little* experience *I've* had. Go ahead! *You* take her down! *You* have a look at Syracuse! Kill us all! Who wants to live forever?"

Such moments with Keim were exquisite and well worth retreat with wounds.

While I absorbed aerial wisdom from Keim, my contemporaries serving other men of equal experience matured in kind. McGuire was learning, and Watkins, and Mood, and Petersen, and Gay, and Carter, and Owen. We now appreciated the niceties of a low approach well done. A failing engine was not an exciting lark but a serious problem to be solved. Fuel, especially in winter, was like an always diminishing bank account and should be expended judiciously. Ice was a phenomenon to be avoided like the plague, and we anticipated the customary uselessness of radios when flying through snow.

It became important to think as well as fly. All of our captains were required by law to choose an alternate airport which they could certainly make should the place of destination prove impossible. We saw that this thinking went much further, and understood that good line pilots held an alternate in their minds for every eventuality. If this did not work out, then they would do that. Expecting the worst, they skipped one emotion when trouble appeared, and thus moved without pausing past disappointment to decision and action.

All of this and much more came to us in time, which was measured and carefully recorded in our logbooks. So many hours and minutes of nighttime, so many of day, and so many of flight on instruments. Together with the dates and the names of those captains we served, it was all set down.

One fundamental of our training had, for most of us, still to be experienced. We had been bewildered, amazed, humbled, and excited. We had not yet been thoroughly frightened or forced to look disaster directly in the face and stare it down. This omission in my own curriculum was corrected on a certain February night.

My escort to fear was a captain named Hughen.

The locale was new to me: AM-23, which designates the air space between Nashville, Tennessee, and New York.

Only the plane was familiar to me. Because the last available DC-3 had been grounded for maintenance, an elderly DC-2 had been substituted to fulfill our schedule. It was airworthy but far from beautiful. It bore a haggard look and its scars were like hard-won decorations. Oil and exhaust flame had left permanent stains along the engine cowlings which no amount of burnishing could ever remove. There were hail dents about its nose, and deeper depressions on both sides of the fuselage where the propellers had cast off countless chunks of ice. A glance at the logbook proved it had flown over ten thousand hours. Someday soon it would be sold off to a more modest line in Africa or China or Central America where it might continue a grubby career for years.

We walk toward the ship in the moonlight. The night is cold and penetrating, without the crispness of northern air. The sky is clear except over the city of Nashville itself, where a thin matting of stratus cloud reflects the surface light. There is no wind and the click of our heels echoes sharply across the concrete ramp. It is just possible to see the vapor of our breaths in the moonlight.

Hughen is a large and dignified man who speaks in short, quick word groups, as if all that he had to say was assembled, chained neatly together, and then released only when ready. He flew the mail in open-cockpit planes and has been with the line so long I must consider that time as forever. The architecture of his face is solid and heavy, contrasting strangely with the infantile smoothness of his skin. He bears one unmistakable talisman of the true early bird—a barely perceptible wisp of mustache which at one time was as much a part of self-respecting pilots as their helmet and goggles. He is quite bald except for a few strands of black hair comprising another wisp just forward of his cranium. These remnants of a pompadour are carefully combed straight back.

Hughen has been considerate and friendly, but the gap between his experience and mine is of such vast dimensions that our relationship naturally remains that of master and apprentice.

We are bound for New York on what should be a four-hour flight. The weather has been forecast as favorable except for a mild warm front some hundred miles to the east. There is no reason to believe it will present any difficulty. There will be eight passengers. They are already waiting patiently behind the wire gate, shuffling about in comfortable ignorance of their immediate future, watching the moon and murmuring the shyly polite little clichés so necessary to strangers embarking on a common journey. Their fates must soon be joined with our own, which is a pity, for on this night they too will know the rancid taste of fear.

Hughen is not happy about the substitution of a DC-2.

"I thought I was through flying these damn things."

But he straps himself into his seat with a sigh of resignation and methodically checks off every control and instrument in the cockpit, calling forth each item from his memory. The ritual performed to his satisfaction, we start the engines and taxi away. In a very few minutes we are climbing toward the moon.

Hughen is a meticulous man and, knowing little of my experience, has worked out the flight plan himself. He has chosen Columbus, Ohio, as our alternate, a convenient place, where the weather is forecast to remain excellent. It now lies far over the night horizon to the northeast. We have sufficient fuel aboard to reach New York and if we should find it closed we have enough to turn about and proceed easily to Columbus. We carry an additional forty-five minutes of fuel to cover any conceivable delay after arrival there. This is the law, and we have complied with it although there is absolutely no reason to believe this reserve fuel will ever be needed.

By the time we have reached our cruising altitude the lights of Nashville are lost beneath the tail. There are times, particularly during day flights, when pilots are much given to conversation in the cockpit, though the noise of the engines and slip stream causes them to raise their voices unnaturally. At night the reverse is true, there seeming to be a muffling of all outward sounds by the darkness until the cockpit becomes a cozy place well suited to meditation. If the night is fair and strewn with stars, or phosphorescent with a moon, then pilots have been known to turn down every light in the cockpit and sit in absolute silence, savoring their uniquely remote peace as long as they can.

On such nights contact with the earth is lost more completely than at any other time. Radio calls from the ground stations are considered an intrusion and answered resentfully. Few pilots are immune to this nocturnal spell. It has a mystical quality which lays a pleasing coverlet over the usual technical thought patterns necessary in a cockpit, and once again the airplane becomes an argosy afloat in space instead of a mere machine.

On such nights, with the horizon lost, it is possible to look down upon certain stars, an illusion which causes the altimeter to become meaningless. The hands pointing to seven and zero could indicate seven thousand feet or seventy thousand or seven hundred miles, for the eerie spectacle from the cockpit is presumably the same.

I have been staring at the moon.

Now, reluctantly, I turn up the lights, place the logbook on my knees, and prepare to mark down our moment of passage over Knoxville. I will radio this information back to Nashville. Based on our ground speed, an easy calculation when a computer is used, I will also report the wind we have experienced and a new estimate of our arrival over Roanoke, which lies to the north.

Hughen has so far done all of the flying and is apparently lost in contemplation of his instruments. He has not spoken since our take-off. I wait, expecting to see the lights of Knoxville before he nods his head to confirm that we are actually over the range station. And the waiting is easy, for there is still the moon.

I lift myself in the seat, inspecting the darkness below. There are no lights of any kind. Instead, the earth is obscured by a veil of cloud which I take to be ground fog. Its presence is unimportant since we have no intention of landing at Knoxville. I toy with my pencil and watch the luminous clock on the instrument panel. The sweep second hand quivers through the smallest units of time, which are now without particular value. The hand appears to move slowly, as it must do to those rich in leisure and safety. Time speeds only when we would halt it.

We are now four minutes late over Knoxville, yet Hughen has made no sign. Thinking I may have missed his signal, I flip a switch at my side and so cut myself in on the range. No, we are still approaching Knoxville. The invisible wind outside must be much stronger than forecast. Twisting the dial on my computer, I find it must be over forty miles an hour. I can solve the equation exactly when I know our exact time over the station.

Now there is a division in the sky ahead which appears to be shaped like a wedge. It divides our forward view into layers. First there is the blackness far below, which has become confused with globules of minor cloud, then the wedge protruding from what proves to be a solid mass. Finally there is an uppermost plateau of vapor, which is almost exactly at our altitude. It is thin, gossamer-like, and relatively brilliant beneath the moon.

Hardly more than a minute passes before we are sliding swiftly along just above the surface of the plateau. The sensation is delightful, for the only way the true speed of an airplane may be visually appreciated is to fly it close to a relatively stationary surface. In barnstorming days we frequently sought this same exhilaration by skimming over the fields and trees, even following the contours of hills as closely as we dared. It was, at least, a stimulating prelude to disaster, which was all too frequently the end result. Such gay foolishness in an airliner is of course unthinkable, but the same sensation can be achieved by finding a flat-topped deck of cloud and flying along its surface until the bottom arc of the propellers slice into it. This is a harmless diversion and when, as now, a moon illuminates a great mattress of vapor, the effect is intoxicating.

I glance at Hughen and find him smiling. What else, when this is fulfillment, the ghostlike, swift, and sensual tonic of true flight? These moments are the sinew of our devotion, the physical excitation to be found in our way of life.

Hughen nods at the tiny glowing light on the instrument panel. We are over Knoxville.

I write down the time on the flight plan form, place a pencil dot on the marking side of my computer, and discover we have been bucking a fifty-mile-an-hour-wind. This is thirty more than forecast and I cannot believe my figures. I repeat the calculation and get the identical answer. I reach across the cockpit and hold the computer so Hughen can see it.

He frowns and takes a moment to smooth the wisps of his hair. "You sure?"

"Yes. I'm sure."

"We'll get a better check between here and Roanoke. Maybe our climb threw your figures off."

"I allowed for the climb."

"Even so."

Hughen turns north for Roanoke as I radio our findings back to Nashville. The moon slides around until it is over my right shoulder. But I have lost interest in the moon. Nashville is sending me a series of weather reports for various cities, and these must be recorded in a special shorthand which most nearly resembles the hieroglyphics of the Egyptians. When the transmission is finished I find that all is the same as on our departure except for Nashville itself, which is now reporting an overcast condition with lower broken clouds.

This is an abrupt change and had not been predicted.

There is also a southerly wind. At Nashville a wind from the south is not good.

"Did you hear the Nashville weather?"

Hughen nods his head. "No matter. As long as New York holds up."

He reaches forward and turns the fuel valve to the right auxiliary tank. Then for a moment he thoughtfully works the wobble pump at the side of his seat to guarantee free flow of the precious liquid. After several strokes, when it is obvious the fuel system is functioning properly, he stops pumping and again retires within himself. I cannot account for his strange preoccupation and believe it must be a personal habit rather than due to any demands of our flight.

I spend some five or ten minutes at my paper work. There are baggage and mail forms, fuel, loading, and logbook to be looked after, in addition to the flight plan. When these are all completed I hand the open logbook to Hughen with a pencil placed in the jaws so he can easily sign his name. I hold the controls while he scribbles with a flourish. And after his name he marks down his seniority number. If my number were 64 I would sign my name with a flourish too.

Enviously, I close the logbook and place it on the floor. Yes, it would be wonderful if my number were 64. When you are young how can you hasten age? What is there to do with youth when you are youth and therefore impatient with waiting? Yet I can only wait and find such comfort as I can in the moon.

It has vanished. There is not even a glow in the sky. Instead we are wrapped in vapor which swoops around the snout of the DC-2 and whips against the windshield. Then we must be in the front which the meteorologists had located almost exactly. They explained that it would lie nearly stagnant in a long trough extending from the Blue Ridge Mountains as far north as Baltimore. Its promised length does not displease me. Certainly Hughen will not wish to fly the full two hours necessary to emerge from this long band of weather. Certainly, when his eyes tire, he will relinquish the controls and if I cannot do anything about my number I can at least add to my instrument time.

There is a new roughness to the air and I become vaguely uneasy. Hughen is absorbed in his instruments and I soon become aware that he is paying particular heed to the outside temperature gauge. It stands at thirty degrees.

I remember from my days in Lester's school that this temperature is supposedly ideal for icing conditions. Yet so far there is no evidence of ice and I am even a little disappointed because the most I have ever seen is a delicate tracery across the windshield. Meteorologists are frank in confessing their inability to forecast the existence of ice in a cloud mass. They seem positive about one thing only. Any cloud holding a temperature between twenty and thirty degrees harbors the potential of ice. It might be there. Or it might not.

The air is still not rough enough to require the passenger seat belt sign. There are jolts, but they are few and far between. I lean back in my seat, thinking about Hughen. How I envy his flying experience! And his fortune, what of that? He was lucky enough to fly when there was romance and stirring adventure—and constant hazard. He came through unscathed to this solidity. His face and body are now those of a comfortable man as secure in his position as the proprietor of a long-established store. He has a wife, two children, money in the bank, and a home. He is a sensible man and serene—certainly not of the swashbuckling type who must sometimes destroy themselves in a search for self-justification. Then why is he still here? Why is he still sitting in a worn leather seat, surrounded by a hundred things of such harsh mechanical nature they can offer him little comfort? Why is he not at home, this solid man, sprawled in a leather armchair? His home will be dark now. It is long past the family bedtime. Yet the head of the house is aloft with the moon.

Our first warning is an insistent hissing in our earphones. It builds rapidly until it becomes an abrasive squealing, the nasty and continuous scratching of fingernails along a slate. The screeching becomes a diaphonic howl and the range signal of Knoxville is buried in it.

Hughen, pained at the sound and consequent lack of guidance, presses his lips tightly together.

"See if you can tune in Knoxville on the D.F."

The direction finder is a completely separate radio installation and is controlled by a tuning dial and a small crank for turning the receiving loop. By cranking the loop a bearing may be taken on any convenient station and thus a navigational line of position established. Because of its construction the loop can often bring in signals when the regular antenna fails its purpose.

I lean forward to crank the loop so that its position is best for receiving the Knoxville range. Nothing. Only the hideous sound of those fingernails.

I turn the volume far down and crank the loop back and forth, a few degrees at a time. Listening intently, both of us press the headphones hard against our ears. Nothing.

"Try Roanoke."

I retune the receiver and rock the crank slowly back and forth. Again, nothing penetrates the screeching.

"Try Charleston."

I am ashamed. The route is new to me and I do not know the call sign of Charleston by heart. I could find it in the book which is in my flight kit, but it is quicker to admit my ignorance and ask Hughen, who must surely know.

"The identification is C.H."

I tune the receiver quickly and crank again. Nothing. Nothing . . . nothing.

"Give Columbus a shot."

I know the frequency of Columbus since it is sometimes used on AM-21. It is far away, but there is always hope in the freakishness of radio.

Yet again . . . nothing. There is no break or recognizable signal to be plucked from the strident discord. We are swallowed in a crazy region of utterly useless sound.

I have been so preoccupied with tuning, listening, and cranking that I have given little heed to the windshield. Now it has become opaque. Our world ends in a gray panel approximately eighteen inches from our faces.

"Start the de-icers."

I flip the switch above my head which will activate the rubber boots, then turn on the landing lights to observe their operation.

Looking back at the wing, I watch the intermittent pulsations of the boots and find their movements strangely fascinating. So this is true ice. It looks more like pie crust. The rubber boots, ponderously swelling and collapsing like elongated hearts, break the pie crust off in great flakes. The rhythm of the operation is a slow one, allowing the ice to form in a thin layer before it is torn apart, spat back at the night, and sucked away.

There is also ice forming on the rim of the engine cowling and the propeller hub. It does not seem to be more than half an inch thick.

Turning back, I find Hughen adjusting the carburetor heat levers. He must reach around to my side of the control pedestal to get to these controls, and I am astonished to see that his bald head glistens with perspiration.

"Too hot in here for you?"

"No."

Hughen is concerned although I can see no reason for being so. This is as nothing to a thunderstorm.

I wonder if Hughen might be one of those pilots secretly afraid of airplanes. There are a very few such men, anxiously nursing their dread until the day when they can retire. Experience has worn them out instead of hardening them. They exist in a half-frightened daze, like punch-drunk fighters, and everyone is sorry for them.

Suddenly someone is throwing rocks at me. There is an erratic banging upon the fuselage just behind my seat. I instinctively twist and dodge, then realize the hammering is also behind Hughen.

"Shoot some alcohol on the props!"

Of course. The propeller blades, like the wings, are accumulating ice, which is retained only until centrifugal force whirls it off. Chunks the size of baseballs are being hurled against the resounding aluminum. And since one blade retains more than another, the delicate balance of the three-hundred-and-eighty-pound propellers is disturbed. An uneven vibration seizes the entire ship. It passes beneath my feet from one side of the cockpit to the other, surging to a maximum, falling off, and then returning again. I do not like this vibration. There is something wicked about it.

I turn a valve marked "props" and labor strenuously at a hand pump which is just behind me. At once the cockpit becomes pungent with the smell of alcohol. My pumping will send the liquid to the propeller blades and supposedly free them of ice.

In less than a minute I am also sweating. Things are beginning to happen very fast. They are not good things.

The vibration is increasing in spite of my pumping. The racket of banging ice is becoming a fusillade. The air is still not unduly rough, but unless the instruments and the seat of my pants are lying, the ship is beginning to porpoise in an unbelievable manner. Hughen is having a very rough time with the controls. Now the sweat is dripping from his cheekbones and he is breathing heavily.

"Try Knoxville again! On the loop!"

He is afraid. I am certain he is afraid. His voice is controlled, but there is the constriction of fear beneath his control. The ordered words come like pistol shots.

I stop pumping, tune the D.F.'s radio to Knoxville frequency, and reach for the loop crank. In doing so, my attention is caught by the air speed. One hundred and twenty miles an hour! Only a few minutes before we were cruising at one hundred seventy. Yet Hughen has not touched the power. A queasy sensation passes through my stomach. The blood rushes to my head until my cheeks feel aflame. My hands are suddenly hot and throbbing. I catch myself working my lips. These I know to be the beginning signals of fear. I cannot seem to stop it.

Because my lips insist on making these silly formations, I cannot say anything about the air speed. One hundred and twenty. We must not lose any more. With a load of ice this ship will cease to fly at one hundred, possibly even sooner.

What the hell is wrong with those fancy de-icer boots? They are not performing the task for which they are intended. Come! Function!

I glance furtively out the window at my side. The blinking red-light indicator shows the de-icers are in operation, but outside there is visible proof that they are lying down on the job. The leading edge of the wing is now one long, unbroken bar of ice. And it is clear ice, rumpled as if there were rocks beneath.

Yes, the boots are working. But they are expanding and contracting *beneath* the sheath of ice and consequently useless! The ice has accumulated too fast for them.

"Get Knoxville!"

I try. I try with all that is in me to hear Knoxville. I strain my senses, allowing the squeaking to sear my brain as I listen for the treasure of a signal. I must hear it, for now a new threat is evident. I am dismayed to see that the altimeters read a mere five thousand feet. We have lost two thousand. We are foundering like a ship. The rate of climb shows we are sinking at a steady two hundred feet per minute, which at least makes for very simple arithmetic. At such a rate we will descend to sea level in twenty-five minutes, whether we like it or not.

Hughen moves the propeller controls to full low pitch. Now I realize that he has every reason to be afraid. We cannot possibly descend to sea level or anywhere near it unless we are ready for surrender. The Blue Ridge Mountains are buried in the night below. We are already below the level of the highest peaks.

"We're getting out of this!"

Hughen pounds his feet on the rudder pedals. They are immovable. The rudder, far back on the tail of the ship, is frozen. There is, of course, absolutely nothing we can do about it. Yet by constant movement Hughen has kept the ailerons free, so a turn is still possible. He must execute the turn very slowly, taking great care not to bank more than a few degrees at a time, for at this speed and with the efficiency of the wings so damaged, a turn can be the introduction to a spin from which, under the circumstances, there can be no possible recovery.

I watch Hughen start into a slow left turn. At once the air speed slips to an agonizing one hundred and five. The ship has abandoned the easier porpoising and is bucking viciously. I cannot believe that an airplane is capable of such idiotic action. There is absolutely no explanation for it.

Hughen is a man tiptoeing along a very tenuous wire. The wire is swaying crazily in the wind, he is being bombarded with rocks, and if he loses balance for one second, we are done for. How can this all have happened so suddenly? Fifteen minutes ago all was as it should be.

"Call Nashville. Get emergency clearance at five thousand. Tell them we are returning on account of heavy ice. Accumulation fast . . . clear ice."

"Do you want me to call first or try to get Knoxville range?"

"Call first. Tell them to clear that altitude."

I repeat the message into my microphone, trying to control the tendency of my voice to become a quavering falsetto. It is I who should be in a leather armchair before a fire. I cannot bear to look at the instruments as Hughen is obliged to do. Their readings are bringing me very close to panic. Where is that rambunctious youth intrigued with the essence of danger? What is happening so very quickly to the young man who thought the present world suffered from oversecurity and produced only mice-hearted men? Captain Hughen, this is all an anachronism. We belong to the modern world and should therefore be secure. Please arrange a remedy for this grievous mistake at once.

One hundred miles per hour. Altitude four thousand eight hundred feet. Still sinking. Maybe if I refuse to look the readings will go away.

There is no reassuring reply from Nashville. I can only assume they received our message and will clear all other planes from our altitude.

A sudden, terrible shudder seizes the entire airplane. At once Hughen shoves the throttles wide open and the nose down.

The shuddering ceases. Hughen wipes the sweat from his eyes.

"She almost got away from me!"

The incipient stall has stolen an additional three hundred feet from our altitude. We must not risk a repetition, and yet the engines cannot remain at full power forever. But Hughen leaves the throttles where they are.

I crank the loop desperately although the hope of hearing anything is dissolved in noise. I abandon the frequency of Knoxville and again experiment with Columbus, which is so much farther away. Then quite clearly I hear a new whine, distorted yet unmistakably genuine. It is interrupted by the code letters C.O. Columbus!

I crank through a null and note the bearing. At once I tune to Charleston and find it also readable.

"I have Charleston and Columbus! Fix in a minute!"

I don't know why it seems so terribly important to know where we are. What *is* important is our altitude, a factor we can do nothing about. If it continues to diminish, our position is of little consequence. Both Hughen and myself would be indifferent as to which of the Blue Ridge Mountains we actually hit.

I manage to take two good bearings when Hughen at last completes his turn. I plot them at once on the chart drawn from my flight kit.

"Here is a fix. Only second-class bearings, but they make sense."

Hughen glances at the two intersecting lines I have drawn on the chart. They show us to be approximately fifty miles to the north of Knoxville—directly over a long hump in the mountains. There is a peak somewhere in this area. Its summit is marked as 4,150 feet. We are now at 4,500 feet and still sinking.

Even as we study the chart we are approaching or leaving the vicinity of the peak. Which it is, we cannot know until I plot another fix. There is no way to make an airplane wait.

"Take another shot in two minutes."

In two minutes the effort might be entirely superfluous.

We have merely nodded to fear. Now we must shake its filthy hand.

Both engines suddenly begin cutting out—first one and then the other. For one awful moment they both subside together. And there is a silence which is not really a silence but a chilling diminu-endo of all sound.

This is the way you die.

At three minutes past two in the morning.

And as suddenly the engines regain themselves. We can feel the surge forward, but we have lost five hundred precious feet! We are below that peak, wherever it may be.

Something must be done about the engines. Nothing else is of any importance whatsoever.

Hughen has yanked on full rich mixture to the carburetors. He switches back to the main fuel tank and works the wobble pump. All the while he struggles to keep the ship in a semblance of straight and level flight.

Again the engines grow feeble. They are stricken with a mysteri-ous disease. We might argue with our flying senses, but we cannot argue with a manifold pressure gauge. Both instruments show a slow and steady loss of power. This cannot be due to carburetor ice. We are certain of that because other instruments tell us the heaters are working.

We lose another two hundred feet. Hughen anxiously jockeys the throttles. He checks the magnetos. Perfect. He seems more perplexed than frightened and I cannot think of a way to help him.

We are much too low. We can only be flying in a valley, but it is impossible to determine which valley since there are several shown on the chart. Nor can we know when this convenient valley will come to an abrupt end. Hughen begins a slow circle. Flying so, we will at least use up less territory.

"Maybe I'd better go back and start heaving things overboard."

We must, absolutely *must,* have altitude.

"Wait. I may need you."

Hughen has switched on the landing lights again and yanked open his side window so he can see the left engine clearly. After a moment he hauls the window shut. Then to my horror he cuts off the fuel mixture to his engine. Starved of fuel, it backfires angrily. At once Hughen pulls the fuel lever to full rich again. The response is like a cheer. His engine is putting out full power once more. He repeats the action with the right engine controls. Again, after a moment's startled regurgitation, a welcome return of power.

We are able to climb at fifty feet a minute!

"Air scoops . . . icing over. Watch them. Soon as the power falls off, cut the mixture until they backfire. Then slam them on again."

I must lean forward to see past the accumulation of ice along the fringes of my side window. It is swelling rapidly and is easily three inches thick in places. Beyond it, in the ghostly light, I can see the engine, now grizzle-bearded in ice.

The carburetor air scoop is an oval-shaped metal mouth on top of the engine. Through it must pass the air, which is as important to any combustion engine as fuel. Without air the engine dies as surely as a drowning human being. Normally, the mouth is approximately four inches wide. Now the reason for our loss of power becomes all too obvious. Even as I watch, the ice accumulates around the lips of the mouth. It builds upon itself, decreasing the size of the opening like a closing iris until it is merely a black hole hardly more than the size of a dollar. The same thing is happening on Hughen's side. Our engines are simply suffocating. Something must remove the ice before it closes their mouths entirely.

Hughen has had the nerve and courage to find a way. By backfiring the engines a tongue of flame spurts from the air scoops. It is not the flame but the force of air from the bowels of the engine which knocks away the closing ice. Two hefty belches seem to do the job nicely. Then there is a wait of three or four minutes until the danger point is reached again. It is a terrible abuse of the engines, but not so bad as asking them to fly through a mountain. Gradually, Hughen is able to nurse the ship to 4,300 feet. But even at full power, that is all. He holds the course reasonably steady on southwest, the direction from which we have come.

Between backfirings I am heavily engaged with the loop antenna. With luck, our position will again become important.

I am able to plot a series of bearing fixes. They show without doubt that retreat might be our salvation. We are crawling across the chart like a wounded insect. But it is very important that we are indeed creating a series of marks rather than a single X, which would, with due finality, designate the very end of all movement. Lower terrain is ahead and presumably better weather. We have actually been in the ice less than thirty minutes, not a very long time to so incapacitate an airplane. And yet the half hour has had the smell of eternity.

Then, quite unexpectedly, we stumble out of the cloud and sail beneath the moon. I refrain from yelling and pounding on the leather crash pad before me only with difficulty.

Hughen, as befits his age and experience, maintains his dignity. His relief is confined to a great sigh, the sound of a shipwrecked sailor throwing himself at last upon a beach.

The propellers fling their final collection of rocks at us, and the vibration which has shaken the ship for so long gradually melts away. We are skating above the plateau again, although its presence is only dimly visible through our side windows. Our forward windshields are solid with ice; hence the moon itself is invisible. But it is quite enough to sense its light.

"Shoot some alcohol on the windshield."

I turn the valve to the proper marking and pump. It is a fruitless procedure. The liquid spews out of small pipes along the glass and creeps between the crenelations of ice. I can see it. I can also see that it is completely ineffective except to fill the cockpit with fumes. It is a stupid arrangement. What could the engineers have been thinking? Somehow the glass itself should be heated.

"I'm getting drunk."

"Forget the alcohol, then. Rig the elephant's pecker."

Hughen refers to a large flexible duct which draws hot air from the main heater. It is hung on a wire and may be adjusted like a fire hose so that its spray of warmth can be directed on any desired portion of the windshield. In very light ice it can, with patience, melt a hole barely two inches in diameter, providing just enough forward visibility for an emergency landing. With this kind of ice it proves as ineffective as the alcohol.

Hughen cannot set up the hose by himself. He is a very busy

man. Though we are flying in clear, smooth air, and thus no longer accumulating ice, the load we already have still renders the ship nearly unmanageable.

It is twenty minutes past two. We know that we have no sound reason to smile at each other, but a smile now seems very necessary —a congratulatory salute directed more to an invisible patron rather than to each other. It is a feeble smile, wanting much in confidence. For we are by no means acquitted; both judge and jury are still out. Still, Hughen is relieved enough to think of our passengers.

"Go back. Explain we are returning to Nashville. Keep moving and it won't take you long."

I leave my seat without enthusiasm. For some reason I am stiff all through my body, as if I had been soundly whipped in a fight. I button my coat and clamp on my cap. Assuming what I hope is an easy manner, I move back past the baggage compartment and open the door to the cabin. Given the choice, I would have closed it at once.

For it is difficult to reconcile myself to this wholly sane and luxuriously comfortable atmosphere. Here are eight people who had been just on the border line of relinquishing their roles as human beings. A very few minutes before, they almost became mixed elements of viscera, bone, and blood, squashed into shapeless blobs which would quiver through the last of life and then be still. Had Hughen lost a mere five miles per hour air speed for even thirty seconds, this could easily have happened. Yet he did not lose those five miles, and as a result the passengers are quite alive. Do they owe anything to Hughen? Not according to the earthy theories of Captain Keim. But I think they do. They owe him for being superbly skillful at his job. They owe him for being enough in love with his work to be where he is instead of at home in his armchair, or better yet—at this hour—in bed.

Their poise astounds me. They could not, of course, see the instruments or appreciate their frightful information, but even here in the cabin there must have been enough commotion for alarm. Two of the passengers are asleep or pretend to be. The others are obviously miserable, yet somehow able to feign reasonable calm. I can only admire them. Helpless and trusting, they had the nerve to sit quite sedately and await their fate.

"I'm sorry. We are returning to Nashville."

The man who sits alone mutters an oath and without further interest returns to his copy of *Time*. I cannot help wondering what he would look like with that magazine as an integral part of his guts.

"I am sorry to tell you we are returning to Nashville."

"Why?"

Why indeed? Because it is the closest place. Because we know the weather is good there. Because the captain knows the field at Nashville, having studied its nature for years, and also it will be much easier for you, lady . . . and because. . . .

"We are returning to Nashville."

"What about the motors? I saw flame. Is something wrong? I felt a little sick."

And "No," speaks the officially appointed liar, "nothing is wrong."

Nothing at all. If I speak the truth it will accomplish nothing. Can I now explain to this man and his wife the cruel and unalterable principles of aerodynamics? Can I say to him while his extraordinarily dull-eyed wife listens without comprehension that this airplane is a scientific masterpiece, intended to remain air-borne at a certain speed carrying a certain weight . . . and yet, because of our newly acquired weight, none of which is pay load, the very basic design of this flying machine has been sadly altered . . . so that all of the previously reliable figures may now be thrown out the window? Can I say that under normal conditions we are supposed to consume ninety gallons of fuel per hour, but for the past hour we have been exploiting our reserve through circumstance, and so consuming twice that amount? And can I say there is nothing we can do about regaining it? Can I say that we have been very lucky?

"We had some backfiring on the engine which is on your side. It's cleared up now. But we think it's better to return to Nashville."

The stewardess is new enough to be frightened. She is huddled on her small seat next to the door although there are many of the regular seats available. She is fussing with her commissary report, as if its completion were a last will and testament.

. . . the coffee was cold when placed aboard . . . the rolls were smashed and there was only half enough butter. . . .

She has her problems.

"What's wrong?"

"Nothing. We're going back to Nashville. You can see the same movie again."

"What shall I tell my passengers?"

"I've told them. Serve some coffee if it will perk them up."

"I don't know what's the matter with those Nashville people. The coffee is always cold out of there. I'm going to report them."

"Do."

"How will my passengers get out of Nashville? Two of them have connecting flights."

"I don't know."

"I don't like that banging against the fuselage. I wish I was back in Los Angeles taking a sun bath. Are you scared?"

"Always."

How a man can parade in front of a woman! How insignificant his fears, how humble his courage. Could this young woman have seen the poltroon within me only a little while ago, the present stuffy stalwart would have collapsed before her eyes. Yet because she is a woman who might see me again, I walk back up the aisle with a confident swagger.

Inside, I am aerodynamically ill. Because Lester, in his school, had taught me to understand aerodynamics. And I do not wish to look like Lester.

After the hypocrisy of the cabin, the cockpit is almost a relief.

"Want to fly awhile?"

I want very much to fly this airplane now that we are in the clear. I want to see what it is like to fly an airplane that is not really flying but merely lingering in the air. After all, Hughen is present to catch me if I fall off the tightrope.

He has reduced the power slightly, but we are still using much above the requirement for normal cruising. Even so, it is barely enough to maintain a faltering one hundred and twenty miles per hour. He waves for me to take over the controls. I flounder uncertainly for a moment, shocked at the heavy, drunken feel of the ship. After a little time I manage fairly well.

The standard radio is tuned to the Nashville beam. It is loud and clear and thus sweet music to our ears. I could almost relax were it not for Hughen. Out of the corner of my eye I can see him fidgeting in his seat. He wipes his face with his handkerchief, opens his collar, then smooths the wisps of hair again and again. His head is in constant motion as his attention alternates repeatedly between the instruments and the window at his side. His fingers drum a nervous, inaudible rhythm on his knees. For a time he tinkers halfheartedly with the heating duct. It has not made the slightest mark upon the windshield ice. Forward, we are as blind as if the oblique sections of glass were marble slabs. We are sitting in a crypt.

It will not be an easy landing at Nashville; therefore Hughen certainly has cause to drum his fingers. But as long as the side windows can be opened, it can be done. In thirty minutes at the most we should be on the ground.

Nashville is calling us on the radio. Hughen quickly takes up his microphone and acknowledges our attention.

"Nashville special weather . . . ceiling estimated four hundred overcast . . . visibility one mile . . . light freezing rain. . . ."

Now then! What is this? We are returning to an airport which little more than an hour before was bathed in moonlight! We are returning because we could hardly have been considered as really on our way. And there was no hint in the forecast that the city of Nashville and all of its environs should do anything but continue to sleep peacefully beneath the moon. It has no right to sour on us. There *must* be some mistake. The operator must be reading a report from some other station.

Luck has a miserly reservoir. It seems that unless you are willing to accept impurities, you can draw out just so much at one time.

There has been cause to believe that we may have consumed our ration for one night, and it is even more certain that we are in no shape to make an instrument approach through freezing rain. Yet outside my window, past the wedding-cake display of ice, there is not a shred of cloud between what has become our private plateau and the moon. This makes it much easier to believe the next report from Nashville will be more cheerful.

Twenty minutes pass. Our course is now west, straight for Nashville. Our propeller ice is entirely gone and the air continues smooth. But we have not lost a millimeter of our wing ice. We cannot will it, or wish it, or melt it, or blow it, away. Where are the engineers again? The wings should somehow be heated. And our rudder is still frozen solid.

We pass through the cone of silence over Nashville station. Hughen takes the controls and starts a gentle left bank. As we circle, the moon appears in my side window. It gives luminosity to the ice decorations around the frame, then slides out of sight. Our traffic clearance has instructed us to hold over the station as another ship is in the process of landing. So we wait and the moon wanders twice across the area of my window. The cloud deck is not far below. Somewhere in it the approaching ship should be plowing through the murk, and when it has found the runway, it will be our turn. We would appreciate it if the other ship would hurry. We have had quite enough of this limited scenery.

Nashville is calling us. Our clearance?

"Message. Nashville special weather. Pilot reports ceiling estimated three hundred feet . . . visibility one half mile. Eastern Airlines missed second attempt approach and is proceeding to alternate. Pilot reports moderate icing in approach. Do you wish further clearance or will you hold? Signed Garrow."

This ambiguous message is actually studded with suggestions. It must be interpreted beyond the mere figures, weighed for its nuances, and applied to our own touchy situation. Translated, it means that for the moment the weather at Nashville is below our company standards, but this may change. Therefore if Hughen thinks he can afford to linger in the vicinity awhile, he might descend for a "look." If he then finds the weather legal, he may land. If not, he is in trouble and he'd better have fuel enough to go elsewhere. It is up to him, and the dispatcher on the ground, who is not influenced by either ice or moon, will abide by his decision. Yet there is a further hint in the wording itself. "Pilot reports ceiling . . ." This is far more trustworthy than a report from a ground observer. Also it was not just any pilot but an Eastern Airlines pilot who decided to pass up the field. This is more than a delicate admonition and one which the dispatcher knows will be understood and appreciated by Hughen. He must now weigh a separate factor which affects the whole business of airline flying. And, after evaluation, fit it in with the more tangible elements.

He must give at least some consideration to the fact that airline pilots are separated into tribes in spite of their common occupation. Gossip has provided legend, which in turn leads to unavoidable generalization. Thus United pilots are considered colorless and sticklers for regulations. American pilots are thought to be a mixed lot, prone to independent complaint and rebellion. TWA pilots, highly regarded individually, are pitied for the chameleon management of their company. Pan American pilots, admired and envied for their long-range flying, are thought to be shy and backward in foul-weather work. The tribes are each healthy and strong in their way, but their characteristics, conditioned by their aerial territories, are as different as the Sioux, the Navahos, and the Cherokees. All of this is recognized as debatable. Yet the legends had to start somehow.

Now it is important for Hughen to remember that Eastern Airlines pilots are singularly determined and clever. They are not given to timidity, and if the pilot now beneath us has refused to continue his approach, then the conditions must be very unpleasant indeed.

Hughen, newly concerned with our fuel reserve, takes less than a minute to join all the factors together and reach a decision.

"We are proceeding to our alternate. Request clearance direct to Columbus instead of via airways."

We will save a few miles by flying a direct course, but it means I shall be very busy with cross bearings. Before the clearance is received, Hughen has already swung off toward the northeast.

In five minutes it will be three o'clock in the morning. It is over four hundred miles to Columbus—at our present speed, some three and a half hours' flying.

On Hughen's demand I check the amount of our fuel.

"We're fat. Four hundred and twenty gallons remaining."

Hughen is not so easily persuaded that all is now well. He holds his computer before him and regards it dubiously. His lower lip slides up to brush along the wisp of mustache; then he shakes his head.

"We're using a hundred and thirty gallons an hour. I doubt if we'll be able to reduce power very much. So we can't make Columbus even in still air and keep any reserve. Get the Cincinnati, Louisville, and St. Louis weather. Ask for the winds aloft."

I call, staring at the ice. If it would go away, then we might fly like an airplane. If . . .

My request is answered directly from New York, evidence that those on the ground are beginning to take a special interest in the proceedings. The reports are not encouraging.

Louisville . . . closed. St. Louis . . . closed. Cincinnati appears on the border line with a five-hundred-foot ceiling, rain, and a mile of visibility. We are homeless beneath the moon. Columbus, our original alternate, which is now beyond our hopes, is the only haven reporting favorable weather. Hughen is biting his mustache again.

The voice from New York drones a report on the winds aloft. I copy the series of figures which presume to reflect the movements of the upper air levels in our vicinity. They are the offerings of an inexact science and not to be trusted implicitly. But they do serve as an omen for good or evil.

I hand the paper to Hughen. Even when things are not going well in a cockpit, there are certain social amenities to be observed, and a man who finds malicious satisfaction in spreading gloom is a wretched airmate. I would rather have kept the winds aloft a secret from Hughen, thus permitting him to concentrate on what was now inevitable.

New York has said that the winds will blow from the north at this altitude and their force will be thirty miles an hour. They will subtract from our speed a like amount and leave us plowing upstream at a time when we need every blessing. It not only means that we *must* land at Cincinnati but Hughen must make his instrument approach unerringly. There will not be fuel for a second pass at the field. We must now consider minutes rather than hours.

Hughen is starting to sweat again. He smooths the pitiful hairs as he reads the figures. For some reason they seem even less in number. At this moment Hughen is the loneliest man in the world.

"Give me a fix every five minutes."

The next hour was checkered with quick change from hope to disappointment, from certainty to doubt, and at last resolved itself into an atmosphere of angry determination. If fate was bound to defeat us, then it should have chosen fewer and more subtle harassments. We might have been tricked into becoming wastrels of time and, feeling entitled to some relaxation, have thrown away as much as five minutes. But we were overly beset and the consequence was a team perfectly agreed that if we were compelled to leave the moon and go down into the blackness forever, it would not be the result of our neglect or surrender.

Our combat against the series of misfortunes was without any sign of confusion. Nor could anyone say, when all was done, that we should have fought in another way. The pandemonium of noise was gone, the radio was so clear we could turn the volume far down, and once more the night enclosed our cockpit. There was then a relative hush, which would have been truly restful had it not been so contaminated with forebodings.

Hughen devoted himself entirely to keeping immediate life in our airplane and yet reserving the last drop of its vitality. He set the propellers in full high pitch and reduced the power until we mushed through the air. He leaned the mixture of fuel so that the proportion of air was increased vastly beyond normal. All of this placed a tremendous faith in our engines, but it cut down our fuel consumption until it was a wonder they ran at all. He was gambling because he had to, but the cards he held were good and he was a skillful player.

Above all, Hughen flew—although the term is inadequate to describe his handling of the airplane. The fact was that he urged it along, his tense body seeming actually to lift the DC-2 every time it appeared on the point of aerodynamic exhaustion. This crisis threatened again and again because as we burned fuel and therefore became lighter in the air, Hughen would correspondingly reduce the power. And so the uneasy relation of weight to minimum speed for flight was set up once more. Throughout this interminable struggle he spoke once.

"If this were anything but a DC-2 we just wouldn't be in the air."

And I remembered McCabe felt the same way about a DC-2 and how on a spring morning he had said I might one day learn to love the machine in spite of its cantankerous nature. The only inaccuracy in McCabe's prediction was that my passionate love affair began at night.

I had more time for thought than Hughen because my work came in bunches. So between radio fixes I not only had moments to fall in love with a haggard and middle-aged collection of aluminum but I had also time to wonder at its presence. The schedule called for us to be flying a DC-3, which would undeniably have had a much worse time carrying this same load of ice. And since our past margin had been nil, it followed that what Hughen had said must be true.

Then why? What combination of events, over which we could not possibly have had the slightest control, caused the last-minute substitution of an airplane that would carry more ice than the type we were supposed to fly? Who . . . what did this? What was luck? Were we, for some reason, more deserving of its mystic attention than others who encountered a series of circumstances— which culminated in their destruction? If we were favored, then I wanted to know why, and so perhaps manage to continue the relationship.

I did not have a great deal of time to twist my way through such imponderables. But I had enough.

A final fix showed us to be twenty miles out of Cincinnati. Just before we flew through the cone of silence, we were called on the radio.

"Cincinnati weather now measures three thousand feet . . . visibility better than three miles . . . wind calm. . . ."

Our rejoicing was short-lived. It expired when I checked the fuel still aboard. Fifty gallons.

The dawn was barely apparent when we slithered out beneath the overcast. Through Hughen's side window I caught a glimpse of the airport dozing in the soft twilight. The man deserved respite for he had been nearly five hours at the controls. But he had two problems still remaining. He had to line up with a runway though he was quite blind forward, and he had to be right the first time. He could not skid the ship and so align it exactly during the last moments of descent. The rudder, in spite of our combined kicks at the pedals, remained frozen. Thus he would be obliged to approach the runway at the end of a banking circle, keeping it in sight as long as he could and then at the last moment straightening out and holding a fixed line of flight. I thought to help him during this maneuver by peering from my side window and calling course corrections. None were necessary. Hughen nailed the runway down somehow and held his descent as if sliding down a banister. He said later that he was not overly worried about the runway. He had a far more serious problem.

Even Hughen had never flown an airplane so laden with ice. By experimentation he now knew its demands and behavior when cruising. But what would happen when those aerodynamic conditions were abruptly changed? Leaving level flight, our angle of attack would be quite different, although presumably this change would be to our benefit. It seemed that a wing so grotesquely malformed with ice would regain some of its efficiency when its attitude was tipped in descent. It seemed. We did not know.

Then when the landing gear and flaps were lowered and contributed their enormous drag, what happened? Normal approach speed was one hundred and five miles an hour. Touchdown to the runway should be at least eighty. In the usual situations there was always warning of an incipient stall and thus time to increase speed and recover. This was something we knew.

But now? How much warning would there be from our distorted wings? Or would there be any at all? How much steeper should the descent be, how much extra air speed maintained to compensate for our infirmity? There was nothing in any regulation about the matter because no one knew.

There was an ancillary complication. Like all airports, Cincinnati had its geographical limits. The southerly side was bordered by a high dike. The runways were black, wet, and slippery from the rain. If the landing was too fast toward the south we might consume the entire width of the airport and slide into the dike. The westerly runway terminated before the passenger terminal, which could also effectively stop an airplane. When an irresistible force , . .

It was like fitting the head to the hat, and Hughen's choice was a beggarman's. It was perhaps best that once we were out of the cloud, he had less than a minute to dwell upon the alternatives. Our fuel meters yelled starvation.

There is a runway. I snap the landing gear down, then the flaps. Our speed slacks off alarmingly. Hughen slams on full power and the engines gulp the last of our fuel.

Hughen banks slightly, daring not to chance more than a few degrees. His face is pale; his eyes dart from instrument to instrument. He allows our speed to increase with the descent. One hundred and thirty miles an hour. I try to convince myself that this speed is not outrageous for the restricted bowling alley ahead. Yet Hughen, sensing the ship through the controls, must believe he needs this speed.

"We're past the wires!"

Hughen flies the ship right down to the ground. Not until the wheels hit does he cut the power. We hit hard and stay earth-bound. There is no life left in our wings for bouncing.

Good morning to the city of Cincinnati.

These were the truths of that morning:

We skated along the rain-soaked runway for nearly one thousand yards and came to a halt directly before the concrete terminal. We were spared the vision of its swift approach because of our opaque windshield.

In all of our fuel tanks there was a total of thirty gallons remaining. Because of the tank design most of this would have been unavailable to our engines; therefore a second attempt to land would almost certainly have failed before completion.

It took the mechanics two hours of hard labor to knock the ice from our wings, engine cowlings, and empennage. In most places it had reached a thickness of four inches.

Nashville was not declared open for flights until past noon. Louisville and St. Louis cleared somewhat later. We were not interested in Columbus since we could never have reached it no matter how great our determination.

We ate a strangely silent breakfast in the airport café. There was really nothing to say and even the click of our coffee cups seemed intrusive upon our thoughts. We did not see the stewardess or the passengers until much later in the morning. They were taken to a hotel for breakfast and for this we were unaccountably grateful. It seemed very important not to see them. It seemed very important not to see anyone and to lean back against the backs of our chairs, blow smoke at the ceiling, and only look at our thoughts.

We could have rested in Cincinnati for the day. And the temptation to do this was powerful, for, having lost both desperation and fear, we were now very weary. We sat for a long time, joined not in conversation but in great sighs.

It happened that there were no local crews available and possibly this influenced Hughen's decision to proceed, although it was doubtful that he felt any pressing call to duty. He simply wanted to reach his home, he said, and lie down, and think things over. I understood his desire and hoped that after he had slept he would spend some time in an armchair drinking beer. On my own, I was still wondering about the substitution of the DC-2 and the remarkable clearing of the Cincinnati weather. And I wondered about the valley into which we descended blindly without hitting anything. And I thought that something must be done about ice on airplanes because next time there might not be a valley.

So we flew on to New York through weather which was not good but merely routine. In my logbook I wrote down the time of our flight from Nashville to New York.

It was eight hours and fifty minutes.

Beside these figures I placed a short notation. "Ice."

☆

V I

OF NUMBERS

☆

AND THEIR POWER TO REDUCE
THE PRESUMPTUOUS QUICKLY

MOST line pilots deliberately cultivate an almost psychopathic modesty which would be intolerable if it were not for the large part genuine and salted with humor.

It would be inconceivable for a line pilot to approach his fellows at the end of a flight and announce that he had just executed a complicated holding pattern without a moment's delay, flown an exact instrument approach, and topped it all off with a perfect landing. Instead he would say, "Well, I barged around for a while not knowing where I was, as usual, and when I finally got the clearance through my head, I managed to locate the range station. Of course, I still have a lot to learn about an ILS approach . . . those needles just never come together quite right for me . . . but this time I persuaded them to meet in the right place, so we stumbled on down until to my complete surprise there was the runway right ahead. Of course, if I could have seen anything it would have been one of my usual rotten landings, but it was raining hard and the windshield wipers weren't operating and so I just sort of waited until the ship landed itself, which is what a man ought to do all the time if he had any sense. . . ."

This is, of course, outrageous twisting of the truth. It is also ostentation. But that is the way it must be said if anything is said at all. If you are a visitor in an airline cockpit, you do not ask the captain where the ship might be. You say, "Lost again?" The reply is also standard. "Certainly."

Likewise, should you inquire of a line pilot if he has ever been afraid, his answer is bound to be "All the time." Which is another distortion of the truth.

Yet the tenor of such replies should repudiate those envious cynics who always hasten to label courage a virtue of indifferent value. Line pilots do not live in an atmosphere of heroism, for that is a very temporary condition better suited to wildly inspired moments in which the hero hardly knows what he is doing. The pilots know what they are doing, right or wrong, always. They wear courage like a comfortable belt, rarely giving it a thought.

But a line pilot is *wary* all of the time, which is an entirely different matter. To be continuously aware you must know what to be wary of, and this sustained attitude can come only from experience. Learning the nature and potentialities of the countless hazards is like walking near quicksand.

In spite of our considerable separation by geographical and climatic conditions, the maturing of Mood, and Gay, and Lippincott, and all the others proceeded in substantially the same fashion as my own.

After the ice affair I flew two trips with Hughen and then no more. This I regretted because he was decent and thoughtful enough to commend my behavior publicly on the night of the ice. His praise helped toward my recognition as a dependable co-pilot, and I was sent off indiscriminately with first one captain and then another. The constant change was invaluable, forcing me to absorb a variety of experience which when added together amounted to decades of flying. I sought out the good in each captain and tried to discard those flying habits which were not so good. In turn, these men passed on their faults and qualities in various ways.

The gigantic Dunn was good-natured enough, but he had a strange facility for making me feel unsure. As a consequence I could not seem to make a better-than-average landing or take-off, or do anything else satisfactorily when I sat beside him. Yet I learned a great deal from Dunn. He was always wary.

Mitchell affected me in exactly the opposite way. He was a remarkably carefree pilot and entrusted me with all kinds of responsibilities which were rightfully his own. He was the first captain to allow me to fly in the left-hand seat, a tremendous reflection of his generosity and confidence, for he then, in effect, became temporarily co-pilot. I did well for Mitchell and pleaded with Robbins to allow me to remain with him.

He could not always arrange it. So I flew with Konz, the former piccolo player, and Dewitt, the much beloved veteran who would one day be so cruelly deceived by the stupid instrumentation in a brand-new airplane. There was Lewis, and Harris, and Macatee, and a brief assignment to Beard, test pilot of the line. Beard was more engineer than pilot and his total absorption in whatever he happened to be testing left those who went aloft with him sitting behind a veil of loneliness. It was also nerve-wracking work and I made no protest when I was transferred back to the line.

There was Miller, who took such a personal interest in my progress that it was almost like being in school again, and Blogett, who was at some pains to point out that since I was not army trained like himself my mere presence on the line offended him.

There was Heredrich, Bidwell, Wood, Hamer, and Macklin. There was Hefner, Fitzgerald, Ricks, and a little martinet named Alessandro. At first I believed that Alessandro hated me, perhaps for some ill-considered remark or minor mistake. In time I learned that his disdainful manner was directed toward every co-pilot who ever flew with him. He was a petty and abusive tyrant who openly admitted that he believed a co-pilot's life should be made miserable for as long as possible. I escaped his attentions finally and crept away wishing him bad luck. It was exasperating to see Alessandro remain unscathed while other, much finer men suffered so much evil.

There was Goeringer and Hunt, Fanning, Hinton, and Ellis. Then Bledsoe, who looked exactly like a young George Washington, and Carpenter, who was vested with the business of putting a final seal of approval on my flying.

From all these men, including the despotic Alessandro, I learned something of my craft. Little by little their skills and ways of thinking contributed to my own resources until they built into a separate entity which was specifically designed to transport and preserve the lives of others. For any professional it was a magnificent opportunity to drain the best from his predecessors. I flew, in all, with some sixty captains. With each one the association was necessarily close. We not only worked within a few inches of each other but we also ate together and normally slept in the same room.

About this time Scroggins and Moore were killed. They were flying through a thunderstorm and suddenly dived into the ground. Lightning could have blinded them or blast effect could have blown in the windows. No one knew the exact cause, but I remembered how Ross had handled our thunderstorm and resolved to imitate his method if I ever became a captain.

Then Fey and Sandegren crashed against Bountiful Peak in the Wasatch Mountains. The Salt Lake radio range was malfunctioning.

There were periods when I again flew with Keim. These lasted a month or more, and we always flew AM-21 to Cleveland. More generous with his confidence now, Keim allowed me to do a full half of the flying regardless of the weather. And he opened the ventilator when he smoked his cigars.

Summer and thunderstorms again. Another winter and spring once more. The back of my uniform shone with the long polishing of so many cockpit seats. The full stripe and the narrower half stripe on my sleeve were tarnished and the cuffs beginning to fray. I made no effort to conceal these marks of service, partly because there were many new co-pilots now coming to the line. They should see in my careful dilapidation that I had been flying much longer than themselves and was therefore deserving of some respect.

And at last there came a day when I took out my first flight as captain. In my logbook there was now carefully recorded three thousand one hundred twenty hours and ten minutes. This was not very much.

It was a sort of traumatic shock to become Don Quixote instead of the Sancho Panza who sits on the right. After waiting so long without true hope, the transformation left me unbelieving until I discovered how very easy it was to accept the luxuries of command.

Boyd, who had first introduced me to a DC-3, eased the transition by coming along on my debut as captain. Now that I had left the peasantry he suggested spending a part of my captain's wealth on a new uniform. The gold stripes, one so tarnished and the other new and now of equal width, made a startling contrast. It was offensive to the eye, Boyd said.

But I thought about numbers and how news of my promotion would spread across the line as fast as an airplane could fly. The numbers. The accursed numbers, to which we were all slaves, insisted that no matter how good a job I did flying, my elevation to command might be extremely temporary. The captain's stripes would remain because nothing could remove my qualification, but they would merely become a rather forlorn advertisement that I was a captain without a ship. And so the very training I had been given in prudence forbade me to invest in a complete new uniform. Instead I simply bought an additional new stripe.

I flew in vast contentment for nearly two months. All of the flights were without incident, and beneath me I saw the summer haze descend again on AM-21. It was my route: I loved it for its beauty and familiarity, loved it even with overtones of jealousy, and I gave to it all of the affection a man can give to his work. While this sudden investiture with authority might have made me uncomfortable on a strange route, here I was at home, knowing my way through the sky as exactly as the names of the men who would greet me on each return to earth. I held no further ambition. I had entered the temple, been set in place alongside Ross and Keim, and I found this new equality worth all that had gone before.

When addressed as "Captain" I found it impossible not to preen my ego, and I took care to see that Pierce and Cudney and Lawless, who were at various times my co-pilots, had little cause for complaint. We were each aware that any day I might be forced to rejoin their co-pilot ranks, and I dreaded the thought of a smile on their faces when the inexorable numbers humbled me. I began a campaign to outwit the numbers, a sort of pitiful, single-handed promotion of the air transport industry. I reasoned that the more passengers we carried, the more airplanes the line must buy and hence my term of command might continue rather than expire. I wrote elaborate flight reports. I went back to the cabin on every flight and tried to convince my passengers that the only sensible way to travel was through the air.

"No, there is no such thing as an air pocket . . . I am sorry about this slight bumpiness . . . that is Utica just over there . . . There is Rome where the Stars and Stripes first flew in battle . . . our ground speed is one hundred and ninety miles an hour . . . delighted to have you aboard . . . please fly with us again."

As the weeks passed, I came very close to begging people to fly again because I knew the numbers were closing fast. My coaxing was indiscriminate. I even included the liars who are standard fixtures in any form of travel. On airplanes the tie salesman becomes president of a haberdashery chain, the maiden aunt becomes *femme fatale*. And there is always the former war aviator who cannot resist explaining what a hell-for-leather fellow he was. His exploits are interesting if only because after a very few minutes it becomes technically obvious that he has never flown an airplane in war or peace, or ever in his life.

Just as the first thunderstorms began to boil on the route, the sword fell in spite of my efforts. Lippincott, who was 16 numbers senior to me, Gay, who was 10, and even Owen, who was but a single number ahead of me, found their way like vultures to the fat carcass of AM-21.

It now became my bitter duty to acquaint these foreigners with my territory. My welcome suited a man arranging an assignation for a stranger with his wife. Gay, smiling the easy way I had previously so much treasured, tried to soothe my choking pride. But I was not to be comforted. The closeness we had known in a cheap and musty hotel when we were both struggling through Lester's school was now lost in pride and greed. Gay, the bene-ficiary of the welfare system, would take my place as captain and I must actually pull out the chair for him. As we signed our names to the logbook, mine now back in the same old co-pilot's space, I said what I had to say.

"Et tu, Brute."

But Gay knew that my scorn was directed only at the system.

Having once flown as captain, I found it increasingly difficult to accept the servile life of a co-pilot. The pain was even more acute spiritually than it was financially. I performed my duties in a sort of envious trance, automatically—all the heart gone from whatever I did. I cursed the numbers, loathing their ability to render me so helpless. I listened to rumors of additional airplanes and found them nothing more. Indeed, the last of our DC-2's were being sold off. I learned that exactly the same disappointments had occurred at other bases. Katzman flew briefly as a captain and was soon superseded by a senior man. Mood, the same. We had been promoted only because we were on the spot.

The miserable numbers! They offered unwanted protection. They were chains, I felt, and they clanked but one dismal song— mediocrity. Yet how they could devise and fix our destinies. For

Gay it might be said that the numbers set the appointment for his death. Had it been possible for us to exchange numbers I might have been the one who crashed into the river near Nashville, and it could have been Gay who lay listening to the mosquitoes in a slovenly town called Corumbá.

☼

VII

GYPSIES

☼

DOUBTFUL OF STATION AND INTENTIONS

I CAME to Corumbá, which is in the very center of the South American continent, because I thought to escape the dictatorial numbers until they were in better temper.

I lay on my back, spread out in the form of a naked H upon the dank and lumpy mattress. Beyond the mosquito netting I could see the framed outline of the window, which extended all the way to the floor. The last time I had looked at the window there was a lizard clinging to the vertical frame, and I had inquired of him how he presumed to justify his existence if he would not devour more of the mosquitoes. But he was a fat and slothful reptile and seemed disinterested in either me or mosquitoes. It was perfectly obvious to me that this lizard had enough seniority so that he could simply coast—which brought me again to thinking how the numbers had contrived to send me so very far from the comforts of AM-21.

If I could have retained my place as captain on AM-21 it is doubtful that I would ever have become involved in international affairs—as I liked to think of my role in this project. Actually my job was to fly airplanes and nothing more.

The State Department had finally become alarmed at the domination of South American airlines by the Germans. They were particularly strong in Brazil, Colombia, and Bolivia. They hired every national they could to aid their own pilots and technicians, and then they hired relatives of those already employed. And then they hired the relatives of the relatives. Thus the Germans and nationalized Germans, who had never really forsaken the fatherland, became an extremely popular force throughout South America. This situation prevailed long before the beginning of World War II and it was carefully nurtured as Nazi ambitions multiplied. While the Germans geared themselves to more extensive conflict, they sent Luftwaffe pilots in rotation to this special training ground. Here they not only learned long-range and jungle flying but gathered invaluable knowledge against the time when it might become necessary to bomb the Panama Canal.

All of this seemed very remote and even a little silly as I lay waiting for the lizard to move, but it was the reason I had come to Corumbá. It was the reason Park slept in a bed across the room, defying with his gentle snoring my conviction that in most tropical regions there exists a special combination of nocturnal factors antagonistic to human sleep.

It was characteristic of Park that he could sleep soundly through the shrieking of the night monkeys in Santa Cruz, or the exhibitionist cocks of Corumbá at dawn. For he was a wonderfully simple man and if he had any nerves I had yet to observe them.

Park was what so many Texans think they are, or would like to be. He was long and lean and hard. His pale-gray eyes belonged behind the sights of a gun barrel and his walk seemed wrong without the clinking of spurs. He was a shy man and quiet spoken.

Park was in command of our airplane, but it was not because of any numbers. We were put together simply because he had a great deal of flying time and no one as yet knew what kind of an operation this would be. We were both learning the hard way.

The Germans had been flying airline versions of the Fockwulfe Courier and the old but wonderfully versatile Junkers 52. Their services over some of the most difficult flying regions in the world could only be classed as superb. It was not surprising that the South American countries in which they operated were reluctant to drive them away. Who would take care of the relatives, so many of whom would lose their jobs? The Yankees? The mothers of most Yankees, as everyone in South America knew, were whores.

The South Americans were only lightly concerned about any rumblings of a distant war, and if anything did come of it and the Yankees were humiliated, why then most certainly no one from Mexico south to Patagonia would weep.

There were more important, more immediately vital considerations. Who would link together the enormity of Brazil? And with what, if the German airplanes were to be left rotting in the sun? No one knew how to manufacture an airplane in Brazil. Few Brazilians actually understood how big their country was. It was no affair of the peon if even simpler compatriots who dwelt in the forest region of the Aripuana River were still shrinking other compatriots' heads.

Money, as usual, forced the final decision. The Germans were deposed. Some went home, others moved over to Argentina. The relatives were left behind, disenfranchised, staring at the nearly empty sky. And now something had to be done to replace the German services.

These were big countries—in total area much bigger than the United States. And the problem, which had to be solved at once, matched their size. Fortunately there were still some native-born pilots who could perform token service if they had the airplanes. The State Department told these countries, "We will give you the airplanes and we will deliver them wherever you desire." And they desired their new and glistening trinkets in Rio de Janeiro.

Thus it was that Park and I came to rest in a place called Corumbá, which is at least on the way to Rio if the approach is made from the west.

A certain sensation known only the day before this dawn still haunted me. I had found it remarkable and wondered if there could be hidden behind those strange moments a value which I might never comprehend. There had been two definite risks involved. Apparently I had been in control of the first while fate commanded the second.

Hitherto, long-range flight out of the United States had been exclusively the province of Pan American Airways. We had invaded their special field as almost complete innocents. We were obliged to learn fast, and our aids were extremely primitive. We were provided with reasonably accurate charts for the coastal regions, but once we ventured toward the South American interior the charts became so sketchy as to be nearly useless.

From La Paz, Bolivia, toward the east and Corumbá, thence almost to Rio, we were required to find our way from a blotchy facsimile chart compiled by a mixture of authorities, all of whom were at least frank in setting down their ignorance. North and south were accurate enough, but there any near resemblance between sketch and the true configurations of the earth ended. The heights of many mountain peaks were simply not recorded. Entire mountains were sometimes misplaced. Rivers were represented by vague dotted lines which rarely bore any relation to the actual courses. Such few towns as were shown were accurately located as far as we knew, but we never knew our exact location when we finally found them and so were never sure.

In Washington we had been told the whole undertaking would be a lark. We had merely to fly the airplanes to Rio de Janeiro, sign them away to the Brazilians, and lounge on the beach until return passage was available. We were told that the airplanes would be a delight to fly—brand-new Lockheed Lodestars.

The last claim was the only near-truth. The Lockheeds performed splendidly even under conditions for which they were never designed.

It had not been long before the first worms appeared in this aerial paradise. It was characteristic of the Lodestars that the right engine invariably began to spit and backfire when all should be well. Because this fault was known and expected, it was more annoying than frightening, but it did fray the nerves when flying over the sea, the jungle, or mountainous terrain. There were three curious angles to this unpleasant habit. The engine never failed entirely, and if left alone for a little time it would smooth in its labors and run perfectly. No one could explain the malfunctioning or seem to correct it. And finally, the left engine never displayed the slightest tendency to imitate the misbehavior of the right engine. It was like living with a dyspeptic.

Our Lockheeds, hastily taken from the factory, were not equipped with oxygen. From Lima, Peru, the Andes must be surmounted before landing in Bolivia. Fortunately, there is a pass which notches the mountains to the east of Arequipa. By standards other than Tibetan, it could not be considered a very easy pass. Its lowest altitude is nearly eighteen thousand feet. It is also a gigantic Venturi, sucking the sea winds from the Pacific and blasting them upon Lake Titicaca and the vast, monotonous *altoplano* of Bolivia. It is a starkly forbidding place, a region of condors wheeling above corrugations so sharp and red they seem to be the bleeding wounds of a butchered earth.

Now, in Corumbá, I remembered the principal color in the pass as red, which it may not really have been. For on our flights there were moments when the atmosphere was purple, and other times when the length of the pass was filled with tiny blue stars spinning concentrically and sliding together as they might in the interior of a kaleidoscope. Yet this was the way the pass had appeared to me, flying on the very fringe of my personal ability to fight anoxemia.

Park said the entire pass was green to him, but we had not the will or breath to argue. Not while flying at eighteen thousand five hundred feet without oxygen. Or pretending to fly. In actuality we sat flatulent in our seats, gasping, staring like idiots at instruments which made no sense, and at peaks which continued shimmering on and on upward to incredible heights. We were not condors, or even trained mountain climbers. As two sea-level pilots we had no business attempting this pass without oxygen. Another five hundred feet high, or an additional twenty minutes in the pass, and we would never have roused from our euphoria. We would not have cared about anything at all.

After staggering through the pass in which the Lockheed flew little better than its groggy pilots, we were able to "let down" as far as sixteen thousand feet. Some of our delusions ceased, but since the Bolivian *alto-plano* continues for hundreds of miles at altitudes better tagged on mountain peaks, we could descend no farther. We sucked at thin air and stared hang-mouthed at a fantastic moonscape. Our altimeters were obvious liars. We were hedgehopping at sixteen thousand feet. To the west and east was the magnificent fencing of the Andes. Many of the peaks were enveloped in snow squalls, and even the lesser summits scraped the sky at twenty thousand feet.

At length we came upon a place called Cochabamba and landed. The airport would have been more agreeable if it were not nine thousand feet above sea level and set in a bowl of rock-strewn hills. There, with the constant wind sighing through its fuselage, rested one of the former German airplanes. It was a Junkers 86, very slightly modified for airline use. The winds of the *alto-plano* had already covered it with fine ochre-colored dust. It could not have been out of service very long, but no one in Cochabamba would say just how long.

I examined the derelict carefully because I had been asked to fly it back to Washington. Our meeting was not love at first sight. I soon discovered that the airplane was a technical monstrosity requiring a crew of at least three men who knew exactly what they were doing. There was no instruction manual of any kind. Some of the flight instruments were of such a strange type that neither Park nor I could be sure of their exact use. And most certainly no one in Cochabamba would be inclined to show me how to fly the thing. Even so, I might have ventured at least a local flight if it had not been for the soft-spoken Park.

He rubbed some of the dust between his long fingers and spat on the earth. I respected Park. He rarely spoke, and when he did, what he had to say was always worth hearing. So I watched his gray eyes as he studied the dust.

"How badly do they want this thing back in Washington?"

"They just said it wasn't really vital, but if I could get it there, it might be interesting to take to pieces."

"A shame no one bothered to cover the engines."

We stood with our backs to the wind and I knew exactly what Park meant. The dust had the hard and gritty feel of emery. There were small drifts of the stuff in the engine air scoops and there was doubtless more ready to filter into the instruments and every moving part of the machinery once the ship was brought to life. No one could say how abrasive its action might be. Nor were there any mechanics who might help us ready the ship for flight.

"Of course it's up to you . . . it would probably hang together . . . but there's no logbook, either, so you'd know what's been done to it . . . and . . ."

Park's voice suddenly faded away as it often did when he had pronounced the meat of his thoughts. He had no use whatsoever for verbal trimmings.

I looked at the drab hills surrounding the airport and saw no promising place to set the "86" down if things began to go wrong. And with the initial take-off at nine thousand feet, things could snowball very quickly. I told myself that I was entirely unfamiliar with the airplane and so could easily be overlong correcting a fault. And overlong here could be a few seconds. Yet I yearned to fly this stranger.

"It won't accomplish much if I take it to pieces on the way."

I was talking myself out of the risk and was very conscious of it. Within me, caution had become such a fatty rind I could almost poke my finger into it.

I had been taught by so many wise men.

"It certainly looks fine right where it is," Park said.

We turned away from the Junkers and I dared not look at it again. Would Ross have flown it? I rather thought he would. As for Hughen and Keim, Hughen might take a quick look and find himself suffering very suddenly from an eye irritation. Keim would grunt and label the entire idea as madness.

But how about the younger men? I thought Watkins might have given it a try, and perhaps Carter. McGuire . . . no. Mood . . . no. Charleton . . . probably not. Peterson . . . maybe. Lippincott, or Gay . . . never.

In excusing my refusal of a challenge, I allowed my thoughts to make decisions for other men who had never heard of the Junkers. It was a very convenient escape. And in seeking escape, I disposed of the first risk.

The second risk presented itself far to the east of the Bolivian heights. It was a straight fifty-fifty gamble. Yet the underlying purpose of this risk removed the sense of folly and substituted that strange and haunting sense of jubilation.

I left my soggy dumpling of a bed and stepped out on the balcony of the hotel in Corumbá where I could look toward the west and the wilderness which now separated us from the Andes. And again I saw those ponderous upheavals, as easily as if they had actually been apparent. The bleak, ghastly, end-of-the-world light brought them over the jungle as in a mirage.

There was something wrong with the Andes. If a natural object can create the suggestion of emotion, then the Andes hated all trespassers. They belonged wrapped elsewhere in their lunar coldness—on the moon, perhaps, but not on this earth.

From La Paz to the harsh eastern lips of the Andes is only a short time by muleback. Perhaps a week. Then suddenly, and most dramatically, the barren, rocky, yellow world of the Bolivian *altoplano* ceases altogether. At once the peaks, both the corpulent and the scrawny, drop straight down into an all-swallowing morass of jungles, sleek and reeking in luxuriance, and they also hate you. They unite instantly in a fierce embrace and there is no welcome for strangers anywhere.

The usual journey by muleback from the Bolivian capital of La Paz to Santa Cruz, which is the first town of any size east of the mountains, requires a month. In the Lockheed it had taken us less than two hours, although we would have been more at ease if we had known the exact height of the peaks between which we presumed to fly. We did not like flying close alongside a peak and discovering its height to be seventeen thousand when the chart indicated fifteen thousand. So we flew to the upper limits of our tolerance and were groggy again.

Once we were certain that enough time had elapsed to clear the Andes, we descended rapidly. And we breathed with the ecstasy of fish returning to the sea. It was solid air, humid and pungent with rotting things—but it was air! We ravished it. We twisted our bodies through it, tried to pinch it between our fingers, and gulping, cried its delight.

We continued to descend until our altimeters said we were at two thousand feet. As we slipped out of the clouds, there was a jungle of jungles; its decay was enwrapped in the steaming ghosts of all the fetid, primeval elements squashed into its ooze. Yet we considered it invigorating because at least it was air.

Santa Cruz was a mud-streeted town with its tile-roofed dwellings protruding like a rash from the green hide of the jungle. And the airport manager was a heavy-voiced Dutchman so sodden with malaria that the flab about his cheeks shivered independently as he spoke. He was very lonely and pressed his meager treasures upon us—two bunks with netting in recent repair, an unappetizing meal of cold beans, and all the gin we wished to drink.

"I live on gin," he announced morosely. "I live on gin because I must also live on quinine, and the gin almost stops the ringing in my ears."

The sweat rained from the dewlaps on each side of his mouth, and across his forehead there was a constant eruption of droplets which no amount of swabbing with his ever-present handkerchief seemed to absorb.

"It is very hot," we said, pitying him.

"It is always hot in Santa Cruz if you do not have malaria. But if you have malaria and if you stay here, you will know it well; then it is both cold and hot at the same time and you wonder what the devil is going to do to you next. Do you believe in the devil?"

I looked at Park and saw that he was not going to answer such a question. So I tried to answer for both of us, equivocating.

"It depends upon what you mean by the devil."

The Dutchman took a long pull at his gin, which was his fourth by my count, and which seemed not to have the slightest effect upon his nearly perfect command of the English language.

"It is the devil who makes one man rich and the other man poor. The devil assigns one man an amusing bitch of a wife who cannot be trusted so far as the market. Or the devil may send another man a good, dull wife who will drown him in boredom. The devil keeps me in Santa Cruz. He brought me here in the first place although at the time I did not fully understand exactly who was responsible."

"Do you like it here?"

"I hate it. That should be perfectly obvious."

"Then why don't you leave?"

His manner changed at once and his voice became patronizing. "It would be better if *you* left—better if you had never come. Because of you many people have lost their jobs, and a job anywhere in South America is a very precious thing."

He sighed, swabbed all about his flushed face with the handkerchief, and sighed again. "I am very very lonely," he said. "I am probably the only person in Bolivia who is happy to see you. Even so I advise you to be careful. Most people here or in Brazil would prefer to see you fail. Some of them may even help you to fail. You can think as you please, but don't forget about the devil."

Later, when the bottle of gin was nearly empty and we had yawned a hundred times, he gave me a handful of quinine pills and insisted I take them.

"Your ears will ring just like mine," he said. "We will be in tune and understand each other."

I slipped the pills into my pocket.

The next morning as we taxied away from his white-clad figure, I returned his wave of farewell. And when I opened my fist, I allowed the pills to drop on the ground.

It is very doubtful that they would have done any good anyway. Certainly not if we lost the second risk, which was by now well under way.

Large areas of our facsimile charts were marked simply UN-EXPLORED. This was particularly true of the region between our shivering, devil-obsessed Dutchman and Corumbá. The Dutchman had more gin than gasoline, but it was only four hundred miles to Corumbá. So we took off in the already steaming morning with just enough fuel to make our destination, plus an hour's reserve. The Dutchman said he would try to communicate with the radio direction finder station at Corumbá and have it operating for our arrival. "But I do not promise," he warned.

Our only concern was the en-route weather and the winds we might encounter. No reports on this were available because, as the Dutchman explained, "The reports would have to come from the monkeys. And why not?"

We climbed through a clammy deck of cloud which was more like a vast steam bath. We flew in a feeble twilight, and the consistency of the cloud was strange to us. It was very thick and so saturated with moisture it appeared we were boring through a solid. We flew east, toward Corumbá.

The Dutchman had told us that we would be flying over an absolute wilderness. "Do not bother to look out the window," he said. "There is nothing to see except the roof of the jungle, and the jungle is all the same."

We flew for more than an hour, both of us strangely uncomfortable and depressed. Yet there was nothing wrong. Even the right engine of the Lockheed kept its manners and displayed no evidence of belching.

Both of us smoked one cigarette after another although the

smoking seemed only to increase our unaccountable depression. My mouth tasted of beans and stalwart Brazilian coffee. I was very glad now that I had not tried to match gin for gin with the Dutchman. He had not spoken of this depressive atmosphere which was so different from any we had ever known. It seemed to be tangible air. It seemed that if I opened the cockpit window it would flow in and bury us.

After two hours we were still flying on instruments, solidly enwrapped in the overcast. We studied the mass almost continuously now, waiting for some indication of a break. Yet there was not the slightest weakness below, or above, or ahead.

I passed the next thirty minutes alternately turning the direction finder and calling Corumbá on the radio. My atrocious schoolboy Spanish brought no reply. So I made a wild distillation of all my linguistic talents and tried Portuguese. Park also tried variations on our theme. The result was the same. Only silence. There was not even static.

Now, checking our fuel again, we both became mildly concerned. And I knew, like hearing the faint tinkling of a distant bell when the ear really awaits a tolling, that tiny excitation of my fear glands. It was not immediate, nor did it surge through my nervous system and leave me quaking as a quick emergency might. It teased and became almost a pleasurable sensation.

We had set our course by the facsimile chart directly for Corumbá. Since our altitude was nine thousand feet our visibility in every direction would be ample to discover Corumbá, though the unknown winds might set us twenty miles either side of the town. It was inconceivable that we could miss so large a settlement even if we never heard the direction finder. Furthermore, it was so situated on the prominent loop of a river that the entire assembly must stand out from an even greater distance.

We flew for another ten minutes and still remained in cloud. Now the time was very near when the most simple equation must be accepted as law. We had flown long enough in the proper direction to be almost upon Corumbá. If we extended this period and direction of flight much longer we must pass it by.

We had still remaining more than an hour's supply of fuel.

So we decided to descend, hoping there might be a clearing at lower levels. On the radio I continued my heartless assault upon the Portuguese language. Park said the Corumbá operator was doubtless so confused and insulted he would never reply.

Suddenly we emerged into true daylight as if the cloud mass had spat an unwanted substance from its interior. We blinked at the glaring sun, smiled, and wiped at our eyes. There were still clouds below, but it was a thin layer of stratus, much torn and riven with great gaps through which the earth was clearly visible. Looking down, we could see irregular splotches of the jungle. The roof of trees was black-green and just above it circled enormous flocks of white birds. Ahead there was a long tear in the stratus deck which revealed an entirely different kind of landscape. As we approached, this appeared to be marshland interlaced with narrow streams, and in one place we saw a multitude of flamingos. And beyond, the jungle ended.

Park was holding out the black facsimile chart. He pointed to the dotted line of the river which supposedly looped Corumbá.

"I don't see a river," he said with such a mixture of disappointment and suspicion that I began to wonder if my tight-lipped frontiersman was not, in fact, a very subtle and clever actor. "I don't see a river anywhere. . . ."

I forgot about the flamingos and joined his anxious examination of all that we could see. It was considerable, for the earth met the sky more than thirty miles away, and yet there was no body of water which might honestly be called a river.

We waited, holding the course to the east. I tried calling Corumbá again. Silence. I began watching the clock on the instrument panel; my eyes were drawn to it again and again although I knew very well that less than a minute intervened between each inspection. And suddenly I knew that Park was doing the same thing. I found this more amusing than worrisome. We were playing a game which was as old as the combination of two men flying side by side in the same airplane. The game has no official name, but it might be called "I-have-nerves-of-steel . . . as you see."

This game is usually played while awaiting clarification or the resolution of a situation which is likely to be distressing.

Park was obviously an expert at this diversion, and I found it extremely difficult to match his nonchalance. He was cheating, though. Three times I caught him moving the facsimile slightly to one side so he could see the clock. Conversation is always held at a minimum during this game and we followed custom exactly.

"Anything on your side?"

"No . . ."

I cannot explain why I so relished this interlude. Every time the sweep second hand made a revolution of the clock face, we consumed another gallon and a half of fuel. Our supply was now very limited; in fact, the inevitable result of this expenditure was so obvious that neither Park nor myself thought to discuss it. Unless we found the river very soon, and Corumbá soon after, our game would have to be played with the utmost determination.

The earth below had thus far offered only two landing choices. When our fuel was exhausted or nearly so, we could select a swamp or the jungle treetops as a point of reunion. I thought that if we survived the impact we should certainly have an interesting time finding our way to civilization on foot—since we were apparently unable to accomplish our desire in a swiftly moving airplane. I saw Park and myself emerging from the wilderness as a pair of aerial Rip van Winkles. While we waited out the last possible minutes for the river to appear if its location was even approximated on the facsimile, I told him of my vision and complained that if I must be marooned with someone, then what had I done to deserve his company. My clumsy humor was lost in his preoccupation with the clock.

I pretended to look for the river, although I was now convinced we had long passed it. Yet even if the decision had been mine, I would not have changed course. It is an axiom of flying that he who starts wandering around when in doubt never discovers his true whereabouts until it is too late. At least, when we went down we would know in which direction to start walking—back where we came from.

I tried, with an elaborate show of indifference to the result, to call Corumbá again. The usual silence.

"I guess the Dutchman was right. We aren't very popular."

I was thinking about Hughen and how very differently I had felt in the Tennessee ice because it had been so immediate, when Park said, "There's the river."

Still playing the game, he kept his voice perfectly calm.

It was not much of a river. It was only a trickle of yellow gravy snaking through the swamps, and it frequently disappeared altogether in the dense mangrove brush. It must have been misplaced by at least eighty miles on our facsimile chart although its direction was fairly true.

The risk which was to afford me such an incongruous sense of jubilation was now at hand.

For, as we approached the river, which cut across our course at right angles, it became very apparent that there was no prominent bend or any evidence of a town. Somehow, because of the unknown winds or the inaccuracies of the chart, we had come upon the wrong section of the river. Which way, then, was Corumbá? To the north or to the south? There was no one to ask except the flamingos and we were in poor shape for exploration. We did not have enough fuel to fly north beyond the horizon and then, if Corumbá did not appear, retrace our flight southward until it did. The same would be true if we first started off to the south. We could only allow a few moments to consider the decision which must now be made. It was not really a decision. It was pure black and white gamble and we recognized it as such. If Corumbá was to the north and we turned that way, we would make it. If not, we would not. Never. At least not in an airplane.

We circled once over the river, postponing the decision perhaps two minutes.

"Which way do you think?" Park asked.

"To the south."

I was not at all sure why I thought Corumbá should be to the south, nor did I have any technical basis for believing it lay in that direction.

"I agree," Park said less surely.

So we turned south along the river. Park set the engines at maximum cruise and I leaned the fuel mixtures to near starvation.

We flew ten minutes in silence, searching the horizon for any sign of smoke or even a break in the jungle. Then . . .

"The river is getting wider . . . I think."

"I hope it's the right river."

Park called Corumbá once, waited without hope, and hung up his microphone. And we were silent again until twenty minutes had passed.

It was during this time that I knew the excitement, the sense of joy, which so puzzled me. The feeling did not diminish, even as my doubts took hold. It seemed that we had lost the gamble and should have turned north instead of south. I looked down at the river wondering about its temperature.

Where the river made a slight twist I saw a collection of logs strewn along the baking mud. Then I saw one of the logs slither into the water and I thought to tease Park with my indifference.

"Alligators," I said, eying his slim figure. "And lean meat is always preferred."

But he had not lost the game and looked down disdainfully.

"They're only crocodiles," he said with the authority of a man who passed them every day.

How long we might have been able to maintain this pretense of calm, how much the steady drumming of the engines contributed to our confidence, or the brilliant sun, or the nearly perfect visibility, was all impossible to evaluate. Perhaps true fear was smothered in the still remaining hope that our choice had been the correct one. As the minutes passed and the needles on our fuel gauges moved inexorably toward the E which meant "Empty," our composure remained exactly the same.

I sat back in my seat, hardly bothering to search the horizon now. For a little time I thought about the numbers.

Another five minutes passed. I wished we had some kind of rubber boat.

Suddenly I saw a loop in the river. It was only a few miles ahead, and there was a red-roofed town scattered along its perimeter. Park saw it at exactly the same moment. He looked at me, keeping his gray eyes expressionless. We did not speak so much as a word now, for to do so would be an open confession of doubt, and this our flying selves would not permit until much later when the pressure had left us entirely.

We saw the airport, such as it was—a flat place on the fringe of the town. As we turned into the final approach, all sense of zest and expectancy left me. I was simply hot and weary. I knew no jubilation in the actual finding of Corumbá. It was as though I had been cheated.

Before I left the balcony I took a long and final look toward the west, where I had re-erected the Andes and spread out the image of a jungle before them; and it seemed to me that this dawn-dreaming had an aura of fancy rather than of fact. Yet the Dutchman was very real, and so had been the two risks.

I shivered though the risen sun was already a hot breath on my back. And I wished I had not thrown away the Dutchman's pills.

There seems to be only one quick and sure cure for malaria and that is removal of the victim to a temperate climate. Soon after my return from Brazil its curse left me, and I made my way like a sailor long from the smells and sounds of his home port toward La Guardia Field.

It was a tonic to enter the operations office, to descend from the moon, swaggering unforgivably, and ho-hoing to those captains who now considered me an equal.

My expansive manner was soon deflated.

While I had been away, Cooper and Owens were killed near St. Thomas, Ontario. Their plane was last seen spiraling down through the night in a right-hand turn. There had been no radio call of distress although there was ample time for a detailed report. The weather was perfect. If Cooper had been conscious, it would have been natural for him to turn to the left. Then why?

The investigators reached only one unsatisfying conjecture. The flight was passing through a region known to be used by migrating fowl. Did Cooper, in a nearly incredible combination of evil luck, collide with a flock of ducks or geese? The season was right for such a meeting. Did they smash through the windshield and blind or stun both Cooper and Owen? No one could truly say, for the report of feathers found in one engine was later proven erroneous.

Fate kept the end of Cooper and Owen a secret forever.

Before Robbins' littered desk I encountered Keim, who had just come in from his Chicago flight. He carefully hitched at his sagging pants before acknowledging my presence; then he bared his fangs, and his snarl was like a heart-warming embrace.

"Well, you silly ass, I see you're back in one piece! Miraculous! You must have flown like I taught you."

"What did you expect?"

"Your effects for distribution to those who knew you well."

"Be patient. I'll be off again in two weeks."

So in easy reunion I remained among my comrades for as long as I could hold their interest, which because I spoke principally of flying in South America was much longer than it would otherwise have been. A pilot's capacity for discourse on flying is virtually unlimited; he may drift away from the subject momentarily, but soon, by some device or accident of simile, he is once again locked tightly to his obsession.

When at last I had exhausted the supply of listeners it seemed better to leave the corporate busyness of the line. It dulled my new pride to see how well things were going without me, and I feared that in too much re-exposure to its securities and comforts I might again slip back into a uniform with a number.

My monologues at La Guardia Field had intrigued Gillette, a pilot who had also been set back by the numbers. He was an excellent man and I persuaded him to apply for a leave of absence and become my co-pilot.

As a conversationalist Gillette made Park sound like a magpie. He spoke mostly in silences. When at last some urgency caused him to lower his reserve and prove the existence of his vocal cords, the emission was barely audible. In the cockpit of an airplane it so visibly pained him to raise his voice above the noise level that I held our exchanges to the minimum, waiting until the quiet of the earth and a drink might ease his tongue. And even then he would employ a silence rather than a sound to express his pleasure or disapproval. He was so remarkably skillful in this trick that he transmitted to his companion a sense of actually participating in the conversation. He could argue or agree with his eyes alone, and since they were ever alert and intelligent eyes, he made a fascinating companion.

Gillette was wiry, deliberate of movement, and proved on our first flight down to Rio that nothing could gain supremacy over his calm. In addition to his skill as a pilot he knew how to operate a radio telegraph key. Through him I hoped some of our ridiculous communication problems might be solved.

I had endured enough of Park's favorite route down the west coast of South America and thence eastward over the Andes. Nor did I feel inclined to revisit the Dutchman and his malaria-laden mosquitoes. So I chose the alternate route, which would take us from the tip of Florida over the Antilles and down to the jungle heart of Brazil.

There were many disadvantages to this eastern route. In general, the weather was not nearly as benign. And this way required longer flights over the ocean for which we had not a single item of emergency equipment. We would also be much longer over the true jungle, but I reasoned that we could bear with these unpleasantnesses if we were spared the miserable altitude problem.

Gillette kept his radio key strapped to his leg and though the whole rig was a makeshift affair, he actually established contact with ground stations a number of times. To know in advance what the weather was doing at our destination was most refreshing— even though the report was fragmentary.

There was an unreal atmosphere about these crude sessions of communication, possibly because at the moment we were so unwanted and certainly unloved. Once we were away from American shores no one gave the remotest damn about our progress or fate. Pan American was supposed to service our airplanes; beyond that they disclaimed all responsibility. Our own government agency was preoccupied with more important matters, and our official Brazilian hosts were only vaguely aware that we were en route. We were two pilots given leave to fly a brand-new and expensive airplane as we pleased, almost wherever we pleased, so long as we eventually reached Rio de Janeiro.

Over the Caribbean, as we floated alone in the sun, quite removed from the regular world of flying, our attempts to achieve respectability flowed through Gillette's clever fingers. His staccato notes sought mainly the weather, although we were satisfied with even the most casual recognition.

"See if you can get Trinidad to take a bearing on us."

A nod, a raised finger, and Gillette in his way replies that he will try. Then the tapping on his leg.

"Did they answer?"

Negative shake of Gillette's head.

"Try again."

A nod. More tapping. He begins to scribble on a pad. He holds out the pad for me to see. Three words are printed there. WHO ARE YOU?

"Did you explain?"

"Of course." But Gillette does not actually voice these words. His eyes pronounce them.

"Try once more and then the hell with it."

More tapping. I fly in a pique because of these rootless arrangements and wonder how long it would take before anyone would know if we went down in the sea. It is a beautiful Sunday afternoon and I should be carefree. Instead, our whole effort seems haphazard and casual. This is nothing like flying the line, and I know that Gillette is already disappointed. I know it from his frown and the way he stares down at the sea, and from the way he works his lips.

"Well?"

The upheld finger again. Then he writes, QDM 345° . . . THIRD CLASS . . . REQUEST ETA. . . .

Gillette's face is eloquent. For a moment I almost hope he is going to speak out and confess verbally that he has shared my sense of being an unneeded ghost. But for him the occasion merits only a thin smile.

"Explain we're landing in San Juan first. We'll give them an ETA later today."

At least someone in all the air space ahead is interested.

When we land at San Juan for fuel, I am not so convinced of our status. I taxi the Lockheed toward the small terminal building. There is not even a baggage boy to hail us.

Gillette cuts the engines. There is the familiar dying whine of the gyros, the easy sense of relaxation flowing through our bodies, and then silence. We remove our headphones and stare at the ramp. No one. Nor is there any sign of a fuel truck. We must leave in an hour or so if we hope to make Trinidad before dark.

"I guess . . . it's siesta time." My voice reflects our orphan loneliness and I try not to think harshly of Pan American. After all, we are not really a part of them.

There is only the brushing of a gentle trade wind and the metallic tinking of the Lockheed's cooling engines to relieve the stillness.

Inside the terminal building it is wonderfully cool and we stand enjoying it while our eyes adjust to the shadows. The long booking counter is deserted. The public waiting room is empty. A telephone rings behind the counter—four times exactly—and then subsides unanswered.

"Well . . ."

An electric fan is whirling on the end of the counter. It is aimed at a place where someone should be standing in attendance and is not. I hold my hand in front of the fan guiding the air toward my face.

"When they siesta here, they really mean business."

"Well, it's Sunday. . . ." The unaccustomed sound of Gillette's voice so startles me I nearly catch my fingers in the fan.

We move toward a hallway because we have heard a scraping sound like someone hefting a heavy chair. There is some kind of life in the room at the end. Now we can hear voices, deliberately hushed, it seems. Someone begins an erratic banging on a type-writer.

There are perhaps a dozen people in the room, several of them wearing the Pan American uniform. They are gathered closely about a radio operator who is tapping slowly on his typewriter. His face is bland, revealing nothing. Before I can speak, one of the uniformed men holds a silencing finger to his lips, then motions us to join him.

The radio operator presses the headphones to his ears. He taps again. And, peering over his shoulder, I understand.

When he is finished there is a long and embarrassed silence.

This is exactly what the operator had typed on a piece of blue paper.

ITEM 86—SUPERFLASH—HONOLULU NAVAL ENGAGEMENT NOW IN PROGRESS OFF HONOLULU—END FLASH

FLASH—ITEM 87—WASHINGTON—WAR DEPT ORDERED ALL MILITARY PERSONNEL UNITED STATES MOBILIZED END FLASH

Modern war is a sort of muddied chaos in which people who are not naturally heroic are obliged to become so, and those most likely to thrill at the bugle charge are often left fixing the plumbing or mounting guard on a whore house.

Most war heroes are lost in the gigantic uncontrolled shuffle. If they happen to have a predilection for disagreement and are lucky enough to have found a favorite charger to mount their passions, then some far removed personality with his fingers hopelessly stuck in the flypaper of complications orders the charger sent away to another land where someone fancies it is needed, but it is really not needed at all. This is called logistics. It is sometimes very trying for those who would be pugnacious.

We were thinking about logistics as we sat at a sidewalk table in Belém, Brazil. It was inconceivable that we should have been ordered to continue after the news of Pearl Harbor, but here we rested in a city which itself was difficult to believe.

Belém, or Pará as it was known until recent years, is a hundred miles up the Amazon River. It is hacked out of a violently beauti-ful and terrifying jungle—a jungle parted only by the river which winds through it like a monstrous gut, and the man-carved wound is the city of Belém. The jungle leans in toward the city, hovering over it, ruling its daily life, ever threatening to suck it once more into its putrefying body.

The citizens seem resigned to their eventual suffocation, and their evening promenade is a listless caricature of the inevitable Latin ceremony. Even a full-scale war, now four days old as far as the Americas are concerned, has failed to stimulate the people of Belém. It is a long way to anywhere from Belém.

I had been sipping at a tasteless and lukewarm beer thinking alternately about malaria and the numbers when Gillette said, "This place sinks me. It's haunted. I'll be glad to leave."

I studied his solemn face and saw that even his mustache had somehow drooped to match his dejection.

I said that at least it was better than Paramaribo, which I would like to forget about but could not.

Paramaribo had been a crazy logistic, more incredible than our continuing to take new airplanes out of a country which, it now seemed, might need them desperately.

Paramaribo is in Dutch Guiana, seven hundred miles to the northwest of Belém. We had landed there for fuel and stumbled upon a forgotten unit of the American Air Force.

The runway at Paramaribo was an asphalt strip recently laid across a scrubby patch of mango brush and semi-jungle. There was no control tower and thus no way to warn us that some idiot had left a steel retaining rod protruding about four inches from the surface. On landing, the right wheel of the Lockheed struck the rod. The tire blew instantly. After a brief wrestling match I managed to bring the ship to a halt without further damage. Waiting for a new tire gave us acquaintance with a group of the world's most frustrated warriors.

For here, in the heart of Dutch Guiana, which was very far indeed from any combat area, we had come upon the bizarre combination of airplanes guarding a mine. The mine produced bauxite, which was understandably valuable, but just how P-40 fighter planes could defend it, or against what possible kind of attack, no one knew.

You had to be among the very best to become a fighter pilot before Pearl Harbor, and these men had been trained to a fine edge of keenness. They yearned to prove themselves in combat and would have joyously taken on any unit of the German or Japanese Air Force if only someone—that magical, never-to-be-found someone—would unleash them. But there was a hole in the earth and they were guarding it against swamp herons, and this sterile adventure was castrating their spirit.

They flew patrols continuously and their hopeless frustration led to the maddest demonstrations of flying we had ever seen. We thought them all demented or nearly so, and yet we could not blame them. They seemed determined to kill themselves in one fashion or another. They shot at the bare sky, the jungle, and sometimes for the hell of it, they said, at each other. The war for which they had trained with all that was in them was passing over their heads. From each empty patrol they returned to their reeking, hot tents to brood on their fate.

Their forlorn and sunburned commander had said they were all bucking for section eight. We understood, because our own mission now seemed so futile, and this feeling had increased in direct ratio to the distance we flew southward.

"There is one thing," Gillette muttered into his beer; "no one is shooting at us. The worst that can happen is maybe getting homesick . . . which I happen to be."

He stood up then and sighed and spoke as if he were already behind the mosquito netting of his bed. And what he said was formula, the prescribed soporific of a working pilot unable to interest himself in groundling affairs. He was only waiting as patiently as he could until there was reason to go aloft again, where he knew the feeling of strangeness would drop away from him.

"I've had it. Good night."

There are certain mornings when the jungle sky seems mainly inhabited by mischievous and weak-kidneyed giants. Shaking a fist at the sky appears only to aggravate this condition, which in the vicinity of Belém normally continues until after dawn is well established.

Because of the lurking cumulo-nimbus the actual sunrise is always riotously spectacular, and then all that has been poured upon the earth begins to steam.

Thus Gillette and I are thoroughly soaked by the time we are ready to start the engines. And we are sullen and unappreciative, not caring at all for the bronze and purple and gaudy yellow of the sky. We are concerned only with the business of the day, which is to remove the Lockheed from Belém and finally deposit it in Rio de Janeiro.

Our soggy rumps make a squishing sound as we settle into our leather seats.

It is nearly six hours' flying time to the next refueling stop at a place called Barreiras, which lies in arid isolation beyond the jungle. And from there it will be another four hours south to Rio. Our food will be a brace of limp sandwiches and a cup of stale warm water. Yet there are certain amenities.

Here, on the eastern route to Rio, the charts are not only gaily colored but meticulously detailed and surprisingly accurate. A swamp is a swamp and clearly designated with symbolic groups of reeds and mangrove quite as graphic as the illustrations in a children's book. Whoever conceived these charts was more than a devoted cartographer and could not have been content with mere facts. Even the green selected to display the vast jungle surrounding Belém is the right green, deep, voluptuous, and forbidding.

Now during the business of setting our altimeters and fastening our seat belts, I blame our strange melancholy on the early heat and the muggy closeness of the cockpit. I blame the two Brazilian mechanics who stand in brooding patience waiting for us to start the engines. And I suddenly realize that no one has smiled at us since our arrival in Belém. Even the boy who lifted our bags into the cabin did so gracelessly, and those few airport employees with whom I had any contact seemed deliberately antagonistic.

I had thought we were doing the Brazilians a favor. Apparently we are villains.

I remember the Dutchman and his gin in Bolivia. "You will not find welcome. . . ."

No matter. All this will pass once we are aloft.

"Clear left!"

"Clear left." Repetition of the command constitutes the first words Gillette has spoken since we left the hotel.

As we taxi away I wave to the mechanics. They ignore the gesture. They only stare.

To passengers, most airports look monotonously alike. To pilots, they are each possessed of innumerable differences. Every airport in the world has certain faults and attributes and these can considerably affect the mood of any pilot. For he is a craftsman, coldly assessing the field of action at hand. As a doctor may balance the technical conveniences of one hospital against another, so the pilot must react to a certain field. He may leave one place with reluctance and gratitude; he may land at another with suspicion and even grumbling hatred.

The airport at Belém is a good one, with long and well-surfaced runways and no surrounding obstructions. There is only the flat jungle enclosing it, which is much better than the fantastic clutter of towers, stacks, wires, and tanks which seem irresistibly drawn to so many airports, as if a powerful magnet were embedded in the center of each.

We splash through two puddles on the take-off run and then are air-borne. There is so much moisture in the air that configurations of vapor ghost along with our wings and about our propellers in a perfect swirling demonstration of the basic principles by which a machine may be caused to fly. Gillette has made the take-off. Once the landing gear is retracted I have little to do except study this phenomenon and reflect upon the marvelous solidity of air once it is moved at speed.

We climb out over the muddy Amazon. The city of Belém spins slowly below as Gillette banks to the south. Now the airport is again off our left wing tip and falling slowly away—a mere hole in the jungle. Habit, a leftover from less mechanically certain times, still compels me to seek for a possible landing place other than the airport as it vanishes beneath the wing. It is worth a smile to catch myself in this ancient act of self-protection—a bemused and inward smile, because the way of thinking is unsharable. Gillette would rightfully mark such meditation as unrealistic and perhaps even a trifle senile. Weren't we blessed with two of the finest engines in the world, and couldn't we easily return to Belém even if one should fail? What difference if the jungle here is like a solid green netting without so much as a single clearing? We are not attempting to penetrate those dark botanical catacombs; we are passing *over* them, which is the privilege of modern man.

Even so, I find such jungle much less inviting than the open sea. This is the only place I have ever been where I cannot conceive of a successful forced landing. I will be glad when this jungle is replaced by terrain which will tolerate optimism. I would not know how to land an airplane on the tops of trees which are so huge and strong and over a hundred feet high.

Now, as we climb into cooler air, our professional interest and vigor return. Across my legs I spread the chart which covers the region surrounding Belém. Like all of the others, this chart is a beautiful thing to behold.

There are a few scattered cumuli hovering over the jungle, and Gillette banks around and between these formations in graceful continuation of our climb. Later in the day we shall be forced to go much higher to avoid them as they gather moisture and expand with the heat.

I glance at the instruments. All is as it should be. Occasionally, as we climb, Gillette moves the throttles forward slightly. He is a good pilot, this silent man. His reserve is not cold but warmed with shyness, and consequently with him there is peace.

In a few minutes we will have flown off and beyond the reaches of this intriguing chart. I begin to fold it, satisfied that it will be followed by many others equally pleasing. Charts are carefully kept in the rack which is above the passengers' seats. I shall take them down one by one, discarding them into the rack on the opposite side of the cabin as their usefulness is ended.

We are still in the climb, just approaching nine thousand feet. I leave my seat and step back into the cabin.

The cockpit of a Lockheed is unusually cramped and the V-shaped door leading aft is barely wide enough to pass my shoulders. I could easily postpone this exchange of charts another five minutes, but I am drawn to the new chart with all of its colorful intricacies as a gourmet must anticipate the details of a feast.

Because there is more space and proportionally less glass area exposed to the pounding sun, it is much cooler in the passenger cabin. So I find it pleasant to linger in the aisle, breathing deeply of the crisper air and thinking about the charts. And I resolve to steal as many as I can carry when this project is finished. And I shall keep them forever. As more than mementos. As stunning, exciting proof that a proper mixture of science and art is not only possible but a blessed union. Someday we would chart the heavens for actual penetration. The positions of the stars and planets will be plotted within a fractional second of arc. But I pray that the representations of stellar bodies will be more than mere blobs signaling to the leanness of purely scientific minds. There are other hungers. Let there be true artists involved who will color a blue star blue, and one that is amber, amber, and pink, pink—accordingly. Otherwise our examination of such charts may produce only an audible clicking sound between our ears rather than a quick gasp of delight. The ancients knew the value of such stimuli, but they often employed art to disguise or excuse inaccuracies. We have little need for such deception. The scientific truths of the chart I shall bring down from the rack are not harmed in the least by artistic embellishment. I treasure their decorations and would be pleased to discover the borders festooned with cornucopias, puff-cheeked faces blowing the prevailing winds, and even, where there might be space, a few jungle serpents.

I must bend and reach across two seats to pull down the new chart. There is a window in line with the seats through which I can see a portion of the wing glistening in the sunlight and most of the right-engine nacelle. These are familiar, integral parts of the ship and so of only passing interest. The glare from the wing is painful to my eyes. I squint against it as I reach for the new chart.

I have the chart in hand and start a half-turn back to the cockpit when my movement is arrested instantly. For past the window I have seen an action which in this first moment is nearly incomprehensible. I am frozen in position, mouth agape, my hand clutching the chart, my brain stunned by what must be a hallucination.

Seconds before, the wing and nacelle were clean. This I know, or I should not have looked away. Now, where the filler cap of the engine oil tank had been, there is a frothing gusher of black liquid. It is not oozing from the hole but seems to explode, vomiting down the curve of the wing behind the engine and spewing across the window.

There is no time to think of a cause. That black stuff is our lubricating oil, our blood, our life. Without it the engine can seize solidly in a few seconds. The propeller will tear itself away most certainly, and the chances of structural damage and a fire are excellent.

Gillette cannot see the engine or the wing. They are behind him. He is gazing innocently at the sky ahead. No wonder, then, that he cannot understand my quick movements as I throw myself through the cockpit door, yank back the right throttle and propeller control, cut off the fuel mixture, and punch the red feathering button above his head. All of this requires hardly more than five seconds.

The Lockheed yaws violently to the right as the engine subsides and the propeller blades feather. Bewildered, Gillette struggles instinctively to maintain his course.

"What . . ."

"Turn back. Back to Belém."

I cut the right ignition switch. Now the engine is quite dead. Glancing back, Gillette sees the cause of my actions. His eyes question me.

"I don't know why. She just blew the oil all over hell! . . . I was standing right there. It happened as if it were waiting for me! Start a slow descent."

Gillette complies and the jungle turns beneath his window.

There has not been time to take my own seat. I am crouched beside him, not dismayed at the thought of losing one engine but at the way in which the loss had occurred.

"I just can't believe it. Why should the oil . . . ?"

We are like stupefied sailors, suddenly witness to our ship's being unmasted in calm airs. There is no logical explanation for such behavior; we are robbed of the very real comfort to be found in technical understanding. A fractured main bearing, a broken oil line, a seized piston, a sticking valve, a hundred things which might require feathering an engine—all a part of our training, our understanding of engine functions. But oil exploding from the filler cap at a rate which must drain the engine very quickly is not in our books—or anyone else's.

And now there is the jungle and only the jungle below, without so much as a pothole clearing. If I had not seen the oil before it was exhausted, we might this moment be diving for the trees and it would be our last dive.

"I was reaching for a new chart. . . ."

I feel the need to explain exactly what I had been about although there is no reason why Gillette should be interested when he has a limping airplane to fly. And why indeed should I care in the face of the new thought which now elbows brutally into my mind and stamps its foot hard on my confidence. What about our good left engine? Would it also choose to go crazy?

I glance ahead. There is the jungle stretching to the horizon, and just beyond, still invisible, would be Belém. Safety.

"Change of plan. Hold your altitude."

Gillette nods. A calm man. Not a suggestion of fear in his quiet eyes. A good man with whom to share a jungle and a sick airplane.

I step quickly back into the cabin and examine the nacelle of the left engine. Clean. Nothing awry. Then back to the cockpit and into my seat. Time now to audit the facts. The oil pressure gauge would not yet have been affected although in a few more seconds it would have faltered. Then the red light above the gauge would have flickered and Gillette would have seen it. But this display would not have occurred until almost all the oil had gone. How about the oil *temperature* gauge? Stupidly, I had not thought to look at it before. How could this be? The temperature was just a few degrees above normal.

"How long has it been that way?"

"I don't know. I haven't checked it recently, but I did so during the climb."

"Was it normal?"

"Yes. Everything was."

I watch the instruments to the good engine warily. Perfect. Gillette has pushed the throttles and propeller controls forward, calling for more power to compensate our loss, but even with extra labor the cylinder heads remain cool enough and the oil only a few degrees hotter. There is no strain. We could fly to the limits of our fuel on this one healthy engine—as long as it remains so.

I have forgotten about the charts as things of intrinsic beauty and, glancing back, regard them now only as primary factors in our discovery of the oil. Why did I go back to the cabin just then, at that exact moment instead of, say, five minutes later? Or four minutes later . . . or three? Supposing I had kept the new charts on the left side instead of the right? Then my back would have been to the window and it would have made no difference when I went to the cabin. Our first knowledge of trouble might easily have been an explosion of the engine. For some reason, as mysterious as the cause of our oil loss, I had to go to the cabin at *just that time*.

"We are very lucky, Mister Gillette."

In fifteen minutes Belém is in sight and we start losing altitude. We spend it cautiously at first, although no man could ask for better support than the good engine has given us.

Engines on an airplane are somewhat like bank accounts. And the arithmetic is equally simple. If you are flying in a single-engine airplane and the engine ceases to function, you are 100 per cent bankrupt. If you lose one out of two engines, you have lost 50 per cent of your security. Losing one out of four engines involves only a 25 per cent cut. The advantages of multi-engine equipment are plainly elementary.

There is nothing difficult about landing a Lockheed with one engine feathered. You must simply bear in mind that the first attempt must be exact and successful, for once the wheels have touched earth you are committed. Under such circumstances every pilot's digestive system becomes alarmingly overactive. Some pilots, when additionally pressed by very bad weather and poor visibility, have confessed an almost irresistible urge to stain their pants.

But Gillette has this approach well under control. His face is a mask of indifference. A wide circle, a gentle bank, and then holding a bit more altitude than he would normally conserve, he lines up perfectly with the runway. He does not call for the flaps or gear to be put down until he is nicely positioned and sure of the field. Then, easing back on the single throttle, we lose the precious altitude rapidly and sink down to the end of the runway. The tires bark less than ten feet from the very end of the asphalt and we have an easy mile to roll. It is a perfect display of control.

Our total flight time, Belém to nowhere and nowhere to Belém —one hour and five minutes.

We stand smoldering in the sun while mechanics strip the cowling from the right engine. These are Brazilian mechanics and there is no camaraderie such as we would know with our own. They work slowly and, as the engine vitals are revealed, ever more unsurely. I cannot put away the thought that they hate us for returning and presenting them with a mystery which must be solved in this screaming sun. Or do they just hate us for returning?

"And be certain," I had ordered, "that you check the other engine too."

I cannot blame their caution or even their show of dislike for the job. The airplane is a new type to them; it drains their painfully acquired assurance, and the curved sheets of glistening aluminum are so hot beneath the sun they should be handled with tongs. But we must discover the why of the oil loss, and the mere fact the filler cap is missing is not enough. Something blew out the oil— something with great force.

In an hour we have the verdict.

"Señor, there is nothing wrong with the engine."

"How can you say that?"

"It is perfect."

The swarthy face of the mechanic is honestly cut and his huge dark eyes entirely sincere. We want very much to believe him. The prospect of waiting interminably in Belém for a new engine is anything but pleasant.

I ask the mechanic how it is possible to lose so much oil if the engine is so perfect. He shrugs his thin shoulders and thoughtfully fingers a ball of waste.

"We drained what oil was left. There was no sign of metal particles. Do the favor to look, Capitan."

He pushes his hand toward us and allows us to prod at a small pool of oil in his palm. The oil is still very hot and I wonder that he can so easily hold it. When we have smeared it about our fingers in a feeble travesty of mechanical detectives knowing what they are about, he offers us the waste to wipe the oil away.

"We have put in new oil and found a new cap. Do you wish now to make a test flight?"

I glance at Gillette, not really expecting verbal comment from his daily word ration, but rather hoping for some signal that he shares my sense of uneasiness. He looks steadily at the mechanic and his eyes are colder than I have ever seen them.

"Will you go with us?"

Mechanics often fly on a test flight after repairs are made, but Gillette's voice seemed to suggest this man should come along as a hostage.

"No, señor. I am not permitted."

"How about one of the others?"

"No, señor. That is also not permitted."

I study the man. His great eyes are intelligent and he carries upon his thin shoulders an obvious pride, a sort of stability I had somehow not expected to find. I ask him if he is absolutely certain both engines are all right.

"Certainly, Capitan."

"Then what are you hiding? Why are you looking at the ground instead of at me?"

A silence, a long one, while he wipes all around his hands with the waste. They are fine hands, unusually delicate for a mechanic's, and I wonder if he has another profession. Back on AM-21 there was a mechanic who was a graduate lawyer and another who had printed his own poetry.

He shrugs his shoulders. "I cannot explain about the oil."

There is nothing furtive about his manner. I believe that he is simply ashamed that he must, on first acquaintance, appear to have failed before these Yanquis. And I am suddenly quite sure that, resenting us, he would much rather have been able to explain exactly what was wrong.

I told him that if we went into the river or the jungle we would return to haunt him.

Two days later in the comfort of Rio, I again thought about the Brazilian mechanic with his reticent manner and regretted my insinuation that he might be concealing a fault. I came to believe that he had tried with all that was in him to discover the cause. Else why would the fifteen-minute test flight have gone without incident? Or why should our continuing flight to Rio pass without the slightest difficulty?

Yet because this whole wretched affair was purely mechanical, there had to be some definite explanation. We pondered upon every conceivable cause all the way to Rio and failed to reach any logical conclusion. There is nothing more frustrating than a crime which contradicts itself, although it did not occur to us until after our arrival in Rio that any crime was involved. We sought mechanical clues only and, finding none of any soundness whatever, at last shrugged it off and nearly forgot the entire business.

Until I talked with a Pratt and Whitney representative in Rio, a chubby-cheeked man who not only knew a vast amount about engines but understood South America and its people as well. I told him of our near-disaster exactly as it had occurred simply to make conversation. I had no reason to expect he would take the pieces of my story and fit them together as he did.

He listened thoughtfully, pulling now and then at his chipmunk cheeks, and it was easy to see that his hands were not those of a man who merely sold engines. When I had finished he was silent for a long time. He belched discreetly and sipped at his beer and looked out over the bay of Rio without, I thought, really seeing it. And I considered that the whole story would have been better left untold. For how could he believe me? An engine, one of his engines, had suddenly spewed out most of its oil, and then it had not. And once the oil had been replaced it had functioned perfectly.

Finally he said, still looking at the bay, "Where was the airplane on the night before this happened?"

I told him we had simply left it at the field.

"And you? Where were you and your co-pilot?"

"At the hotel."

"Who was guarding the airplane?"

"No one. Why?"

"It probably wouldn't have made any difference since the guard would only sleep under the wing anyway."

"Then?" This was a mechanical puzzle, a problem of metal and lubrication. I could not see how a guard asleep or awake could possibly provide an answer.

"The trouble with most pilots is that you are spoiled. And lazy. You have never taken the trouble to learn mechanics properly."

"There are times when there are things I would rather not worry about."

"If you were not so innocent you might have considered that if someone poured a cup of water into your oil tank the result would be exactly as you've described. It would take no more. As the oil heats, so does the water, until it becomes steam. Then as the process continues the pressure builds and something finally has to give. In your case it was the filler cap. Very fortunate for you."

"What about the other engine? It remained normal."

"But how much longer would it have done so? You said the temperature gauges stayed normal on both engines, which should prove even to you that the heat of the oil was only an accessory to the event. It was the temperature of the water that counted. It is possible that in another thirty minutes the same thing would have happened to your left engine. But I think it more likely someone bungled. Either they did not put enough water in your left engine or were interrupted before they could finish the job. It wouldn't have made a great deal of difference. If you had not actually seen the oil let go you would have had all the trouble you could handle and probably more."

And just then, like a child who has known his first brush with evil, my innocence departed. I had been thinking according to a puerile code, like so many Americans. Our heroes were always cleanly wounded in the shoulder and even our villains died hygienically. No one was ever shot in the rectum or sliced across the testicles.

There could be only one explanation to our sudden loss of oil. Whoever had arranged it was a knowledgeable man. It made no difference if his effort had been inspired by a passing of money or simply hatred. He must have calculated how long it would take for the steam to build in the tank. And he, or they, must have known that of all places in the world, a successful forced landing in the near vicinity of Belém was impossible. What remnants of Gillette and myself or of the airplane might be found among the trees would never offer any answers to the most thorough technical analysis. The steam would have long gone. The obvious deduction would be that the Yanquis had failed because they did not know what they were doing. And, if necessary, other examples would be arranged.

"Such a thing can become very discouraging," I said, deliberately matching my voice to the stilted words.

"That was undoubtedly the idea. Because of your coming someone lost his job."

But the thing was over and I was strangely reluctant to talk about it more. What continued to possess my thoughts was a less tangible complication, a question yearning for an answer which I supposed would remain as elusive as the actual identity of our would-be saboteur. My mind held fast to that hot morning and the moments of coolness in the cabin. I could so easily re-enact every moment. Again—why had I gone back to exchange the beautiful charts at that precise moment?

How many times would I, in whatever innocence, be compelled to choose the right time? As with Beattie in the night sky between Buffalo and New York . . .

VIII

RULE BOOKS
ARE PAPER

✵

THEY WILL NOT CUSHION A SUDDEN MEETING
OF STONE AND METAL

AFTER one more flight to Rio my body again became
host to malaria, and by the time the macabre en-
tertainment had passed, the South American project was also
finished. We never learned whether our enterprise had achieved its
full purpose, for all auxiliary projects were now gobbled into the
maw of the burgeoning war effort. An enormous, pent-up national
energy had suddenly been released, and aviation in all its aspects
fizzed and hollered and kicked with the intensity of rebirth.

The airlines no longer wistfully hoped for passengers to keep them alive. Seats to any destination were difficult to obtain, and even those long reserved were subject to priority surrender. The planes of our own line worked continuously, and Lester's school was said to be jammed with men training to fly them.

And everywhere there was confusion and argument and alarums and pettiness. The hysteria of Pearl Harbor had yet to evaporate, and the echoing cry of indignation from the American people now sounded like a traumatic screech rather than a determined roar of anger. The true leaders did not yet have their bearings. The still-unyoked multitude milled in Babylonian turmoil as their pundits cast them adrift between selfish opportunism and impossible visions of nobility. The paradox affected every endeavor and it paraded in brash nudity through the erupting complex of aviation.

The airlines, standing obsequiously for so long, had at last tasted recognition. They rooted like hogs, and their appetites soon proved insatiable. Though technically wards of the government, they kept a calculating eye on those routes which would one day offer the best business potential, trading and maneuvering slyly against each other for future gain. And sadly, in this sudden growth, there began a perceptible change in company-employee relationship. In far less time than it had been created, the aura of a common devotion allied against hazard and discouragement vanished.

To all of this we returned in some bewilderment. The teletypes in the operation office at La Guardia chopped away continuously at the long rolls of yellow paper, and it seemed they did so with special urgency. Robbins, minus a few hairs, was still at his post, although his air of defiant leisure was gone and he gnawed often at his pencil. There were several new faces behind the dispatch counter. A few of them were those of young women, which filled us with wonder.

Ross had finally abandoned AM-21 and was flying to Chicago. Keim had done the same and grumbled that there were so many new changes in flight procedures no man could keep up with them. Boyd had been called away to the Air Force, his reserve commission activated. Others had soon followed him—much to their distress, because an airline pilot called back to the service too often found himself flying a desk. Since this was tantamount to imprisoning their spirits, those who held commissions and had still to be called, watched their incoming mail with increasing anxiety.

A considerable increase in scheduled flights soon absorbed the available time of the senior men, and the need for qualified pilots reached so far down the list that it passed my humble place. And so, once again I flew as captain over loved and familiar AM-21 and was well content in spite of the miserable winter. My co-pilots who shared the frigid cockpits were an assortment of men whose numbers were higher than my own. Davenport and Brink; Ditfurth, who was ever ebullient; Matucha, who was nearly as silent as Gillette; Lawless, who was soon called back to the Navy; and Johnson, who was destined to share flights of longer duration than either of us could ever imagine.

I saw and heard little of my contemporaries from Lester's school except for Mood, who was also now flying as captain on AM-21. The rest were scattered elsewhere over the line, and to all of us the war remained remote.

Brown was killed during an instrument approach at Salt Lake. His co-pilot was Miner. Soon afterward Shank and Nygreen crashed at Miles City, Montana. In both events the investigation hinted that the pilots were to blame—which might have been more easily acceptable if the principals had been around to defend themselves.

As if in recompense, the pilots at last won a minor battle which had lasted too long. We persuaded the lines to install wing tip and tail lights on our planes which would flash instead of remaining fixed. The steady type had too often been mistaken for a star or distant light on the earth below. As aerial traffic increased beyond all predictions, we were haunted anew by the specter of collision. The new lighting mechanism cost a great deal of money, but now, with full loads, the lines were forced to admit they had the necessary funds available.

As the blizzards left AM-21, there was recorded in my log a

total flying time of four thousand one hundred twenty-four hours
and five minutes. This was neither paltry nor a great deal. It generally matched the time of my contemporaries and was enough to
mark us as seasoned pilots. We were beginning to know what we
were doing—most of the time.

Yet such is the swift tempo of airline progress that no pilot can
long rest upon his past or everyday experience. He is almost continuously in school, studying new devices and methods in addition
to his routine sessions with the Link Trainer, or sweating through
instrument flying checks with his chief pilot. And then there are
physical examinations to be taken at least three times a year: two
for the government and one for the company. Consequently, the
hours spent in the actual flying of an airline pilot's schedule and
that given to attendant assignments are about equal. These extra-
curricular activities are never seen by their passengers, though
upon them much of their intrinsic safety depends.

Those of us based on the east coast were occasionally soured
with envy as we passed the lumbering Pan American Clippers
bound over the Atlantic or, even worse, the seaplanes of the newly
formed American Export Airlines. We regarded this last organization as an upstart and though we were confined to domestic flights,
considered them rude invaders upon our private domain. But the
boundaries separating airline pilots are severely drawn; hence
social intercourse between pilots of one line and those of another is
uncommon. There may be an exchange of pleasantries upon meeting, or sometimes a renewal of an old acquaintance, but the rule is
ever toward clannishness, and pilots regard those flying for another
line as foreigners subject to a quite different, if momentarily interesting, society. There is also more than a hint of professional
snobbery among the men of every line, each convinced that the
methods, techniques, and demands of the other airlines must be
somewhat inferior to his own.

The numbers are partly responsible for this curious lack of
rapport. The seniority numbers dictate, not the man, and it is as
rare as a transfer of citizenship for a pilot who has been any length
of time with one line to resign and join another. Should he attempt

it and succeed in doing so, he must start all over again at the bottom, regardless of his experience or capabilities.

It was therefore a mystery and a surprise when several of us were invited to attend a special school conducted by none other than the dour McIntosh who so harassed my early days in Lester's school. And the mystery was further deepened by the subject, which proved to be celestial navigation.

No one could account for the strange selection of students. For once the numbers had been openly defied. Seniority ranged from veteran O'Connor's 33 to my own precarious 267. As usual, there was no one beneath me on the totem pole, a situation to which I was now accustomed and perversely beginning to enjoy. McIntosh had become greatly mellowed and proved himself a wonderfully patient and superb instructor.

The purpose of the school was not too clearly stated. It seemed there was a possibility we might do some over-ocean flying, although when, or which ocean, or with what kind of equipment, no one even pretended to know. Nor was any explanation offered for our oddly matched student body. O'Connor, who learned to fly in World War I and thus held immeasurable seniority over us all, and who had more air time than most men in the world, seemed incongruous alongside such comparative juveniles. He was gray-headed and gray-eyebrowed, but there were no other indications of his age. His weathered face, which had known so many thousand winds, was extraordinarily youthful, and his blue eyes sparkled merrily from behind spokes of sun wrinkles. His face was altogether an Irish caricature and he was inordinately proud of his ancestry.

There was also present the mountainous Dunn from AM-21, bland and vastly relaxed outwardly, although his quick comprehension of all that McIntosh had to explain soon revealed that his ease was only physical. There was Sisto, obstreperous and alert, as he had been in Lester's school, and the handsome, cavalier Watkins, whose beauty had only been enhanced by two years of maturity.

There was Bledsoe, pink-cheeked and dignified; and Robinson, a traditionally fiery Virginia gentleman. These two men were sometimes known as "the twins" because they were nearly inseparable and their careers had been identical since they had been Air Corps cadets together.

There was Hay, a shy man with a long and noble face. His complexion was so all-over red he appeared ready to burst into flame, an impression which was misleading since he was habitually self-contained.

There was Smith, a quiet and much loved man because of his wonderful simplicity, and Davidson, who, along with Boyd, had guided me through the painful metamorphosis from co-pilot to captain.

Davidson was a perfect specimen of what an airline pilot should be, according to popular conception. He commanded instant respect from everyone without the slightest show of effort. His gray eyes, wide set in a sandy face, were alert and completely honest. His jaw was square and firm, his manner gracious and confident. Although he was only of average height, he gave the impression of being much taller, and his powerful frame was obviously in splendid condition. He was, moreover, one of those rare men whose physical appearance was entirely fulfilled by his intelligence and ability.

Later, others came to this makeshift school, and among them was the silent Gillette, and also McGuire, who had nearly forgotten his Carolina mule.

We were all equal in at least one respect. In the beginning none of us knew a star from a planet, much less how to employ their movements and differences to guide us through uncharted skies.

McIntosh, in his methodical, pipe-puffing way, reminded himself that he was dealing with a supercharged audience and began to lead us cautiously through the heavens.

We were formally introduced to the sun and made acquainted with its habits. One by one we met the common navigational stars, and in time it became a minor triumph if we could utilize their altitude and azimuths to fix our position within five miles. My own success was frequently hampered because I seemed to have a predilection for focusing the octant upon the wrong star. The results provided McIntosh with fleshy opportunities for embittered comment, although tatters of my pride were preserved because I had much company in this confusion. It was one thing to find the Big Dipper and quite another to recognize the difference between Castor and Pollux on a hazy night.

None of us had much success in discovering the dragons, scorpions, lions, and reclining goddesses so imaginatively inscribed in the night sky by the ancients. Nor did it then impress us as significant that our less than exact observations were taken from the security and comfort of a very steady hangar roof.

The school lasted a month, and then, as if the authorities regretted its creation, it suddenly expired. We were left with a sort of half wisdom and considerable wonder as to what we should ever do with it. A few of us took octants along on our regular flights and I occasionally astonished passengers by attempting sun sights between such obviously adjacent cities as Rochester and Buffalo. There was never time, of course, to calculate or plot these observations until long after my return to earth. I was often hurt by the discovery that if my sights were to be believed we had been somewhere over the middle of Lake Erie. Yet all of us persisted because of the method's peculiar fascination and, ignoring the ridicule of many who claimed we had lost our reason, eventually managed a fair degree of accuracy.

To no avail. There was a long and unaccountable lull. Our new-found knowledge began to mildew in neglect and we plodded through the sky saved from boredom only by the special trickeries of a boisterous spring. When its arrival was firmly established, every visual attribute of AM-21 was enhanced, and the solid packs of stratus between New York and Cleveland separated into delightful and friendly little bundles of nimbus. The quick changeability of the weather matched the rumors which now began to pass among us. We were all to be taken into the Air Force. We were to serve as pathfinders for bombers over Germany. We ourselves were to instruct in navigation. And the most shocking of all—Pan American would soon take us over.

None of these rumors had the slightest basis in truth. They were only the background for a pattern which had already been set. It was a scheme in which at first the numbers had little influence, yet one which would control our lives for years and violently terminate some of the finest.

Davidson hailed me as I passed his office. I set down my flight bag reluctantly because I believed that he might again tell me of a setback to co-pilot. Or it could be a ricochet from a recent passenger who had refused to extinguish his cigar on the stewardess' request. I had told him that unless he did so immediately I would land in the nearest emergency field and leave him marooned. He complied with a snarl at my arrogance and a promise to see me fired.

Davidson said, "How would you like to go to Presque Isle?"

I asked where such a place might be.

"In Maine."

"How long would I be gone?"

"Five or six days. Perhaps a week."

"All right."

It did not strike me as peculiar that I failed to ask for more information though I had not the vaguest idea where in the state of Maine Presque Isle might be, or what I should be doing there. If Davidson had asked me, that was enough. Nor did I know until the following morning that a complement of ten crews had been similarly lured from their comfortable routines.

This was the very beginning of what later became the world-girdling Air Transport Command.

And it was very much of a beginning: hesitant, tangled in cross purposes, and at times nearly chaotic. The army personnel at Presque Isle, which proved to be on the northern border of Maine, was beside itself with chagrin and confusion. They were suddenly invaded from the skies by a force of civilian air crews which jammed every facility. Our ten crews were relatively easy to assimilate since somehow our impending arrival had been duly announced through channels, but a much larger group of TWA planes and crews arrived wearing white caps and thin white shirts as if they were still flying through the heat of Kansas. While we were sent off to billets in a nearby tourist camp and advised to look after our own feeding, no one had the faintest idea what should be done about the hapless TWA crews, much less why they had been ordered to come in the first place. As the teletypes sought an answer from Washington, some recklessly inspired officer ordered their airplanes loaded with the contents of a freight train which had been standing alongside the field. Nothing was weighed. The airplanes were simply loaded until they were full. No one bothered to inform the TWA crews where they were supposed to fly their cargoes. Just as the loading neared completion an order came down to unload the planes again. The weary curses of the G.I.s had barely subsided when all of the TWA crews were ordered back where they had come from. They flew away to the south, quite empty and as thoroughly bewildered as those who had called forth these logistic phantoms.

The citizens of Presque Isle, hitherto mostly dependent upon the price and quality of potatoes for gossip, found new zest in the presence of our men. It was a lovely little town surrounded by undulating hills of trim potato fields, each delivered of drabness by bordering pine trees. A swift and clear river meandered down from the hills and paralleled the main street. The long early-summer evenings at this latitude allowed the sun to linger affectionately upon the tree-shaded streets and erased the look of stolid respectability from the houses, lending them instead an air of enchantment. There were delicious fresh lobsters to be had cheaply in the hotel, and on Tuesday nights the same establishment featured a New England boiled dinner which thoroughly converted the most skeptical of our company.

And since Presque Isle had so long hungered for new events, and

because it was the sort of small American town where nothing un-
toward would escape discussion, we were soon subject to both
direct and indirect examination.

Why had we come? Were we in the army? Then if we were *not*
in the army what were we doing flying army airplanes?

Anxious to make friends, we did our best to answer such questions, but it was difficult, for the only truth was that we did not
know the answers ourselves. Nor could we explain why it was that
if indeed we were pilots, none of us wore any emblem which might
support our claims. We could not seem to convince our listeners,
either male or female, that the wearing of symbolical wings elsewhere than on a uniform was frowned upon. It was a hoary axiom
of flying that young neophytes were possessed of three things in
lieu of actual air experience—large ornamental wings, a large and
complicated wrist watch, and a penis to match the assembly. In time
a few of our more romantically ambitious crew members sent away
to a mail-order house for the largest wings they could buy. They
reported immediate and thrilling social progress.

We were assigned four airplanes which in normal utilization of
crews would leave one as a part-time spare or permit its substitution for others under repair. These airplanes were a patchwork
collection of our standard airline DC-3's. Where the brown army
paint had already begun to peel, we could see portions of faded
lettering which had once identified the proprietor airline. Two of
the airplanes were haggard with age and one which had survived a
crash on United soon became known as "No-go" because of its
tendency to take forever to reach flying speed. It also displayed a
remarkable habit of flying a trifle sideways once it was coaxed into
the air. The most diligent and clever manipulations of controls and
trim tabs could not correct this exasperating fault. Smith said, in
his mild way, that while he appreciated its strength of character he
would prefer an airplane with a lesser passion for the earth. Its
disinclination to fly became more vicious with heavy use, and
finally it led one of our company to his death.

The other airplanes were new military versions of the DC-3, a type soon to become much trusted and beloved. These were C-47's equipped with two Pratt and Whitney engines and furnished with metal bucket seats. They flew splendidly through a variety of nearly impossible conditions and never betrayed us.

Our long-inbred caution received a severe shock when we learned of the weights we were expected to fly. In the same airplane we had been held to the law of 25,346 pounds. Now we should lift a presumed 31,000, an increase which left us dubious because it canceled our ability to fly on one engine until long after take-off. Moreover, the loads were not accurately weighed but merely estimated. This led to some interesting surprises. Distribution of the loads in the airplane was purely a matter of convenience. We were rarely in proper trim and at length became quite accustomed to flying either nose or tail heavy.

There were other innovations to remind us that the conservative days of airline flying were no more. We were assigned radio operators, who squeezed themselves into a cubbyhole behind the captain. In spite of this confinement their horizons were limitless, for their wireless telegraph keys had a vast communicative range; and so it was the pilots restricted to human speech who became the isolated. These skilled operators had been hastily recruited from the security of their airline radio rooms and were generally of such a peculiar nature that we despaired of ever fully understanding them. They kept much to themselves, lost in esoteric electrical discussions. These were the men, so long unseen, with whom we had talked on our regular schedules. For years they had been only voices, and now we were not quite sure they were real.

We were also assigned a flight mechanic, and most of these men we had known before. They flew with the airplane, curing its various ills only after we had landed. They were all thorough professionals of long experience and we trusted them implicitly. We could only hope the reverse held true.

Additional fuel tanks had been improvised in the cabins of the planes. These were of composition rubber and were connected to the regular fuel system by a makeshift and rather fragile series of pipes and valves. Yet they must have been efficient, for we smoked near them often and suffered no harm.

A plywood table had been erected directly over the tanks on one side of the cabin, and upon this we applied ourselves to the business of long-range navigation. We soon discovered the table also made a tolerable bunk. When so employed, it occasionally caused a certain lack of harmony among the crews. Since none of the airplanes had automatic pilots, the co-pilot was held captive in the cockpit while the captain fulfilled his secondary function as navigator. After a prolonged session with McIntosh's still unfamiliar azimuths and declinations, the captain would sometimes be quite overcome with ennui. He would stretch out upon the table to consider his findings more comfortably. This frequently took a considerable time, and the anguished cries of the co-pilot demanding relief were lost in the drumming of the engines.

So it was that in only a few days we threw off our cloaks of conservatism. We were almost totally independent. The army told us where the cargo was destined. How, and when it arrived, became our individual responsibility.

None of us believed this pleasant and relaxed situation could endure for long. But we underestimated both the perception of our military masters and also the formidable task to be done. It did not occur to us that the Army Air Force, preoccupied with training for actual combat, lacked experienced men for such an endeavor or that they also recognized the values of a tight professional group which would be operating free of elephantine officialdom. Using us without danger of interference or superior restriction, a general could accomplish far more than he could with his own personnel. The last thing they wanted us to do was join the army.

At first we flew cargo and army technical personnel to a place called Goose Bay in Labrador, returned to Presque Isle, and repeated the flights on a twenty-four-hour-a-day basis. Because they are not of flesh and blood airplanes presumably cannot tire; hence the leather cockpit seats were often still warm as one flight crew replaced another.

The actual flying proved to be simple enough. I was amused to find that once again we were flying with charts much given to the word UNEXPLORED.

Northward beyond the St. Lawrence River, the land seemed stunned into silence, still waiting for first breath, as if not yet sure of its liberation from glacial ice. And the pattern past all the horizons was monotonously the same—a seemingly endless repetition of deep and quiet lakes cupped in primeval forests. It was nearly impossible for a stranger to distinguish one lake from another, and in these skies everyone was a stranger. There were no radio aids of any kind except at Goose Bay, where a feeble and notoriously unreliable range station had recently been installed. Thus we were obliged to rely upon the primitive dead reckoning of our open-cockpit days and often found it expedient to hold firmly north until we picked up the wild Hamilton River. We would thence follow its twisting course eastward until at last we stumbled upon the flat projection of land which contained the airport.

In good weather the flight was child's play. But occasionally the season abandoned its assigned character and gave us the back of its hand. Then a solid overcast would descend upon the granite outcroppings and hang graceful stalactites of vapor between the higher trees. The rain replaced all useful sounds in our earphones with the whining and screeching of tormented animals. Yet all this was done facetiously, with whorelike teasing instead of violence. The worst days never produced the ugly thunderstorms which were now commencing their march across AM-21, nor was there even mildly rough air. Instead, the impression of any real threat was withheld, the weapons dulled, as if we were being persuaded to remain hereabouts for the winter—and then, if we had the nerve, to match cunning.

Our heavily loaded airplanes were so soggy in spirit they responded like ailing whales and could not be urged above the overcast where we might have a chance for a sun sight. Thus we were often compelled to creep like furtive thieves along the very treetops, skimming the lakes so low we could sometimes see fish jumping, stealing our progress bit by bit through gloomy caverns of cloud.

My co-pilot Johnson had the nose for such flying. For it was a small, saucy, turned-up nose, ideally suited for pressing against the windshield as he sought the quick loom of hazards and opportunities ahead. His eyes were doll-like, deceptively innocent, and his pink and nearly beardless face was that of a very healthy baby. His hair was a cropped mass of golden ringlets, and as he peered thoughtfully ahead, he became a hopeful child yearning before the window of a candy store.

In truth, Johnson was a flying leprechaun capable of astounding mischief. He was resolute, absolutely fearless, and so utterly devoid of nerves that he could fall instantly into a deep sleep though all hell's noises might be vying for his attention inside and outside the airplane. Even the loss of an engine or a ticklish fuel predicament could not stay him from his slumbers. Perhaps this was why, at the age of twenty-five, he carried a special folder of identity cards to prove he could buy a drink.

Our radio operator was Summers, a man of pungent vocabulary and fiercely independent spirit. He wore glasses which he seldom bothered to clean even though he was nearly helpless without them. Yet for what he lacked in keenness of sight he compensated with the most delicate auditive powers. He could wrest a signal from the silence of a tomb, hearing it long before our detection, or he could separate and identify a puny fleeting *dit-dah* from roaring pandemonium. His sending "fist" danced lightly upon his key and was much admired by his colleagues.

Tetterton, our flight mechanic, was a genial bull of a man who had forsaken a career as a racing driver so that he might more completely realize his love for fine machinery. Engines were not mere assemblies of metal, gears, oil, and cylinders to Tetterton. He cared for engines as living creatures, speaking to them softly as he worked, cursing and cajoling in accordance with the particular behavior of each.

These men, wrapped for indefinite periods in an aluminum cocoon, were typical of all the others. Their faith in me as we proceeded into the relatively unknown was difficult to justify. I was embarrassed by its completeness, and touched by the thought of their volunteer status. They could, in distrust or disaffection, have left me at their will and sought more prudent commanders. I led them quite helplessly into many questionable situations. Some of these were entirely of my own doing, and others occurred as natural developments in our new existence.

All of us had much to learn and there were no instructors save ourselves.

Thus we were often obliged to throw large portions of the rule book away and fly by our wits. No one, for example, except Lowell Yerex's colorful airline in Honduras, knew much about flying cargo by air. We learned one night that there was more to it than just heaving assorted material into the cabin and closing the door.

Our first cargo for the north proved to be portions of a radio station which would one day serve to guide bombers and fighters toward the European theaters of war. The pieces were mostly long steel girders, pre-cut, for later assembly into an antenna tower. We hardly glanced at the piles of metal as we passed through the cabin on our way to the cockpit. It was a provocative night and we were intrigued with the subtle pleasures of making a take-off we should never have attempted on our regular line.

The field at Presque Isle was officially closed to operations because of fog. It lay with deadening serenity upon the ground and there was not even a suggestion of wind to brush it away. The visibility was less than fifty yards. Yet we had practiced blind take-offs many times and were confident of our ability to make one under genuine conditions. The technique was simple enough—a matter of lining up precisely with the desired runway, carefully setting the gyrocompass, concentrating on it, then taking special care to hold course within a degree or two. It was customary to make such take-offs every time a chief pilot held an instrument flying check, but then, of course, he had perfect visibility from his side of the cockpit. Here, there would be none for either Johnson or myself.

We followed the taillights of a jeep to the end of the runway and swung around until our magnetic compass matched its direction.

We set gyros, altimeters, and carefully completed the cockpit check list of instruments, engines, and controls. This we carried out from memory, our voices chanting the sacrament as priests before an altar.[4]

We were ready. Johnson turned our radio to the range station so we could climb out on the proper leg. Summers was in his crypt behind me. Tetterton stood waiting in the dark passageway which led back to the cabin. Past the moisture-laden windshields we could see a single pair of lights on each side of the runway. Beyond, only a void.

"All set?"

A moment of anticipation. Then a common urge silently to bless the engines.

I did not switch on the landing lights because the fog would only reflect their brilliance and annoy us.

I shoved the throttles forward, jockeying the rudder pedals slightly to compensate for the initial surge of power, and devoted myself to the instruments before me. We gathered speed.

Normally we allowed the tail of these airplanes to rise of itself until a satisfactory angle of wing attack had been achieved. The change of attitude occurred at approximately fifty miles per hour and the airplane was held on the ground until flying speed, or better, was acquired.

I sensed nothing wrong until we had passed sixty miles an hour. The tail had not left the ground. I shoved forward on the controls, spun a few turns on the stabilizer wheel. The tail rose very slowly. I considered it unimportant, concentrating my entire attention on holding a perfect gyro course. I thought I could still slam on the brakes and stop if we drifted off the runway. The runway lights were now looming swiftly out of the fog and sliding past like rocket balls. Then, to my astonishment, precious seconds before I had intended, the airplane left the ground.

We had bare flying speed and I heard Johnson cry out. His warning of a stall was superfluous for I was shoving forward on the controls with all the strength within me. And I could not move the controls! I spun the stabilizer as far forward as it would go. We were shuddering into an uncontrollable climb which could only end in a blind spin. My altimeter read less than a hundred feet.

I yelled for help from Johnson. He threw himself on the controls. The nose *had* to go down.

Tetterton, alert to our dilemma, yanked up the landing gear.

We shoved forward on the control yokes until our muscles locked. Our blood pounded up to our faces in stinging pin pricks and our breathing became grunts of desperation.

Yet we could not move the controls an inch forward. If we relaxed only an instant the yokes would fly back in our laps. We might hang for one second before we fell off in a final dive through the fog.

"Tetterton! Go back! See what—"

He had already gone.

We dared not ease off the throttles. If we were to climb so against our will, then we must maintain all possible speed and power. This was the most basic law of flight. To consider the strain on the engines was useless anyway. We had not a hand to spare from our frantic pressure on the controls.

The air speed lingered. It refused to pass ninety miles per hour.

"Tetterton!"

There was no answer.

But Summers swung out of his niche and asked what I wanted. His complete unawareness of our predicament was almost a relief. Even watching us, breathless, and held rigidly in our positions like grotesquely posed statues, he failed to show fear.

"He's back in the cabin. See what the hell . . ."

Summers dodged into the darkness and we waited, hypnotized by the quivering needle of the air speed.

The engines remained howling at full emergency take-off power.

Gradually, hardly daring to believe the instrument, we watched the air speed needle creep past ninety-five.

We saw it at ninety-six.

We saw it at ninety-seven.

Then the air speed held, and slid to one hundred. We wanted to cheer. At last we had an airplane in hand. For now we could feel the controls; there was give—as sudden and wonderful a feeling as only a resilient woman could provide. We breathed. We luxuriated in the sensuous feeling of command and control. During those awful moments we had been little boys, although we struggled like men. Our need was speed, which for these moments of time was better than love.

It was again like an introduction to dying, without quite passing the barrier. And I thought, This is not like the ice with Hughen, or the cold mental remains of instant danger with Beattie. Or the visual shock of spewing oil over the jungle.

This was a quick revelation smashed at our senses while we were blinded, and my heart would not cease its throbbing.

But the airspeed crept past one hundred and five and then one hundred and ten. We could even ease our pressure on the controls although the stabilizer was still rolled all the way forward.

At last we broke out above the fog into a glorious parade of stars. I wanted to hear a band.

Johnson, the nerveless, wonderful Johnson, said, "Jesus . . ."

Then he wiped the beads of sweat from his pink forehead and said once more, "Jesus . . ." There was no hint of an oath in his voice. Nor was his word a prayer of gratitude. He was simply expressing as best he knew, in the most formidable phrase he could then muster, an indirect appreciation of his escape. "Jesus." He savored this name softly and shook his head in wonder.

We found that one man could hold the controls, so I asked Johnson to reduce the power carefully. Each succeeding moment brought more sensitivity to the controls. We were approaching seven hundred feet, a safe altitude. Our air speed was steadily climbing, and we could see.

There was now time, as we climbed toward the stars, to consider our near-catastrophe. It had obviously nothing to do with our blind take-off. Each minute the airplane was beginning to fly as it should, so surely and with such comparative ease that I could now roll back the stabilizer to a decent position.

Finally, Tetterton came forward and leaned between us, panting. His shirt was splotched black with his sweat and the veins on his hands stood out like heavy worms. And he at first also found himself wanting for some means properly to express his woe. So he bowed his head in weariness and lighted a cigarette. Then, staring vacantly at the floor, he hoarsely and reverently repeated Johnson's exact verbal refuge. "Jesus . . ."

"What?"

"Those frigging steel radio towers! They should have been tied down. When you jammed on take-off power, they all just naturally slid to the tail! Must have been a couple of tons of 'em. I dragged the pieces forward fast as I could. Summers helped."

Then Summers, glasses steamed with his own heat, said resentfully, "A thing like that might kill a man."

I could easily visualize their struggles in the dimly lighted cabin as they fought to drag the heavy girders up a floor inclined at least twenty degrees. And, far worse, they could not have known at what instant the floor might violently reverse its angle and tumble them into eternity.

We had nothing further to say on the incident, for in fact Summers had said it all. So we remained silent, each man wrapped in his thought, trying to behave as if nothing had happened.

Summers went back to his radio cubicle and switched on his light. He pushed it down close to his tiny desk so that its glow would not spread forward to the cockpit. In a few moments I heard him clicking away at his key, a thin, delicate sound which inexplicably prevailed above the engines; and I wondered with whom in the world he could be conversing at such a time and whether he would mention that his fortune had so recently demonstrated its perfect match to our own.

Tetterton remained in the dark passageway behind us smoking. And I sensed, more from his observant silence than anything else, that he was still troubled. Finally he leaned forward between us so that he could look out at the stars, though his true interest was almost at once revealed to be elsewhere.

"How long did you leave the engines at full power?" he asked so casually that it was as if he were speaking of a time weeks before. He said it as primly as a spinster inquiring the length of a sermon unattended, and I thought, Good God, how can he care for the time when the engines have just spared his life? Yet I knew the reason for his question and took a moment to delight in it. And I wondered at how fixed a man could become upon his special pursuit. The dentist attacks an ailing tooth not seeing the whitening knuckles of his patient squeezing the chair. The printer discovers a typographical error and is wounded, though the error may be infinitely less damaging than the words. Now Tetterton suspected me of abusing his engines and he wanted an accounting in spite of his deliverance.

"I haven't the faintest idea. I wasn't exactly watching the clock."

"How high did the head temperatures go?"

"I wasn't watching them either."

Tetterton made no attempt to conceal his frown of disapproval. The parallel wrinkles across his forehead became deeper in the subdued cockpit light and he turned his head owlishly several times, directing his amazement first at Johnson and then at me. We had, his eyes accused us, been grievously delinquent.

"We're supposed to fill out the logbook. What am I going to put in the spaces for engine take-off and climb?"

"How about . . . I love you."

The forehead wrinkles became gashes and his lips compressed until they were nearly invisible.

"Thanks," he said with the heavy mockery of a man betrayed.

☼

IX

VALHALLA

☼

THE TORTUOUS ROUTE THERETO

THE airport at Goose Bay was a single strip of gravel which had been bulldozed through the trees. There were also several temporary wooden buildings mainly occupied by men of the Royal Canadian Air Force. They had recently become the rather surprised hosts to a vanguard of American Air Force units.

Just south of the field the Hamilton River quieted, spread itself to join with the sea, and thereby formed a considerable bay. Its eastern extremity had long been known to mariners as Hamilton Inlet. Prior to the establishment of the airport the only inland habitation in this region was a Hudson Bay Company Trading Post at Northwest River which served the frugal needs of a few trappers. All else for hundreds of miles about was solitude. To the north and west, the charts openly confessed complete ignorance of tremendous areas, not even bothering with the apology UNEXPLORED.

Yet in this unforgiving wilderness, to which everything of any size had to be brought laboriously by sea, there was now such energy and focus of activity as no trapper could conceive in his most drunken delirium. For Goose Bay was being transformed while the bewildered caribou watched from the forest. And the salmon crowding in the Hamilton River discovered new and unnatural hazards to frustrate their urge to spawn.

There was not to be found a particle of good in any of this. Even the most warlike, the most devout and obnoxious worshipers of everything modern, regretted the intrusion. Everyone who came to Goose Bay was openly ashamed. It was impossible to find any thrill or satisfaction in this rape of the primeval, yet because of a distant and basic hatred between types of their own species, not even the wisest of men could offer an alternative. For Goose Bay was poised in a global position most convenient to flying the Atlantic as well as the vitally strategic lands to the north of the fifty-fifth parallel. Furthermore, its natural weather was considerably more favorable to aerial operations than the fog-bound fields of Newfoundland. Its peace was doomed.

There were several separate groups engaged in flying across the Atlantic Ocean by one route or another, but in no respect could any of these operations be judged frequent or routine.

There was the Canadian Ferry Command, a civilian outfit controlled incongruously by a railway.[5] This was a picturesque one-way operation, ferrying Lockheed Hudson Bombers to the United Kingdom. The air crews returned to Canada by ship, or flew back as passengers aboard Royal Air Force Transport Command airplanes. The R.A.F. westbound flights were extremely spasmodic and marred with tragedies, but the ferry service itself performed superbly and finally delivered a great many bombers. The pilots involved were a heterogeneous group recruited from everywhere and included some of the most colorful aeronautical soldiers of fortune ever to find themselves engaged in a common effort.

There was a painfully cautious Pan American Airways operation, flown in general by exactly the opposite type of men. Hampered by regulations as well as facilities, their service was sadly lacking in frequency as well as dependability. In winter they abandoned all North Atlantic ventures.

Plucky little Northeast Airlines had just begun some exploratory flights with a few planes like our own.

Finally there was American Export Airlines, which was short-lived and so occasional of operation that few were aware of their tribulations.

Thus the skies over the Atlantic were nearly as lonely as they had been for Lindbergh. Someone was obviously of the opinion we might serve as a nucleus to remedy this situation. And they further conceived that Goose Bay must eventually serve as a launching platform for a multitude of bombers and fighters, manned by inexperienced crews, who would disdain the prevalent custom of pickling aircraft and shipping them by sea.

There were many obstacles to be conquered before this could be done, and there were as many pessimists who said it could never be done. The visionaries, as always, found they must be their own strength, for the hairs of pomposity prickled upon the skins of the incumbent authorities, warning them to smother this new attack upon the impossible. Fertile imaginations were ridiculed and occasionally thwarted, which was only a repetition of history; yet, likewise, they mainly triumphed in the end.

It was true enough that little fuel was available and the means for transporting and storing the precious stuff had still to be constructed. Radio navigational aids, except in the United Kingdom, were scanty, and those very few operating were far from reliable. Weather analysis and the forecasting of winds aloft were so random and speculative that it was pure folly to trust anything drawn on the charts. There were no facilities for the handling of either men or planes in any numbers. And winter was coming.

Into this we flew, not to be plagued by bullets but always beset by the fiendish technical complications of modern war.

They were still building the control tower when we landed at Goose Bay. Our mere arrival was such an event that a welcoming committee stood waiting for us. And to my personal delight there was Boyd, the gilt of his new major's leaves glistening in the morning sun. With him was Clark, a red-faced, red-haired, stocky man whose speech sounded like the staccato explosions of a firecracker string. Though we all came from the same airline, I knew Clark only by reputation as a brilliant and provocative mind, so remarkably quick in thought that he frequently reduced slower thinkers to mumbles. Clark was now also just returned to the army and his major's leaves were as new as Boyd's.

There was a third man looming over them both, and his face was that of a disenchanted walrus. He wore the leaves of a lieutenant colonel, and I saw that they were tarnished with age. Before I could leave the cockpit he called up to me in a voice that seemed to shake the airplane.

"Did you bring any whisky?"

I explained that someone in Presque Isle had put a case of milk aboard and that it should be near the door.

"Milk!" The disgust in his voice was monumental. *"Milk?* Milk is for babies!"

This vast, effervescent man was Hassel, a famed arctic character better known as "The Fish" because of his insatiable appetite for anything that could swim. Long ago, when all aviation was very young, he had landed a faltering Stinson on Greenland's icecap. He was automatically given up for lost, but somehow, during the following year, made his way to civilization. In spite of his misadventure he came away with an abiding passion for the north. Hassel, his rasping voice a torch of pithy expletives which he directed upon humble and glorious men alike, was held in great affection by all who knew him. But his scorn for protocol and his iron independence demolished every hope of promotion.

Boyd took my hand as if we had flown from the moon and said, "Welcome to White Pigeon."

And at once I was returned in thought to a more tranquil period when I had served briefly as his co-pilot. We had found ourselves flying a plane chartered from our line by a political team junketing around the United States. Our passengers displayed a constant and abnormal interest in their exact location—information we seldom had ready at hand. And so we would assume a solemn mien and point out a town, or village—any one visible would do—and we would say, "That is White Pigeon."

Regardless of our actual location this answer seemed to satisfy all curiosities completely.

Still grasping my hand, Boyd said, "Captain, do you like movies?" And I was very aware that he smiled at his emphasis on the word *captain*. It brought to me a sense of well-being, for I also remembered the first day he had introduced me to a DC-3.

"It depends," I said warily.

"These have everything but sex."

And Clark said, "The army is going to kidnap you."

I found the implication flattering, and when we had slept we saw a travelogue which was intriguing in spite of its concentration upon a single locale. The film was taken from the cockpit of an airplane flying along the western coast of Greenland. There, we were to deliver the girders.

Over the humming of the projector Boyd said, "There are three fiords, as you see. You will also notice that all three look exactly alike as you approach. But only *one* is the right fiord which leads to the field. The others are dead ends and you are advised to stay out of them unless you have learned how to back up an airplane."

Very interesting, I thought, especially since Davidson had said we would be back in New York by now.

"The little island you see off the mouths of the fiords has a range station on it, but it's not reliable. So don't trust it with a letdown toward the shore. The field which we call Bluie-West-One is sixty miles up the *correct* fiord just at the base of the icecap."

"Ah . . ."

"You will not actually see the field until you have made the last turn around that cliff; then it will appear all of a sudden so you'd better have your wheels down a little early. It's a single runway with quite an incline. You always land uphill and take off downhill, regardless of the wind. You have to land whether you like it or not."

"But . . ."

"If the weather is overcast you may have some doubt about being in the correct fiord."

Watching the film I could easily see how such embarrassment might occur. I could not detect the slightest physical differences between the fiords. Yet Boyd knew his airline pilots. He was a connoisseur cleverly displaying an irresistible collection of jewels. He knew that we gave constant lip service to the dictates of safety and howled like Christians condemned to the arena if any compromise was made of it. He knew that we were seekers after ease, suspicious, egotistic, and stubborn to a fault. He also knew that none of us would ever have continued our careers unless we had always been, and still were, helpless before this opportunity to take a chance.

"There you see the wrecked freighter. It is about thirty miles up the *correct* fiord on the north side. If you do *not* see that freighter you are in the wrong fiord."

"Nothing to it," Clark said, rattling off a barrage of outlandish names from his marvelous memory. Sukkertoppen . . . Angmagssalik . . . Upernavik . . . Narsarssuak . . .

The films were obviously taken in fine, very clear weather. Somewhere in my memories of Rockwell Kent, I seemed to remember that Greenland weather could be otherwise. I inquired.

"There is some fog and low stuff at this time of year, so if you find the fiords are closed, just save yourself for another day. Turn around while you're still off the coast and come back here. And don't go exploring. You'll need all your fuel. Sometimes our communications leave something to be desired. Sometimes messages are a bit slow due to one thing or the other—like just now we haven't been able to contact Greenland for three days."

"Then you won't know when we arrive there?"

"We will in time. We need something to fill up the files."

"And if something goes wrong en route and we have to ditch?"

"That's just too damn bad," Hassel said with a nasty chuckle, "Put your trust in God and Pratt and Whitney."

They were that night, it seemed, our only friends.

It was nearly thirteen hundred miles across the Labrador sea to our dubious destination. And our only alternate was our place of origin, which meant that to return ever, we would have to squeeze every last drop of fuel from our tanks. If the North Atlantic winds chose to increase, we simply could not make it with dry feet.

We ignored this possibility as we slid eastward beneath the stars. There were no life jackets on board, much less a life raft of any kind. There were no ships on the ocean interested in our destiny. Yet each of us had been provided with a parachute. Just what we were supposed to do with these we could not imagine. Tetterton found that, when laid out upon the girders, they made a reasonable bed.

There were other sobering discoveries as we eventually reached cruising altitude. Neither Johnson nor myself could make the airplane truly fly. Instead, it floundered through the night, mushing along like a caravel, sinking hundreds of feet the moment we tried to relax. And our occupational resentment against aircraft engineers mounted with the passing of each interminable hour. As men of less learning will do, we cursed the engineers and their facile playing with graphs and slide rules. For it had been the engineers of the line who had set up the new long-range cruising procedures. These were impressive paper instruments, calculated, we knew, by men dripping with scientific degrees. Hence we dared not question their findings and consequent formulas. They knew. We were bumpkins told by our betters to hold the carrot in front of the mule just so, and were at first appalled and then righteously indignant when our charge refused to move.

The engineers had applied their ubiquitous slide rules to a hypothetical flight of this duration and found that we might indeed become impoverished for fuel if we operated the engines in the normal fashion. They had concluded that we should set the propeller revolutions at a mere fifteen hundred per minute, instead of the customary nineteen hundred or two thousand. The engine engineers, after consulting their slide rules, resolved that such procedure would do no harm to their machinery providing we refrained from using too much manifold pressure; which was the same as saying thin ice will support you indefinitely or at least until the arrival of spring.

We now found these theories were producing certain interesting phenomena. A deathly quiet pervaded the airplane which was not in the least mitigated by our peculiar isolation. Switching on the landing lights, we found it possible to follow the individual propeller blades as they sliced ponderously at the night. Johnson, lulled by the sonorous rumble of the engines, fought to keep awake. Tetterton had succumbed entirely back in the cabin, and Summers, stretching again and again to the limits of his cubicle, yawned so lustily we could hear him in the cockpit.

As the captain, I could not so easily accept our situation. The graphs proclaimed that at such a power setting and altitude our air speed should be one hundred and thirty miles per hour, which, I mused, certainly set the clock back to Lindbergh, since his speed was in the same plodding range. But the indicator before me read only one hundred and fifteen, with occasional giddy forays toward one hundred and twenty. No amount of patient experimentation with the controls seemed to improve matters. A pilot always reflects the tenor of his flight, and if the airplane with which he is charged performs miserably, then he is equally dejected. If he doubts the cause he may even indulge in self-pity and so in my growing discomfort I told Johnson that we were mired in the sky.

"How's that?"

He blinked his china-doll eyes and made a pretense of being alert.

"If this keeps up we'll be old men before we arrive anywhere."

"True."

I was pleased with Johnson's way of answering. Sometimes he

dredged up phrases from the depths of his native Confederacy, and with his magnolia and julep accent they sounded so exactly right.

Later, just before dawn, I went back to the cabin and took up my octant. I held it first to my ear and turned gently upon a small knob protruding from its side. When I heard a faint squeak I knew that a chemical bubble had been formed within the instrument which would serve the same purpose as a horizon. I stepped over the slumbering Tetterton and applied myself to a window where I could best see the star Dubhe, at the lip of the Dipper.

McIntosh had predicted that my frivolous disregard for light-years and millenniums of space would one day lead me into the greatest navigational mistakes since Columbus discovered Japan. I was determined to prove him wrong. So I peered into the eye-piece and sought most carefully in the octant's ghostly field for my special star and no other. To clinch matters I hummed "Star dust." At last, convinced that I truly beheld Dubhe, I tried to move it into the center of the quivering, luminescent bubble. This was not so easy and my humming gave way to profaning the inadequacy of an airplane which caused me to squat like a baboon while playing the wizard.

Johnson, I whispered, please fly more smoothly so that I may catch this recalcitrant pinpoint of light, which is God knows how many million miles away, and hold it locked within this antagonistic bubble, which is three inches from my nose.

Finally, tensed into position, I began clicking at the octant's trigger, holding to Dubhe as if I would shoot it down. The trigger activated a pencil which made vertical marks on a small metal drum. These I averaged and noted the resulting altitude on a scrap of paper together with the time according to Greenwich.

I repeated the process with the star Arcturus, which hung like a thrilling amber blob, somewhat higher than Dubhe had been and more toward our tail. And again, in the face of beauty, I blasphemed the acrobatics necessary to bring it into view.

Then I moved back to the toilet, which reeked of disinfectant, but had at least one attribute. There was a small rectangular window in the ceiling and through it I could see Sirius, cobalt blue and glistening, as if it were swimming in a private sea. Here I could actually stand for my observations and I was so far removed from our lazing engines that there was no sound save the brush of the slip stream against the ship's skin.

I left Sirius reluctantly, for it was of all stars the most flamboyant, and I was beginning to regard it as a newly acquired friend. So far removed from other stars, its very remoteness seemed to match our loneliness.

Tetterton roused himself from his couch of parachutes and watched while I devoted myself to the books and charts on the navigation table. Twice he asked if I knew what I was about and I answered him shortly, for my confidence was as fragile and demure as the bubble in the octant. This was the first time I had attempted to plot a position from the stars that would really count. My wits, dulled by lack of sleep and the irreconcilable sensation that we were flying in a homeless balloon, deserted me again and again until I nearly despaired of my arithmetical errors. But at last I sorted them out and, cheating only a little, brought the three lines representing the stars observed into a reasonably small triangle.

"There," I said, pointing with a flourish at the intersection, "is where we are. Or were, when I started all this."

Tetterton was unimpressed. He twisted his fists in his sleep-laden eyes and said that if we still had so far to fly he might as well go back to sleep.

Forward in the gloom, Johnson and Summers awaited me. Beware of the hearty man, I thought, for he lies to his flesh and blood. So I answered their questions cautiously, not wishing to share my secret misgivings. Yes, we were doing all right. The wind was on our tail, averaging about twenty knots, and so things were not so bad as they seemed. The star fix? Good enough. Really, there was nothing to it. But we must talk to the engineers next time there was an opportunity and question this ox-cart speed. It was an abuse of the medium, an insult to the Wright brothers.

I eased into my seat and took the controls from Johnson. He

yawned once, tilted his head backward against the steel surface of the oxygen bottle, and almost instantly slipped into unconsciousness.

There was nothing to do now but hold course and wait.

Fighting weariness, resenting it because I knew it to be an ill partner to flying, I smoked one cigarette after another until my mouth was resinous. Gradually, as our fuel was consumed, the ship became lighter and I could manage to fly it with some degree of ease. Johnson slept on quite peacefully, and since I had not seen Tetterton for over an hour I assumed he was likewise so fully confident of our immediate future that the resting of his body remained important.

I twisted around for a look at Summers, who had switched off his light. I could make out his vague outline in the darkness and saw that his headphones had slipped down until they encircled his neck. He had propped his head on his folded arms, turning it askew so that he looked like a wounded sparrow.

Then it was still important to rest. The most important urge, at least, for this somnambulant interval of time. My companions were separated only by air from an ocean which they had never seen. Therefore the ocean hidden in the darkness existed only as an idea and they had found the idea uninteresting. They had left a wilderness without a backward glance, and their physical beings, the marrow and fluid of them, were moving toward a greater wilderness, of which they knew nothing. This was occurring at a considerable speed in spite of our crying complaints for more. Yet they slept. Because they held deep faith in a supreme being? I presumed they did although I should have been chary about challenging them on such ethereal support. Faith in Pratt and Whitney, a business institution engaged in the manufacture and sale of machinery? Of course. But someone had to tend this stalwart combination, else they would also fall asleep. Where was the trust, then? I wondered. Who sang the lullaby? Ho! I was suddenly very lonely. And I found it agreeable.

For loneliness, I thought, is an opportunity. Only in such a state may ordinary minds, spared comparison with superior minds, emerge victorious from thoughts which might prove perilous to explore in company. Loneliness presents no challengers to undermine by argument and stipulation those comforting theories born of it. Loneliness is not deadening, even for dullards who contrive against the condition because it forces them to think. Unless men are transformed into true imbeciles and simply stare at nothing, or play with their physical toys, then loneliness can form a magic platform which may transport the meek to thoughts of courage, or even cause the scoundrel to examine the benefits of honesty. Mere physical separation from other human beings can energize new conceptions for those usually incapable of any mental experiment. Yet to be thought lonely is automatically to be pitied, which is an insult, since pity is most loudly offered by the patronizing and hypocritical. Pity for the lonely speaks of uncleanliness and rejection (poor fellow, he is not as admirable as I know myself to be); thoughts so often nursed by those terrified of separation from the mass.

Here sustained in space by a heartless machine, I sank into loneliness gratefully because there was, for whatever time the condition might last, no limitation upon my fancies or conceits. And it seemed to me that Johnson and Summers and Tetterton accepted unconsciousness as a duty, as a proof to themselves that all was as it should be. I did not envy them. They had simply died momentarily and willed me a legacy of night beauty few men could ever contemplate alone.

Venus rose to signal me from the eastern horizon and it was so brilliant and inconsistent in color, changing at once from yellow to green to purple and then reversing the show, that I thought for a time it was another aircraft equipped with special lighting devices. But Venus steadied in time, proving its identity. Tagging along behind it like an errant child, a small star arose, and I watched it being chased upward by the dawn.

There was now a pause in everything. The night heavens appeared indecisive and reluctant to accept the invasion of foreign light. I changed fuel tanks and carefully reset my gyrocompass with its magnetic brother. And when I looked out at the sky again only moments later, I found the conquest well under way. My fatigue left me, subsiding in direct proportion to the gradual lightening of the sky. My eyes continued to burn, I touched often at the prickly stubble of my beard, and my legs were stiffened from so little burden. Yet I was otherwise comfortable and could not believe when I reckoned by the clock that I had been held in my seat for three hours. Staring ahead, I thought that if such beauty could prevail I might willingly fly on forever.

The stars still maintained themselves importantly, but now the new light revealed a rumpled deck of stratus hanging just above the sea. There were fragmentary breaks cut out of this cloud deck through which I could observe the still black ocean. Upon the surface I saw occasional gray structures which I finally realized were icebergs.

Then against the horizon I saw a series of warts in silhouette. They were sharp-edged and I supposed them to be optical illusions, a final adventure in my private trance. But they persisted like the stars and slowly enlarged until I knew they must be real.

There, then, was the enormous mass of Greenland, and I could not look away from it. It held me as it took on coloration and I finally distinguished the warts as the peaks of great mountains. And all about them, choking their gigantic necks, lay the awesome icecap. This all-embracing coverlet formed its own horizon and stretched north and eastward beyond my comprehension. I had never in all of my flying seen anything to compare with this fantastic exhibition and I thought that if Hassel had fallen in love, then it was understandable, for he had certainly loved extravagantly and well.

This magnificence, I reasoned, must be shared regardless of my companions' determination to pamper their bodies. Otherwise my loneliness might become ingrown with selfishness, cherished too long, and thus sour all that had passed before.

So I prodded Johnson into wakefulness and, like a proprietary master of ceremonies, swept my hand across the windshield. I asked him how he liked such staging for his return to life. He blinked and looked long at what lay outstretched before us. Finally, when I began to fear that he was not impressed and that he might, incredibly, have no comment to make, he spoke a word so appropriate I wanted to clap my hands in applause for man and scene together.

"Jesus . . ." he said softly, in exactly the same wonder-filled way he had spoken of our deliverance from danger the night before.

Then I called to Summers, who released himself from his headphones and came forward to stand between us. He said nothing, but in a moment he went hurriedly back to fetch Tetterton. Soon our four heads were aligned and we crowded upon each other like standees at a theater. And my joy became complete. For these men, each of so different background and nature, at once cast off their drowsiness and joined the mood. We began chattering and our voices were those of small children enraptured with a show. See this . . . see that! Look there! Who could believe this? Holy mackerel!

In all of the times I later came upon the continent of Greenland, the crew members invariably expressed the same wondrous exhilaration.

Tetterton was the first to discipline his senses and he asked about our fuel. We checked the amount remaining and found it almost as impressive as the scenery. We had consumed so little fuel per hour at first we were incredulous; yet checking and rechecking we proved the amount.

"We're fat."

"Wonderful!"

We regretted our castigation of the engineers. Obviously, they knew.

"We're over an hour ahead of our estimate!"

Our estimate to where? It was some time before I began to frame the question because any reason for doubt came upon us slowly and was so foreign to our visual experience that there was no standard for judgment. Yes, there was Greenland and obviously mountains. We were flying directly toward them and they were definitely not hallucinations. Still, they remained nearly fixed in size, utterly belying our progress.

We looked down to reassure ourselves and saw the flocks of stratus sliding beneath us as they should. Then surely, by now, the mountains should appear larger and their details better defined. But they remained, after twenty minutes, nearly the same. After a further twenty minutes there was a barely perceptible change, as if the mountains wished merely to guarantee we had not lost our minds.

"We must have picked up one hell of a head wind!"

So near and yet so far. We fidgeted in our seats, waiting. We tried to take a bearing on the radio range recently installed near the mouth of the fiord and at last succeeded. The bearing showed it to be only a little to the north, which spoke well for our course but did nothing to fix our speed.

The sun rose to glare in our faces. I watched a projection of land far to the north and identified it as Cape Desolation. It protruded from the low deck of stratus and I could gauge it easily against the metal framing of my side window. It did not seem to move at all. And yet, thanks to our lesser weight, the air speed now stood at a reasonable one hundred and forty-five.

The sky above was bald, the sea smooth, and the stratus latent. From these signs I was convinced that at worst the favorable westerly winds had fallen calm, and that a contrary head wind did not exist. And I realized at last that we had perceived the mountains of Greenland from an incredible distance. And who knew how high they really were? Once again the region over the icecap where the highest mountains stood was marked UN-EXPLORED.

So much for our gaining an extra hour of fuel! So much for the engineers and their listless caravel, floating instead of flying in the sky. We must still suspect their calculations. Perhaps with these dilatory tactics we would actually consume more fuel for the over-all flight than if we had perked up and truly flown. We questioned this among ourselves, theorizing with the solemnity of those uncertain of their theories. Finally we decided this was hardly the place for experiment. It appeared that we would soon have quite enough of trial and error. For all of the visual deception to which we had been subjected was at last revealed.

The icecap formed a dome, like the curving top of a gigantic pie. And the mountains, which had become bronze in the light, fringed the borders and penetrated the surface of the pie dome as if some demented baker, unable to control himself, had cast them about for decoration. The stratus nestled solidly against what we assumed must be the coast line, thus forming a low-level coverlet which concealed any evidence of entrance to the mass. All of this display extended approximately north and south, dribbling away in perspective with such perfect clarity that we could see the entirety of western Greenland from Cape Desolation to Cape Farewell.

The stratus tightened as we crept toward the land, and we knew that beneath it there could be no such feasts of vision. So, instinctively, we held our altitude until the direction finder indicated we had passed over Semitak Island. Only then did I find myself wishing we were over Syracuse and that I knew what must be done next as well.

We slipped into the stratus and were at once enveloped in gloom. We held straight down, watching the altimeters unwind with increasing concern. For a pressure altimeter is not accurate unless it is recently set to the immediate locale. It can easily be wrong by five hundred feet or even a thousand.

"Summers! Can you get an altimeter setting?"

"I'm trying."

We maintained the descent, waiting as the day became an eerie twilight. All enthusiasm had left us. We were comforted only in the thought that the sea was a flat surface, and unless the stratus extended right down to the water we should see its blackness in time to level off or climb away.

I heard Summers grumbling that everyone in Greenland must be asleep. Our altimeters read eight hundred feet, and even the nerveless Johnson was beginning to squirm in his seat. A blind man likes to know his corridor.

I resolved to let down a further one hundred feet and no more.

If then there was not some significant change in the overcast, the balance of risk would be all on the wrong side. I shouted over my shoulder again to Summers.

"Any contact yet?"

"Nope!"

"Keep at it!"

"Why not? The electricity is free!"

Oh, you early morning humorist, Summers! We can see and you cannot know what it is like to see and yet not be able to see what you desire—or your humor would tend more to irony.

Tetterton, standing on tiptoe between us, had a more vertical line of sight than either Johnson or myself. Nor was he distracted by the instruments. Peering over the nose of the ship, he announced that it was all dead black ahead.

And before he had finished his sentence we emerged from the underside of the stratus and there, enveloped in murk, rolled the ocean. It was dead black and greasy. The horizon was lost in a fine mist, but I estimated the visibility at a mile, perhaps a little more. Enough then, if it became no less. Enough if we proceeded alertly, for there were no uncharted obstructions in the sea; a truth, I found almost at once, which applied to most of the world's oceans but not here. For an iceberg loomed out of the water almost directly on our course. Its sharp peak extended upward until it seemed likely to puncture the bottom of the overcast. The black ocean sloshed ponderously against its base, surrounding the berg with a skirt of green froth and so making it a beautifully wicked thing.

Momentarily I indulged in "ifs." I had no notion how big an iceberg might be. This one matched a mansion. If it had been higher, and if the overcast a little lower, and if we had let down at just the wrong place . . . I promised myself never again to let down over these waters below three hundred feet, unless I could see. We were learning.

As I banked sharply around and reversed course toward the coast it became painfully obvious the lessons had just begun. We must first find Semitak Island as a progress check and then creep on toward land to seek out the proper fiord. I slowed our speed to one hundred and twenty, which might not be exactly creeping but would at least allow us a few extra seconds to avoid any further surprises.

We continued through the mist holding a hundred feet above the sea. Summers yelled that he had contacted Bluie-West-One, and we set our altimeters to correspond with their reading. He also said the weather at the field itself was overcast at three hundred feet and the visibility better than two miles. Our informants did not know what kind of weather prevailed in the fiord.

Johnson said he was hungry.

The visibility diminished as we approached land, and the icebergs became more numerous, although none were as grand as the first we had seen.

I eased the ship down to fifty feet and found the visibility better. I also thought that there is a limit to all things. This was a heavy airplane, not a little acrobatic ship maneuverable in a trice.

"Once we put our nose in that fiord there won't be any coming out again," I said, half hoping Johnson or Tetterton would suggest we come back another day.

"True."

And again Johnson complained of his hunger.

A jumble of ocher rocks proved to be Semitak Island. It swept past our right wing and became lost almost instantly in the mist.

Now for the fiord. The *correct* fiord. We held on straight for the shore line.

We would very soon be committed. The distance between the island and the mouths of the three fiords was only two miles. How could we be sure we had entered the fiord in the middle unless it was possible to see the other two? Eenie-meenie-miney-mo . . .

"All right if I reel in my antenna while we still got it?" Summers yelled.

I agreed that he should. His transmitting antenna was a seventy-five-foot length of wire hanging down in an arc from the tail of the ship. A metal weight known as the "fish" was fastened to the end of the wire. Summers did not want to lose his "fish" if it chanced to strike the surface of the sea, and I could not blame him, for spares were unaccountably hard to obtain.

We came upon squadrons of small pancake bergs, confusions of torn floe ice ribboned with green, and then a collection of rocks scattered like heavy dung droppings upon the sea. Almost at once we became aware of solid apparitions off the end of each wing. The masses were dingy in the mist, achromatic, and only occasionally stained with reality. But they were *there* undeniably, and they seemed to fold around us. We were, I became uncomfortably certain, entering a fiord. Eenie-meenie . . .

There was no time for protracted consideration. Either we must turn around at once or accept whatever came to us. I hesitated and any alternative was lost. The masses closed in more tightly on each side so that room for a turn seemed out of the question. There was no retreat. We could not go up. The fiord was far from straight, and a climb on instruments would very likely lead us to collision with its vertical walls. We could descend perhaps another twenty feet, but if we did, then we must thread our way deviously between a clutter of bergs which now appeared everywhere ahead. And the space between them was not always sufficient to pass our wingspread even at an angle. Thus we were flying in a tunnel, squeezed between rock, water, and cloud.

I cursed my original lack of caution, knowing now that we would pay a toll of one kind or another in this fiord. I could not think of any pilot who would have been such an utter fool. Entering a known cul-de-sac at sixty feet! To forgive my guilt, I determined we should get off as cheaply as we could. My mind raced to match the swiftness of our passage, trying to avoid the ultimate folly.

I told Johnson to keep a careful check on the time. Thirty miles to the wrecked freighter. That would be approximately fifteen minutes—if there was a freighter in this fiord.

Time now. A time of self-reviling. Time to face my stupidity, see it mocking, almost hear it hurled back in evidence by the gradually closing walls of the fiord. Time for the smell of true fear erupting within my aching belly, the flushed hot face again, the chill waves surging upward along my arms, evaporating in cycles from my scalp, and taking with it the last residue of my confidence.

Summers, having left his cubicle, said, "This sure as hell better be the right fiord." And I hated him for it.

Otherwise a terrible silence prevailed in the cockpit. No one made a sound as the bergs floated past just beneath our wings. The water of the fiord changed from black to a vivid, breath-taking green, but its beauty was lost on us. Somehow the color seemed to make the bergs look larger.

Nine minutes passed and we sought eagerly ahead for some sign of the freighter. There was a trifling encouragement now, for the cloud deck had risen. I followed it upward some forty feet until we were easing along just beneath. And the mist had lessened. We could now clearly see that the walls of the fiord were teethed with small ice cakes where they met the water. We could maintain an altitude of eighty feet, a dizzy height compared to our original penetration.

Then Johnson saw the freighter and I saw it and Summers and Tetterton saw it because all our eyes sought nothing else. And together we yelled the pleasure of our discovery. The freighter lay as predicted against the northern wall of the fiord, listing slightly and down by the stern, rusting and drab and broken—and very, very beautiful.

No woman was ever ravished with such affectionate eyes as this pitiable hulk. I wanted to paint a huge sign along her hull saying, "Here a fool found salvation."

Though the field was still invisible beyond the coming twists in the fiord I told Johnson to announce our arrival to the control tower by voice and obtain the wind.

I took a last fond look at the freighter and followed the contours of the fiord, which began to curve sharply to the left. Then very suddenly the fiord widened. On our right we saw a long landing strip which appeared to have been laid without regard for aero-dynamics upon the lifting threshold of a mountain.

"As advertised." I sighed and signaled Johnson to put down the landing gear.

But Boyd and Clark and Hassel had neglected much in their description of Bluie-West-One. They had failed to tell me it was so without comparison in setting, or that its visual impact made it nearly impossible to concentrate upon the minor technical problems created by its location. Here, at the very end of the fiord, lay a tremendous bowl in the mountains. The bottom was mainly filled with such an expanse of green water that several small ships could be accommodated. The calm surface was speckled white with icebergs squatting sedately, like families of gulls. The runway of the field continued its incline to a slope which rose ever more sharply until it joined with the brooding base of the icecap. This gigantic barrier then rose upon itself and where it met the overcast there was a thin line of blinding white light reflected downward by the sun. It was like a cold and savage frieze bordering the roof of a prodigious ceremonial hall. It led, I knew, to limitless and mysterious snows.

We glided down toward the end of the runway holding more speed than usual because landing upon such an upward incline would certainly cancel the need for brakes. Just as Johnson lowered the flaps I saw the runway to be of the new steel matting. When the wheels touched and our landing roll began, it made a clanking noise more terrible than my first DC-2 landing with McCabe.

But I cared not. A fool was at least a little wiser. And this place, I thought, in full understanding of Hassel's passion, could easily be Valhalla.

✺

X

A LONELY,
UNLOVED SHIP

✺

FINDING HAZARD THE MORE BITTER
WHEN MATCHED WITH TRIFLES

MERE beauty could not stay Johnson from his fixed
intent. His button nose sniffed at the lean and
invigorating air of Bluie-West-One, detecting a fragrance un-
associated with the tiny wild flowers, lichen, and outcroppings of
moss scattered along the cliff sides. His nose took a firmer bearing
than had our direction-finder on Semitak Island and led us surely
past the regular army mess until we reached a long wooden building. It proved to be a dining hall operated by the airport construction company.

In this place there followed such a memorable meal that Johnson fell asleep sitting up, which was not so surprising as his faulty sense of timing. He was overcome before the pies arrived.

We were still yawning over our coffee when a major arrived to hold me in brief consultation. He said that the steel girders had been removed from our airplane and another cargo substituted. The major fanned a sheaf of papers toward me and explained we must leave at once. I pointed out that we had just arrived and had not measured a decent sleep since our departure from Presque Isle two nights previously. The major muttered something about our ignorance of a war and added that we might finish our coffee. I thanked him for this consideration of our ease and began a sorry discourse on the ability of a single airline crew to change appreciably the course of a world's conflict.

He fluttered the papers again and told me of our new cargo and destination—and much of the weariness left me. For I saw that he spoke with the longing of those who must send others to places they have not seen themselves. I pitied him because here was a willing warrior hopelessly separated from any principal fray and he knew it; and knowing it, he was striving very hard to conceal his disappointment. So I agreed we should go as soon as we could gather our wits.

I looked at the slumbering Johnson, who now lay outstretched upon the bench and wondered at Hitler's far-reaching influence.

"Wake up. We're going to Iceland."

"Where's that? Where . . ."

"Over the hill they say."

"What hill?"

"The one with the snow on it."

"Sure . . . of course . . ."

Johnson's eyes were still glazed, and it was obvious he had never heard of Iceland, nor did he care how far over any hill such a place might be. Yet it was typical of the man that he was willing to go without further inquiry. We could as well have been bound for Tibet and his answer would have been the same. Johnson might regret the pie, but never his destiny.

Summers was of a more inquisitive mind. He wanted to know what in the name of God kind of cargo we were taking to Iceland.

"Toilet paper."

"You mean a whole airplane load of—"

"This is war, men," I said bravely. There was obviously a logistic crisis in Iceland and I thought again of my fighter-pilot friends chained to a bauxite mine in the jungles of Dutch Guiana.

There was no sound of bugles to inspire our take-off, and the airplane climbed as if we were dragging a stout cable. Its lethargy matched our mood while I tried to soothe Summer's worries. He was concerned how he would ever explain this unromantic mission to his grandchildren. "Just what the hell am I going to say when they ask me what I did in the war?"

We chose to spiral directly up from the runway until we could eventually break out on top of the overcast. This was unashamed barnstorming, but we wanted no part of the fiord again even as an exit from Valhalla.

I watched Johnson, who was doing the actual flying and was again reminded that he was one of the few so-called "natural" pilots I had ever known. His physical handling of the airplane was matchless, and now as we slipped into the overcast and he switched to instruments, his flying held beautifully sure and steady.

I could not think of an answer which might wholly satisfy Summer's concern. Examining our situation, I found opportunities for heroism slim. Our cargo was of a poor nature to justify a dash for the barricades, and whatever swagger may have originally invested our crew was long lost in unshaven grubbiness. We had not uniforms or insignia, unless the small winged device on our caps could be considered as anything more than an advertisement for our employers. We were wearing our regular line pants, shirts of our choice, and fur-lined leather jackets hastily tossed our way by a sullen supply corporal in Presque Isle. We were dirty, ripe with body odor, and clinging rather forlornly to the one thing which remained stable and familiar—our business of flying. No one had explained how or when we would be paid, where—if ever—we would sleep again, or how we should eat. Our total funds amounted to eleven dollars and fifty cents, most of which belonged to Johnson. All of these confusions were of no consequence, but we would have felt more at ease if we at least knew who commanded us. In almost every case our brief contacts with the army had been warm and co-operative. Officers and men seemed to look right through our weird collection of uniforms and they gave us the same welcome they offered any of their own. There was no resentment on either side, which led us to believe the army was as confused as ourselves. The heroes, it appeared, were yet to come and we were like the anonymous property hands in a Chinese theater, seen but not seen, moving things here and there so that the stage would be properly set.

There were a few other odds and ends aboard in addition to the toilet paper. A new Allison engine for a fighter plane had been lashed to the cabin floor. Since there were no fighter planes in Greenland, I thought the man who had originally missent it must have been a very grand personage, certainly not given to minor errors. There were also several bundles of ordinary brooms placed aboard so I assumed it was at least going to be a tidy war. This belief was strengthened just before departure when a pair of enlisted men shoved two filing cases and forty metal wastebaskets through the door. The baskets were telescoped into four neat stacks of ten each and were the only items for which we carried manifest papers. Apparently they were considered valuable since the papers were in quintuplicate—a military whimsey which nicely divided responsibility among so many that it was difficult to hold one person accountable for anything. Likewise, someone would eventually have to answer most cleverly for our orphan Allison engine.

Such space as remained in the cabin was filled with an unknown number of racks holding fragmentation bombs. I could find no record of their weight and wondered how much their presence aboard had to do with our soggy rate of climb. The individual bombs were very small, fit for a plane flown by Santos-Dumont or Blériot, but I thought they at least added a certain note of glamour to the proceedings. I told Tetterton that if we should be so unfortunate as to have an engine failure he should at once open the door and heave out the entire lot. It seemed to me they might be effective if the Red Cross in Iceland was planning a Fourth of July celebration but could hardly affect the outcome of the war one way or the other.

I beckoned to Summers, having thought of a few things which might evoke a certain cynical wonder in his grandchildren if nothing else.

Coming from his cubicle, he blinked uncertainly at the light. I told him we were spiraling upward from the bottom of a bowl, the sides of which were stouter than iron, and that Johnson was keeping our spiral tight because we had only a vague idea how large the bowl might be.

I explained to Summers that there were certain fundamentals lacking in this flight and if he brooded on them long enough he might consider himself either a hero or a fool. Once we were above the overcast there would be the icecap, which we *assumed* was clear of cloud. We did not know, nor did the charts offer any detailed information, how high this icecap might be. It was said that to surmount it an altitude of at least nine thousand feet must be held, which in itself presented a problem. For several hours, until our fuel weight lightened, we could not possibly maintain an altitude higher than six thousand feet on one engine. Therefore, if either engine should fail, our flight must terminate within a very short time.

And then there was the business of alternates, which was now reduced to the utmost simplicity. When we emerged from the confines of the bowl, it would be near suicide to attempt a return descent upon Bluie-West-One in the same manner. We could have a go at the fiord again by turning back to the west, but unless the weather had much improved, this held little appeal. Once we started eastward across the icecap, then, we were committed to our destination of Reykjavik, and I confessed complete ignorance of what the weather might be there. The army had not received a radio report from Iceland for the past twenty-four hours.

Summers said he would see what he could do about a report when we had reached cruising altitude.

There were other embarrassments which I felt compelled to share with Summers, and with Tetterton now, who thrust his head curiously into the lecture. These were things the major had confided in me with all the winks and mysterioso of a soldier sharing secrets with a civilian, against his better judgment. The Germans had established a weather station on the east coast of Greenland. If we saw them we should steer clear, a bit of advice which I considered somewhat less than complimentary to our judgment. Between Greenland and Iceland there were supposed to be a number of U-boats. These should be reported, but also avoided. In the vicinity of Iceland it would be possible to encounter long-range German patrol planes. These were said to be heavily armed and we should avoid any close association with them. The major did not explain in any detail how one plodding DC 3 could escape such predatory beasts. Yet the most likely inconvenience, the major had said, might well originate within our own forces. Long before approaching Iceland we must be very careful to identify ourselves properly by radio. Should we fail in this, such radio aids as Reykjavik offered would be shut down, which would not make the place any easier to find.

The approaches to Iceland were patrolled by fighter planes, and the pilots, nearly starved for action, were reported more than ordinarily trigger-happy. Summers had been presented with a special code kit to make friendly signals in the air, and I asked him now if he understood its complications.

"Well . . . I guess so."

According to my calculations, we would arrive over Iceland with one hour's fuel remaining and just as the brief subarctic night began. En route, then, there would be only the sun for navigation. The winds aloft had been roughly estimated by the army meterologist as favorable and the weather good. We were not to rely on any of this, however, since the prediction was two days old and based upon very scanty reports.

Watching the faces of my comrades, I could see that I had said enough. They were not in the least frightened or even outwardly concerned. They seemed to be only in a state of sleepy wonderment, content to believe that if I had agreed to leave the earth in the first place, I must have complete confidence in our safe return. I thought of Park and Hughen, and Ross, and Keim, and Lester and McCabe. And for a moment of the numbers. This was our world, bedraggled and obscure for the moment, but still familiar in tone. I saw no purpose in dwelling further on my personal doubts and suspicions.

We emerged from the overcast and were stunned with light. The sun skewered our tired eyes on hot little pins and we drew in our shoulders instinctively, as if recoiling from a heavy blow. It was some moments before we could bear more than a glance beyond the windshields. Then finally I saw and understood once again Hassel's strange love affair. For here was enchantment such as few men had yet beheld.

The icecap surged upward from the overcast in a great rumpling tidal wave of snow. The protruding mountain peaks we had seen from afar now appeared much higher than had been alleged. A few most certainly bettered ten thousand feet. We had been warned to approach the icecap with care, for in certain combinations of light it merged so gradually with the sky that there was no visible horizon. And since no one professed to know its exact height, maximum possible altitude was also recommended.

On this morning there did appear to be a faint division of light marking a horizon, but it was ephemeral and untrustworthy. So as Johnson turned northeastward we resolved to fly on instruments, rejecting the invitation to depend upon our eyes. Since we were quite in the clear the sensation was deeply disturbing, like flying toward a constantly retreating wall.[6]

As we proceeded across the icecap I began to mark down various mountain peaks where the chart offered only blank spaces. I also marked their approximate altitudes.

Johnson nursed the ship to eleven thousand feet, which altitude, he drawled, was as damn-all high as it would go. And once more we brought back the propellers to satisfy the dictates of the engineers. And again the eerie silence fell upon us. We proceeded thus for almost two hours, holding oxygen masks to our faces now and again in a dogged effort to keep awake.

Later the horizon became more defined and we could clearly see the enormous camber of the icecap as it rose gradually from the west, held nearly flat in what would be the center of Greenland, and then fell away gracefully to the east. We were silent and each thoughtful in his own way, measuring ourselves against this garish, brooding wilderness, and there came upon us a certain spell, so powerful that when we were occasionally required to make some technical comment concerning our fuel, or course, or speed, the urge was to speak in whispers, which we did as nearly as we were able. And as we continued, assimilating little by little the dominant hostility of this land, we knew the sensation of being dwarfed to nearly zero proportions; we became far more diminutive than even a thunderstorm could render us. We were less than gnats in the sky and were accordingly cleansed of ego.

Finally the icecap sank beneath us and we perceived the erratic range of mountains which fringe the eastern coast. We began to descend, following the contour of the snow until it broke away entirely and tumbled into the sea.

The vagaries of the chart made it impossible to mark exactly where we left the land, but at least I could record the time and so have some speed basis for later navigation. There was considerable pack ice crumpled against this eastern shore, and Tetterton yelled that he saw a walrus basking in the sun, but since none of the rest of us could detect the slightest sign of life on the ice below, we called him a liar, which at once led to further accusations; and thus, in a return to human sound, we managed to break the spell. The badinage spurted from our flapping lips overeagerly, as if too long withheld. We clutched at the normalcy of our jests, allowing them to be as dull in content and as tainted with the obscene as we pleased. We were again sticky little men reveling in vulgarity, farting and hollering and adjusting our genitals, and preening our stubbles of beards as well as our fancied souls. And it seemed to me that men were never intended to play at Gods, which they should be if they would dwell comfortably in such places as the ice-cap of Greenland.

When this mood had held us long enough to burn out any lingering traces of fineness or inspiration, I went back to the table in the cabin and busied myself for a long time with shooting the sun. I took several lines of position and worked out our radius of action. What I had told Summers and the others was now fact. Considering our fuel supply, the only dry destination we could reach on earth was Iceland.

We left the last iceberg behind, and the waters of Denmark Strait remained ominously calm. There was no indication of any assisting wind as we drummed monotonously through the afternoon. Evening came on hastily, but the sun itself remained above the horizon. Yet it was now too low for a decent sight and only served to lend the sea a reflection of its anemia. Gradually a high, thin overcast shelved across the sky leaving only a luminous blob where the sun had been. A few formless and isolated clouds appeared just above the water and were later joined by others until the sea was obscured entirely. Johnson, long at the controls, said something unintelligible in the middle of a magnificent yawn and turned up the cockpit lights.

I asked Summers if he had been able to make any radio contact with Iceland, though I knew beforehand that he would have told me of any such good fortune. He had been clicking away at his key, swearing and tinkering with his equipment for the entire afternoon. He peered at me resentfully through his smudged glasses as if my question offended not only him but the reputation of all wireless communication.

"No. But I worked O'Connor's operator. They just left Goose Bay. And Smith has left Reykjavik west bound."

"When?"

Summers shrugged his shoulders and said that all signals were skipping about the atmosphere in a way they had no damn business doing and if I would just be patient he might eventually have more news.

So I turned back and was patient though sorely discontent. I wanted to reach beyond the tight confines of the cockpit and touch the minds of other human beings, if only electrically. Preferably these confidants would be Robinson or MacDonald or Smith or Dunn or Pharr or Hay, any of whom would have understood my frustration in not knowing what the winds might now be doing, or exactly where we were.

Our situation was approaching some kind of resolution whether we were ready or not. We might overshoot the shores of Iceland if we held aloft much longer, and there were mountains on Iceland which were just as hard as mountains anywhere. We could see ahead after a fashion, since there still held a weak twilight between the lower level of cloud and the high overcast. But the visibility forward was steadily becoming less and in a very short time it would not exist. As it was during our original approach to Greenland, we had no way of knowing how closely the lower level of cloud pressed against the sea.

Iceland is not very large. An error of fifty miles could cause us to miss it entirely, and I had not been able to take any navigational fix for over four hours. Johnson had been playing with the direction finder almost continuously, though without result. We should long ago have picked up some kind of signal from Reykjavik, yet the only sound of any consequence had been some rather primitive music from a station in Morocco.

I asked Summers if he was certain he had sent out the properly coded identification signals. He held a metal folder toward me. Its interior contained miniature tracks upon which there were small sliding tabs. These could be adjusted to a previously agreed-on formula according to the date and hour.

"Figure it out for yourself. I set it up just like they told me."

I declined. My brain was like a limp salad and held enough confusion without the seasoning of an intricate code machine. I turned back once more to our direction finder. How dare they turn off their signals? The precious nature of our cargo was going unappreciated. Yet Iceland's welcome continued to be a cold silence.

Armies, being faceless entities, are useful targets for complaining men whatever their time or nationality. There is nothing quite so satisfactory as cursing "the army," particularly when serving in one. We indulged ourselves in this special pleasure, postponing decision as long as we dared. Until finally I knew our nerves were once more in for a strumming.

Iceland *had* to be near, regardless of its coy concealment. The only question remaining was how near. I told Johnson to start a descent.

We slipped into the lower level of clouds at three thousand feet and it was instantly night. We still had time to spare, which meant room to spare. By letting down so early in the hunt we avoided any possibility of overshooting our mark or colliding with it. A humble hands-and-knees entrance, I thought, but one befitting the conditions. We continued down.

As we passed through one thousand feet and then five hundred, I began to squirm in my seat. We were still in heavy cloud and were spat at more frequently as we plunged into light rain showers. I grumbled to Johnson that this seemed to be our day for low-altitude maneuvering.

"It's really tomorrow, isn't it?"

"It can never be tomorrow if you're alive."

I remembered the fine four hours of sleep the morning before yesterday and was momentarily ashamed of my softness. The only hardship was having to think. Now the machinery creaked when it should spin, because the elements were not co-operating.

We passed three hundred feet and I told Johnson to hold altitude. We were still in cloud, deaf and dumb and blind. What the altimeters said could be a lie.

"Take her down to two hundred and hold."

Johnson pursed his lips and I was strangely pleased to discover that he was not, after all, inhuman. There were fibers of nerve buried within him and at last they had been touched. He became a grim kewpie as he eased the ship down another hundred feet.

"Summers! Can you raise anyone?"

"No!"

I fiddled with the direction finder briefly and twisted my headphone jack in a hypocritical attempt to prove this silence was only the result of a poor connection. This moment of research was pure stalling. I knew very well the connection was firm. I also knew that we must continue down now until we could see the sea, and it must be now and not ten minutes from now. I hated the idea. How much deeper was the sky? There should be some way to reach out a finger and poke downward until the end became wet—then we would know.

I remembered Summers' past concern for his aerial "fish." It could keep us from swimming whatever remained of the distance to Iceland. Using it according to my plan might also be very hard on the nerves. But it would be better than nothing.

"Summers!"

He came forward at once though still tethered to his equipment by his headphone wire. His glasses were steamed from the unnatural heat of his body, and I thought that his hands must be very hot and moist, like my own, always an early sign of fear.

I told him quickly of our predicament, though I knew he must be generally aware that all was not well. It was an excuse for delaying action a few moments longer and I seized upon it hungrily. I wanted time to assemble all the gall within me—much needed if my scheme was to be accepted as anything but madness.

The antenna wire was wound upon a reel set beneath the floor of the airplane. There was a small removable hatch over this reel, and by reaching down through it a man could grasp the trailing wire.

"You may lose your fish."

"Why, for Christ's sake?"

For this bauble alone, Summers seemed concerned.

"We're going to let down until we can see something. I want you to hold on to your antenna wire as we descend. If you feel a jerk, yell your head off. Then we'll stop going down."

"It only hangs down about fifty feet—maybe less. It don't hang straight, you know."

"I know. Fifty feet is fifty feet."

Summers hesitated, reluctant, like any good workman, to part with his tools. Then he turned back without a word. I watched him as he lifted the hatch beside his cubicle and knelt over it. When he reached down for the wire his bald head shone in the dim light from the cockpit. Behind him I could barely make out the figure of Tetterton standing motionless in the shadows. Summers looked up at me and the light reflecting on his nearly opaque glasses concealed his eyes. He said that he was ready and wished it had taken him longer to be so.

I found it necessary to take a deep breath before I could assume the proper mask of indifference and join with Johnson in playing the same game Park and I had played on a hot afternoon in Brazil. Finally I made a prodding gesture and Johnson started down. Perhaps it was the lack of illumination, or fatigue, but this time the incongruous sense of jubilation I had known with Park was totally absent. I fought fright successfully, only because I knew Summers' "fish" must strike the water first.

I turned the cockpit lights completely down and yanked open the side window as Ross had taught me so long ago. Then I waited, revived by the roar of air, trying to ignore the roiling in my belly, staring out and down until my eyes seemed sucked from my head.

We passed through one hundred feet according to the altimeters.

"Should I keep descending?"

"Yes."

A quick glance at the compass. Johnson had not varied his course more than a degree. But his voice had cracked to a falsetto.

"See anything?"

"Not yet."

I glanced back at Summers, but in the gloom I could not be sure whether he still had his hand on the wire. I was sorry for him because from his supplicant position in the darkness he could see nothing. I could, at least, delude myself.

Johnson continued down and I begged again of the night. The last time I looked at my altimeter it read eighty feet. I determined to ignore it. I leaned to the window until the slip stream ripped at my hair. After a moment I saw, or thought I saw, a deepening in the blackness. It was lost at once as a hissing rain lashed the windshields. I drew back from the open window. A silliness. Must not wet shirt.

Then Summers cried out so piercingly that I could have heard him had I been standing on the wing. He had lost his "fish." Seconds later I saw the black ocean and was appalled at its nearness.

There was no need for me to signal Johnson. The shout from Summers had been enough to make him hold his altitude. He knew well enough that water struck at this speed would be as firm as concrete.

Scud swept past beneath us, clinging to the water, but we appeared to be otherwise in the clear. The rain ceased as quickly as it had come and I told Johnson we would set our altimeters at forty feet.

"Hold that."

Johnson complied perfectly, his eyes fixed to his instruments; and I thought that my voice echoed the mandates of Ross when he insisted the variation of a few feet might be a sin.

We continued so for some twenty minutes while Summers tried again and again to contact Iceland. But, he said, without a "fish" to stream his antenna properly, he looked for little success.

At last we saw a division ahead, slicing between the overcast and the sea, and this subtle offering from the night greatly encouraged us. The division took on strength and became luminescent. It increased until it overcame the twilight and we saw it as the lights of a city.

"That must be—how do you pronounce it?"

"Reykjavick." I answered as if I knew.

Johnson, now once more a hoyden doll, asked me what language they spoke in such a place and I told him the field was operated by the R.A.F. The people in the control tower would undoubtedly understand English.

We passed over the shore line and saw that the field itself was set in the heart of the city. Johnson called the control tower and an English voice tonelessly relayed the wind force and direction.

Johnson looked at me in hurt bewilderment. "I thought you said they spoke English here."

"The man is a Cockney. It's a little special."

"Well, I never heard the like."

Nor had the control-tower operator. As we circled the field, there followed a long and confused verbal exchange between the deepest South in America and the equally regional Limehouse. The topic was inhospitality. Johnson charged our hosts with being cruelly indifferent to our navigational needs. The result was a hilarious impasse at Johnson's expense, successful only in driving away all of the fears and some of the weariness we had guarded for so long.

I learned later that there had been a mix-up, not uncommon to partner nations at war. We had been given the wrong code for the day and had been reported as "approaching enemy aircraft." The fighter planes had been out looking for us but had never thought we should be skimming the sea.

Which did not greatly disturb us as we stumbled into a Nissen hut and fell upon our cots.

☼

XI

THE NUMBERS

☼

IN A WICKED, VENGEFUL MOOD

THUS, in timorous austerity, we began a type of flying which only a short time previously we would hardly have dared consider. Our methods were of necessity crude and highly individual; certainly they were frowned upon by those slavish to any book of rules. Except for O'Connor and MacDonald, who volunteered from the start, those of great seniority on the line made no attempt to displace us. It seemed we were welcome to hang ourselves, and our elders would eventually cut us down for decent burial. Meanwhile we were thought irascible and over-venturesome by our more conservative colleagues, most of whom were content to sit back and see what happened.

We were not altogether naïve. McIntosh and experience had taught us better than we knew. Consequently there were no more than minor alarms during this exploratory period and only our frugal equipment prevented us from accomplishing more. Even so, the service, if it could be so dignified in name, grew rapidly and then compounded in extent until our primary efforts seemed as nothing. On the North Atlantic route new airports were torn out of the wilderness far north of Goose Bay. These were the "Crystals," known as "One," "Two," and "Three," and "Bluie-West-Eight,"[7] which, like its southern Greenland counterpart "Bluie-West-One," lay at the end of a long fiord. Stephensville in Newfoundland was building, and Gander enlarging its facilities and lengthening its runways.

Elsewhere similar projects were under way, some in actual operation and others still in the embryo stage. There was a shuttle service to Alaska, flown by men of our own line. I learned with the swiftness of aerial rumor that Lippincott and Gay and Owen and Charleton were among the pilots. We had left the innocent days in Lester's school far behind. There were also reports of activity in the South Atlantic, of new fields in Brazil, Ascension Island, and Africa. As far as we knew they had yet to be used. United Airlines and Consairways were experimenting with a service across that part of the Pacific which remained still free of Japanese domination. The baptismal halls through which America proposed to send a final host of fledglings were being readied everywhere.

Our special gauge to this tremendous endeavor was Goose Bay, which grew so quickly before our astonished eyes that we hardly recognized it. Through all of this, Hassel fumed and swore and labored so mightily that he was at last sent off to his beloved Greenland, where he was content. Boyd was promoted to a lieutenant colonel and transferred to Presque Isle. Clark disappeared, and soon the faces which greeted us in Goose Bay were those of strangers.

Our original group remained intact, but our status continued so confused that not even Davidson could clarify matters. This was creating a cross tangle of authority and certain rumors which infuriated us all. While no one questioned the value or hazards of our early flights, it was said we were being paid so highly that we must retire as wealthy men. The truth was that we had no idea what we would be paid, and for the first six weeks we were not paid at all. Even later it took some fairly dramatic pleading to receive our regular line salaries. Since we maintained ourselves, this illogical arrangement was often embarrassing.

By this time we had willingly abandoned the eighty-five-hour-a-month flying limitation and simply flew as needed. As a result we were perpetually tired though far from exhausted, and most of us could have taken a great deal more. But our constant state of transit, existing mostly in airplanes moving from Iceland to Greenland, to Labrador, to Maine, and back again, left us strangely rootless and timeless. We slept when we could and sometimes ate three breakfasts in succession. The simple pleasure of the same cot in the same barracks, a tiny haven where a man might keep his rudimentary treasures in place, was impossible for us to devise. We could not indulge in even the wistful childishness of pin-ups, or hobbies, or become a part of the makeshift communities which had already established themselves at every place we landed. Loyalty to an immediate group, the venerable savior of all men engaged far from home, was difficult for us to realize because we seldom saw our counterparts. We were without easy identity and our movements were marked only by careless greetings or by distant farewells.

We lived in and out of our flight bags, they being our true and only home. Thus, if we were not actually flying or sleeping, we were often lonely and at a loss to occupy ourselves. Some of us simply sat and stared, rising automatically when the call came to break the trance and start again over the horizon. Others absorbed themselves in various remedies for our all-prevailing constipation, the inevitable result of long cockpit confinement and irregular diet. A few played cards when they could find enough companions, and there were spasmodic expeditions through whatever literature was at hand. Very occasionally we would find ourselves on the ground when the local army movie was shown. These we attended to a man. Otherwise we yearned for amusement of any kind and the dullest of us came to realize it was an appetite like any other. Strangers everywhere, we were obliged to provide our own.

My own solutions to this problem were many, although none were very successful. I made crude sketches of my companions and even less skillful portrayals of the environment in which we flew. I also made many notes for this work, hoping thereby to save my mind from mildew. And lately I had taken on a new fancy which had already brought threats of mutiny from my crew. I had purchased a mouth organ in Presque Isle, which was a grievous mistake in the eyes of Johnson and Summers, for I soon established a shocking inability to carry a tune. Since we no longer carried flight mechanics along with us, Tetterton was spared my concerts.

In spite of the others' comments I considered my renditions rather melodic as long as we were in actual flight—"Home on the Range" sounded particularly stirring against the accompaniment of two powerful engines. At least, I thought, it kept Johnson awake, although the effort of blowing at any altitude above five thousand feet made me dizzy.

Our oddments of special flying knowledge had increased until they now composed a respectable bounty. We knew the remote fields of the North Atlantic as well as we had once known our domestic routes. We knew how to sneak into them in bad weather and how best to escape when the planes were overheavy. We knew the summer moods of the ocean itself and could estimate winds with remarkable accuracy by merely aligning the waves with the metal stripping of our side windows. Our celestial navigation, dependent mostly on the sun because the nights were hardly of any duration, became realistically valuable. Our points-of-no-return took on honest significance because new facilities were constantly being provided and we knew the fat pleasure of having someplace worth returning to. McIntosh flew with us frequently, observing and checking our skill. One of our number, finally exasperated with the sickly air speeds, decided the engineers were in error and took it upon himself to set the propellers at their normal cruising speed. He was right. He arrived at his destination with more fuel than he ever had before. We all adopted his experiment and never returned to floundering.

Thus we flew through the days and slowly lengthening nights until the North Atlantic air space held all those small familiarities likely to satisfy the professional pilot.

Yet it was plain to everyone concerned that our time was limited. Just as we were becoming more than a curiosity and fulfilling those needs for which we had been chosen, we must now retreat before a new and uncompromising enemy. Even at the low altitudes we were compelled to fly, the winds sometimes achieved sixty miles an hour. Two-engined airplanes simply could not return westward across the Atlantic against such contrary forces. In September these winds began to blow. When they carried the first snows across the lakes and forests of Labrador we were sent away southward like weakling birds, and most of our original group was assigned to the army four-engine school in Smyrna, Tennessee.

The highly revered Pedley was killed near Palm Springs, though it was not of his own doing. With him as co-pilot was Reppert. Flying an airliner in peaceful skies, they were victims of a mid-air collision with an army airplane. Pedley's number on our line was 4. His long and magnificent flying record made this particular ambush of fate especially hard to understand.

Our training at Smyrna was devoted if perfunctory. Murray, a most skillful young army pilot, took me in hand for six hours and demonstrated the rudiments of flying a Liberator bomber. The instruction took place all in one day and that was the end of it. None of us had opportunity to try landing one of these rather peculiar flying machines at night. We were still innocent of a legend already attached to the cargo version of the Liberator which was to be our lot. It was said that the assembly of parts known collectively as a "C-87" would never replace the airplane. Eventually these aeronautical botcheries were held accomplice to the death of big Hunt, who had flown on AM-21, and of Charleton, who had shared Lester's school. And one of them nearly put an end to the long career of O'Connor. They were an evil bastard contraption, nothing like the relatively efficient B-24 except in appearance. In time they betrayed each of us in various ways and there was a tendency to approach one as if it were an angry bull elephant—to which they somehow bore a startling resemblance.

These so-called airplanes had not only the four engines but a considerable cruising range. The amount of cargo or personnel we could transport was likewise greatly increased. Consequently, they were thought the answer to the winter winds of the North Atlantic. In them we could fly nonstop to England and, by refueling at either Iceland or Greenland, return westbound with reasonable predictability.

No one knew, as yet, that the C-87's could not carry enough ice to chill a highball.

The soft-voiced MacDonald was the first to discover this miserable shortcoming. In the winter night he encountered a mild front just south of Greenland's Cape Farewell. He sought to climb above it and was proceeding nicely when an innocent frosting decorated his windshields. It was so thin and light in consistency that he ignored its slow accumulation and was in conversation with his co-pilot when the C-87 quivered as if stabbed in the midriff and instantly fell off in a wild spin. Two thousand feet later MacDonald brought the ship back to normal flight and while waiting for his heart to subside developed an understandable contempt for the C-87. The amount of ice which caused his involuntary dive toward the freezing sea was much less than he had frequently carried in a humble DC-3. Soon afterward, in almost the same locale, I had an identical disappointment, although MacDonald's experience had made me wary and we managed to recover more quickly. We thought, perhaps unfairly, that the "Davis" wing was to blame for this pernicious habit. It was designed for efficiency at very high bombing altitudes and had no place in our present efforts.

We had now been provided with life rafts and vests, a solicitous gesture which was as touching as it was ridiculous. No voyage upon our winter seas in such craft could be anything but a brief and torturous postponement of the inevitable. It was natural, then, that we gave our utmost attention to remaining aloft. Preoccupation with calamity was far from constant, but it lurked always in the background of our thinking. It was served up juicily during the long cockpit nights, bandied back and forth among the crew members in the merriest speculation—an historic habit of men and small boys whistling in the dark.

The C-87[8] had other built-in evils. It was a ground-loving bitch, and with heavy loads it rolled, snorted, and porpoised interminably before asserting its questionable right to fly. The failure of any one of the four engines on take-off was an extremely serious affair, a part of which was due to its hasty conversion from bomber to transport plane. The balance was never exactly right in spite of our constant experimentation. The flight controls were heavy and insensitive compared to other airplanes. This was particularly true at the lower altitudes.

The illumination in the cockpit was inadequate for intensive bad-weather flying. Small bouquets of tubular lights were placed haphazardly throughout the flight deck, and the quality of light produced gave us the blind staggers after hours at the controls. It was a cold, morguelike luminosity which seemed to pull our eyes slowly from our heads—when the system worked at all. For the entire installation displayed a faithless cunning which sometimes revealed only our tempers. All of the lights would often fail simultaneously in the middle of an instrument take-off. The shouts of rage from both pilots could easily be heard above the sound of the engines as we sought to persuade the C-87 to leave the ground and at the same time pound the lights back into commission. Smart co-pilots kept a flashlight handy.

No one knew how best to winterize the C-87's we flew, which created a continuous series of minor crises. Landing gears would not go down when they were activated and sometimes they would not retract. On one occasion Dunn flew about for hours with one wheel up and the other down. This ludicrous, storklike attitude canceled the pauper's choice of a decent belly landing.

The pitch of the propellers was controlled electrically. At least once during a flight the mechanism was bound to freeze, which left us helpless to reduce speed properly or climb out of adverse weather. The transfer of fuel from the reserve tanks to the operating tanks was necessary on every flight of any duration. It was a nervous and an odoriferous business. All smoking was stopped while the smell of high-octane gasoline marinated the entire airplane. We stopped smoking because the connecting hoses invariably leaked, some enough to make troublesome puddles on the floor. A high-octane wading pool is something you can't throw out the window. Throughout this eye-burning transfer process we also kept the radios silent, with the idea of preventing explosion. It never seemed to trouble any of us that the fuel transfer pump was also electric and gaily threw out sparks within a few feet of the hose connections.

Finally, the C-87's had a heating system which was of two minds —both malicious. When it chose to function it produced a sirocco that left us gasping on the flight deck, while our few miserable passengers shuddered with cold. When the system refused every effort to make it work, we all shivered together. The reputations of C-87's and the maledictions heaped upon them grew in accord with the outside air temperature, which was often fifty below zero.

There were certain good things about C-87's. The engines were magnificent. Mechanics like Ulbrick and Tetterton, who worked in such cold that they dared not touch a tool with their bare hands, had nothing but praise for these engines. This was most fortunate because the same men were driven nearly out of their minds by the constant frivolities and idiosyncrasies of the frozen hydraulic and electric systems. The devotion of these men and all their kind, working on snow-swept ramps in jaw-aching cold, forever impressed and shamed us as we watched them from the comfort of a warm dispatch office. Consequently we saved our feeble complaints until we were in the air, well out of hearing of those whose noses dribbled continuously and who regarded painful frostbite as just another annoyance.

The C-87's had speed, which algebraically lessened the effect of head winds and cross winds on our flight plans. Their ability to fly very high enabled us to surmount all but the most vicious fronts. Their range allowed us the luxury of "pressure-pattern" flying whereby we could take advantage of the most favorable winds. We did our best to remember these blessings even if the winter often negated their value.

Our home remained the cockpit, but it had now changed in many ways. We continued to wear pieces of our airline uniforms supplemented by heavy fur-lined leather flying suits and boots. Our individual crews had expanded until they had become a small family. It was obvious that the captain of a four-engined airplane had quite enough to occupy his attention without the details of navigation. So we were assigned a "navigator" who minded the actual positions, graphs, and flight plans. These were usually young men previously employed by the line in various earth-bound jobs. They volunteered for McIntosh's course in navigation, raced through it, and suddenly found themselves over the middle of the winter Atlantic. The first man assigned to my own crew celebrated a double debut. It was not only the first time he had tried to put his navigation into actual practice; it was the first time he had ever been up in an airplane. Something near terror struck him when he made his first mistake and thereafter his assistance was meager. Yet, like all the others, he learned very quickly, and soon a good navigator became a prize well worth a captain's scheming.

We were also assigned flight engineers. These men were not veterans like Ulbrich or Tetterton but apprentice mechanics who had also volunteered. They maintained the airplane as conditions would permit, transferred fuel, kept the endless records on engine performance which had previously gone almost ignored by the pilots, and froze with the rest of us.

We continued to operate mainly from Presque Isle. The potato fields were now covered with deep snow and the inhabitants in hibernation according to their annual custom. At the airport, Boyd was already a full colonel and in direct charge of our endeavors. At Prestwick in Scotland, which stood at the other end of the operation, the red-faced Clark now held sway in his most explosive manner. For some reason, he was still a major.

We flew a mixture of airplanes, the C-87's serving the longer flights and the two-engined C-47's still plodding faithfully on the shorter overland legs to Goose Bay and the Arctic "Crystal" fields.

At "Crystal Two" Miller was killed. He was a strikingly handsome young man of great charm and considerable intelligence. He had recently been promoted to captain and was flying the notorious "No-go," that same airplane which had caused each one of us concern as it became our duty to fly the thing. Miller began his take-off in blowing snow and the visibility varied from moment to moment. The wretched "No-go" was characteristically reluctant to leave the ground. It lingered an instant too long. One wing struck a high snowbank bordering the runway and in the resulting cartwheel much of the forward end of the airplane was demolished. The co-pilot escaped without injury. The circumstances of the accident were strangely similar to those which had years before left Lester's body in ruins. But Miller's fortune was not so kind. Grievously cut in his left leg, he bled to death before proper help could arrive.

Fatalism was flimsy protection against such tragedies. It was easier to think that Miller, like so many others, had been killed doing what he wanted to do. Our minds were always technically prepared for such melancholy events, and thus nearly devoid of emotional protest, but our hearts were not so easily resigned.

The same debonair Beattie who had shared a sticky night in which an outlaw plane nearly terminated our careers was once again my co-pilot. We flew many times across to Scotland and he suffered unduly since I now carried an instrument to match the size of the airplane. I had forsaken the mouth organ for a concertina, which I kept in a box near the left rudder pedal. It was my fancy to render "You take the high road and I'll take the low road" immediately before take-off. The result was a superstition among our crew which was quite baseless. It began as a joke and was ultimately awarded that peculiar half-belief by which civilized men under stress do betray the actual thickness of their cultivation. If I performed the tune without error, the omens were for a good and easy trip across the ocean. If I drew forth sour notes, difficulties could be expected according to their number. Unfortunately my talents had not improved in the slightest—a deficiency, we were forced to admit, that seemed verified by the elements.

There were still only a few C-87's available for our use and even our redoubtable mechanics could not keep them all off the sick list. Consequently the questionable privilege of flying the larger machines soon revolved upon seniority, of which the veteran O'Connor held the greatest.

Those humble in seniority, like Miller, were assigned to fly the two-engined C-47's on flights to Goose Bay and the Crystals unless one of the larger planes became available to fly the ocean. Thus, once again, the numbers took over the regulation of our private destinies and once more the numbers composed themselves in a way which at times made some of us feel like a ball spinning in a roulette wheel.

We had been scheduled to fly a C-87 to remote BW-8 (Thule). We had not been to the place since summer and the prospect intrigued our entire crew. The spell of Greenland persisted and all of us wanted to see if the magic was even more powerful in winter. Our special desire for the flight was magnified by pride and to some extent by the insatiable curiosity of all airmen. Bundled in fur and leather, we discussed the flight enthusiastically on the way to the airport.

Apparently O'Connor shared our interest. At the airport a sergeant informed us that we had been replaced. O'Connor would take the flight. As a sop to our spirits we were to leave immediately on a relatively simple flight to Goose Bay in a C-47. The navigator and engineer, superfluous on the smaller plane, returned to their beds. My own disappointment turned to resigned bemusement when I found the change had been devised only an hour before. So I scribbled a note and carelessly flipped it in O'Connor's mailbox. These were the exact words: "Thanks for the bone, you old bastard. I hope you have a nice *long* flight!"

I regretted this childish reaction soon after we were air-borne. But it was too late. By the time we had returned to Presque Isle,

O'Connor would be well on his way. Sometime during that freezing night we shared the arctic sky.

It passed, and then another, and on the following morning every pilot available at Presque Isle was summoned to a room near Boyd's office.

We stood in stiff, formalized little groups, a handful of army officers on one side of the room and the airline men opposite. I sought out McGuire, who had just arrived, and asked if he was ever going back to his Carolina mule. He answered softly that he still held the prospect in mind, after which the embarrassed silence was broken only by the occasional sluffing of our fur boots, or the crash of a match igniting. Then, as if resenting the quiet, two radiators began a crazy banging. It was extremely hot in the room and most of us had removed our leather jackets.

Boyd entered, calling each man by name from the remarkable storehouse of his memory. He confirmed the rumor about O'Connor which had held us in such silence. He was indeed missing, information which particularly distressed me, for every word of the note I had left him rang through my mind.

Boyd, sucking thoughtfully on his pipe, told us what little he knew. O'Connor had arrived without incident at BW-8. He had remained there only long enough for refueling and a hot meal. With seventeen sick and injured men as passengers, he had taken off again to the south and was not heard from again until he reported a position in "the vicinity of the St. Lawrence." Radio reception had been poor everywhere and the balance of his message was garbled, but enough could be deciphered to assure us he had been in trouble. He had encountered ice, which was unpleasant enough in a C-87. Worse, he was uncertain of his position because he had been unable to climb above the weather. His navigator was unable to take a celestial sight, nor could he manage any believable radio bearings.

Matters then seemed to have snowballed on O'Connor in their wondrous fashion. A supercharger on one engine failed, and he was doubtful that he could clear even the low mountains just south of the St. Lawrence. His message concluded with the advice that he was "turning back northwest." This made no sense whatsoever. If his reported position was anywhere near correct, he would be turning toward a frozen wilderness which was almost entirely unexplored. On the latest chart which Boyd displayed, a few rivers and fewer lakes were vaguely represented by dotted lines. The remainder, to the shores of Hudson Bay, was a blank.

"That's the fix, gentlemen," Boyd said, kicking at one of the radiators, "and it isn't a good one. Not in the month of February."

We discussed the fix, giving to it our combined knowledge of the earth and the skies covering the thousands of square miles between BW-8 and where O'Connor had last thought he might be. It was easy enough to visualize the pressures upon him: he would not have slept for more than twenty-four hours according to the times recorded. With ice and a failing supercharger, the ship must have flown like a grand piano. All of the miserable faults of a C-87 had combined to defeat a man who must have already been very weary. It was even easier to appreciate his situation if he were still alive. Outside our overheated room, with its obstreperous radiators, the temperature was fifteen degrees below zero. Wherever O'Connor might be, it was undoubtedly much colder. I could not resist thinking of the numbers. On the surface at least, it was only the impish, unpredictable numbers which had placed O'Connor in that airplane instead of . . .

Boyd led the discussion, asking each man to say what he would do if faced with the same situation. The answers were all basically similar and were generally prefaced with the reservation that it was one thing to sit in a warm room and say what a man might do, and quite another to be sure how any man would react when besieged by weather, confined by the inexorable limitations of time against fuel, and bleeding with mechanical failures. A few men said they just didn't know what the hell they would do other than commence their prayers.

There is always a dunce present in any meeting of more than ten men, and now the attention-seeker proved to be a lieutenant who began a long analysis of what O'Connor should have done instead of what he might have done. He was an enormous man with a roast-beef face; altogether the physical type to be valued in a rough environment. He made a strange contrast to young Thomas, a slight, terribly shy airline captain, or to Catchings, whose physique and bald head better suited a bank official. We were later to discover that this lieutenant, who concluded his inept tirade by volunteering to lead us all to O'Connor's immediate rescue, possessed the courage of a gazelle. We were all grateful when Boyd lost patience and silenced the man.

He then read us a message supposedly received from a Coast Guard cutter which had been in communication with a distressed airplane. The plane was not identified, but the pilot was alleged to have said he would try a landing in the water off the coast of Nova Scotia. There was something wrong about that message; it had a taint of phoniness which we could not analyze exactly, and yet it was there. Someone suggested it might have come from a German submarine wishing to confuse a search for O'Connor, which was as good an explanation as any. Instinctively, we all mistrusted it. Boyd said attempts had been made to contact any Coast Guard cutter in the area for further confirmation. None had replied.

Yet the message agreed with our various opinions as to what we would do if similarly challenged. Why should O'Connor have said he was turning away to the northwest when such a course must take him away from even remote contact with human assistance?

Vaughn, a major who knew the north country far better than most men, said he thought O'Connor might have reached a very intelligent decision. In spite of the vagueness of the charts, he believed that most of the immense area to the northwest of O'Connor's last position was relatively flat and certainly he would favor such land. Vaughn made sense and put his case aptly, but we clung to the idea that the message had been misunderstood. We finally agreed that had the choice been ours, we would have proceeded back toward the ocean and let down to layers of warmer air. To the east there would also be Nova Scotia, where there were several fields good enough for an emergency, and if fuel exhaustion prevented reaching one of these, we would try a crash landing along a beach. In any case, we were all certain that whatever the fate of O'Connor and those with him, they could not survive long in such temperatures. There could be no leisure to our search.

Boyd outlined its planned proportions and we were impressed. Every available airplane would be diverted to the search. Additional crews were already en route to relieve us when we could fly no more. Bush pilots were standing by in Montreal if needed. Northeast Airline crews would join with us and so would those few army pilots available.

"But it's a lot of geography," Boyd concluded, "and we haven't very much to go on."

We left the hot room, which was now nearly suffocating, and clumped into the operations office. We found the weather over Nova Scotia to be fine for a search. Less than two hours after Boyd released us, we were in the air. We carried full tanks of fuel and a great deal of stuff to be dropped when we found O'Connor. Our human conceit, which must have been shared by O'Connor and his unhappy charges, allowed us to believe that his location would be easy to discover. How could anyone miss a big airplane outlined against the snow? Moving ourselves so swiftly, and with the visual vantage of eagles, we must spy him in a matter of hours. We proceeded eastward in great confidence, having forgotten the trickiness of sunlight, the size of the earth, and the puniness of mankind.

We had just crossed the waters between the mainland and Nova Scotia when Summers yelled from his cubicle. A message was coming through from Presque Isle. It was relayed from O'Connor himself and this is what it said:

AM ON A LAKE ABOUT FIVE MILES LONG APPROXIMATELY FOUR HUNDRED MILES NORTH ST. LAWRENCE ON A COURSE OF THREE HUNDRED THIRTY DEGREES. ALL WELL. NO INJURIES. URGENTLY REQUIRE FOOD AND SUPPLIES.

We yelled and pounded each other on the back as if it were ourselves who were so miraculously alive. This celebration was duplicated in the several airplanes already aloft, for our unadmitted

conviction had been that O'Connor would never be found alive.
No one injured! He must have done a superb job. I was greatly
relieved because I esteemed O'Connor, and the notion that my
churlish note might have somehow cursed his flight still troubled
me.

We immediately turned from Nova Scotia and set our courses
northwest. Rapid calculations dispersed some of our shame for not
taking O'Connor at his word and so stubbornly beginning the
search in the wrong direction. Catchings, who had come along to
assist and lend additional eyes, spun his computer and found we
had enough fuel to fly the four hundred miles north of the St.
Lawrence, search for at least an hour, and finally make Montreal.

Johnson frowned at the outside temperature gauge, which at
this altitude recorded twenty-five below zero. He puckered his nose
and shook his head. "Jesus, they must be cold."

There were four airplanes in this formation, all C-47's. We
spread out in a line across the clear sky so that our total point of
view would cover a maximum area. The farthest plane to the west
was barely a speck against the afternoon sun and at times became
invisible. We communicated easily by voice radio and, until we
had long passed the ice-laden St. Lawrence, kept up a constant
chatter, like so many loquacious geese in flight. Much of this
conversation was gay and foolish since we rarely had the opportunity to fly in company and, with the assurance O'Connor was
alive, it was like a holiday. None of us anticipated any difficulty in
finding him before the sun had set. And the weather, except for
the extreme cold, was glorious. We were comfortable enough in
our heavy suits, and each plane reported in tones of wonder that
the heaters were functioning as they should.

We now penetrated a new world to which we lacked a polite
introduction. Soon after we passed the St. Lawrence the details on
our charts became less in number, until finally there were only a
few dotted lines here and there. Yet the earth below was rich in
prominences. These we began to sketch in on the blank spaces of
our charts. We placed the various terrain features as accurately
as we could, at first as an amusement and eventually in the reali-

zation that they constituted our only guide to the region. It became necessary to identify these discoveries. We named a river the Johnson River, and its equally frozen tributary the Cotton Blossom Fork. We named a snow-swept hill which was devoid of timber Mount Catchings, after the baldness of his head. A frigid marsh-land became Sleepy Lagoon. Boyd was honored with a magnificent frozen waterfall, and Vaughn with a large snow-covered lake. There were so many lakes our supply of names ran short and we began to number them.

Finally, what had commenced as a diversion became a very serious affair. For we discovered that our magnetic compasses were behaving in a thoroughly reprehensible fashion. They were the single unit upon which all of our navigation was based and had to be trusted implicitly. Now they were malingering and apparently given over to fraud. Because of our relative proximity to the earth's magnetic pole, we were already compensating for thirty degrees of variation, which caused our compasses to read northwest when we were actually flying north. We were long accustomed to such differences, but there was no justification for their increasingly erratic behavior. The compass in our airplane would hang well enough on northwest for minutes, and then swing slowly and drunkenly around until it was indicating south. There it would linger uncertainly, then swing either west or east, pause, and in time return to its senses. We were mystified and increasingly concerned. Had this same thing happened to O'Connor and, if so, how could he be certain he had flown a straight course of three hundred and thirty degrees? Furthermore, his passage had been at night, and presumably on instruments, so that he would not even have had the sun for reference. And as for the sun, it was now sinking rapidly. The snow had become a feeble golden color and the western sky laced with long spatulas of cirrus clouds.

We began to realize that finding O'Connor might not be so easy as we had supposed. With empty charts and wandering compasses we were having difficulty keeping track of our own positions.

At length we came upon a considerable range of mountains. These extended from horizon to horizon, roughly east and west, and thus lay almost directly across our course. There was absolutely no recognition of their existence on the chart. If O'Connor had flown over them in an ailing airplane, then he must have slipped through one of the few passes. They were austerely cold mountains and strangely forbidding, as if they marked the frontier of the true arctic from relatively easier regions. Where the wind had swept the snow from their granite summits there was now a hard bronze glaze reflecting the last of the sun. We named these the Wynn Mountains.

Beyond the mountains all signs of timber ceased. There were only vast areas of glacial desolation interrupted by occasional lake formations, and all of it locked in cold death by the snows.

We called to each other rarely now because we were listening so anxiously. But after passing the mountains we seemed to feel the need of friendly voices.

"Seventy-eight to thirty-four. Do you know where we are?"

"I do not."

"Hear anything?"

"Negative."

We kept a constant radio guard on two distress frequencies. O'Connor's heartening message had been sent from his ship's radio, which should be powerful enough to give us a bearing. He also had a small emergency transmitter known as a "Gibson Girl" because of its shape. Though it would have to be cranked by hand it was also capable of sending out a signal upon which we could take a bearing. We listened in vain.

Somewhere in this endless wilderness twenty-two men were gradually freezing to death. They were huddled on a pinpoint in the middle of nowhere. They must be very hungry and exhausted from the cold. If they could rise only a moment and view their incredible prison, they would have every reason to be afraid. Where was that grizzled Irishman?

"Hear anything?"

"Negative."

We saw the plane so many times the sightings became monotonous. And always it would prove to be an outcropping of rocks, or a shadow in the snow, or a clump of brush along the shore of a lake. Our desire transformed the most unlikely features into the shape of a C-87 and we felt obliged to examine each one. These investigations took precious time and each disappointment cut into our sum of hope, until very little remained. O'Connor had said he was on a lake about five miles long. He could not have known there were hundreds of lakes about five miles long dotting the terrain like confetti. And on none of them could we spy a real airplane. We had no idea how cold it might be on the ground. Our temperature gauge lay hard and lifeless against its ultimate peg—at forty below.

Now time commanded us. Another ten minutes and we must turn for Montreal or eventually join O'Connor in the snow. We called to him again and again, pleading for a single bearing. There was only silence.

We held on through the twilight, trying to convince ourselves that in these last minutes O'Connor must send a signal. Certainly every man on that lake must be straining his senses to hear the sound of our engines echoing in the empty sky. It was like calling down a bottomless well. Halloo there . . . do you hear me? If they would only build a fire we should see the smoke.

O'Connor must be here. He must be there. This lake? That lake? That one?

At last Catchings studied his computer and held it before me. There was not even a thread of choice remaining. Our fuel would last just so long. We must leave the area immediately. I banked away to the southwest in what I hoped was the general direction of Montreal. One plane of our formation had already been forced to depart and now the last pilot agreed he must also turn away.

So ended, in complete discouragement, the first day of the search for O'Connor.

✦

XII

COLD

✦

EXHAUSTING, UNRELENTING, MURDEROUS COLD

WE were aloft early on the following morning, renewed in energy, and with some confidence
restored. We were also convinced that O'Connor's course must
have been as uncertain as our own. He should have been able
roughly to judge his distance flown, but he was possibly somewhere to the east or west of his intended course. We would look
for him first in the region around Lac Mistassini, one of the few
actually indicated on the chart, and then work eastward.

Presque Isle radio had been in successful communication with O'Connor during the night. They had urged him to send bearings at regular intervals, but he had replied that his batteries were capable of only one more transmission. This was most disheartening although the fact that he was still able to think shrewdly when his brain should have been frozen cheered us. He said he would crank the Gibson Girl frequently.

A Hudson Bay trading post far to the south of where O'Connor believed his position to be reported a night surface temperature of seventy below zero. Yet the cold brought and maintained one great blessing. The visibility was again excellent.

We knew that several more planes were now in the air although they were unseen. Because we were all on a common frequency, we could hear them chattering as they left Presque Isle and Goose Bay. I recognized the voices of McGuire and Watkins and remembered that Watkins was flying as O'Connor's co-pilot during the same period I had flown with Ross. The numbers, I thought, were becoming curiously jumbled.

Shortly after noon, as the planes approached the most promising area, the radios became silent. Everyone was listening for O'Connor.

Then a lame duck quacked, bursting rudely upon the stillness. It was the intrepid lieutenant complaining of his compass. The disgust of many shook his earphones as he was unanimously rebuked for airing his troubles. We needed silence, absolute silence, lest we miss the faintest signal from O'Connor.

In the cockpit we rarely spoke.

Returning to the same general area should have been an easy business and we did manage at last, thanks to our crudely drawn representation of the more prominent rivers and lakes. Without this aid our visual impression might have tricked us, for every feature of the land seemed to change in conformation and size from hour to hour. In the morning the same lake did not appear at all the same as it had in the afternoon. And every lake seemed to qualify as being "about five miles long."

We had flown as far north as Egg Lake and then turned about

to the southeast, our eyes inspecting each feature of the terrain as faithfully as we could chain our flagging interests. Hour after hour of lakes, each one so similar to its neighbors, passed beneath us. The total effect was stunning and after a few hours became so soporific that Johnson had a terrible struggle with himself. Only the thought of O'Connor's now truly desperate situation kept him awake.

We began to pass through occasional veils of snow which trailed downward from the cloudless sky. These crystals glistening in the sun were not really snow but minute particles of ice formed in the super-cooled air. We had a long and perplexing session with our right engine, which took on such a spasm of coughing and backfiring that we despaired of ever taking full power from it again. The trouble seemed to be created by a lack of sufficient carburetor heat in the right engine, which in turn normally supplied heat for the plane's interior. Now if we turned the heater off, the engine ran fairly well. So we alternately froze and then sweated with nervous concern, and wished O'Connor would choose less alien places to land his airplane.

"Hear anything?"

"Negative . . . negative . . . negative . . ."

"HOLD IT!"

We had about thirty minutes of gas remaining for the search and the sun was again very low when a faint peeping sound enlivened our earphones. It endured for no more than twenty seconds, but it was there—unmistakably O'Connor. We took a bearing on the signal. It subsided before we could achieve any degree of accuracy, yet the general direction was straight ahead. So we flew on, waiting for a repetition, holding our breaths, scratching at the thin coating of frost on our windows for a better view of the earth. We waited ten minutes; then the signal came again. It was louder, so we must be flying in the right direction, but again so short our bearing was only approximate.

The right engine began another ruckus and threatened to quit entirely. We disregarded it, so intense was our desire for a further signal. We were afraid to call the other planes lest our transmission

drown O'Connor's relatively feeble hand set. We waited ten minutes
more, and then another ten. No signal. We circled once, then flew
back over our course in the hope O'Connor would hear our engines
and start cranking again. Our eyes searched every lake. Nothing.
We rechecked our fuel supply, telling ourselves there were always
a few more gallons than shown on the gauges. If we could be
positive of our position and assume the winds would hold light, the
flying time to Presque Isle would be approximately six hours. It
seemed we had exactly six hours' fuel remaining. O'Connor!
Damnit, man! Crank!

So easy to demand from our perch of relative comfort. We
could not understand why O'Connor would select these last precious minutes to abandon his efforts. But no sound came, and we
turned south once more. With numbed fingers we sketched in
the general shapes of the larger lakes and marked a low range of
barren hills which were the only distinguishing feature of this area.
We must locate this same lonely expanse on the morrow. For
O'Connor was no longer lost. We knew he was down there, somewhere in that wilderness . . . waiting. And if our hands were
numb, his must be ever so much colder.

In spite of his tremendous vitality, O'Connor was far from a
youngster. He could, if he had chosen, have remained flying comfortably between New York and Boston. And he could thereby
have slept in a bed at night instead of a wilderness. The irony of
his position matched that of his radio operator, a man who had
left the Merchant Marine because he had been twice torpedoed
and considered he had asked enough of fortune. Such men were
worth saving for there were never enough in the world.

Long after nightfall we landed at Presque Isle with some twenty
minutes of fuel remaining. Ten of those minutes we would gladly
have exchanged for even a glimpse of a plane on a lake. The
mechanics worked all night trying to make our right engine behave
itself.

So ended the second day of the search. We told Boyd of the
signals but confessed we had not known our true position during
the whole of the afternoon. The signals could have come from

directly below our plane or a hundred miles away. There was no way to prove anything.

We were all agreed that O'Connor's most likely position occupied the center of a unique triangle which would place him almost equidistant from Montreal, Goose Bay, and Presque Isle. Therefore he was so close to the maximum round-trip range of any C-47 we could not devote enough search time on arrival. Boyd eliminated this handicap by commandeering two C-87's in which we could search much longer. McGuire would fly one of these planes, and the other would be mine.

Presque Isle was now swarming with pilots, air crewmen, and various experts on almost everything. There was endless theorizing by these aerial detectives, spiced as frequently as he could find an audience with the latest adventures of our stalwart army captain. We who had tried searching true desolation soon wearied of the elaborate errands of mercy proposed by those who had once spent a summer fishing in Canada, or knew how to drive a team of sledge dogs. No dogs could remove O'Connor from his captivity. Nothing could, except a continuous run of luck and that must begin very soon.

Just before we slept a message came through that O'Connor had been found. Watkins, flying westward out of Goose Bay, had literally stumbled upon him, and dropped food and blankets. Like ourselves, however, he was flying on the last of his fuel and was obliged to leave immediately. This was indeed the greatest of accomplishments and we had a great deal to say about the luck of the Irish.

There was now only one grievous hitch. After crisscrossing a thousand miles of sky, Watkins did not know his own true position when he saw the stranded airplane. Nor did he pretend that he could ever find the place again.

Binkowski was our flight engineer in the C-87, for which I was most grateful. If Binkowski said the airplane was in good health, then it was nearly a guarantee the C-87 would snort and bellow on schedule and we would not abort this important day of search because of some mechanical outrage. Binkowski was a fair-skinned, blond young man, of deep religious convictions. Behind his little jump seat at the rear of the C-87's flight deck, he had placed a small brass-framed triptych. An unusually bland Madonna panel occupied the center, and I envied Binkowski for the peace she seemed to bring him. I could not decide whether he bore his treasure with him in mistrust of all C-87's or hoped, in the doing, to remind us of our sins. In either case he would have sufficient reason, for most of us were at best irresolute polytheists.

On this morning Wynn had replaced Catchings in our airplane, and Beattie had taken over for Johnson. Wynn was new to the north country and to C-87's, which was the only reason I continued to hold down the left-hand seat. He was much senior to me, yet because of his unique tolerance no protocol hindered our relationship. He was a dynamic and mischievous spirit, so quick of movement and bubbling with the most rapid conversation that he seemed constantly on the brink of physical disintegration—which was a deception, for Wynn was nervous only in his moments of relaxation. On demand he could settle his lean face into the firmest lines of concentration, his eyes would cease their darting, and he would become, in a trice, the coolest of pilots. But he was also an instinctive actor and delighted in holding his listeners spellbound while he passed quickly from the absurd to bleak tragedy.

"A C-87 does not really fly," he explained to the bewildered Binkowski, who had not broken his contemplation of the Virgin since we had reached cruising altitude. "No, indeed, it does *not* fly. It is merely a crude form of levitation."

He favored Binkowski with his most sardonic and evil wink and left him to think his way through such nonsense.

With our extra speed we could reach the search area in about four hours and remain in the vicinity long enough to find O'Connor. Wynn's effervescence was contagious and with a four-engined airplane which thus far behaved perfectly, we proceeded northward in full confidence. We located Boyd Falls and Mount Catchings and the Johnson River, and were much pleased at their familiarity. As our compass began its unpredictable swinging we reached the Wynn Mountains, which their namesake surveyed as if they were truly his own. Then we were again in the wilderness of the lakes and even Wynn fell silent. We were fixed to the windows, staring at the frozen earth, and waiting for the slightest sound in our earphones.

This day the February sky had lost nearly all its former cold blue and was instead a pale and jaundiced white. It was as monotonous as the snows except for a festooning of mare's-tails. Too often they foretold high winds and bad weather. In this region the result could easily be a long series of blizzards which O'Connor was ill-prepared to withstand, and which would certainly halt any attempts at rescue.

Rescue remained a matter for the future. We had still to rediscover O'Connor. The lakes were now beneath, the same lakes in the same area we had been over the day before, but there was no sound in our earphones. Again each one of us knew the certainty of spying an airplane on a lake, only to discover after more careful examination that whatever object we concentrated upon was only an illusion. The process was intermittent but self-creating, causing us to rise suddenly in our seats, gasp, twist our heads this way and that like puppets, and finally subside in embarrassment at our repeated gullibility.

In the middle of the afternoon we picked up a signal which offered more than just a bearing. It said, "Return same place" over and over again. Where was the same place? We believed we were already over the same place. If the message was for Watkins he was far over the horizon also looking for that same place.

Before the signaling ceased we managed a valuable bearing. We called to O'Connor's radio operator begging him to keep up a continuous series of long dashes. We were fishing in the depths, but this was more than a nibble. If they would send long enough for our automatic direction finder to swing, it would all be over.

"He's on again! We've got him!"

Wynn was in a frenzy of excitement and even Beattie was bereft of dignity when the direction finder swung sharply around and pointed to our right. I banked immediately and put the ship on the exact course indicated by the needle. The signals became much louder. He should be dead ahead. But if he was, we could not see him. The great hoglike snout of the C-87 blocked off our forward visibility. I jinked the ship a few degrees left, and waited. A fine sharp signal came once more. We had him now. It was a certainty. I rose slightly in my seat trying to see past the others who were pressed to the flight deck windows. But none of us could discover an airplane on any of the lakes below.

The signal came again, so loud we were obliged to move our earphones. The needle began a rapid swing until it pointed nearly vertically to our course. Still no one could recognize an airplane.

Binkowski had left his Madonna some time previously and had been observing the earth from the cabin. Now he rushed forward, calling to me and pointing.

"There he is! Right by the shore!"

I pushed the C-87's nose down so we could all see. And still there was nothing to enliven the empty lakes below. I doubted Binkowski, a reaction I should never have believed possible. Yet he was insistent. He kept pointing and we all tried to follow the inclining line of his arm.

Then very suddenly I felt more insignificant than I ever had before. We were all, for one humiliating moment, squashed into our miserable little bone and flesh units and the multitudinous cells of us became one cell, thereby establishing a proper microscopic relationship to all things of creation. We were men like O'Connor, and as men here in such environment, we were physically insects of the lowest order. Find O'Connor? Without the radio to guide us and Binkowski's keen and worshipful eyes, we could have passed over him fifty times in vain. O'Connor, how did you become so small, so Lilliputian in dimensions that you rudely shock all of our senses? In fact, you are now shown as a traitor to the vanity of man, for we cannot see you at all, nor any of your species. Our eyes are only drawn to your airplane, which is over a hundred feet in breadth and length. And yet it too is so terribly small. Compare yourself to it, as you have caused us to do, and weep for your nothingness. Remember you are as we are, which is such a mortifying station the mind must accept it altogether or reject it altogether. The hesitant middling ground is strewn with the wreckage of men's sanity.

I began a large circle over what we at once christened Lac O'Connor. We radioed every plane in the sky so they could take bearings on us. Montreal also took a series of long-range bearings and Sydney in Nova Scotia did the same. All of this took some time, which we knew to be a strain on O'Connor's patience, but it was very necessary if he was at last to be exactly located.

Circling, I had leisure to appreciate O'Connor's almost incredible situation. The lake was as he had described it. His airplane appeared to have stopped just to the south of the shore. To land a C-87 safely on that lake in the middle of freezing arctic night was certainly magnificent airmanship. All of the skill of O'Connor's long career must have been bunched into those vital last seconds and now he could justly claim a victory.

While we continued to circle I scribbled a note which left me in considerably better spirits than had a previous communication to the same man. Influenced by Binkowski and his mellowing triptych, I wrote:

> THANK GOD WE FOUND YOU
> MORE PLANES COMING AND
> WE'LL HAVE YOU ALL OUT
> IN A FEW DAYS.

I inserted this note in a box of chocolate bars and asked Wynn, who would supervise unloading our supplies, to drop it first.

When every interested plane and station was satisfied, we had a rare moment of triumphant joy with a C-87. I peeled off fighter-pilot fashion and dived for a low pass at Lac O'Connor. The maneuvering was intended as a salute to every man on the lake. They returned it with much arm-waving. We swept over their heads too fast and hence could recognize no one, but our chandelle when we reached the end of the lake was designed to gratify their excitement. Exhibitionism, I hoped, was here forgivable.

When the show was completed, we slowed and prepared for the serious business of dropping supplies so they would land in convenient places. One thing puzzled me while I waited for word from the cabin that Wynn was ready. I had noticed a long arrow made of what appeared to be pine boughs laid out in the snow. If it had been a cross, then I would have known O'Connor realized how difficult his special lake was to separate from any other. But an arrow?

I banked for the first dumping pass and slowed to a near stall. Beattie frequently called off our flight speed so I could concentrate on a flight path straight for the waiting men. We came in very low and on this descent I could easily recognize O'Connor's face. He was standing beside the arrow pointing to it and alternately waving his arms. I assumed his excitement was overwhelming and thought I understood his gestures as a simple demonstration of joy. Near him stood another man who genuflected like a pilgrim before Mecca and afforded us great merriment. Spirits must have remained very high in that stranded party if they could keep their sense of humor. More credit, we thought, to the indomitable O'Connor.

We made three additional passes over the field before all our supplies had been dropped. Each time O'Connor pointed to the arrow and made gestures which I could only believe were an invitation to land. With Wynn and Beattie I discussed the possibilities. We quickly agreed that a landing could accomplish nothing and might very well end in disaster. O'Connor must know this. Apparently it had snowed heavily since his arrival, for there were no visible tracks to mark his landing. He was standing thigh deep in snow when he made the signals.

While we sought an answer, the first supporting plane arrived. It was Captain Lord of Northeast Airlines flying a C-47. We welcomed him on the radio.

Lord made his passes over the lake and we saw O'Connor signal in the same fashion. Finally Lord called us on the radio and asked us to stand by. He believed that with his much lighter and slower plane he could make a successful landing. We wished him luck and watched apprehensively as he began a slow descent. If he could land, there would presumably be enough men on the lake to shovel a short runway. Then he could begin taking people out a few at a time.

The wheels of Lord's C-47 brushed two light marks near the end of the arrow. The ship settled ever so gently and then suddenly vanished in an explosion of snow. When it had settled we saw the airplane buried to its wings and our meek decision was confirmed by a discouraged voice on the radio.

"Oomph! I'm stuck!"

We now had more mouths to feed. On the long way back to Presque Isle we watched the torn clouds very high aloft and found no peace in them.

Factual events rarely arrange themselves in convenient or dramatic sequence. Yet here the revelation of more important matters would be justly suspect if the true line of events were even once adjusted. The various real dangers, displays of courage and cowardice, plus certain inevitable sacrifices, all occurred *after* O'Connor was located and so composed a sort of grand anti-climax.

Soon after Lord had joined O'Connor other planes arrived over the lake and the pilots felt no temptation to try further landings. They dropped their supplies and left. All of this amounted to a fair collection of food, stoves, blankets, and cigarettes. There were also magazines and playing cards to help pass the time until some scheme could be devised for the actual removal of the men. The food supplies would be sufficient to last for a few days, but we would have to return with more at frequent intervals. My own message to O'Connor promising their release within a few days was exceedingly premature. I had written it in a moment of great exhilaration and had failed to analyze the true dilemma.

The little community now existed on a flat cake of ice a very long way from any assistance. Presumably they could continue in good health for so long as they were careful and we were faithful with supplies. If we failed they must resort again to such occasional nourishment as owl soup (which they had tried and found very unappetizing), or if they were lucky they might shoot a ptarmigan. They could not long survive on such a diet of semi-starvation for their greatest and most frightening enemy—clutch-ing, soundless, and absolutely unforgiving—was the extreme cold. It was with them like a poisonous shroud every moment of the day and night. The haggard O'Connor's battle had just begun.

We set off for the lake on the following day loaded with tents, shovels, axes, and all manner of additional gear to provide shelter. It seemed very possible that the party might be spending a long time on Lac O'Connor, if indeed they could escape before the com-ing of summer. Against this dismal possibility, arrangements were under way for bush pilots in small ski planes to establish refueling stations on the lakes between Montreal and Lac O'Connor. Hop-ping froglike from lake to lake, they could eventually fly the entire distance. It was to be a long and laborious operation. Meanwhile our sole business was the continuance of food and shelter.

Our fourth day was an abysmal failure for everyone save the meteorologists, who would have wished otherwise. In spite of the meager reports they received from the general area they had dis-covered a warm front which they claimed would bring winds of such velocity we could never make our goal and have fuel enough to return. Consequently the two-engined airplanes were grounded, but we believed a C-87 should have ample reserve.

We were wrong. Our heavy, lumbering C-87 became a helpless butterfly. It danced in the air, trembled and bounced and writhed in such a continuous paroxysm of violent fits that there were times when we could not read the instruments. The wings flapped as if they were responsible for our elevation, the great double tail twisted alarmingly, and we were constantly jammed down hard in our seats or thrown against our belts. All four engines nodded angrily on their mounts and the entire assembly of parts seemed determined to separate. Neither Wynn, nor Beattie, nor myself had ever seen anything like such turbulence except in the maw of a thunderstorm, and our half-jokes about the inherent strength of a C-87 became ever more feeble.

At last we surrendered, but not because of the turbulence alone. We estimated the wind to be at sixty miles an hour and directly on our nose. The visibility ahead was fair enough, but the ground was completely obscured in blowing snow. Even if we were lucky enough to find Lac O'Connor under such conditions we could not possibly execute a useful drop. So, with our tail between our legs, we turned back to Presque Isle.

During the night the wind diminished and it began to snow heavily.

Far to the north of the Saguenay, beyond even O'Connor's special wilderness, a blizzard was conceived because a heavy mass of air met, took, and raped a lighter, more delicate mass of air. It howled down from Hudson Bay and from the Belcher Islands. It swallowed Cape Sandy and obliterated the Great Whale River. It screeched toward O'Connor's refuge where he waited in ignorance of its being. Its stealth in approach, strewing Christmas card snowflakes before it so prettily, gave no hint of its inner fury. Only science could reveal its spiteful character and for once we trusted the meteorologists. They said the blizzard had not yet reached Lac O'Connor. Nor would it, they believed, for some twenty-four hours. After this preparatory stage we should accept the fact that O'Connor could not be reached for some time.

Because of the nature of the weather on this fifth day we rejected the unhandy C-87 and returned to our faithful two-engined airplanes. We knew the route now and believed we could follow it well enough if we could keep visual contact with the earth. Hedgehopping, we thought to locate ourselves by the prominences we had named and so be less at the mercy of our untrustworthy compasses. The cloud ceiling at Presque Isle was very low, but we intended to slink along beneath it. The snowfall was spasmodic, becoming quite heavy at times and then subsiding to sprays of little body. It was much warmer than it had been for weeks, yet the dull gray sky and the foreign appearance of our home airport in its new formations of snow depressed us.

We set off with five airplanes, one of which was flown by our bombastic lieutenant. He had been stomping around in the snow long before our actual departure and the clouds of vapor from his anxious breathing served as a fitting background to his words of fire.

If we were to give full credence to his behavior this man was fearless, although he had not as yet once reached even the general vicinity of Lac O'Connor. Something always developed within his airplane—a rough engine or a faulty radio or frozen propeller controls—which forced his return to base. Here too the poor bull of a man must have been at constant odds with the fortitude which obsessed him and the true timidity which ruled him. For we saw him frequently terrified of badge authority, cringing in the presence of Boyd, who was half his size, and ever obsequious to anyone of higher rank. We concluded sadly that he was a worshiper of power and, in his greed for even a sip of the brew, had performed his own emasculation.

None of us cared very much for the first hour of flying. The terrain between Presque Isle and the St. Lawrence was easy and rolling, but the top of the mildest hill can become the rending summit of a mountain when it is hidden in cloud. We were frequently obliged to slip between the hills, taking such advantage of the shallow valleys as we could. The visibility deteriorated to less than a mile as we proceeded, and in the snow squalls became somewhat less. It was not safe flying. All of us knew this and accepted the fact with such wry remarks as came to our minds. Catchings' southern drawl came over the radio.

"There's a very limited future in this."

Someone else: "I forgot my snowshoes."

Another: "On Donner . . . on Blitzen."

We reeled in our trailing antennas for fear of losing them and hugged the contours of the earth. All manner of objects, both human and natural, loomed suddenly out of the white mists ahead. It was as impossible as it would have been unwise to fly in close formation. Each pilot drew away from his nearest companion and sought his separate way between squalls and terrain.

It was no surprise to any of us when the lieutenant's voice rattled in our earphones. And it was full of such honest misery we could only pity him.

This time he made no claim of mechanical difficulties. He simply stated that we were all crazy. We had no business flying in such conditions and he was getting out. He would climb through the overcast to a sensible altitude and return to Presque Isle.

We urged him to hold a little longer. We told him the weather was bound to improve although we knew as well as he did that any such prediction was based upon pure wishing. We must remain low regardless, believing it impossible to climb to a higher and safer altitude, fly for five hours on instruments, and then descend with any hope of recognizing our location. The course to Lac O'Connor was inflexible. If we lost it visually for any appreciable length of time, our compasses invariably led us astray. And O'Connor desperately needed what our airplanes contained.

The lieutenant said he was sorry. And that was the last we heard of him. I began to doubt my opinion of the lieutenant, for a man could not be altogether lacking in courage who would so publicly display his funk. He knew he could not be forgiven and he must have known his censure would be unspoken, which is the most severe punishment of all. No one would ever ask him why he turned back, or suggest that it would have been more admirable if he had persevered. The guise of politeness, even a touch of jollity, would be his slap in the face and it would sting for as long as he had any contact with those who had been witness to his desertion. He had chosen loneliness and there was nothing we could ever do to regain him. The rest of us continued in hypocrisy, frequently afraid yet compelled onward by our even greater fear of each other.

My own resolution often reached the vanishing point. Beyond the St. Lawrence the squalls thickened, whirled around each other in ghostly dances, and finally united in those meager tunnels through which we managed to squirm our way. We would only occasionally catch sight of each other and more frequently lost the course entirely. It seemed hopeless and even more foolhardy if we dared to approach the Wynn Mountains, but there was suddenly a large break revealing their lower foundations so that we were momentarily encouraged. But the barren outcroppings of granite, the minor indentations, sheer cliffs, and dark crevasses we had known, were smoothed over with snow. Now the range presented only a series of domed teats, joining upon each other until the highest were lost in the overcast. At length we found a promising valley columned with snow showers. We slipped through it to immediate disappointment.

Nothing in the land beyond was recognizable. All of our carefully plotted landmarks had magically disappeared or had been so changed in contour and character by the heavy fall of snow that we failed to identify any of them. Our compasses, bewitched as ever, required us to fly due west or east for a full five minutes before they would settle enough to set our gyros. Then we could carry on north again. The process, in such visibility, caused us to wander back and forth across a course we now could only assume to be correct, and consequently we wasted precious time.

Here in the wastelands of lakes, the visibility finally increased to a mile or so, but the cloud ceiling prevented us from climbing above a thousand feet. Thus we must come upon Lac O'Connor exactly, neither too far to the east nor to the west. An error of two miles would carry us past it, unseen and unseeing. The chances of stumbling upon O'Connor as Watkins had done were about equal to the multitude of lakes against one. We called repeatedly for radio guidance to the lake, but no sound came. It was understandable that we might not be expected guests in such weather, but the rationalizing did little for our spirits. We had found O'Connor only to lose him again.

We milled all about to the limit of our fuel and then turned away in dejection. Actually we were never sure, nor could we ever be, that our searching on this day occurred anywhere near the right area.

Unknown to us, McGuire was searching the same skies in a C-87. He had thought to locate O'Connor by radio alone and was obliged to remain much higher, within the overcast. When no signals came he was also compelled to turn toward Presque Isle and, in the doing, found a measurement of his fortune.

The fuel tanks of a C-87 were constructed of a self-sealing

rubberish material, as were those of its bomber counterpart. Because of the extreme cold on these operations it was customary to seal off the air venting pipes to these tanks with masking tape. Thus, when the airplane was on the ground, moisture condensation could not collect just inside the pipes, freeze, and thereby choke the breathing of the fuel system. When the airplane was prepared for flight, the masking tape was removed.

Just before night fell McGuire's engineer discovered this vital chore had not been performed on two of the tanks. From the astrodome he could see the vents only a few yards away, yet he was helpless to reach them. Horrified, he informed McGuire, who did some rapid thinking and yearned for the simplicity of his Carolina mule. The engines had continued to function only because the rubber tanks were slowly collapsing. How much longer could they squeeze out the needed fuel? McGuire found out soon enough. One engine backfired and quit without further apology. Shortly afterward, the second engine also ceased to function.

McGuire was flying a C-87 on instruments, at night, over unknown terrain, with two engines out on the same side. This was something less than a pleasure, but not his major concern. All of the remaining fuel on the crippled side of his airplane was unavailable to him. As a result he simply could not reach Presque Isle or any other recognized airport. It seemed as if he might be the unwilling imitator of O'Connor.

He radioed his impossible predicament and learned that there was a new field still under construction on the north shore of the St. Lawrence. It was much too small for a C-87, but it did have a radio range. McGuire calculated he could just make it if nothing else happened. This was good, but now there came an additional evil.

When he arrived over the airport he was told the only lights outlining the short and snow-swept runway were a few kerosene flares. And the weather could not have been less hospitable. The ceiling was far below limits—its actual height, unknown. The visibility was half a mile—less, in the periods of heavy blowing snow. The wind was strong across the runway.

Every trick and device McGuire had ever learned since he first clutched the controls of an airplane, all of the knowledge acquired in Lester's school, and his subsequent thousands of hours' experience as co-pilot and captain, now asked for a reckoning. And to this he must add more than a soupçon of luck, plus a heavy seasoning of pure nerve.

The final ingredient was courage, which McGuire summoned through his fears when he cut back the two throttles and sank into a white void.

True to his profession, McGuire said later it was a rotten instrument approach. He was referring to his minor technical misdemeanors, as if they were important at the time. His critique deliberately skipped the fact that the airplane was flying askew, everything below was foreign to him including the nature of the terrain, and they had to lengthen the runway before the C-87 could be flown away again. Nor would he mention how he swept down through the squalls, caught a mere glimpse of the runway, then somehow squeezed the ship into its limitations, and landed without scratching the staggering beast of an airplane. All of these things he passed off as inconvenient tribulations which it would be in poor taste to discuss. He acknowledged a surging in his bowels when they passed downward through two hundred feet and there was still nothing to be seen; but the thing anyone was asked to understand was his technical clumsiness in wavering from the beam an occasional degree or two, or, preoccupied with his troubles, momentarily allowing his air speed to exceed or fall below those exact amounts prescribed for flying in perfect conditions. It was he who was fraudulent, anyone must understand, and the ultimate success was achieved in spite of his efforts rather than because of them. Overmodesty can easily be the reverse side of pride and hence intolerably false; but if it is contagious and constant to the bearer, and if he assumes it with wink and humor to conceal honestly the details of personal exploit, then it may be admirable and also delightful. It was a code to which nearly all of us were happily bound.

Two days passed while the snows loaded the earth. We waited

in warm impatience while the mechanics fretted over our planes. From the overheated operations office with its banging radiators, we could watch the mechanics trudging out to the line of half-buried airplanes and then jogging stiffly back when they could no longer stand the cold. And they were very cold, for wind had come along with the snow and penetrated every protection. Most of the mechanics were muffled to their bleary eyes and had deliberately rubbed grease on their faces against frostbite. But they suffered it anyway and would tenderly minister to each other when the telltale white areas appeared.

We stood about, smoking and cursing the weather, and kicking at the radiators with our soft flying boots, and saw in the raw-meat faces of the mechanics only a reflection of our uselessness.

We went again and again to the weather room, interfering with and annoying the meteorologists with our questions, prognostications, arguments, and unhappy derision. We stood before the teletype machines defying them to repeat their dismal utterances of continued bad weather from every station, and the machines, as if in stuttering revolt against such persuasive attempts by human beings, always stood their ground. There were, of course, no reports available from the search area itself, but reports from Montreal and the few Hudson Bay outposts to the west were sufficient to draw a general picture and would normally show the earliest improvement.

I had brooded upon our failure to find Lac O'Connor by hedge-hopping. The present storm must alter the appearance of the terrain even more radically and it seemed we might once again be defeated because we could not recognize our way. The capricious behavior of our compasses at a vital point along our route was still mysterious, but it was proven well enough and some means must be found to circumvent it.[9]

We now knew the approximate latitude and longitude of Lac O'Connor. But this was an arbitrary as well as invisible point in space and the problem remained to bring ourselves upon it. Our barnstorming tactics had succeeded and would again eventually, yet the process was dangerous in bad weather and ripe with frustrations when the weather was good.

So we went to Boyd with a plan and found him, as always, receptive. We proposed leaving Presque Isle at night and at an hour which would permit us to arrive over Lac O'Connor, or at least in its vicinity, just after dawn. We would employ celestial navigation to keep our course, using the stars in lieu of our eyes. We would take fixes as frequently as possible, every half hour or so, and thus have an almost continuous warning of any deviations from course. The very last fixes would be taken just before the stars faded, and the concluding distance to Lac O'Connor should then be so short we could hardly miss it. In addition, a message would be sent to O'Connor and Lord describing our intentions and stating our approximate time of arrival. If they would then set up a fuss of radio bearings, an oil fire with as much smoke as they could manage, plus flares when they heard our engines, they would have visitors. Most of us were now convinced O'Connor had no idea how difficult he was to see even when we were on top of him.

To all of this Boyd agreed, and improved in detail. Among other things he suggested better navigators than our already rusty selves. These men would keep us toeing the line.

We took off the following night, climbed above the still-lingering overcast, and placed our trust in the stars. Our compasses could be as clever as they pleased, for now their dishonesties were rediscovered so frequently they could not long deceive us.

For this first attempt, which was admittedly experimental, we used only three airplanes and flew in loose formation. It was a beautifully smooth flight, free of incident for a change, and we were as jovial as we could be about the cold. Ordinarily we would have amused ourselves with complaints of such minor discomforts —the itching misery of our oxygen masks, which were designed only to fit the face of a baboon, the theft of our sleep, the cold coffee, brittle sandwiches, and the slow all-pervading fatigue for which our heavy flying suits were partly responsible. But there was none of this. We were all too conscious of the men on a lake hidden in nowhere, and of their true ordeal.

The last fixes, obtained just before the stars disappeared, placed us some fifty miles south of the area. We started a slow descent toward the broken overcast as the light increased and called to the lake for radio bearings. But the silence in our earphones remained undisturbed.

We were in cloud only a few minutes and then slipped out beneath. I began to doubt the wisdom of the plan, for nothing I could see in the half-light was recognizable. The snows had obviously been very heavy and the rippling mass of lakes and low hills might have been anywhere. I wondered if our original estimate of O'Connor's latitude and longitude had been in serious error, or would we in these last few minutes pass right on by because we were again at a low altitude? Already the question of fuel had entered our thinking and each minute of silence subtracted from our ability to remain in the vicinity.

Suddenly the silence was broken and our direction-finder needles swung with wonderful precision. O'Connor was not straight ahead, a situation which could only have been miraculous, but he was a mere ten degrees to the left of our course. Moreover, we thought him to be near, since the signals were of strength. We banked at once and followed the quivering needles.

He was farther away than we could have believed, and our impatience stretched the distance. Dawn was well established when we saw a series of red and green flare balls explode and glisten against the white horizon. We could not yet observe their origin, but they were still in descent when we passed over a ridge of intervening hills and at last swooped down upon our quarry.

Two days later I made a final flight to Lac O'Connor and was then assigned elsewhere. O'Connor, Lord, and their companions, were as well found and fed as could be wished under the circumstances, and a considerable assembly of men and machines was now combining to effect their actual liberation. O'Connor was among the last to be taken from his frozen home, a retreat made in justifiable pride, for all of his charges, even those who were sick and injured before they ever left Thule, emerged in good spirits and health. Their most grievous wounds were a few mild cases of frostbite. They were on the lake, in all, nearly three weeks.

O'Connor rested briefly and then, indefatigable as ever, went out to Assam, where he became chief pilot of an even more difficult and sensitive operation—flying the Hump into China. I did not see him again for a year, and then under quite different conditions.

The doings at Lac O'Connor did not terminate with the departure of its discoverer. Wynn remained in Presque Isle to conclude the adventure in a remarkable and appropriately determined fashion. Everyone was distressed at the idea of an undamaged airplane finally sinking into the lake when the ice melted. So a snowplow was flown to the lake in pieces, reassembled by a crew who made their own acquaintance with pure cold, and a short runway was cut across the lake. The C-87 was filled with a minimum of fuel, the engines revitalized with special heaters, and when all was ready, Wynn took a deep breath in an instinctive attempt to increase its lift and flew the thing out.

The same airplane was eventually sent to the Hump as if in dogged pursuit of its former master.

XIII

HEAT

IN MOST MEN THERE LURKS A LESSER MAN,
AND HIS PRESENCE SMELLS IN THE SUN

KEIM peers down at me from his upper bunk Acropolis, wigwags an eyebrow, and snorts, "It's raining like a cow pissing on a flat rock."

He has been lying stark naked except for a magazine spread across his ample belly and his opinion of the rain is accurate, for when the night rains deluge Brazil no other manifestation of nature seems to exist. And in Natal where we lie in a sort of moist coma, as if we were oily, odorous condiments suspended in some grand solution, the rain drowns everything.

The dismal little city of Natal is situated on the easternmost tip of Brazil, where someone originally set it down because there must have been an empty place. It is unlikely that anyone foresaw its convenience as a base for airplanes spanning the South Atlantic to Africa.

Our container is an old house with tile floors in the Brazilian fashion. Now the tiles are wet with water spewed inward through the open windows and their uninspired designs are obscured by mud, cigarette butts, flight kits, bags, pieces of ancient magazines, and the remains of a cardboard Christmas tree.

There are five principal rooms in the house, all of them jammed with crude wooden bunks set in double tiers. The rooms are vertical in shape, the distance from tiles to cracked plaster ceiling being considerably more than from wall to wall. Hence we live on top of each other in every way, including those moments when a fitful sleep can be found during the fleeting coolness of pre-dawn. The rest of the time it is very hot and the air within the rooms is always a suffocating solid.

The guest list in the house varies according to the whims of the C-87's which we fly from Natal to Ascension Island in the middle of the South Atlantic, and thence to the Gold Coast of Africa. At times there are as many as five crews in residence, which would be twenty-five men, and at other times there are only one or two crews. Regardless of the number present, there is only one toilet, which seldom works.

There are also numerous permanent guests who openly resent our invasion. These are a collection of winged and ambulatory insects which would thrill the most sophisticated entomologist. The spiders are especially clever and industrious, more so than the fleas, which in our expert opinion seem rather languid and almost foolishly suicidal.

The policemen of this cramped community are the lizards, all of which are fat and so surfeited with conquest they can hardly move on patrol. I inhabit a bunk opposite Keim's. He delights in reminding me that were it not for his careful tutelage on AM-21 I should long ago have killed myself. My only defense is to point out that in spite of his precious seniority my ocean experience at least now exceeds his own.

I am watching a lizard which is affixed to the window frame exactly as I had viewed a similar Brazilian lizard long ago. Beyond the lizard there are thick vertical chains of rain glistening in the single light which hangs from the ceiling. Keim has opened his magazine, resting it upon his slowly heaving belly.

"You'll ruin your eyes."

A grunt. "Screw my eyes."

"If you flunk your next physical it will give me much pleasure to say I told you so."

A grunt. "I can see two fleas fornicate at a thousand yards."

"Then kill that mosquito on your toe."

Keim swings his magazine in the general direction of his feet, which sends the mosquito across to me. This pleases him so much he lights a cigar.

I had done my best to avoid assignment to Natal because I honestly feared a return of malaria. I was also reluctant to have anything more to do with C-87's. Yet their very perversity appeared to have been so influential that no conniving on my part had thus far been successful in separating us for more than brief periods.

I try to forget the heat and stink from the nearby toilet by thinking about C-87's and how I seem fated to live or die with them. It has been over a year since I saw O'Connor standing in the snow and my assignment upon leaving the northern latitudes had been typical. Of all things, I became an instructor in C-87's. This had proved to be a mixed pleasure and occasionally a source of irony because some of my students were veterans who had at last chosen to fly the oceans and would therefore fill any vacancy to which I might return. Except for the various idiosyncrasies of the airplane itself, the instruction had been easy work, for such men as West, Ingram, the miniature Burns, Johanpeter, and Brown were wonderfully adept and proved immediately that they belonged at the top of their profession. The red-faced, much tattooed Carter, with whom I had attended Lester's school, was also a student, and the sad-eyed Charleton another.

Keim growls across the murky, putrid chasm between our cots. "What did you claim you did with all the—" His eyebrows wigwag a willingness to be deceived, which delights me.

I know he is referring to the long flight from which I have just returned. It had been a remarkable journey in three ways: the first because the sole cargo was millions in Chinese paper money, the second because the flight circled half the world and the co-pilot had proven himself to be the only living human being who could never be taught to fly, and the third because it had almost made me a person of dubious historical fame. I had nearly destroyed one of the seven wonders of the world.

Finally, although it was not a part of the flight itself and therefore could not be considered a reason for my present mood, I had as a consequence of the flight come face to face with cowardice discovering it within myself. The revelation had troubled me so deeply that I had not yet managed to forget about it. I kept remembering and seeing the plug-ugly, boastful face of the lieutenant who had also strewn dust on his self-esteem, and I had been wondering if such displays were intrinsic and of the being-permanent, or were only temporary peelings and crackings of the kind which now marred the ceiling above my head.

Partly to avoid such ruinous thinking, I have invented a harmless fable with which I hope to bait Keim. There is sufficient truth in the game so that I hope to continue it indefinitely. Anything to relieve our boredom.

"How much of it did you really steal?"

"I sort of lost count."

"How the hell can anyone lose count?"

"If you are surrounded by beautiful Chinese girls and those mandolins are strumming, you can lose count of a lot of things— especially if it's only money. What's a million here and there?"

"You're a Goddamned liar."

"It makes me more comfortable to have you believe that. But I really don't think there will be any investigation anyway. One of the packs just broke open and the stuff was lying around on the floor of the airplane . . . and, well, it was only *Chinese* money. . . . You should have been there. What a blast!" I yawn elaborately.

Everyone in the crew house knows the airplane had really been full of money, a fact I am sure Keim has checked. The part about one of the packets' breaking open would be more difficult to verify because the supposed windfall had occurred more than fifteen thousand miles away.

"Don't you have any left?"

"I'm not saying. I might get back to China again someday."

It is easier and much more rewarding to play this game rather than see a coward in the sun again. But I dare not elaborate too much lest Keim tire of the whole thing. Later I may suggest indirectly that some preposterous sum is still in my flight bag and at least lure him into a suspicious glance. But it is not any fabrication which persists; the truth is far more difficult to lose.

Keim falls silent and I return unwillingly to the sourness of my speculations. The rain seems to nourish them, and so is to blame. The rain, the dribbling, gurgling, incessant rain washes me right back into that bake-oven cockpit and I look out of it again to estimate the long black runway at Agra, India.

We had come a long way—from Natal to Ascension Island, to Accra on the Gold Coast, and thence to Kano in Nigeria. Then on eastward, flying through a haboob which shook the C-87 mercilessly and because of its swirling columns and veils of red dust concerned us greatly for the engines. Then to earth, if it could be called that, in a place known as El Fasher, which was deep in the Sudan. One of the engines had developed a serious oil leak and we thought to land for a few hours and fix it. Yet when we were ready for flight again the starter on the number two engine fractured its vitals and even Franko our engineer could not repair the damage. So we waited eight days in searing heat until a replacement arrived. On several occasions I had resolved to take off on three engines, starting the fourth by windmilling, but even before I began to measure the chances I knew such a procedure in a loaded C-87 could only end in our destruction. The runway was barely long enough for a *four*-engined take-off. Even that would have to be made just at dawn, before the sun robbed the thin high desert air of what little lift it could provide.

As Johnson was the finest natural flyer I had ever known, so the co-pilot of this accursed odyssey was even worse than I had once been. It seemed my grandmother could have been taught better technique in a few hours, and most grandmothers would have taken more interest in their task. He could not hold anything like a true course, and the one landing I had so recklessly given him ended in such a near disaster that my historic performance with McCabe seemed the work of a master. He was, in every execution of his office, completely inept, and long before the entire flight was done the others of the crew begged me to keep his hands off the controls. He was terrified of all airplanes and C 87's in particular a reaction I might have forgiven him, but his remarkable inability to perform the simplest of flight maneuvers caused us all to loathe his presence.

When we had at last departed El Fasher we came down for fuel in Khartoum and then again at Gura in Eritrea, where skilled mechanics did their best to stuff the troubles back in a Pandora's box of an airplane. Eventually we flew over the Red Sea to Aden, and then to Salala, in Arabia, where one of the propeller governors went wild and we were obliged to land in some haste.

By now I was beginning to suspect that this flight had a more than ordinary quotient of evil poxes. This C-87 had either been grievously maltreated or was the original caldron in which all of the sinister essences common to the type were brewed. The direction finder would not work at all. The nose wheel refused to come down unless Franko crawled into the snout and kicked at it with all his might. The controls were flabby in one flight attitude and iron stiff in another. The flaps would not go all the way down and the cabin door would not close completely. The windshields were so scratched that they appeared to be laced with cobwebs and the plexiglas above our heads as well as the side windows were a muddy opaque yellow from too many suns. The entire airplane possessed a peculiar vibration which was quite unpredictable and which we had observed in no other C-87. We could never discover the cause of this and finally stopped our investigations because we were so occupied with other tinkering.

In addition to the money, we carried one passenger, who suffered his own sorrows through our continuous calamities. This was Hill, a large and splendid English officer in the Royal West African Frontier Force. We came to love this man for his humorous dignity, his indestructible calm, and his magnificent walrus mustache. He left us and our miserable machine convinced that all Americans were mad as well as inefficient.

We limped to Karachi, and then on to Gaya in India, and finally stumbled into Chabua in Assam. Here, from a field beside a tea plantation, flights over the Hump began. Near here, Charleton would soon perish when one of the engines on his C-87 quit at take-off. Near here, big Hunt would also die against the dike of a rice paddy.

Big Hunt, a superb pilot, would die alone. In his no-nonsense fashion he would most bravely challenge a C-87 to kill him, and lose the battle. Bound over the Hump to China he would acquire a heavy load of ice and the C-87 would behave in a typically vicious fashion. On his orders the members of his crew would bail out to relative safety, though they would spend nearly two weeks walking out of the jungle. And one of these men would be that same torpedoed radio operator who had been so cold with O'Connor.

When he would at last be alone with his adversary, Hunt would apparently conclude that he could still win. And he would ride the monster down to his death.

This was the way things had been and would continue to be on the Hump; but when I sat waiting and sweating at Agra, estimating the runway and trying not to be completely dogmatic about our hapless co-pilot, both Hunt and Charleton were still very much alive. They were merely en route to their final appointment.

I prefer to think of Agra instead of Chabua, because now it is a wonderful escape from my moldy insect orphanage of a bunk. It is amusing to think of Agra because it does not represent an inner defeat, the re-examination of which I should like to postpone as long as possible. It is not amusing to discover you have several times set yourself up as judge and then find you are open to identical judgments. It is not amusing to pose as a swashbuckler and find your sword is made of tin.

While most airports in the world are surrounded by industrial junk, Agra is fantastically endowed. There is a border of dark green trees along the northern side, and just beyond the trees there is the Jumna River, which eventually joins the Ganges. Almost on the shore of this river, otherwise alone in its incredible and mysterious beauty, stands a monument to love—the Taj Mahal. Its dome and delicate minarets are just visible beyond the trees, for the runway points at them straight as a cannon. Any airplane taking off in this direction therefore becomes a projectile, which is ordinarily of no consequence. It is easy to maneuver away from an object so small as the Taj Mahal.

We have completed the pre-take-off check of the C-87 and are agreeably surprised to find all in order. It is unbearably hot, the true torch heat of India, and I have duly considered it because no airplane wing exerts the proper amount of lift in hot air. The very factor of flight will diminish in direct relation to the increase in temperature. Agra is one of the hottest places in the world.

The cabin is filled with various mechanical parts of crippled airplanes being sent to Karachi for repair. They are very heavy but no one knows how heavy since the usual practice of filling the cabin until it seems "about full" has prevailed. Chabua, always short of fuel, had rationed us to a thousand gallons of gasoline, which had been a blessing in disguise. The C-87 had taken off almost like a real airplane. Therefore, here at Agra, I ordered a like amount of gasoline and no more. The distance to Karachi would be less than four hours' flying and gasoline weighs six pounds per gallon.

Ahead the runway wriggles in the heat waves and appears foreshortened. Buzzards wheel against the blank and garish yellow sky and the only relief to our eyes is the black line of trees marking the northern limit of the field. I will bear those trees in mind, for in the extreme heat they will influence our flight in the same way trees on AM-21 had done. Just over their tops there will be a layer of cooler air which will be descending like an invisible waterfall. I will gain as much altitude as possible before reaching the trees, knowing some of it will be lost in passing.

We have developed a rather peculiar method of persuading C-87's to leave the ground. It is open to argument, but most of us are partial to this procedure. We stand hard on the brakes and then shove the throttles forward. We hold hopes and position until the snout of the airplane attains the attitude of a bull at point of a charge. This creates some fifteen seconds of noise and turmoil which is perhaps more heartening to the crew than of technical value. Finally the brakes are released and if the C-87 has any guts whatsoever, it lunges forward in a reasonable facsimile of a mechanism promising flight. There are some who say this initial ceremony is a waste of time and fuel, and is even harmful to the desired result. Those few say cavitation of the propellers stirring up the same air space will cancel any advantage, and no one can say they are wrong. I join the majority and prefer the illusion of liveliness to the sublimating effect of just allowing a C-87 to roll on its way.

After a suitable interval of hoof-pawing I release the brakes and goad the C-87 down the runway at full throttle. It is a ponderous, dreamlike business at first, but this is always so. There is time to think of Gainer back on AM-21 who once said in his wonderful way, "I told Orville Wright and I told Glenn Curtiss, I told both them fellers their danged things would never fly."

Such thoughts are fleeting because I already sense something is wrong. We are halfway down the runway and have only achieved sixty miles an hour. I glance quickly all around—at the instruments, the engines, and the remainder of the runway. Appreciation through habit is nearly instantaneous, but understanding is not. What the hell is wrong now? Even this C-87 has never behaved in such a leisurely fashion.

Yet all is apparently in order. These are the moments of truth in a pilot's life when he must decide within seconds whether he should abandon take-off and jump the brakes or fully commit his airplane to flight. There is still room for choice. Finding nothing amiss, I hold forward. There is the cremating heat to blame.

Eighty miles an hour. We need one hundred and twenty and I should prefer one hundred and thirty. The trees dance toward us, wavering in the sun. Ninety. The choice is gone, other than a certain plunging through the trees.

One hundred. I haul back tentatively on the elevator controls seeking response. Very mushy. A glance at the engine head temperatures and a quick resolve not to look again. With their task less than half done the engines are already far beyond the allowable heat. A flash memory of Tetterton moving steel girders in the night . . . of Johnson and myself shoving on the controls. How many times can a man—

One hundred and ten at last. I can raise the nose wheel a little, but not yet enough. We just cannot clear those trees. But we must try.

There is no time to be afraid and besides I will not admit fear ever again. Not after my exhibition in Chabua.

I haul back on the controls. The C-87 leaves the ground, sinks back, bounces on one wheel, then staggers aloft in a mushing half stall.

The trees are no longer there but here.

We clear them. I can count the leaves. A flock of buzzards explodes before us. We sink back toward the trees and are going to hit.

The trees are a thin fringe along the river. Our tail is just past them as we sink below their tops. We are for an instant in the clear, over the river. Full power. Air speed one hundred and thirty and still sinking.

Now, a new obstruction, dead ahead. The Taj Mahal. They are making repairs. Much of it is covered with scaffolding and I can see the workmen moving about. I can see the folds in their turbans. I can see their mouths open as we approach. I cannot see any beauty.

The quickest and surest way to finalize a semi-stall in an airplane is to turn it. Pressure on the rudder, a trifling bank of the wings, subtract those few critical miles of speed which keep it flying. But I *must* turn or they will have much more repair work to do on the Taj Mahal.

There is one crazy hope. It is not written in any book of aerodynamics. Park told me about it long ago. But I have never tried it, nor has anyone else on a C-87.

"Franko! Full flaps!"

He slams down the lever. The C-87 collides with a soft invisible wall. The air speed falls off and everything shudders. But we balloon upward a hundred feet almost instantly—barely enough to clear the spike of the first minaret.

"Now ease them up slowly!"

Franko complies and we sink again. But speed is returning. And I think we can clear the next minaret without turning. It flashes past. I see a group of workmen cringe against the scaffolding. The Taj Mahal is gone. We swoop down beyond it and with agonized slowness begin picking up enough speed for a halting climb.

It has all taken less than twenty seconds. In that space of time I grew much older. Say, in wear and tear, some several years.

Now lying quite safely in my Natal bunk, the incident deserves a smile. What a way to observe a thing of beauty. What a way to become notorious. And once again it had been because of factors over which I had no control.

Only a few C-87's had fuel gauges and we were warned to disregard the readings of any we happened to encounter. Therefore the amount of fuel in the tanks was taken from the man who actually filled them, and he took his readings from the meters on his truck. In most of our operations the requirement was for full tanks anyway, so the metered amount became mere bookkeeping.

We never discovered whether it was an error in the truck meter, or if the soldiers obliged to stand on that scorching metal wing misunderstood my order, or if the sun had rendered them incapable of caring. Whatever the reason, we had over a thousand gallons of unused fuel aboard when we landed in Karachi, which meant that on our escape from Agra we had been burdened with a minimum overload of three tons. Combined with the heat, this linking of incidental circumstances very nearly destroyed the Taj Mahal. And some admirers.

I look across at Keim. I can tell him about the Taj Mahal, or Hill the Englishman, or make up a story about the Chinese money.

"I swear he was the worst co-pilot I ever had."

Cigar ashes are delicately flicked toward the tiles. "Now you know how I suffered when you used to fly with me."

I cannot tell Keim about the afternoon in Chabua. He would hear me out fairly enough because beneath his crustiness there is a deeply sensitive man. But when I was done, I am certain he would say from the stone foundations of his practicality, "Well, for once you used your friggin' head."

And that would not be satisfactory. It would merely provide an excuse which I had already fallen back upon and leave me in dread that someday it would happen again. It would leave me fragile, with a hole inside which might fester and spread until cringing became habit.

It was one thing to avoid knocking down the Taj Mahal through an act of desperate self-preservation and admit even jokingly that no thoughts of saving its beauty were involved; it was another thing entirely to admit the afternoon in Chabua had ever occurred.

The ubiquitous Clark directed operations at Chabua. Here, on the other side of the world from the North Atlantic, nothing had changed in his staccato manner except the phraseology. He spouted a new parade of names as easily as the tongue-twisters of Greenland. Now it was Kitsing . . . Kumming . . . Tezpur . . . Iruphal . . . Likiang . . . Tengchung. In a few months he had transformed himself from an expert on arctic geography to an old China hand and was also a fair authority on the Himalayas. There was nothing phony about it. Clark's enormous enthusiasm for any project kept him delving and absorbing while others slept.

When Clark squeezed his sponge mind, he expected the droplets of energetic enthusiasm to inspire anyone within range, regardless of his weariness. Failure to react led to immediate classification as a dullard. So I protested little when he strapped a gun around my belt and announced that in spite of the fact my money-laden flight had officially terminated in Chabua, I must at least see what it was like to fly the Hump over to China. I would go as co-pilot to a Major Sweeney.

I pointed out as gently as possible that while my interest in his operation was considerable, a question of category was involved. I was a civilian and carried a card which identified me, however ridiculously, as a noncombatant. This placed me somewhere between the U.S.O. and the Salvation Army. The Japanese were holding much of the area over which we would fly and their fighters did what they could to harass the operation. If we met with any of the misfortunes Clark had so vividly described, wouldn't it be rather embarrassing to explain my status and his gun? Some memory of francs-tireurs—those engaging in hostile actions without attachment to a recognized military band—led me to believe they were denied prisoner-of-war treatment and summarily shot.

Clark was as resourceful as he was versatile. "That we will fix instanter!"

And instantly I became a major, if his gold leaves were to be believed. I thought that if necessary I could make up a serial number.

When the Burma Road was closed by the Japanese, the Chinese forces still fighting for their homeland were cut off from almost all allied supply. The complete conquest of the Chinese mainland was only a matter of time, unless some means could be found to furnish the hordes of tennis-shoed troops with the most necessary instruments of war. There had been in the past some occasional flights from India to western China by China National Airways. And so it was thought feasible to enlarge upon these infrequent flights and eventually create an indestructible supply line if a vast military organization was set to the task. There were difficulties in abundance, and the eventual cost in lives and material dirtied all the claims of later-come generals who would boast of the million tons moved on a certain day from A to B.

First there was the terrain, which was awesome in its natural attributes and frequently gruesome were the stories about the tribes who dwelled in those few places fit for even savage habitation. The true Himalayas, which included Everest and the even higher "K-3," fenced the route to the north. The winds from Tibet swept down across this gigantic range and spent their power upon the mountains which intervened and divided Assam from China. These mountains were impressive enough even compared to their mighty neighbors, and to surmount them safely in an airplane required an instrument altitude of sixteen thousand feet. The only alternative was to follow the tortuous passes, an extremely hazardous procedure unless the weather was perfect, which it rarely happened to be.

The weather was easily enough handled. It was dismissed by a general who one day announced that "From now on there will be no weather."

This marvelous dictum was lost on the elements. The next monsoon season brought the kind of weather monsoons had always brought to the Hump. For the people who are called upon to defy such conditions in an airplane, it is simply and truthfully the worst weather in the world. Every combination of meteorological ugliness and treachery is present over the Hump during monsoon season, and no general save God will ever change it.

There was a paucity of airplanes to assail the Hump, and in the beginning there was only a nondescript assortment, most of which were impoverished for spare parts or actually grounded because of their lack. There were some C-47's. These airplanes were in no way suited for the operation because their two engines could not carry them high enough to clear the Hump with any load. Consequently they were often forced to snake their way through the passes and too many young Air Force pilots were killed in the doing. So many others made variously successful crash landings in the mountainous jungles that a special search and rescue unit was soon designated. They were always very busy.

There were also some new Curtiss C-46's being ferried to Assam by a group of Northwest Airline pilots. These were as eagerly awaited as Christmas toys by those for whom the Hump had become a way of life and death. The C-46's also had only two engines, but they were very powerful. When the C-46's finally arrived and their multitude of mechanical troubles solved, they served well enough.

Men to fly and men to fix were always in pitifully short supply. The distance over the Hump was short—three to five hours according to the destination in China—but the distance to bounteous sources of parts, gear, fuel, and all the impedimenta required of such an enterprise was more than halfway around the world. Consequently, those who flew the Hump in actuality, or merely wished the planes on their way, labored under incredible handicaps. Only the utmost resourcefulness, devotion, and courage kept any sort of operation going. Their efforts made our feeble accomplishments on the North Atlantic seem a comparative holiday, and those who retained their nerve, resolution, and at least outward sanity had well deserved their decorations. They were very tough men—raucous, profane, fatalistic, and disillusioned to the point of abandonment. They were quite unrecognizable as so-called "soft" Americans and existed carelessly month after month in an atmosphere of alarm, physical hardship, frustration, and disaster.

Sweeney and I are returning from China. The weather has been neither very bad nor very good over the Hump. For me it has been interesting to fly a C-87 equipped with two machine guns in the nose. These I have enjoyed firing at imaginary Japanese Zeros obliging enough to appear directly ahead and in our line of flight. Since the guns are fixed, neither Sweeney nor I can conceive how they could be anything but a momentary nuisance to the most stupid foe.

Because we have worn oxygen masks almost the entire time of our acquaintance, the only opportunity for conversation has been on the ground in China while coolies unloaded the airplane. But we are of like mind about C-87's and many other things aloft, so that in only a few minutes we have evaluated each other. Pilots of considerable experience are not strangers for long, or they have silently elected to be strangers forever. I like Sweeney and believe he returns my regard. He is easy of manner with his crew and his airplane, a man who speaks eloquently enough when he has something to say and otherwise holds his silence. He is of medium height, sandy complexioned, with strong freckled hands and very powerful about the shoulders. He has been generous in showing me all of his local lore, as if I were a favored relative come visiting from a different world. I have tried to reciprocate with rather stale information on the North Atlantic.

We break out of the overcast to the east of Chabua, pick up the Brahmaputra River, known to my host as the "Brahmaputrid," and I start a descent. Chabua Field is in sight and I am concerned with lining up on the single runway. The afternoon sun is brilliant. By the time I signal the landing gear down we are sodden with sweat.

Now, near the center of the field, we can see a column of black smoke curling upward. Sweeney shakes his head and his lips tighten.

"Let's get down. Someone's bought it."

I tighten the leisurely approach, for the source of the smoke is unmistakable. A C-47 sprawls flat on its belly just to one side of the runway. There are flames licking at the base of the smoke. A number of men are milling about the plane.

We land through the smoke and roll past the burning C-47. I taxi swiftly to the nearest bunker and cut the engines. Sweeney leaves me at once with the explanation that he must do what he can.

I wait, a spurious major, saddened at the thought of the men who must have been in the plane. The wreckage is halfway down the runway, perhaps a quarter of a mile from where I stand. I am deeply impressed with the continuing activity on the field. One airplane lands through the smoke; two others take off in succession, disappearing for a moment as they pass through its writhing column. Such nonchalance is hard to understand and I wonder if I could do the same if the men were my known and valued comrades.

Sweeney returns in a few minutes. He is driving a jeep and is smiling.

"They got out all right. Everybody okay. I told those damn kids not to be in such a rush to raise their gear, but they never listen." He told me the pilots were recently arrived and were both twenty-two years old. I wondered if they would make twenty-three and asked what had happened.

"Lost one engine just as they broke ground."

There is no fire-fighting equipment at Chabua so the C-47 is simply left to burn itself out. By the time we arrive, it is reduced to a pyre of two engines askew and shapeless metallic forms. There are no other witnesses to its final cremation. Apparently even the plane's young pilots have lost interest and left the scene.

I take some photos of the still-burning remains, a little ashamed of my ghoulishness, and remembering the first airplane I had ever owned was consumed in much the same way. While I am so engaged an officer stops by Sweeney in a weapons carrier. He reports something briefly, and drives away.

When I return to the jeep Sweeney is downcast and smoking hard on a cigarette. "We lost another C-87 to the hills. It happened this morning . . . after we took off."

Again I ask what had happened.

"We don't know yet. There were eleven men aboard. Someone is supposed to have seen them go down. Cut a big path through the trees."

We sit for a time in the jeep, Sweeney seeming reluctant to leave although he has left the motor running. We talk more of the C-87 broken and scattered somewhere in the distant mountains than of the smoking ruin just behind us. And we confine our thoughts to purely technical courses, speculating in a heavier manner than is usual during such post-mortems. And among other things we are of the opinion that Clark is secretly hoarding a bottle of whisky and that it has been a long day and if we approach him properly he might be persuaded to share at least a thimbleful of his treasure.

The wind has changed a little, swinging the column of smoke across the sun.

Sweeney moves the jeep to the edge of the runway but must wait to cross because a C-47 is taking off. We can hear its engines snarling ever more loudly, and then, since we are pilots and there- fore quite incapable of ignoring any take-off, we turn to watch the plane leave the ground.

From our position, the smoke column obscures that part of the runway opposite the wreckage. When the C-47 has emerged from the smoke it is already about fifty feet in the air. The landing gear has not yet been retracted and by the flight attitude, which approximates a steep climb, I assume the airplane must be empty. Otherwise the pilot is asking a great deal of a C-47. Two or three seconds pass and then there is a distinct backfiring from the right engine. The sickening sound multiplies upon itself. I know in- stinctively that the pilot is going to lose that engine—or perhaps he is only simulating a loss and will at once return it to power. Surely, if this is the real thing he will shove the nose down and land again. There is still ample length of runway remaining and the gear has not been retracted.

We watch, fascinated but not yet truly concerned. Sweeney and I are like old medics watching critically from the gallery while an intern performs his first very simple operation.

The plane passes us, faltering, sinking to perhaps fifty feet. Come on, son! *Do* something! A C-47 is the most air-kindly and forgiving of all airplanes, but you must not abuse it. You have time, but not all the time in the world!

And then suddenly, to our horror, there is no time.

The C-47 appears to swerve toward us, then banks abruptly away. It seems to hang in the air, the wings tilt, and it plunges toward the earth at an oblique angle. The wheels are still down. It hits the runway, bounces crazily into the air again, and comes down hard on the right wing tip. Instantly it is torn from the run- way and plunges nose first into a high mud embankment on the opposite side.

The hollow, rending *carumph* as it hits is an awful sound, and then for an instant there is an uncanny silence. Sweeney and I are stunned and still disbelieving our eyes when the silence is torn by a cannonade of explosions. Great sheets of flame blossom from the cloud of dust.

All of this has taken place no more than two hundred yards from where we sit in the jeep. We could cover the distance in seconds. But we sit motionless and undoing, thinking of nothing except that first frightful impact. Our mouths are open, our eyes staring. There are no obedient muscles in our bodies, and our brains are paralyzed.

Sweeney groans—a deep, agonized exhalation of air and strangled sound from his inner being. The pilots are dead. We do not even consider the possibility of their survival because the entire nose of the airplane is telescoped back until the engines are smashed against the mudbank.

Both Sweeney and I have been trained by long experience and association to act quickly in an emergency, yet now we sit like two clods, waiting, listening to the beginning snap of the flames . . . waiting for our guts to unravel, waiting in terrible fear that we might hear a human cry from a thing—which is all it could now be—inside that airplane and we would have to go and try to drag that thing or pieces of it to a place in the dust where it could expire in its own smoking jelly.

I do think to go toward the plane, but there is no response from my body. It sits, separate from me, shocked static.

Sweeney is the first to find his wits. Some twenty seconds have passed. In that time we could have been alongside the plane.

His words are lost in a booming explosion as the fuel in the right wing ignites. It is followed immediately by a series of sharp cracks and the bee whine of bullets.

"The damn thing is full of ammunition!"

Still we have not the gumption to move. Even our natural sense of self-preservation is locked. We just sit, idiotlike, watching the fire and hearing the bullets. More seconds pass.

A long line of men is running toward the plane. They are strung out along the runway in groups of two and three, their legs pumping fiercely. They are yelling to each other and their khaki figures are entirely unreal to me. I cannot, in this bad dream, even be sure where they are going. Certainly not into that holocaust.

We hear the howling of a siren and see an ambulance turn onto the far end of the runway.

The khaki figures swerve around the tail of the airplane and yank open the door. They seem unaware of the bullets, or uncaring; I do not know. I do not know anything except that we could have been at that same door at least a full minute before those living men.

Almost at once four bodies are pulled out of the door and dragged away from the smoke. One finds his own feet and then they are all lost in the men crowding around them. The ambulance arrives and a colonel jumps out. We see him pointing and hear his brief commands. We see all of this and the ambulance draw away as if we were judges at a show and have a perfect right to wait listlessly for the finale. I cannot explain this. I cannot understand such remoteness, or link it with what I thought myself to be. Perhaps we were also dead.

There is a dull thumping explosion in the center of the fuselage followed by a rising ball of fire. The men turn and run away in all directions. One of them has come toward us and Sweeney calls him further. He is a young G.I., his face streaked with sweat and dust. Sweeney finds voice enough to ask the toll.

"The pilots have had it. There were five passengers. We got all but one. They're shaken up but okay."

He leaves us after a moment, returning to whatever he has been doing, which, considering his rank, is probably menial work. But he leaves in courage, as he and the others arrived, running half the length of the runway to engage an obvious danger without a sign of hesitation.

And we sit. Now, even if we would, there is nothing we can do.

"Let's go get that drink. I'm sick of us."

Sweeney sighs. I must assume that he is equally ashamed and incredulous at our behavior because his record alone proves him to be anything but a timid man. Then why had we, for certain vital moments, been overwhelmed?

At once I find a premature excuse by reasoning that there is cowardice buried in every man, as well as unknown quantities of courage. Either force can be unpredictable, at times obedient to call and discipline and at other times the reckless or the cringing despot of the will.

We drive to Clark's quarters, which also includes the Command Office of the field of Chabua. The house had originally been the principal dwelling of the tea plantation and is reasonably comfortable. We drive all the way in silence.

We bring no news to the alert Clark. He is fully informed on the details of the triple calamity and conceals his distress as best he can by a constant series of calls on the field telephone. Red-faced and sweating, a master of his business, he passes out sympathy and censure in his staccato manner. It is encouraging to see him try to get at the roots of the troubles, demanding and beseeching, and know that he is all and honestly intent upon preventing a recurrence. We sit in cane chairs watching this whirl-wind of a man demonstrate the better qualities of a flying officer. He can fly a desk as well as he can an airplane.

Clark is on the telephone.

"There's no damn sense in losing men or planes unless you're a combat unit . . . and this isn't supposed to be."

By my count on this day which is far from ended, fourteen men have been lost.

"If I could only get some top trained mechanics. . . ."

By my count on this day which is far from ended, three airplanes have been lost.

"Send a signal straight to Washington. Send it to New Delhi, Karachi . . . everybody who can read. Tell them we want real mechanics . . . now . . . and I don't give a Goddamn how you phrase it. If they aren't here in two days I'll fly down to New Delhi and kidnap every man they have. Yes . . . put that in the signal!"

I am beginning to understand why Clark is still a major. And why there continues to be a reasonably efficient Hump operation when there might have been a shambles. Even now, with two airplanes still smoldering on each side of the runway, the sound of engines at take-off power flows intermittently through the open windows. The house trembles and Clark's voice is lost as they pass over the house.

When he is done with his telephoning we delicately mention the possibility of refreshment. Clark at once questions the legitimacy of our birth, our crassness, base habits, and fixations. He reluctantly produces a bottle of whisky and without removing the cap discourses at length upon the value of the contents against cobra bite.

"And there are a hell of a lot of cobras in this area. I must think of myself. Just the other day I saw one—"

A sergeant enters the room and there is no nonsense about knocking or saluting. It is unnecessary. The esteem in which he holds Clark is unmistakable in his manner and voice.

"Bad news, Major. We just dropped another one. A C-87 back in the tea patch. Nobody got out."

There is not the slightest change in Clark's face. He could still be talking about the cobra. But his eyes are suddenly emptied of life.

"How many were aboard?"

"Eighteen all told, sir."

"All the gears cranking?"

"Yessir. There's nothing more we can do for now. Lieutenant Parker will be here with the details in half an hour."

When the sergeant has gone, Clark reaches into his desk drawer and takes out three tiny glasses. He pours about one eighth inch of whisky into each glass and then firmly recaps the bottle.

There has been no word spoken since the sergeant's departure. Clark raises his glass. "Great place, isn't it?"

We drink. By my count, thirty-two men gone. And four airplanes. It is only five o'clock in the afternoon. The Hump. Not to be confused with a combat operation.

The Natal rain has ceased, which seems to give the mosquitoes even greater energy. Keim enjoys some protection from his cigar smoke screen, but the patrols zoom and chandelle actively over my own bunk. I suppose that someday my regrettable behavior in Chabua will diminish in importance, but the fact that it could have happened at all may not fade so easily. Sweeney and I were both pilots, which may have contributed to our timorousness. For it is a rare thing for any pilot to observe as a bystander the beginning, the middle, and the end of an eventuality. It was a thing we knew could happen to us although there was neither time nor perception for such thoughts during the few moments of enactment. Then it must have been our instincts which were appalled, an unconscious refusal to believe that what we saw was happening at all. Our life was flying, and to have that life suddenly turn about and deny us was the shock of a father smitten by his daughter. We knew that such things happened but did not admit it could really happen to us. The evils which had slain our comrades in the past were usually explainable, but they happened at places remote from our direct observation, and only chief pilots or those authorities charged with investigation ever saw anything more than long-cooled samples of wreckage. In Chabua this protection had been removed. And the ugliness petrified us.

The rain begins another cascade. I hear a weapons carrier pull up in the street outside. I know from the sound of the brakes that it is a weapons carrier because I have been transported back and forth to airfields in so many weapons carriers that they have become like a matador's carriage. And I know the sounds which will follow. There are a few shouts, the shuffle of feet, and the thump of flight bags heaved to the ground. Another crew has arrived from somewhere in the night, and voices are still charged with their efforts and the need to yell over the sound of four engines. There is no way to be sure where they have come from until they enter the house. Then, be it Africa or Trinidad or the United Kingdom, Keim and I will glance down from our bunks and ask the same questions. How was the weather? How was the food? What is new? And if we fail to ask, our impoliteness will be punished. We will be told at greater length.

I recognize a familiar voice cutting through the others. The hoarseness, the phraseology, is unmistakable. O'Connor. I have so long held a question for that man, nursing and relishing it because for once I believe it possible to catch him without a ready answer.

I swing down from the bunk and pull on my mosquito boots. Because of their improper curing they stink, but everything in Natal stinks, and the boots are only a symbol of our station.

I run for the front door and there is O'Connor just emerging from the sheets of rain. He is soaked to the skin, his cap is on the back of his head, and his flight bag hangs soggily from his hand. It is my intent to hit him with the question before he can get his bearings. I want to know the reason for his arrow of pine boughs laid out in the snow. And I must know why he had made signals to land. I intend to ask him if he was just lonely or intent upon breaking my neck. The riddle has been with me too long.

But suddenly my challenge is tasteless and the sarcasm I had intended not even worthy of utterance. For O'Connor moves into the light from the doorway and he is at once the oldest professional in the world. His gray hair is matted with rain and his whole body sags with weariness. This is a man who has come a long way, not just on this night, but on so many years of nights when his way of life kept him aloft. He is a scarred warrior, accustomed to discomfort, danger, and travail. He is not to be defeated; for having so many times emerged victorious, no other outcome enters his thinking. His home is in his flight bag, his wardrobe a rumpled uniform, and his office in the sky. Now, coming to a miserable house which he has never seen, in a foreign land he has found but never observed in daylight, he is home from the office. He is, for this moment, the weather-worn symbol of us all.

He squints up at the light and the rain spatters on his face. He halts, hesitating before the doorway, and his position is almost exactly the same as it was when I last saw him standing in the snow. Seeing me, he smiles, and his face becomes a thousand crinkles. He calls out hoarsely, "What in the hell are you doing here?"

"The same as you. Welcome to Brazil."

I am greatly relieved. There will never be a right time to ask about arrows in the snow.

✧

X I V

FORTUNE

✧

WHERE IS THE MAN WHO SURVIVES
WITHOUT . . .

O'CONNOR had a penchant for the tough. He went on
to the Hump, where he flew with distinction. I enjoyed better fortune—at least temporarily.

The greatest single boost to long-range over-ocean flying was the
introduction of the Douglas C-54, later to become familiar as the
DC-4. It was, in every sense, a wonderful flying machine. It could
carry a great deal of cargo *and* ice. It was easy to land in difficult
situations and left the ground with enthusiasm. The flight deck

was efficient and comfortable. The airplane had phenomenal strength and striking versatility. It was a joy to fly on instruments, maneuvering almost as easily as its little predecessor, the DC-3. And above all, it had the same reliability.

There were certain faults in the early C-54's. The wing tanks leaked so badly that the mechanics used every type of paste including chewing gum to stop the flow. Furthermore, the fuel system was not perfected and more than occasionally an air lock formed between the big auxiliary tanks in the fuselage and the engines. This sort of thing caused all four engines to quit at the same time, but such was the quality of the airplane itself that even this embarrassment failed to discourage us. We would try various combinations of valves, cross-feeds, and pumps until order returned, and we rarely lost a serious amount of altitude. In time, this trouble was remedied and the airplane very nearly became the perfect machine.

The engineers were still experimenting with the C-54's when we first began to fly them across the Atlantic. Aircraft engineers are ever reluctant to leave well enough alone, which is as it should be, but they are sometimes unable to give their improvements sufficient practical testing. And those sometimes can become the curse of the regular line pilot who rediscovers, to his distress, that slide-rule theory does not always prove itself in day-to-day action.

Not long after my romance with C-54's began, it was nearly terminated.

We were bound for Scotland with a full load of cargo. We took off from La Guardia Field on a sparkling morning and were in every way easy and content with our lot. I found it a morning to be agreeably surprised at the progress of men. Keim and I had set one of the first airliners down upon this same runway. Long before La Guardia Field was created I had flown a little biplane out of the identical spot. It was then only a patch of cinders beside a tawdry amusement park known as North Beach.

The four engines of any plane are numbered for easy identification. Number one is the farthest out on the left wing, number two the inner engine, and three and four in corresponding positions on the right wing.

The take-off on this morning was normal until just after the landing gear had been retracted. Whereupon the number four engine quit abruptly. I was more chagrined than concerned and immediately began the necessary trim corrections. We passed over the end of the runway in good order at some three hundred feet. The waters of Flushing Bay were now below.

The C-54 flew beautifully on three engines in spite of the full load of cargo and fuel—for some ten seconds. Whereupon the number three engine regurgitated, fell away entirely in power, caught again, subsided, and after much nursing maintained in a very rough fashion about one third power. Two engines out on the same side is nothing to be trifled with even in a C-54, but there was still no reason to believe we could not make it back to the field. We had lost altitude, settling to one hundred and fifty feet.

Opposite La Guardia there is a foul-smelling island built of refuse from the city and upon it is a municipal prison. The waters of Flushing Bay encircle this island and on the northern side become the East River, which flows toward Hell Gate and Manhattan.

In twenty seconds we were alongside this island trying everything we knew to keep the two ailing right engines alive. Now we were barely able to hold one hundred feet without approaching a stall. The entire airplane was shaking in vicious spasms.

Suddenly the number two engine failed in exactly the same manner as had the others. It would quit for approximately five seconds, then unexplainably catch again and return to full power for ten or fifteen seconds. The resulting surge of power over-revved the propeller until I was certain it must tear itself from the mount. Now engines four, three, and two all joined in this mad contest of weakness and strength, surging and expiring, backfiring and howling like tormented wasps. At moments all would malfunction simultaneously and then separately return to life.

Only the number one engine, far out on the left wing, held absolutely steady at full emergency power. I had not touched its throttle since we first rolled into the take-off. We lost an additional fifty feet of altitude and I banked as much as I dared, intending to circle the north side of the island and there ditch the airplane before we reached the swifter waters of the East River.

The flight deck was a shambles as the hooligan engines posed a constantly changing dilemma. Throttles, mixture controls, and propeller controls were all so out of kilter as we sought to coax the last bit of power from each engine, or prevent its over-revving when it caught again, that it was nearly impossible to perform our standard emergency procedures with any degree of efficiency.

Thirty seconds after we had left the runway we were fifty feet above the water, the radio operator was calling May Day, and the navigator counting his beads. The co-pilot, the engineer, and myself were a stiff, erratic ballet of darting hands.

Fear and fright are two different things, the emotion of true fear requiring time for culture and preferably a period of helpless inactivity. Then fear breeds upon itself because it is a hermaphrodite capable of endless reproduction. Fear is a contagious disease, spreading from its first victim to others in the vicinity until it is powerful enough to take charge of a group, in which event it becomes panic. Fear is the afterbirth of reason and calculation. It takes time to recuperate from fear.

Fright is only the percussion of fear. It snaps rather than rumbles and its explosion is instantaneous. Likewise, fright is self-destructive, being more of an instinctive physical reaction than it is an emotion. It hits, explodes, and may be gone as quickly, if it does not have time to ignite the keg of fear. On this morning, time was in short supply.

Fright is as unpredictable as it is quick in arrival because its fuse is either visible or audible. It may even benefit its target. In fright, clear thinking is often possible and the triggering of muscles and joints accelerated to a marvelous degree. Thus, in such a transitory state, are people sometimes able to survive situations which should by all reason be their end. On a morning such as this one, a man may find each hand performing the work of two, his entire body vibrant and his thinking electric.

Sixty seconds after the first engine faltered my left hand and both legs were entirely engaged in trying to satisfy the physical demands of mere flight. The airplane and its burden weighed over thirty tons and composed a mass which must be kept in motion at an absolute minimum of one hundred and ten miles per hour. If this speed were not sustained, flight would cease and the law of gravity prevail. In an airplane there are two sources of speed—power from the engines, of which we were presently almost disinherited, and diving, which must involve a loss of altitude. We were poor men, having already squandered all but fifty feet.

There are sixteen basic engine controls in a C-54. In the same manner there are thirty-two ancillary switches and knobs by which various other functions of each engine may be controlled.

There are thirty-two instruments to inform on the health or ailments of each engine. In an emergency, all of this congress must be given heed and quickly disciplined. An incorrect appreciation or a wrong movement can compound whatever original difficulty exists.

All instruments except the set concerned with the number one engine were now frantic with pernicious gossip. They screamed invective, spite, and intermittent betrayal. At moments they were so palsied with the tremors of the airplane we simply could not absorb their messages quickly enough to relate intelligence with action. Yet my one free hand and those of the co-pilot and engineer, moving swiftly in fright, somehow united to pull or push the right lever at the right time and so maintain an average of power which was enough to pass along the north side of the island, accomplish a bank, and aim the airplane back toward La Guardia. The control tower said we disappeared behind the island, which is some thirty feet high.

To correct trouble in an airplane its source must be known. We sought energetically and with the single devotion of minds in fright for a plausible cause. But there were not enough seconds.

It was less than a mile to the edge of La Guardia. We limped, porpoising with each explosive surge of power as the engines revived. And when they failed we sank toward the water again.

The ensuing seconds brought a new complication. The control tower had no reason to believe we would reappear from behind the island so quickly. They were only aware of our troubles and were still absorbed in clearing the field of other traffic. A commercial DC-3 was in the middle of take-off—rolling down the only runway available to us. We were on a direct collision course. I wasted two seconds praying the pilot would see our threatening approach and bank away as soon as his wheels left the ground. Our own ability to turn was nil. We clutched at a mere thread of hope that we could reach the edge of the field.

A final surge of power came at the precise instant I had lost even hope. It lasted for perhaps ten seconds. This brief span of time was tangled with complication and instinctive action. The DC-3 broke ground and banked steeply off to the east. We snapped the landing gear down and the wheels touched the very edge of the runway almost simultaneously. The flaps were still in the process of extending and the co-pilot was still asking permission to land as our nose wheel banged down on the concrete. I had not touched the throttles to reduce power. We landed with everything we had.

The total air time was three minutes, something of a record in a four-engined airplane. Our relief soon changed to bewilderment. Taxiing toward the hangar at normal speed, all four engines performed sweetly.

We stopped in front of the hangar. I stood on the brakes and separately ran each engine up to full take-off power. Number one behaved perfectly, as it had all through our brief misfortune. Our affection and respect for that engine were maudlin. The others backfired outrageously and threatened to jump off the wing when full power was applied. The noise and fuss were so clamorous that I considered it a rude public display of our difficulties. With the whole field looking on, it was treason to our mechanics, an advertising of their dirty linen which would not be appreciated. So we shut down all the engines as if hiding a blush and waited while the gyros whined down. A group of men had emerged from the hangar and were trotting anxiously toward us.

The first man to appear on the flight deck was Hoyt, our chief of maintenance. He was stocky, blackhaired, and his almost crimson cheeks contrasted so spectacularly with his olive skin that his face seemed more of an oil portrait than real. Hoyt would have everyone think he was easygoing, but in truth he was intense, utterly devoted to his complicated machinery, and always fretting about it.

The relationship between the men who fly big airplanes and those who fix them is harmonious because it is based upon professional respect. It is also a most delicate relationship; however undeserving, the pilots are traditionally covered with tinsel and the fixers are not. Both groups are proud men, but the pride of the mechanics is not so easily paraded. The pioneer "grease monkey," his overalls splotched with varnish dope and his hands black with grease, is long gone. Unless he was ambitious and disposed to learn constantly, such pioneers could not survive against the increasing technological demands of each new aircraft. Many of them simply faded away. They were replaced, unless they became, of themselves, men who thought and lived in ever-spiraling complexity.

A modern airplane is a labyrinth of electrical and hydraulic and mechanical combinations, all of which must function with scientific reliability. The multitude of devices conceived by man in his restless efforts to increase his mobility sometimes overwhelms those inheriting the final Machiavellian assembly. Hence, there are experts on hydraulics, electronics, plumbing, radio, and engines, and each is so absorbed and confined that he is nearly blind to the provenances of the others. No man can master all of these things, although Hoyt came very close to doing so.

Now, because we knew each other well, and because on such occasions there was custom to be observed, Hoyt asked me most casually if I had experienced some trouble. And, on my part, there was also custom to be followed; so I answered that after three minutes in the air we had become bored with flying and had decided to give it up for the day. I then pointed out that our decision might have been influenced by the fact that our engines had developed a trifling though mysterious malady. I outlined the nature of our difficulty, as if Hoyt had not heard the exhibition of a few moments before.

Finally I added that I was growing older at a pace which was not to my liking and would Hoyt please tell me what was wrong with all but one of his Goddamned engines. Now that the airplane was on the ground, they automatically became "his" engines.

I was surprised when Hoyt appeared only mildly interested and waved one hand wearily toward two young men who had followed him to the flight deck. I knew them vaguely, yet would have recognized them anyway, since their thoughtful mien, bow ties, and white shirts with pockets sprouting pencils and slide rule clearly marked them as engineers.

Brilliance rather than wisdom characterized these men, and their very remoteness from our daily tasks made any definite relationship with flight crews almost impossible. We regarded aircraft engineers as curiosities, probable geniuses, and therefore special people to be politely avoided lest their erudition prove our shallowness. Except for Brink and Speas, two engineers who had considerable flying time, we also found them rather dull company.

Now one of these young men said to me, "Captain, we're very sorry about this and frankly cannot understand it."

"Can't understand what?"

"The plugs."

"*What* plugs?" I thought to hold my tongue for it was risky business provoking engineers who could prove a man an oaf with a flick of their slide rules. But a twinkling in Hoyt's eyes seemed to support my curiosity and he carried an abused air which indicated our difficulties were not entirely his affair.

"You see, Captain, we have been experimenting with this new type spark plug. They proved out perfectly on the test bench so we believed they were ready for a service check. The new plugs are in three of your engines, but there wasn't time to install them in the fourth."

"What a damn shame!" Again I saw in Hoyt's eyes that he shared my dismay.

"Apparently these new type plugs broke down under the heat of full power take-off, which leads us to believe our test bench data must be in error. We'll have to analyze it further."

They were so sincere and totally unaware of the very near consequence of their experiment, I could not distill the residue of fright within me to even pretended anger. Yet the opportunity for righteousness was irresistible. So I thought to knock their brilliant heads together with sarcasm and began by telling them that I was not qualified, nor had I recently received any pay as a test pilot. Furthermore, I was a very feeble swimmer, and since the waters of Flushing Bay were reported filthy, the rest of the crew were similarly uninterested in bathing. I suggested they conduct their own test flights in the future and recommended an empty airplane with a minimum of fuel aboard for such projects. "It will float better," I said, "in case there has been some slight miscalculation in your figures." I concluded with a brief speech on ethics. I admitted the show might have been more sporting for them as played, but asked if it might not have been almost equally so if they had at least dropped a hint about their substitutions.

It was wonderful fun, at the expense of the engineers. But I thought they had already had theirs.

We waited for the rest of the morning while the old and reliable type of plugs were installed in the engines. Our take-off and flight to Scotland was so without incident that I found time to brood upon man's technological progress and remember that he often stumbled before gracefulness was attained. And I tried unsuccessfully to think of some way whereby I could do my own stumbling.

From Scotland we flew to Marrakech in North Africa and thence back to La Guardia, where two letters awaited me together with a highly technical report on the guilty spark plugs.[10] One letter was from the chief pilot's office requesting some explanation as to why I had landed with a full load of fuel plus cargo. This was against regulations. The other letter was from the control tower censuring me for landing before proper permission had been obtained. The letters were three weeks old. So I confined my answers to the promise that I would be good and never do anything like that again. I could not know how time would uncover the wishfulness of such a naïve statement.

There was now a growing stability about all of our over-ocean operations which had hitherto been almost entirely absent. Over the Atlantic our operations were vastly extended and every day increased in number. Now, we usually by-passed Presque Isle and flew eastward directly to Goose Bay, or Gander, or Stevensville in Newfoundland. Goose Bay, where Boyd and Clark and Hassel had once stood beside a single gravel runway, was now a mammoth development of concrete and steel, and the wilderness trembled with the continuous sound of airplanes. It had become the launching platform of a multitude of bombers en route to the European theaters of war. Most of these were "Flying Fortresses" flown by anxious young men with peach-fuzz beards. Many of them were about to embark upon their first ocean flight and a large proportion would never return. Their figures were walking leather and their accouterments so numerous that even the most dramatically inclined found it difficult to swagger with conviction. Headphone wires dripped from their flight caps, oddments of survival gear from their leg and shirt pockets, daggers banged on their hips, and the majority were armed with heavy 45-caliber automatic pistols. They made a great deal of noise, but behind their bravado we recognized the earliest mixture of fear and defiance. These were the brave aerial children who would soon go down in flame and history as the Eighth Air Force. Later, when we brought them back, the accouterments were gone. They wore medals instead and all the innocence was gone from their eyes. Now, before their massive ordeals, they came to us shyly and inquired about the Atlantic skies, as strangers might ask the way. And we reassured them as best we could, feeling old and doubtful of our usefulness. Most of them flew by way of Greenland and Iceland as we had done in what seemed the long ago. We usually had the decency to refrain from telling them how this had been.

We served the North African as well as the European theater of war. Thus we moved in a series of aerial voyages from the various take-off points on the North American continent to Scotland or to

England. Or we would set course to the southeast and land at Terceira in the Azores, proceeding eventually to the United Kingdom or Casa Blanca or Marrakech. We would sometimes reverse all of this and return the opposite way via Iceland; or we might return the long route via Dakar in Senegal, crossing the South Atlantic and landing at a new field in Fortaleza, Brazil. Then we would grind northward past Belém, the Guianas, the Antilles, and Puerto Rico.

Operations in the Pacific were even more extensive. After reaching the Hawaiian Islands crews flew westward to Australia via Johnson Island, and later, as the war progressed, served all of the many Pacific bases including those in Alaska.

When we left New York we had no idea how the routing of each flight would be ordained. In part, weather was a factor because we always sought the most favorable winds. Our cargoes consisted of every conceivable item from special bombs to surgical instruments. As U-boat harassment eased, our proportions of cargo also diminished, for much of it could at last be sent by sea. The space was taken by personnel: at first, much-needed technicians, fighter pilots, medics, and paratroopers, and finally just wistful G.I. Joe. We returned west with occasional batches of German prisoners, pilots who had completed their missions, wounded, and all the depressing junk of war, including those individuals known as "Very Important People."

Most of the pioneering was done with, but not all of it. Catchings, together with Arden, spent one winter flying "Project Icicle." In a C-54 equipped with special instruments they set off regularly to find and accumulate as much ice as they could. They were supposed to report on its effects and discover, if they could, the best ways to avoid or conquer it. In addition, they were asked to investigate more scientifically the various evils of North Atlantic and sub-arctic winter weather. No one envied their research, but they seemed to enjoy it and their eventual contributions to our knowledge were most valuable.

Every major airline in the United States was now involved in these tremendous undertakings. For all of the air crews, contrast was so routine that they thought nothing of waving farewell to pink-faced Scots in the night and, after a dreamlike period of suspension during which nothing was to be seen, swooping down in the dawn over Mohammedans bent toward Mecca.

There were pleasures and distresses according to the season and the geographical areas. We came to know them all, as we had formerly known our more humble domestic routes. Some of these things we loved and others we hated. We became both wary and confident in our knowledge. We knew that the airports in Newfoundland and Nova Scotia were cold hosts in the wintertime, and treacherous when summer arrived. Heavy fog at dawn and evening made these places always suspect as either destinations or alternates. We learned to expect an encounter with what could almost be considered a permanent front lying approximately six hundred miles to the east of Newfoundland. In winter this front contained varying amounts of ice, but seldom enough to start the train of fear. In summer, particularly in late evening, it was given to thunderstorm activity. These fomentations shook things up merrily enough but were in no way as vicious as those we had known domestically.

As an amusement, we could often estimate our general location by the character of the skies both above and below. East of Newfoundland the sea was usually hidden beneath a low level of stratus cloud. Farther east, after the front had been negotiated, this deck of cloud would become broken, or vanish altogether. In the middle of the Atlantic the weather was rarely uncomfortable, and here in the summer we expected large areas of calm.

We learned to respect the so-called "Icelandic Low," which on the weather charts spun like a tremendous phonograph record pinned to the island. In summer this Low brought heavy rains and enough cloud to make an instrument approach to the airport a normal procedure. In winter it could wind up so tightly that the resulting winds required us to keep a careful eye on fuel consumption. These gales occasionally achieved a velocity of ninety miles an hour aloft, which would force us to turn back if westbound. Eastbound, of course, the flight became a sleigh ride.

The enrichment of our knowledge was hastened by necessity, and it was constantly refertilized by mutual exchange of information and opinion. While waiting to take over the next leg of their flight, crews would meet in Goose Bay, or Iceland, or Prestwick, or the Azores, or Morocco, and always the talk would be of flying. Crews bound in one direction would meet with crews bound the opposite way and learn at first hand from those just landed of the weather awaiting them. This was much better than the inherent uncertainties of a weather map. Like Pony Express riders, we had a better idea where the Indians were. These meetings usually took place in the operations room and were unavoidably of short duration because the incoming crew would be tired and more often ravenously hungry.

"There's nothing in the front. It looks bad. There are a few anvil heads around, but we went through at eight thousand and only hit a little rain. . . ."

"That Spanish station is jamming Gibraltar again so don't expect anything from it. . . ."

"You'll go like a bomb until about thirty degrees west; then you'll hit the wind and stand still. Better take some extra fuel for the wife and kids. . . ."

"The whole U.K. was stinking when we left, but by the time you get there this front should go through and you'll have a fine ride. . . ."

"How are things in Accra?"

"Good, if I could ever find the place. I always seem to arrive at night and it always rains at night and the rain knocks out the range so we hunt around the coast of Africa until we get lucky and some native waves a lantern. . . ."

"The runway at Lagens? Has some new dips in it where the rain washed the earth away . . . like a roller coaster. . . ."

Thus, from jest, from imprecation, gripe, and a sort of steady capillary action, we absorbed an entirely new world which previously no man knew very much about. The waters below us had been navigated for centuries, but the experience gained thereby was nearly useless to us who must telescope voyages normally requiring many days into a period of hours. Our sea was of all three dimensions; we sailed it sitting down, without either the benefits or confinements of tradition, and we were obliged to develop our own sense of what was right and what was wrong.

We learned to know a front which habitually lurks to the west of Ireland, roughly paralleling the fifteenth degree of longitude, and we found it mostly static and harmless except in the summer, when it could breed some nasty thunderstorms.

We learned that off the Gold Coast of Africa, beginning almost exactly with every muggy evening twilight, the elements would erect a lofty barrier such as few men had ever seen. Here were the fathers of thunderstorms, the grandfathers, and the monstrosities of all their issue. These gigantic cumulo-nimbus, shouldering against each other for air space, were brilliant with inner fires—not those spasmodic flashes of lightning which characterized the northern variety but a continuous blossoming of yellowish light as if the interior of every cloud held a blast furnace. We found in time that this spectacular wrath was usually a bluff, and the ferocious appearance more frightening than anything we would find inside. There would be moments of extremely heavy rain, then nothing more.

We learned that the distance between the Azores and Bermuda had a magical way of expanding beyond scientific truth. This was especially true when west bound for Bermuda. It seemed, without logic or visible cause, always to become the longest, dreariest flight in the world. Here we fought monotony, which was rarely present elsewhere, but there was also a relatively permanent front in the region of fifty degrees longitude. This diversion could, at any season, become a malevolent area sprouting every form of meteorological harassment, and it was here that Keim suffered a lightning bolt in his aerial rump. No one could ever explain how lightning managed to shoot upward, but Keim's airplane was struck in the belly only, leaving a considerable hole and fusing all radio connections. Keim swore that he himself became so highly charged his hair stood on end for hours afterward.

So from the Hebrides to Sudan, from Ascension Island to

Thule, and from Baffin Bay to Natal, we came to know, in certain ways, the atmospheres and a corresponding quarter of the earth better than we knew our own homes. Unlike the sanguinary record on the Hump, the whole of our route was, for a time, remarkably free of anything save minor incident and alarm. It was difficult to believe this could continue, particularly since the regular domestic routes which were presumably easier flying had meanwhile claimed the lives of Stiller and McClure and the veteran Carpenter, who had first passed upon my captaincy. Also taken were Dryer and Brand, and along with them went my old friend and contemporary Gay, whose winning smile had never failed to brighten Lester's classroom or the cheap hotel in which we had once studied and hoped. I hated to think of his smile extinguished forever because of such a thing as ice. They went down in the same area where Hughen and I had so sweated on a winter night.

Then disaster struck our own route and it hit viciously. Golden, flying a C-54, crashed into the houses on the south side of Prestwick airport. Fortunately, the houses were not occupied, but all aboard the aircraft perished. Soon afterward, another C-54 struck the railroad embankment on the western side of Prestwick. It bounced once, exploded, and all were gone. Both tragedies occurred at night and in heavy rain.

Even so the old-timers of our line at last showed great interest in our activities. I viewed their arrival without bitterness, but with something less than enthusiasm, knowing their seniority numbers would soon return me to the bush league and all the knowledge and experience I had so far managed to accumulate would not save me. There even came the highest of priests, and every physical characteristic of this man was exactly right for the role he carried so easily. He had flown the mail with Lindbergh on Robertson Airlines. As he spoke, his strangely delicate hands flew graceful little glides, dives, and chandelles, and his face came alive as can only a man's who is totally in love. His features had the bone structure of an American Indian, his skin was a nutty brown, and his eyes were wise and humorous behind the fences of sun crinkles surrounding them. His hair was jet black and straight, which only increased the legend that he was a descendant of Cochise. To stand before him was to join a lazy, soothing dance, for his lithe body was never still, swaying as he shifted weight, gliding and slowly twisting as he wished to emphasize a point. He was like a comfortable, reliable old boot and in many ways he resembled one.

This was Sloniger and his seniority number was . . . ONE.

In air time, Sloniger ranked with Parmentier, Geysendorfer, and Smirnoff of Royal Dutch Airlines. In this exalted group there were also Jones, Travers, and Kelly-Rogers of Imperial Airways, Freng and Knight of United Airlines, Codos of Air France, and the legendary Mermoz of l'Aeropostale.[11]

Like his fellow peers, Sloniger had begun flying during World War I and had kept at it continuously ever since. He had not spent thirty consecutive days on the ground for twenty-seven years, which gave him over twenty thousand hours! These men were kings and received homage befitting their records. All of them were a special and wonderful mixture of intelligence, dexterity, canniness, courage, and humility. Like ancient chieftains endlessly engaged in both foreign and tribal wars, they had to possess all of these things to survive for so long.

I had never seen Sloniger before and so knew him only by name, reputation, and the wonder of his unique number "One." And here, on the Atlantic, we met only briefly before the pressure of his followers defrocked me. I certainly had no idea that one day our fortunes would become lashed together under circumstances of hazard, frustration, and near despair, through all of which Sloniger would display the most admirable loyalty to one of his subjects.

I managed a tenuous hold upon the route which I now regarded with the same affection I had once held for AM-21. Yet after a few months the inevitable numbers again took charge and I was once more relegated to the ironic business of introducing my numerical superiors to the satisfactions of four-engined aircraft. Even this period of instruction was most temporary and I was soon squeezed back to my place in the peasantry. The only assignment available to me was inglorious and uncomfortable—Natal, where they were still flying the cantankerous C-87's.

My service in exile was blessedly short. After three flights across to Africa the old malaria returned in such an odious fashion that I was confined to the army hospital. When I had regained enough strength to walk without reeling I was returned, a seedy lump, to the remedial influences of more temperate latitudes.

There was now recorded in my logbook a total of five thousand six hundred and twenty-two hours and thirty-nine minutes. It was so little, but closely matched the flying time held by all of us who had been together in Lester's school—McGuire, Mood, Owen, Watkins, Sisto, Lippincott, Katzman, and Carter. Gay and Charleton had closed their logs forever and soon there would be one more uninterested in time.

The times were in figures, the dull specifics which were supposed to record nothing more than the passage of intervals in our lives, and serve as official recognition that a certain amount of experience and consequent wisdom had dribbled into our aerial selves. The numerals, in summation, represented much more than this. For they said that our marrows had been both frozen and melted, our quotients of courage drained and replenished, and our ability to act in fear proven. The numerals established us as solid citizens of the skies—though not yet to be considered as true aristocrats. Altogether, the numerals stated that we knew how to remove ourselves and others out of our natural element, in all seasons, and in all circumstances and conditions, and return the lot safely to earth.

And they also made an important announcement: Our luck was exceedingly good.

✵

X V

A HOLE

✵

SO SMALL, BUT OF EXQUISITE DESIGN

To suggest, even by inference, that captains should
be given sole credit for moving a multi-engined airplane from one place to another would be the ultimate in strutting
dishonesty. Each man in the crew has his manifold duties, and
unless he performs them well, the captain is sorely tried.

A captain of any aircraft was, and is, exactly what the ancient
and honorable term has always defined. Regardless of the circumstances, regardless of whatever human temptations may invite this

man to shift or even share blame and responsibility, he must refuse them. Otherwise he is a man moving in hypocrisy, thieving the respect with which he so freely adorns himself and betraying the very basis of the faith which is always offered to him.

It is a rare captain who is not heavily conscious of his duty; even the most lighthearted recognize that theirs is a special appointment and jealously guard the tradition that whatever misfortune occurs on any flight is fundamentally their fault.

Even so this maxim has been twice denied. In the one case it was sheer deception bordering on insanity, and in the other an incredible and shameful attempt to shift the blame for a disaster upon others of the crew. The eventual results were satisfying to those who felt obligated to live and fly by the code. Mercy had no place in our thinking because it has no place in such a potentially lethal instrument as an airplane. The first man died in disgrace and by his own hand, and the second was repudiated forever, through permanent loss of his license.

As the C-54's became more abundant and the whole enterprise of flying the oceans matured, the stature and line of command became ever more pronounced. A good crew was treasured by any captain and each did his utmost to assemble a group of aides whom he could trust. There was open competition for skillful co-pilots, navigators who could work with accuracy and calm, radio operators who would stay alert through a long flight, and engineers who would turn the proper valves at the right time. In this internecine and sometimes amusingly petty warfare, the seniority numbers played no part. The most junior captain was entitled to connive, cajole, and maneuver at will in capturing the best of men.

For various reasons there were always substitutions in any crew and inevitably a certain amount of subtle trading. Captains and crew members tried to achieve what they hoped would become the ideal unit. However, it was sometimes possible for crews to stay together for long periods of time. The result was that a navigator was known as one of "So-and-So's" crew, or a co-pilot as having been long with "So-and-So." They were accordingly either envied or pitied.

On our line Robbins was still charged with this sort of thing and, in the process of making his constant deals of assignment, lost even more of his hair. I continued to seek his counsel and shrewd aid, contriving by flattery which he saw through instantly, and pleas which he professed touched him deeply, to gather and hold excellent men. Thus the only crew member of whom I ever had true complaint was the hapless co-pilot on the flight to China.

My usual comrades aloft were such men as Robertson, who soon became as trustworthy a co-pilot as Johnson had been.

Robertson was an extraordinarily powerful and darkly handsome man. His features were classic Greek in line and his forbearance almost unbelievable. He patiently tolerated a continuous needling from all of us on the subject of his masculine beauty and never mentioned that should we prod him too hard, he could have easily broken any one of us into small pieces. In contrast to his physique, his voice was soft and melodious.

And there was LaFrenier, who became one of the finest and most versatile navigators I would ever know. Perhaps it was because of Robertson's muscular presence that LaFrenier seemed frail, but he was in fact a slight man with strangely delicate hands. He was cheerful almost to the point of exasperation, and if he was not whistling merrily, he was singing popular songs—the saccharine lyrics of which he was devoted to memorizing. He was never discouraged by our sour reception of his efforts when he persisted in whistling through a thunderstorm, or sang through a blizzard at four o'clock in the morning. LaFrenier was nearly fearless and in several situations displayed an *élan* and faith in our continued future which was heartening to behold. He was a devout Catholic, observing all the rites of that demanding religion. We all envied him a little in his unswerving belief.

To my regret, Summers, the radio operator, had somehow been stolen or lured away during one of the many shifts of scene. He was eventually replaced by Bradford, who was equally proficient with his key. Bradford was a big man, often silent for extended periods. But then he was in love, and we knew he was in love and did not cease our chiding of him until he finally married the girl.

Our flight engineers were more difficult to keep in the family and so we were never able to know them as well. They would make one flight and then perhaps another, after which they would be gone. Millington was an exception and somehow managed to stay with us for many flights. He was even darker of complexion than Robertson, enthusiastic, and ambitious—and, more important, possessed a thorough mechanical knowledge of the airplane.

Every crew, eating together, sleeping within a few feet of each other, and flying together, naturally developed certain special methods and customs within their family unit. These were the trifles and rather pathetic little trimmings which eased friction among those compelled to live so closely. They offered amusement when physical weariness and the instinctive urges for a more stable existence disturbed us. One crew disdained the tedious box lunches normally furnished on flights and carried a special commissary bag in which they stored whatever delicacies they could buy or steal. The engineer made an ingenious stove which could be plugged into the airplane's electric system, and while others breakfasted on limp sandwiches, the members of this crew enjoyed ham and eggs, hot rolls, and really fresh coffee. In our envy we developed a near hatred for their cleverness.

Our own crew was more given to personal eccentricities. Perhaps LaFrenier sang so lustily because he had survived sixty-three flights across the Hump in C-87's, which was reason enough. Bradford was a storehouse of cookies, always replenished on those occasions when he returned to his love. He was generous, but also a careful rationer, so that the supply often lasted two weeks. The crumbs mixed nicely with the droppings of the cigarettes which I now affected to roll by hand.

Our pre-take-off ceremonies had become rather elaborate and were strictly observed. A movie star of great natural beauty had presented us with her photo, on which she had written sentimentally of her desire for our safety and well-being. As we started the engines, LaFrenier would thumbtack the photo above his navigation table and carefully adjust the nearest flight deck light so that the picture would be most advantageously illuminated.[12] A chance meeting with a great theatrical personality had produced a black garter, having upon it a colorful rosette.[18] This Robertson would solemnly bang on the knob which was normally used to set one of our horizon instruments. At the end of the runway, when all of this nonsense was done and the engines had been checked, I would take the concertina from beside my left foot and quickly render "You take the high road . . ." It made no difference that LaFrenier might be singing some other tune at the same time. The sound of the engines mercifully subdued everything.

It was after such embellishments to our technical preparations that we were ready for take-off from Stevensville, Newfoundland, on a gloomy August morning. We were all in excellent humor in spite of a certain strangeness created by the absence of two of our regular family members. Ditmeyer sat at Bradford's place behind the radio, and Braseman had taken over as engineer. We had slept well, the weather forecast for our arrival time in Scotland was encouraging, and the winds throughout the flight were predicted as most favorable.

Hence the rotten weather at Stevensville itself could not depress us. The cloud ceiling was a bare four hundred feet, and the visibility somewhat less than a mile in the intermittent rain squalls which were typical of the season. We knew that we would leave all of this behind in an hour or two, because the condition did not extend far over the ocean. We did not know that in a much shorter time we might question the authority of those little trophies now set up as household gods.

Stevensville airport is situated at the end of a long, fingerlike bay which is confined between a considerable peninsula of rolling hills and a wide arm of the Newfoundland mainland. The barren hills on both sides of the bay are of like design, but somewhat higher to the east. The bay extends in a northerly direction for several miles, where it is eventually cut off by the land. Here, at first, the upward slope is gentle from the shore, so that an airport could be built. The whole establishment tilts toward the sea and the runways at their northern ends are higher than their southern extremities. Because the normal approach to the airport is from the bay, this lack of plumb is more aid than handicap to aircraft. Beyond the fringes of the airport the rock-speckled hills rise abruptly and finally achieve the full dignity of mountains.

These mountains extend toward the north and east and after a time diminish gradually until they melt into the glacial terrain which prevails to the coast line. Because of the mountains the minimum instrument flight altitude in the vicinity of Stevensville is six thousand feet. And descent below that altitude must be accomplished when the pilots can see, unless they are actually flying the approach leg over the bay.

This did not concern us. We were bound for Scotland and had no intention of returning to Stevensville. There were thirty-four military passengers sitting on bucket seats in the cabin.

We took off in a squall and the rain instantly found its way through the framing of the windshield and dribbled on my left knee. We plunged into the solid overcast only a moment after we left the ground. I was at once much occupied with the flight instruments and trying to kick my concertina box to a dry place beside the rudder pedals. I could hear LaFrenier singing of some unrequited love and knew that his vocalizing was only an accompaniment to his recording of our take-off time, course, and the laying out of his charts and graphs. Robertson nursed the throttles with his big hands, keeping the engines at proper climb power. Braseman, the engineer, eased the flaps up a few degrees at a time. Thus all was pleasantly normal and the whine of the Stevensville radio range faded rapidly in my earphones. We were on our way, another morning, another flight over the ocean, another entry in our logbooks.

The airplane was new and climbed well, so that proceeding upward through the heavy overcast became an exhilarating business. Like any craftsman whose tools seem to have a sharper edge than usual, I indulged in a certain smugness and self-appreciation —in this event because I could so casually hold exact course and rate of ascent when the visibility was nil. I could even feign temperament, using the dribbling rivulet of rain as a foil and cocking half around in my seat to escape it.

After a little time I noticed that Braseman had not yet settled down to his book work of recording engine temperatures and pressures. Instead, he was tinkering with the lever controlling the hydraulic system. The lever was on the floor beside Robertson's seat and could be pulled up and back by inserting two fingers in the face plate. I glanced at Braseman.

"What's going on?"

"I don't know. I can't budge it."

"Let Robertson try."

Braseman relinquished his grip and stood back.

Robertson placed his fingers in the hole and heaved until his face flushed. We laughed at his mighty struggles, because the relatively weak must always relish the physical defeat of the very strong. But soon our laughter subsided. If the lever could not be moved, the entire hydraulic system which controlled the raising and lowering of the flaps and landing gear must remain in continuous operation until the engines were shut down. The hydraulic oil would circulate all through the maze of piping at high speed and under great pressure. We were not certain if this was bad, but since it was abnormal we were reasonably sure it was not the best way to start out on a long flight.

"Maybe if we put the flaps down and then bring them up again it will help. The pressure should be released long enough. . . ."

We put the flaps down and brought them up again. Neither Robertson nor Braseman could move the lever.

"Let's try putting the gear down and then retracting."

I resented these diversions because they would interrupt the smoothness of my flying, but we put the gear down and brought it up again. In spite of our combined efforts the lever remained flush with the floor.

LaFrenier stopped singing.

We were eleven minutes out of Stevensville and had just reached seven thousand feet, which was to be our cruising altitude. A bitterness had stained the morning. As I leveled out and settled the plane on course, it seemed to me that a flying man had enough to do without concerning himself with a complicated mess of hydraulics. Well enough, I thought, to understand its principles, but the intricacies of valves, poppets, pipes, should be classed as et cetera. My business was to set the plane smoothly and surely on the west leg of the Gander Range as soon as it could be heard and thus send us nicely on a fixed departure from shore. Yet secretly, guiltily, I knew that the hydraulic system was also my business, and I should be able to correct the fault.

I tried to recall what I had learned about hydraulics in Lester's school, but the fragments of ignorance outweighed those of knowledge and I could not think of a thing to do other than what we had already done. I fell back on reasoning that Braseman was the engineer and would eventually come up with the solution. Meanwhile the intensity of the rain had increased, which brought on so much static I could not surely identify the signals of Gander Range.

LaFrenier started singing again.

Robertson glared at the lever, gave a final hopeless tug, and then appeared to forget about it. We passed out of the squall and I was pleased to see the needle on the direction finder swing around on the Gander signal and point straight ahead. Now if Braseman would only fix the confounded hydraulic system we should be well on our way.

Where *was* Braseman? I suddenly realized that he was gone and had been absent for several minutes. I glanced over my right shoulder, intending to say something about first things first if he was back in the crew compartment having a cup of coffee. Braseman?

In turning, my eye caught a dull red glow at the top of the instrument panel. I forgot about Braseman momentarily. Now one of the fire warning lights was misbehaving, which was so common an occurrence in a C-54 that we had all long lost faith in their dire reports. They were small red glass boxes behind which a bulb was supposed to light up if a fire developed in any of the engines or various compartments in the airplane. But they cried wolf too often. Some malfunctioning, which the engineers had so far been unable to correct, caused them to light up across the instrument panel like a crazy pinball machine and sometimes report fires in all four engines when absolutely nothing was wrong. Occasionally the lights would flicker and then go out or they might remain on for hours—in which case we would remove the bulbs to avoid the glare. We were certain our senses, supplemented by the regular engine instruments, would inform us of any fires quite soon enough.

But this red light was marked "B," which meant that the alleged fire was in the cargo bin beneath the floor of the crew compartment. Robertson frowned at the light and said, "Now, what . . ."

I was disgusted. Where was Braseman and what about the hydraulic system? Then I remembered that a considerable assembly of the system was located in cargo bin "B." Perhaps if Braseman was down there working he might have bumped against the heat-sensitive switch and somehow set off the warning light.

I had just resolved to turn the flying over to Robertson and investigate when Braseman came running forward.

"There's a hell of a lot of smoke back in the passenger cabin! And it's starting to come up through the floor in the crew compartment! I think we'd better . . ."

Whatever it was that Braseman thought was lost upon us for he brought smoke with him like a devil's veil. But it was thin smoke still and I believed Braseman must be exaggerating—until I turned in my seat to look back at the crew compartment. LaFrenier had pulled back the curtain. Smoke, becoming heavier by the moment, gushed into the flight deck.

And fright took instant command of us all.

Braseman was tugging at the hydraulic control lever. "We've got to stop it working. . . ."

I saw the fire signal light marked "B." It was now a bright red. I pulled the extinguisher lever, which would flood the compartment with CO_2. The red light continued to burn and, if anything, the smoke seemed to become heavier.

Fright alone instructed me. I put the ship in a tight left bank, holding it until our course was reversed and we were headed back for Stevensville.

"Ditmeyer! Get an emergency clearance. Six thousand. Returning Stevensville."

LaFrenier called to me. "Twenty minutes back to Stevensville!" His voice was unnatural in its gravity, but then he had the wit to add a refinement. "Twenty minutes . . . *mais ou menos!*"

Mais ou menos—an old Natal way of expressing almost anything in doubt from the price of mosquito boots to hopes of transfer. LaFrenier said it exactly right, as if he really didn't care.

The smoke was thickening but was still no worse than in a crowded barroom. Now it had taken on a faintly acrid smell.

Braseman and Robertson were alternately tugging at the hydraulic lever. There were many profanities.

I saw the hydraulic pressure gauge beyond Robertson's right arm. It read three thousand seven hundred pounds! Something was going to give.

Twenty minutes—nineteen, maybe eighteen now.

We were on instruments. We could not descend because of the terrain. This was suddenly the slowest airplane in the world.

I cranked Stevensville on the direction finder. The needle swung around and held steadily. I saw my hand tremble when I took it away from the instrument. Where the hell was our clearance?

Ditmeyer seized the back of my seat and pulled himself forward.

"Cleared to cruise six thousand. Stevensville weather, three hundred feet variable . . . one mile . . . light rain . . . field closed."

I saw the field in my mind too clearly. It would be exactly as when we had left with the lower cloud base enveloping the rock hills and the runway ends dissolving into vapor. We would have to go through a long approach procedure—out over the western peninsula, turn, and back up the bay, thence creeping toward the sea edge of the field. Allow eight minutes as a minimum for the whole business. Eight minutes more pressure to build and a fire to smolder.

"Braseman. Lift the hatch. See if the fire is out."

He went back to the crew compartment. LaFrenier held the curtain aside. We watched Braseman pry at the hatch in the floor.

He raised it an inch or so and slammed it shut again. Smoke spewed up at him. He began a fit of coughing.

LaFrenier. Pray in your special way. Pray hard, if you will.

Now the smoke rushed forward. My whole body began to shake. My feet would not stay still on the rudder pedals. I coughed to conceal my trembling. My thoughts were a wild whirling mixture of frantic possibilities and technical demands. Should I chance a descent, hoping we might find a break down below? Land wheels up along the side of a hill or perhaps in a swamp? Suicide. Not a chance in a million. But anything was better than fire in the air.

Fright had passed. Fear, true fear, now possessed me. I felt it throughout my body like a devouring ague and I saw myself beginning to flounder, as if I were utterly detached. Our altitude had slipped two hundred feet. We were fifteen degrees off course. I thought I heard the others talking, or perhaps they were shouting. Their voices were without intelligence—mere sounds in the smoke.

It was suddenly much thicker. We were all coughing and our eyes wept. I could no longer see the instruments clearly or even Robertson, who sat so near.

All of this persisted for perhaps one minute. Then, as if he had emerged from the smoke, I saw Ross. And he was holding lighted matches in front of my nose as we descended into Newark. And I saw his sardonic smile and heard him say again, "Steady."

And the cringing left me. Fear remained, but I had it under control. Ross had said, "In this business we play for keeps."

Now let's get about that business.

I yanked open my side window. Doing so would create a draft in the ship, I knew, but we had to see and breathe. Smoke rushed past my face and my eyes protested. After a moment I closed the window.

Twelve minutes to go.

Looking at the red light, Braseman asked me if he should shoot some carbon tetrachloride into compartment B since the CO_2 had apparently failed. I rejected the idea, fearing the creation of poison gas.

Robertson opened his window, breathed deeply and shut it again.

The army sergeant in charge of the cabin appeared at my side. I asked him how the passengers were behaving.

"They're scared. What shall I tell them?"

"Anything."

Nine minutes.

I asked LaFrenier if he was certain of his estimate.

"Mais ou menos . . ."

Stalwart LaFrenier.

We could no longer tell if the smoke was getting better or worse. We endured it as long as we could and then opened the windows just long enough for quick relief. We were drowning in smoke, but so far there was no flame visible.

I tried to visualize compartment B. It could be entered from the belly of the ship, which was impossible in flight, or it could be entered through the floor hatch, which now seemed quite as impossible. The compartment was not very large and was used for stowing either cargo or baggage. It seemed an unlikely place for a fire.

Six minutes. The direction finder needle was steady now. When it began quivering we should be almost over the Stevensville range station. Six minutes and add eight more for the approach. I knew the last eight were going to be very long minutes.

My intestines were seething. For a moment I thought I would soil my pants.

I forced myself to explore B compartment again mentally. There was a mess of hydraulic pipes running through it. Because we could not disengage the system the oil would be passing through the pipes at tremendous speed and under increasingly greater pressure. The result would be heat—also of increasing intensity. There was a blockade somewhere. A very small poppet valve could set us aflame.

The compartment was lined with a heavy cloth padding. The pipes ran between the padding and the aluminum skin of the ship.

If the overheated pipes set the padding afire, then the skin would go next. And aluminum burned like a torch.

How silly to die because of a bit of metal I could hold in the palm of my hand.

Time could be our final enemy on this morning. How long did it take a smoldering piece of cloth to ignite and serve as kindling for aluminum? Two minutes . . . ten minutes?

There was a hand bottle of CO_2 hanging between the crew bunks. I told Braseman to pry up the hatch again and shoot the contents into B compartment until the bottle was exhausted.

When he had done the smoke became unbearable. Yet if we opened the windows a terrific draft would be created.

We needed three more minutes to the range station and then those eight for an approach. I resolved to cut some corners and make the approach in four.

We coughed, sucked at our cupped hands, and writhed in our seats.

Robertson had the good sense to clamp on his oxygen mask.

I imitated him at once, pressing the mask hard against my face. The result was extremely painful. Somehow the smoke seemed more concentrated in the mask. Two daggers probed my nostrils. I threw the mask on the floor.

Robertson and Braseman had abandoned their efforts with the control lever. I could not blame them. Physical effort was intolerable with suffocation so near.

But I *had* to concentrate. Ross was holding the match.

The direction finder needle began to quiver. Even our gasping subsided. We lived on little half-breaths.

Now, at best another minute.

A spasm of rain lashed the windshield and we passed into moderate turbulence. I wanted very much to hit the range station exactly. It was very important.

The turbulence ceased and suddenly a lightening in the overcast caused me to glance out my side window. And that instant I believed in miracles. For there was a hole in the overcast which shafted almost straight down. And at the bottom of the hole I saw the crisscross design of the Stevensville runways. The hole was of no greater dimensions than our wingspread, and optics caused it to appear even smaller at the bottom. But there, six thousand feet below, was our salvation.

Under ordinary circumstances I should have ignored such a sucker hole. They were snares for the foolish. The hole could close as quickly as it had opened. If we were caught circling blind between the rock hills, we would be in an even worse situation.

I had only a few seconds to accept or reject the invitation.

I saw it as an offering of time.

So I impulsively chopped the throttles full back, wrapped the ship in a near vertical bank, and tried to stay within the vaporous confines of the hole. I yelled at Robertson to slam the landing gear down and shoved the nose over in a steep dive. It was a crazy maneuver in a big, heavily loaded, four-engined airplane. Such violent acrobatics belonged in an air circus, but we needed minutes.

We spiraled down in a near vertical bank. Our high right wing sliced continuously through the walls of the hole. But I could see from my side—straight down. And the crisscross pattern of the runways revolved like the spokes of a slow turning wheel.

The only sound was the erratic backfiring of our engines and the rumbling of our slip stream. Somehow our steep angle of attack seemed to reduce the smoke. I could see that the runways were wet with rain.

Robertson called for an immediate clearance to land.

We were descending at two thousand feet per minute. The airplane was extremely stiff on the controls, yet it behaved like a fighter. I renewed my love affair with Douglas airplanes though a two-headed monster now arrived on the scene.

We could not use any power and stay within the confines of the hole. The engines were cooling far below prescribed limits. We could only hope they would catch again and give us power when most needed.

Passing through three thousand feet, I saw that the hole extended only to the perimeter of the field. The adjacent buildings were hidden beyond the misty lips of the shaft. How much room would there be *underneath* the cloud mass? We needed maneuvering room to break away from our spiral and execute a landing.

We could not see the bay or the hills or anything else except the very center of the field. It was a beautiful target, but we had no wish to make a bull's-eye.

I tightened the spiral until our cheeks sagged.

I now was so involved with these problems I almost forgot about the smoke or what might be happening in compartment B.

Not a word passed between us as the earth rose swiftly.

I wished LaFrenier would sing.

At four hundred feet there were tatters in the mouth of the hole. I eased the bank and gunned the engines twice. They protested in a long series of backfires, but they caught.

At three hundred feet I saw a dim division in the overcast, then a faint scraggly line which marked the shore of the bay. If we could make the water we could make the field on a level approach, though the ceiling might be almost nil.

I rolled the ship out of the bank and made a final dive for the scraggly line. We held our breaths until it became a definite reality.

Robertson handled the throttles for I had no time to consider engine pressures. We were at two hundred feet, heavily loaded, and the gear was down. There was no horizon and the smoke in the cockpit remained. The field was now behind us and we were over the bay. My sole devotion was air speed. Too little and we would stall, too much and we would overshoot the field when we reversed the course. As I began the final turn Robertson called out continuously.

"One sixty . . . one sixty . . . one fifty-five . . . one fifty-two . . . one *forty-five* . . ."

We were headed back in the direction of the field. I called for fifteen degrees of flaps.

"One forty . . . one forty . . . one *thirty* . . ."

Where was the shore again?

There . . . and the end of the northeast runway. Both loomed very suddenly ahead.

"Full flaps!"

We swooped down and as the wet runway slithered beneath our nose I saw fire trucks waiting in line. Before the landing roll was completed we had yanked open the windows and gulped at fresh air.

There were several curious things about this morning, one of which had to do with the almost instant deterioration of some men's judgment when pressure is relieved. There was also a serio-comic display of the acumen characteristic of crowds in fear.

And there were other things we could not analyze so blithely.

In the first instance I was so grateful to be alive and on the good ground that whatever thinking processes had so far compelled me ceased altogether and at once. For what I did automatically, with the fire trucks trailing uselessly behind, was to taxi the airplane at high speed to its usual loading position and there stop it. This position was directly over underground tanks which contained many thousands of gallons of high-octane gasoline. Fortunately the fire crews extinguished the still-minor conflagration in compartment B before my stupidity could create a holocaust.

Next, the heavy smoke in the cabin created understandable concern among the passengers. When it seemed they were very near panic, the sergeant in charge of the cabin told them there was really nothing to worry about since what they saw was only *carbon monoxide*.

This statement, incredibly, broke the tension and the passengers relaxed.

Finally there was the weather. The hole through which we had descended closed completely five minutes after we were on the ground. Whether the minutes saved prevented a full fire and an inevitable mid-air explosion remained conjecture—but this fact was undeniable.

In the weather office we learned that our blessed hole which was so precisely over the airport had been the only known break in the cloud mass for seven hundred miles.[14]

✦

X V I

A PRETENDER

✦

HOW ONE FINE MAN IS ILL-USED BY FATE
AND ANOTHER DARES DECEIVE IT

No ONE of us could find a satisfactory explanation of why the handsome Watkins ceased to exist. At one moment he was alive and reporting on the radio in his normal, vibrant voice. There was the usual hint of contemptuous mischief in his tone which even electronics could never eradicate, and then there was—silence. Moments later his lithe body was mixed with bits of machinery and the hard earth and stone of a mountain ridge near Stevensville. It was the same ridge which might have taken us, had we not cheated the fire.

Now Watkins was dead, the Watkins who had stretched his long legs across the way of Lester pacing a classroom so long ago, the Watkins who had first sighted O'Connor in the wilderness, the joyous, exuberant Watkins was gone without a hand flipped in farewell, and this seemed altogether incongruous. He had struck upon the ridge which enfolds the bay to the west. For no conceivable reason, that was the last of his nights, and it was of no comfort to consider that four additional minutes of that night would have seen him quite safely on the ground. Then he could have swaggered down from his ship as was his way, cap tilted jauntily, grinning as if he was about to divulge some very special secret.

But Watkins was denied those four minutes. The technical result if not the reasoning for this was obvious. By design, decree, or accident, the distance between his swift-moving airplane and the earth had suddenly been reduced to nil. It was nearly impossible to believe that a pilot of Watkins' experience and cleverness could have made a mistake of such consequence; therefore we sought in every way otherwise to excuse and forgive the tragedy.

So Watkins joined Gay and Charleton; and since we had all been comrades in Lester's school, I could not resist a gloomy counting of numbers which had nothing to do with seniority. In the process a little more of the gaiety leaked away from my own flying, for it seemed that such gaiety would ever be poor mimicry of Watkins, and he should be respected even in absentia.

Soon afterward Bethel and Smith flew into a thunderstorm near Hanford, California, and their airplane came apart in all components.

Twenty-six days later Snowden and Bamberger hit the mountains on an instrument approach to Burbank.

Forty days later McCauley and Eitner did almost exactly the same thing.

Forty-three days later, near Rural Retreat, Virginia, Stroud and Brigman flew into the mountains.

We could too easily identify ourselves with these men. Yet the confidence which lures a man to a life of flight in the first place is almost indestructible. He believes, he *must* believe absolutely, in his personal fortune and destiny. It is, therefore, always a status in which an overly inquisitive attitude is dangerous, and prolonged brooding becomes intolerable.

Thus the constant shuttling back and forth across the Western Hemisphere continued remorselessly and the loss of individuals could not stay it any more than a rock can interrupt the surf. Very few of us had any idea that when the war was done every ocean sky would echo with the faint drumming of aircraft engines. We thought the peacetime citizen of the world would return to steamships and we would, if lucky, return to our regular domestic flying. Month after month my own pattern remained like the others— ascent, cruise, and descent, from and into Greenland, Scotland, France, the Azores, North Africa, Brazil, Bermuda.

On all of these flights LaFrenier stood his post as navigator, singing his repertoire of maddening lyrics, cheerful in spite of an occasional cursing from those who lacked his sublime faith. I trusted LaFrenier as implicitly as any commander of a long-range aircraft can trust anyone but himself. Robertson remained as copilot most of the time although his place was sometimes taken by a small and extraordinarily defiant Irishman named Donahue. Another occasional intruder upon Robertson's province was Mays, whose mind had not had time to fix itself inescapably in the grooves of professional flight and who therefore, during the long nights over the ocean, became a welcome stimulus to each of us.

The Germans had surrendered. There were now six thousand five hundred seventy-two hours and twenty-seven minutes in my logbook, and thus far I had never put a scratch on an airplane. Possibly this had something to do with my appointment as cocaptain on a special flight with the diminutive Burns. In a travesty of every major Roman victory, we flew General Mark Clark from Paris to Chicago, serving as charioteers to a carefully manufactured triumph. Others of our group were identically engaged in delivering Generals Eisenhower and Patton to the convenient adulation of multitudes in New York and Los Angeles. Our enthusiasm for these special flights was somewhat less than the supposed honor involved. For a long time we had been flying litter ships, bringing back the wreckage of younger men whose marvelous triumph was breathing. In sharp contrast to the accommodations provided the generals, these ships were arranged three and four litters high along both sides of the cabin and were always overcrowded. They stank of every elimination which can escape from the human body, but mostly they reeked of quick decay, shock, disinfectant, and blood. Yet none of this seemed to matter, neither the bottles hanging alongside the litters and connected by tubes to the occupants, nor the collapsed areas of blankets where limbs should have been, nor the astonished eyes of a hurt creature peering from a bundle of gauze. Litter ships were an innovation and a majority of the men in them were but a few hours out of combat. Almost before they had time to contemplate their personal disasters they were on the way home. Thus, in spite of wounds, their spirits were unbelievably high and a sort of ecstasy pervaded the whole ship. And the ugliness, which was the reality, was somehow defeated.

When the Japanese surrendered I managed a leave of absence. I convinced myself there was now need and opportunity for contemplation without the accompanying sound of engines. I had looked suspiciously at my crumpled, beaten flight bag and wondered if it must be my close companion forever.

So I went to one of the few places in the world where no airplane was likely to be seen and wandered about long, white, desolate beaches, as an alcoholic might force himself into denial. I should have known better, having witnessed others attempt the same separation. For I knew of no man who had flown as a way of life and ever succeeded in turning his back on flight.

My own attempt was a quick failure.

It was June and the return to AM-21 was such a dreamlike regression to a former life that even the summer fields and trees and the various subtleties of each familiar airport seemed to have resisted all change. Yet nostalgia was soon mired in boredom. I no longer found it satisfying to fly a little DC-3 in a series of hedge-hops over the countryside. I felt confined, and the red-faced, volcanic Clark of Labrador, Scotland, and the Hump, who came along on the first flight to reintroduce me officially to my old

route, understood perfectly. He shared this readjustment to domestic flying and also found it an uneasy spell of fretting and
restlessness. After giving so much to the development of long-
range flight most of us felt we might have some little right to
inherit certain ocean routes. This soon proved to be a childish
delusion, born in complete innocence of power and politics. Pan
American took all but the crumbs and we were greatly disappointed.

Meanwhile Stoner and Baker had crashed against Thing Mountain in California. Once again the true reasons for descent below
the known level of terrain baffled the investigators.

It was far easier to explain how luck had turned upon Keim,
the ultraconservative of flying men. His caution and craftiness
against weather and the misbehavior of machinery should have
assured his flying for many years.

I reached the hospital as soon as I could. And there lay Keim
upon a rolling table. His ruddy face made the same contrast with
the sheet as it had so often in frowsy hotel rooms and the miserable
bunk in Natal.

I stood looking down at him and saw only a faint bruise on his
forehead. His mouth slid to one side of his face and he rasped a
greeting which convinced me nothing could be very wrong.

"What the hell do you want?"

"I heard you had an accident. I didn't have anything else to do
so I thought I'd stop by and waste some time."

Knowing any insult would please him, I said that while I had
always suspected his head was abnormally hard I never thought
he would try to prove it so violently. Then I asked him what had
happened.

His growling answer was muted, but the insolent scorn was still
there.

"We landed just after midnight. It's on the logbook so, by God,
I can prove I was sober. I was driving the co-pilot and the stewardess home. A drunk rammed us at the intersection. I was thrown
out and hit my head on a curbstone. We were all shaken up but

no one else was hurt. I have a hell of a headache. So what else is new?"

I thought what else was new and wondered if this was the time to tell him.

"I'm flying to San Francisco this afternoon."

An eyebrow waggled, but he remained silent for a moment. Then he said, "Since when did they stretch AM-21 to the coast?"

"Sloniger called me. He's chief pilot of a new service started by a steamship line. I'll be flying to Honolulu."

"You're an idiot. What about your seniority? What's one ocean or the other? All oceans belong to Pan American, irrevocably, absolutely, by order of God and the President of the United States."

I told him the steamship line had immense financial resources and all would be well.

"They'll lose every dime they've got."

I left Keim perfectly confident in his future, for even as I went out the door he was grumbling peevishly about the stupidity of my decision. That, I thought, is a perfectly normal Keim. The king of crosspatches was still on his throne.

So I left with a light heart, savoring the thought that if the steamship air line did survive, my seniority number could hardly be higher than two, and even Keim would have to admit that was a pleasing number to hold.

I could not know that Keim would soon be called upon to demonstrate a new and far more difficult kind of courage. Nor could I envisage the difficulties and one very near disaster awaiting me.

In a week I was wearing a new uniform and it was ever so fancy, with embroidered golden wings, four gold stripes, and a white-topped cap to frost the display. Accustomed to operating luxury liners, the steamship company was determined to fly in style. They provided the most luxurious airplanes anyone had ever beheld and every resource of the great company was placed at our disposal. It all promised wonderfully well, particularly so because the veteran Sloniger was in direct charge of the flying. If he had surrendered his precious number 1 on our own line, then certainly I could risk my miserable 267.

We waited impatiently as the preparations for the first flights were completed. And during this time I met Captain Dudley.

Sloniger explained that Dudley had been employed by the steamship line even before he had arrived. "We sort of inherit him," he said.

Dudley was a fascinating personality, so beguiling in manner that it was easy to become his willing audience. He was a lover of complication and theorizing. I envied his ability to manipulate a slide rule as if it were an extension of his fingers. My own wet-the-end-of-the-pencil technique of solving long-range flying problems was obviously inferior.

According to Dudley, all of the long-range flying either Sloniger or myself had done in the past had been wrongly accomplished. If we were to believe his elaborate series of graphs and charts we were lucky to be alive. We could not specify how Dudley managed to cast such a spell over us. We had only to examine our own records against his to bring us to our senses, but his persuasiveness was of such magical quality that we failed to do so—until later. And all of this time I was additionally distracted by the haunting, inescapable notion that I had seen or known of Dudley somewhere before.

Dudley was a big man and heavily built, although his sallow complexion and baked-potato physique gave no suggestion of either good health or strength. His eyes were gray and distant and at first it was difficult to detect the wildness in them. His evangelical style of speech was inoffensive because there were always threads of humility which he wove through his phrases so dexterously they were to be sensed rather than heard. The total effect of any argument or even daily commentary by this man was mesmerizing—so lulling to reason that he could make the most outrageous statements utterly convincing.

Dudley's face was peckled with time and peculiar indentations which were more like the rotting of loam than a souvenir of some pox. These minute craters gave his features a crumpled, indefinite look, as if he could change their context and relation by simply molding the skin with his fingers. Sometime during the war he had crashed in a training plane and as a result bore a long scar which extended from the lobe of one ear to the center of his chin. In spite of his physical shortcomings Dudley was abnormally vain and never seemed to miss an opportunity to view himself in any mirror.

I first began to wonder about Dudley when he stood overlong before a mirror in the hangar washroom one afternoon pushing at his malleable face and thoughtfully caressing his scar.

"How do I look?" he asked.

"What do you mean, how do you look?" It was simply a question uncommon between men and I could not think of a proper answer.

Then his voice became almost demanding. "I asked you how I looked?"

"You look fine. Just like you did a while ago."

I remembered that this was the second time he had found a mirror in that one day.

"Do you think people notice my scar?"

"What difference does it make?"

"I wish it didn't go so far down on my chin."

He stood there fingering the scar, kneading his tactile face, and muttering some complaint about his luck which I found easier to ignore. I left Dudley still absorbed in self-adoration.

I was unaware that Sloniger, ever the wisest of pelicans, was also having difficulty understanding Captain Dudley.

This weird mistrust, entirely without cause, became even stronger soon after we took off on the steamship line's inaugural flight to Honolulu. Since this was a very special event attended with considerable ceremony, Sloniger himself was in command. I served as his first officer and Dudley was designated as navigator. He had let it be known that among his other accomplishments he held a master mariner's license and had been captain of several ocean-going ships before his heart led him to flying. In this he was as totally convincing as in any other aspect of his career. Since nautical lore was my hobby I had hoped to learn much from

Dudley, but thus far he had always managed to elude my earnest questioning.

Dudley boarded this flight with an astonishing collection of paraphernalia. In addition to his octant and hack watch, he carried a great bundle of charts, a heavy folder of graphs, extra triangles, an antiquated air force wind computer, and a set of parallel rules which would have seemed more appropriate aboard a Cape Horn square-rigger. He solemnly distributed this gear over an enormous navigation table which he had caused to be built into the space normally used for crew bunks. We were busy with our flight duties and paid little attention to him.

It was a magnificent, clear night and we flew into it with extra zest and satisfaction because here again was a fresh enterprise and we were entrusted with its actual execution. In the morning we would be in Honolulu and if our much-promoted arrival marked new competition for Pan American, then the work would be doubly sweet.

My respect for Sloniger was enormous and so I had no objection whatsoever to flying as his co-pilot. Watching his leathered, thoughtful face in the subdued light of the cockpit, intrigued as always by the easy, flowing movements of his expressive hands, I found it very right and delightful to be over the sea again and to talk with Sloniger about other flights now long completed, and what this one would signify.

We flew westward for almost two hours before Sloniger cocked his head and said in his easy, always unhurried way, "I wonder what's happened to our navigator."

Customarily the captain is given some kind of a report at least once each hour and the course being flown is verified. We had not seen or heard from Dudley since take-off.

I said that I would go back and have a look.

Since he had appropriated the crew compartment for his duties, Dudley worked behind the green curtain which was designed to keep light from the flight deck. I found him bent over a collection of graphs which were totally unfamiliar to me. He appeared to be in deep concentration. Having done my own navigation and being thus very aware how certain questions can come at just the wrong time, I stretched my arms and pretended to take the kinks out of my back before I asked him how we were doing.

"I haven't taken a fix yet."

For a moment I stood listening to the steady drumming of the engines, which were only a few feet from us and directly in line with our position in the ship. I was shocked. Could I have misunderstood Dudley or was he joking? According to our time in flight we must be nearly four hundred miles from land and yet he had not bothered to make any check against wind or course. I looked at his chart, which covered the ocean area between the California coast and the Hawaiian Islands. There was not a mark on it.

"I think the skipper would like a fix right now. We've got a position report coming up in ten minutes."

As if Dudley didn't know, I thought—or certainly should know. "Sure."

He picked up his octant and watch, then turned off the light. After several collisions with the bulkhead in the forward passageway and a brief entanglement with the green curtain, he managed to mount his navigator's stool. So placed, his head projected into the Plexiglas astrodome, enabling him to observe the stars. It was a strangely clumsy performance for anyone accustomed to navigation, but I considered his size in relation to the confined space and for the moment thought little of it.

I rejoined Sloniger on the flight deck. We waited.

Ordinarily the navigator of an aircraft requires about eight minutes in his astrodome. During this period he can easily take observations on three stars and a skilled man who has taken the trouble to precompute the various altitudes and azimuths usually prefers to shoot five stars. When he is done with the actual octant work he descends from his stool, completes his final calculations, and graphically plots the various intersecting lines of the position on the chart. All of this requires a maximum of fifteen minutes, and quick men like LaFrenier could often be finished in ten.

Twenty minutes after he had mounted his stool, Dudley was still in the astrodome.

Meanwhile, for lack of anything better, Sloniger had given the radio operator a position report based on his own dead-reckoning. He was squirming unhappily in his seat, glancing back at the dark shadow of Dudley's bulk and looking at me quizzically, as if I could provide an explanation.

I was about to ask Dudley if he was stuck permanently in the astrodome when he descended. Moments later the light in his compartment flashed on. We waited. We waited in reasonable patience because Dudley's peculiar spell was still upon us and we had no doubt that he would soon appear with a satisfactory explanation for the delay. At last Sloniger told me to go back once more and investigate. Previously, Dudley had been almost fawningly ever-present. Now he shunned our company.

I passed through the green curtain. As before, Dudley was bent over his table. He had taken off his uniform coat, and his shirt was soaked with perspiration. He pointed at his chart as if he had just wrought a miracle.

"There we are!" he said grandly.

I looked at the lines on his chart, which formed a wide isosceles triangle, the interior of which could easily have represented an area of fifty miles. It reminded me of the very first celestial fixes I had plotted in Lester's school and was just about as useful.

I asked him why he had only shot three stars.

"All I could get. There's some scattered clouds above us."

I could not remember having noticed any clouds during my time on the flight deck, but Dudley being Dudley it seemed unreasonable to question his word.

"It took me a long time to get things lined up," he added. "I seem to have something in my right eye and that's the one I'm accustomed to use. You know how that is."

I did know how it was, but I hardly expected him to lift the lid of his eye and ask for sympathy.

"Do you see anything?" he asked, rubbing his eye and then pulling the lid up and down again.

He went to the mirror over the washbasin and poked at his gum-like face while he rolled his eyes around and around. Then he seemed to become entranced with his scar and for a moment I thought he was going to ask me how he looked again, but he did not.

I suggested he take his position report forward to Sloniger.

"I was just going to do that."

Then I asked him if he would mind if I took a fix, explaining it had been a long time since my last efforts and I needed the practice.

"Go right ahead. Sure, any time."

I did need the practice. It had been nearly a year, and relying on LaFrenier had spoiled me. Standing in the gloom of the astro-dome, I was very glad that I had at least made it a custom person-ally to take one fix on each ocean leg of our Atlantic flights. But one fix is a bare minimum to maintain skill, and I thought La-Frenier would have had glorious fun chiding my ineptness. I was so rusty it took me almost as long as Dudley to descend from the astrodome with observations of Capella, Rigel, and Dubhe. And I was all thumbs when it came to plotting the lines.

At least, I thought, my triangle is smaller than Dudley's. I was more pleased that the position it indicated agreed very reasonably with Dudley's plot. Then the fleeting notion Dudley might not be altogether sure of himself was ridiculous. I wanted very much to believe he was as expert as he claimed. After all, he would deter-mine our point-of-no-return, our course changes and drift, and our fuel reserve. And we must depend upon his calculations for a best plan of operation if we should be so unfortunate as to encounter strong head winds or lose an engine.

Now only one thing remained to disturb me. When I stood in the astrodome, I had seen no indication of Dudley's scattered clouds. The heavens had been an explosion of stars, hundreds of which dribbled right down to the darkness that was the sea.

Throughout the balance of the flight Dudley remained strangely aloof. However, he did furnish us with the proper series of position reports. They were always slow in coming but matched our own dead-reckoning calculations so closely we had no further cause for concern.

The "steamship" airline was set up so that we flew a gigantic triangle with the tips at Los Angeles, Honolulu, and Seattle. We would frequently bisect this pattern by flying directly from Oakland to Honolulu or vice versa. Passengers could purchase a round-trip ticket which gave them the choice of flying one way and taking the steamship the other, as they pleased. If they wished they could ship their heavy baggage on the line's surface ships at no extra charge. The food on the airplane was served at a regular table, steamship style, and had to be seen to be believed. Partridge or guinea hen with wild rice, squab, pheasant, magnificent stands of roast beef with truffles, plus the finest wines and liquors, were all included. The meals were served by a professional steamship steward complete with napkin over forearm. The two stewardesses were chosen by a committee obviously concerned with beauty. Flight crews were paid full salary whether they flew or not, and our consequent enthusiasm for this dream airline was exceeded only by that of our delighted passengers.

All of this troubled Pan American, and their determination to eliminate such competition became even grimmer. Our airplanes were full and theirs were not. There was every indication that in a few years this would become the finest airline in the world. Pilot, navigator, and engineer applications came in from every recognized airline, which enabled Sloniger to keep the standards so high that few could qualify.

Since Dudley was already employed, he was at first taken for granted. It was my lot to uncover a fault in him which soon led to minor defeats and eventually to pure tragedy. For I commanded the second flight to Honolulu and Dudley was assigned as my co-pilot. Smith, a fine navigator of much experience, took over the navigational duties. I was delighted with the entire crew.

But Dudley was far from content. He kept muttering about his temporary assignment as co-pilot and said quite openly that our positions should be reversed. He pointed several times to the four gold stripes on his sleeve as if the gaudy bits of cloth could remedy the situation. This was a new Dudley to me—a more puzzling man than ever. I was sympathetic to his complaints at first and then tried to be amused because I thought that for just one flight he was behaving childishly. Hoping to divert his thoughts and soothe his pride, I asked him to take the left-hand seat and do the flying for a spell.

He sat down grumpily, heaving his bulk from side to side as if it were impossible for him to find a comfortable position. The airplane was flying on the automatic pilot and from time to time he would adjust the control knobs slightly according to need of altitude or course. The work seemed to ease his resentment and I tried to forget that a man who had offered so many refreshing ideas on long-range flight seemed to be of less personal stature than I had supposed. And I was now convinced my memory had tricked me. I had never seen or met Dudley before.

There was a front approximately halfway between San Francisco and Honolulu. Moderate to heavy rain plus some turbulence had been reported by other planes which had flown through it. When we entered the eastern fringes of this weather area I asked Dudley to take the ship off the auto-pilot and fly manually. I much valued an auto-pilot, but along with most other captains I also believed they were potentially dangerous in heavy turbulence. There was no way of estimating how much rough air we should now encounter.

Dudley made no move to disengage the auto-pilot. He sat at ease, running the tip of one finger along his scar, staring at the curlicues and intricate liquid designs the rain was creating on the windshield. I thought he might not have heard my request and repeated it.

"Why? We're doing all right."

A regular co-pilot would have been obliged to obey, but Dudley was in a different position. When one captain flies with another, mutual respect and understanding preclude a direct order.

I told him I would be more comfortable with the auto-pilot disengaged and added that perhaps I was getting old.

Now Dudley leaned across to me and began in his most winning way to tell of a thunderstorm he had flown through a few years before. Again the spell descended. It was of such peculiar power that I believed him when he described the wildness of the storm. I had learned to expect Dudley would emerge the hero because his sense of flying modesty was unpredictable, but throughout this adventure he remained a sorely distressed man—saved by the auto-pilot. It had brought him safely through turbulence he himself could not have mastered.

"All the same I think we'll fly for a while without this one."

I waved my hand at his control wheel and saw him reach for it. Then I yanked up the auto-pilot release, levers. This was my prerogative and even Dudley recognized the futility of protesting. I went back to a study of the weather chart and then had a brief discussion with Snow, the engineer, about transferring fuel. I was so engaged for perhaps six minutes when I noticed our magnetic-compass heading was some twenty degrees to the south of what it had been. I began a search of the shelf area beneath the compass which is a catchall in every airplane. I expected to find a wrench or a screw driver which some mechanic might have forgotten, or perhaps even a camera light-meter left behind by a member of a previous crew. Of all the instruments in any airplane the ancient and honorable compass is the most fundamental. Its very simplicity makes it trouble-free and it can be relied upon absolutely—unless someone carelessly leaves a piece of metal nearby.

There was nothing on the shelf except a pack of cigarettes. I lighted one and watched the compass suspiciously. Slowly, a few degrees at a time, our course was swinging more and more to the south. This was like searching for O'Connor. There must be an iron mine in the middle of the ocean.

I looked at the two gyro compasses which were merely mechanical echoes of the basic magnetic compass and were set according to its dictates. They all matched within a few degrees. It was inconceivable that Dudley would have changed course so radically without advising me, yet there was no other explanation.

"Whither are we bound?" I asked in a way that I hoped Dudley would take as a joke and reply with a sensible reason.

"Bound?" He looked at me as if he had not understood, and

again I saw the strange emptiness in his eyes—almost, it seemed, an inability to take in what I was saying. I pointed at the compass.

"That way lies Tahiti. Much as I'd like to go there, I don't think we have quite enough fuel to make it."

"Oh . . ." Dudley looked at the compass as if he'd never seen it before. Then, to my astonishment, he started a turn to the left which would only compound the error.

I said, "Hey . . . hey . . . hey . . ." and waggled my thumb to the right. And, very slowly, Dudley obliged. I glanced over my shoulder at Smith, the navigator. I wanted confirmation that I had not dozed off and had a sudden nightmare. Here was an airline captain turning over twenty-five degrees off course and not knowing it, or apparently not knowing it, and then, in an effort to correct, turning the wrong way and apparently not knowing *that!*

The look on Smith's face was quite enough. I had not been dreaming.

We flew on in embarrassed silence. The intensity of the rain increased for a time and with it came some light turbulence. I turned on the "seat belt" sign and after a very brief period turned it off again. Yet in my estimation Dudley was flying all over the sky. He managed to hold our course within five or ten degrees, but now his altitude was varying from three to five hundred feet within a matter of minutes. I was appalled at his seeming lack of co-ordination. Finally he said that he had suddenly developed a stinging headache and asked if I would mind relieving him. He wondered aloud if he had eaten something before take-off which might have poisoned him.

We exchanged seats and he seemed much relieved. Later, when we emerged from the western extremity of the front, he took over the flying again. There was a half-moon and a vast pastry shop of ghostly puff cumulus clouds below. Above them the stars glistened, and in such an environment Dudley at once regained his vast confidence.

This peculiar Jekyll and Hyde behavior continued throughout the round-trip flight. Dudley flew well enough when we were in fine weather, but when instrument conditions prevailed he became morose and his technique was incredibly bad. He said that a considerable time had passed since his last spell of instrument flying, an explanation which at last convinced me something must be very wrong with Captain Dudley. An experienced pilot returning to instrument flight after long separation may take a few hours to regain smoothness and absolute accuracy, but he does not wander all over the sky.

In a moment of misguided generosity I decided to give Dudley the landing when we returned to Oakland.

In all the time I had spent instructing in this type aircraft I had never witnessed such a performance, and it occurred to me that I could have taken any man on the street, placed his hands on the controls, and said, "Now there is the airport and the long strip of concrete you see is the runway. Aim the airplane at the end of the runway and just hold everything until you feel us hit."

So flew Dudley—straight at the earth. I could not believe my eyes. In the last seconds, when it became all too obvious he was frozen on this suicidal track and had no intention of flaring out our glide angle, I hauled back on the control column and we hit on three points instead of on the nose wheel alone. We were going so fast it took nearly the whole of Oakland airport to stop. My flying nerve fibers twanged even more shrill a note when I saw that Dudley seemed pleased with his performance.

The next day I reluctantly told Sloniger that I thought Captain Dudley needed a flight check before he was allowed to take out a flight under his own command.

All airline captains must take a flight check every ninety days. In this way faults are corrected before they become habit, and various emergency situations are created: fires are started, engines cut out, radio and electronic failures simulated, and unusual navigational problems presented. Pilots are graded according to their performance. Failure is extremely rare and even then it is usually the result of a minor mistake which is corrected after a few hours' practice on the specific maneuver.

Such checks are inevitably more complicated and likely to hazard than any regular passenger flights. An airline pilot accepts this as a part of his livelihood, although it is easier to forget those occasions when the practiced emergency becomes the real thing. Nilsen was killed in this way, as were Elder, and Stehle, then Hearn and Day, then Weeks and McKeirnan, then Winkler, Christensen and Kennedy, then Galt and Render, then Angstadt and Worthington, then Garrard and Gessner, then Kocher, Wilson and Moen, and then Swain, Jeberjahn, and Job.

"Simulators" fixed to the ground, in which any emergency or problem can be artificially reproduced, have done much to cut this toll, but any learning demands a penalty, and in aircraft there is still no substitute for the genuine. An airline pilot is paid for more than sitting grandly aloft and watching the lovely white clouds float past.

To this principle Dudley apparently did not subscribe. He was furious when Sloniger advised him a check flight was due and he went through all manner of excuses and procrastinations to avoid it.

I was blessedly absent when the unavoidable debacle took place. Once again Dudley flew the airplane directly into the ground and only quick action on Sloniger's part saved the landing. But this was as nothing. While aloft Dudley was required to perform various maneuvers on instruments. The cockpit window on his side was covered with a louvered device known as a hood. His performance, when he could see no farther than his instruments, was atrocious. Yet Sloniger was determined to give him every chance to prove himself. He set up a routine navigation problem which was customary on all check flights. The confused, sweating Dudley flew in circles and impossibly erratic courses for over an hour without finding his goal—Oakland Airport. It was almost directly beneath him throughout the entire procedure.

Sloniger was more puzzled than exasperated. How could a man of Dudley's experience be so wrong on every count? He had no choice but to ground him.

The intrepid Dudley was not in the slightest abashed. Instead, he accused Sloniger of deliberately seeking to confuse him, of unfair demands, and many other prejudices. He would see his lawyer unless he was returned to flying status at once. He insisted on another check flight to prove his arguments.

Sloniger obliged. He arranged for Dudley to fly with a government inspector who could not possibly be accused of partiality.

If anything, Dudley's exhibition before the inspector was even more grotesque. It was so bad the inspector insisted on retaining Dudley's license until he could set his aerial wits in order by rest or practice. It was then that Dudley's fantastic, real-life fairy tale collapsed in the processional style of Greek tragedy.

"Captain" Dudley could not turn over his airline transport license to the inspector simply because he had never possessed one. The only license he held was a "Commercial" and even that relatively simple ticket failed to carry an instrument flight rating. He had never flown any ocean. Almost all his logged hours were entirely a product of his imagination. The only airline experience he had ever had was a few weeks on an eastern airline, after which he was discharged "for lack of aptitude." Almost everything he knew of navigation, his celestial work, his experimental graphs, and his complicated theorizing had been painfully acquired from books and a careful memory for what men of actual experience had said.

To my own astonishment, I subsequently discovered that the salt-encrusted old master mariner had never actually held a sea command. And finally, through a series of clues, the persistent fancy that I had known Dudley before resolved itself. He was the man who had not only talked himself into an eastern airline but had previously employed his verbal magic on the same men of the State Department who had sent me off to South America. There had been a special mission to study the rubber situation in the Amazon country. The airplane employed was a small seaplane and Dudley was the pilot. He considered it unnecessary to trouble his employers with the mere detail that he had never flown a seaplane. By a sequence of wonders he managed to fly the seaplane all the way to the Amazon without serious incident. There his incredible luck ran out and he destroyed the airplane during an attempted landing. Fortunately neither Dudley nor his passengers were injured.

In some respects Dudley was a very brave man although his

twisted courage and monstrous gall eventually led him to tragedy. Certainly he was not entirely to blame for the temporary success of his deception. During the entirety of my own career, *no person* ever asked to examine the actual bit of paper which set forth my qualifications! Nor did anyone in authority ever bother to check my logbooks.

So our inclination was to pity this sick man rather than to vilify him. There was a sort of grand pathos about Dudley. It was not until his crazed ambition led to the death of innocent passengers that we held him in loathing. After his brief affair with the steamship airline and the discovery of his hoax, we were certain that he would vanish discreetly from the aviation scene. We again misjudged the man.

XVII

A CERTAIN EMBARRASSMENT

. . . THE URGE TO SHIFT BLAME BECOMES EVEN UGLIER WHEN THE ACCUSED HAS LEFT THE FEAST

BELOW, the night fog has stolen in upon San Francisco Bay according to custom. It is no more than a hundred feet thick and hence a glowing amber from the lights within its depths. The towers of the Bay Bridge and those of the Golden Gate protrude above the fog like channel buoys in a nether-world sea. And the hills to the west and north of the city form dim islands floating upon an ocean of vapor. There are stars above all this and the visibility is unlimited.

We are bound for Honolulu again. Drake, an ex-navy transport pilot, occupies the first officer's seat. He is given to courtly manners and his military parlance is still much with him. Smith, the navigator, is behind him. He waits in the darkness of the flight deck until we have reached cruising altitude. He is blond, soft-spoken, and very tall. Standing near him in the flight deck gloom is Hayes, equally as tall. Both men are much given to apologies when their six-foot-three bulks collide.

Hayes is the second officer, also ex-navy, and also an excellent pilot. He will relieve either Drake or myself as the flight progresses and hence there will always be two men on actual flying duty. They do things properly on this airline.

Vaclavick is crouched in his cubicle, directly behind me. He is a first-class radio operator with a passionate resolve to improve himself. He reads constantly and even now, a few minutes after take-off, he is lost in a technical book. He is reading with a flashlight, cupping his hand around the lens so the light will not trouble our forward vision. Except for the intervals when he is actually engaged in receiving or sending a message, Vaclavick will read until we land in Honolulu. Then on the return flight he will read again. I cannot account for the endurance of his eyes.

Snow is our engineer. He sits between us on a leather jump seat which is usually removed after we have reached cruising altitude. He is a sandy-haired, drawling young man and an excellent mechanic. He can fix almost anything.

All is familiar and satisfying. The airplane is exactly the same type I flew for so long on the North Atlantic except that new engines of greater power have replaced the older models. These are known as "Dash-13's" and enable us to climb faster and make better cruising speed. There are other improvements to the scene. We are all rested and well fed. Our uniforms are clean and so are we. The en-route weather over this area of the Pacific is usually benign—almost to the point of ennui. This is the sort of thing a flying man accustomed to other skies can hardly believe. It is an old lady's run, with earthly delights at either end, and the dream appears indestructible.

There are thirty-three passengers back in the cabin and several babies. It is pleasant to think that in the morning they will be smothered in flower leis and welcomed by a Hawaiian band.

The Golden Gate drops away beneath us, and beyond the coastal fog I can already see the whipping flash of the Farallon light.

I hear Vaclavick shifting his communication channel over to ocean frequency and then there is only the steady snoring of the engines to mark our progress upward.

The special sound of these new engines is reassuring. They seem to give youth to the airplane, which, like every aircraft now engaged in long-range flying, has seen war service. The newer types, designed specifically for airline use, are still in the testing stage.

The air is perfectly smooth. Hayes and Smith are in amiable argument about the best way to age meat. I am certain Snow will interrupt them as soon as his engines are settled down in cruise. Snow is one of those men who knows a little about nearly everything and too often compounds the offense by being right.

I pull off my headphones, hating the things. They are too heavy and have hardly changed since the days of Marconi. It is enough that Drake and Vaclavick will be listening. A captain is entitled to certain physical comforts. If the crew insists on treating him as an old man regardless of his age, then it is his amusement to loll in privilege. He must, unless the balances of command are newly revised, pay for it in some manner anyway.

A few thousand miles to the eastward, the numbers are still the principal factor of influence. McGuire will be plying the same night sky somewhere between Chicago and New York. So will Lippincott and Dewitt. Dunn will also be there if he is flying this night, as will Ross, my early mentor, and Catchings, and Mood. Hughen, now a chief pilot, might therefore be at home and I wonder if he is still smoothing his wisp of hair. And Robbins, with huge crew lists of unfamiliar names before him, will still be tinkering with schedules and times. But it will still be the numbers, and not Robbins or anyone else, that decide who flies where and when. Bittner must be in southerly skies, nearing Memphis perhaps. And Johnson, a more dignified kewpie now because he is a captain, will also be there. O'Connor will be in or out of Boston, again such a fixture on his old route that the regional birds are said to cry his name. Peterson will be sharing his particular sky. I have been concerned about Keim. A rumor claims he has been removed from flying status—for how long no one seems to know. If the rumor is true he will not be in any sky.

We pass through nine thousand feet and set our altimeters to standard pressure so that our readings will correspond with all other airplanes flying over the Pacific. Compelled by habit, I scan the instruments before and above me, absorbing their readings at a glance. This, when all is so well, becomes an easy thing to do. After staring at the same face for thousands of hours, one instantly recognizes the most minute change of expression. And usually the reaction to intelligence transmitted is automatic.

Now one of the fuel flow needles flickers. The entire movement requires less than a second and the actual travel of the needle point is barely a millimeter. It is the flick of an eyelid, a tic, and then the needle is steady again.

There are four needles which indicate the flow of fuel to each engine. They are primarily intended to aid us in calculating consumption and reserve, but the needles are activated by a hypersensitive mechanism and so serve additionally to warn of incipient engine difficulties. They are not alarmists but have been known to cry wolf when only a puppy is near. This is particularly true of a DC-4A, in which we are now flying.

The fuel system in this type is a tangle of compromises created because the airplane was not originally designed to fly great distances. Consequently a valuable portion of the fuselage which should carry paying passengers is still taken over by large auxiliary fuel tanks. These are in a separate compartment aft of the flight deck.

Because of these tanks and other plumbing idiosyncrasies a certain amount of air frequently plagues the entire fuel system. The engines belch and spit, a circumstance which is never comforting over any ocean. Yet the spasms seldom last very long, so in time we have become almost inured to the fault. There is a considerable difference between expecting trouble and the sudden beast which jumps from security corner.

We pass through ten thousand feet and for a moment steal an additional hundred feet so we can descend back through it. In the doing the ship can be set flying in a slightly nose-down position. Thus, "on the step" we will add better than ten knots to our air speed and also satisfy our sensual appreciation of flight. A mushing airplane, regardless of its speed, becomes a miserable contraption to any dedicated pilot. He absorbs this unhappiness through the seat of his pants. There is no reason to believe this will ever change regardless of aircraft design. A good pilot becomes morose and irritable in spite of what the most modern instruments proclaim unless his ship is "on the step." He will work endlessly to achieve that delicate angle and for this once and only once will prove the instruments wrong and the hair tips of his sensory powers more honest. When the instruments finally admit additional speed, then the pilot is doubly content, for he has proof that the instruments are not his absolute master and he is not as yet altogether a mechanical man.

We slide back down to exactly ten thousand. Snow eases propellers and engines into cruising power. It is a matter of pride that this be done without the average passenger's becoming aware of any change. We are not being paid to excite their nerves and we are honest workmen.

I glance at the fuel flow meters again. The needles are steady. Snow moves the mixture controls into cruising position, one at a time. We are on the step and I am well pleased with the cramped little world over which I am to preside for some twelve hours.

The Farallons slide out of sight beneath the nose. Drake reports our passing to air traffic control.

I bend forward, intending to set the auto-pilot in operation. The fuel flow needle to number one engine jumps and the engine backfires. A profanity.

"Full rich on number one."

Snow complies at once. The engine smooths. The needle is steady again.

"Looks like the same old—"

Number three needle jumps erratically. More backfiring.

"Full rich on number three!"

Snow yanks up a second lever. Smoothness returns. But there is to be no peace.

Now numbers two and four are popping. Drake switches on the fuel booster pumps above his head. They seem to have little effect. Snow moves all four mixture levers to emergency rich. The backfiring is general for a moment and then subsides. We shoot alcohol to all four engines, then apply carburetor heat. All is tranquil again. The whole embarrassment actually endures for less than a minute.

"Air or ice . . . one or the other. . . ."

If it was carburetor ice we are a little ashamed because then we would have been caught off guard. But such ice is uncommon to the Pacific.

Snow rubs his heavy farmer's hands together. It is a gesture of frustration—an engineer suddenly bereft of pride. He loves these new Dash-13 engines.

I try to console him. "It's not the engines, it's air. The same old crazy plumbing system."

Air will finally be sucked out. It was expected. There is no reason to be concerned if the engines will now run again in cruising mixture. It has always been so before.

Snow moves the mixture levers back to cruising mixture, gingerly, suspicion clouding his face. He moves the levers one at a time.

All is as it should be. The air must be gone now. We have eliminated the possibility of carburetor ice by maintaining the heat.

I wave the controls to Drake, who smiles and shrugs his shoulders. I know his gesture is in reference to the backfiring. We have all seen this happen before. Now it is over and we are relieved. Vaclavick was only momentarily distracted from his book.

Smith rips off four pieces of Scotch tape and fixes his chart to the table. Snow opens the logbook and starts to write down the engine readings. He will not bother to record the coughing and spitting except in his injured thoughts.

Some pilots prefer to fly with the instrument lights turned full up and others favor semidarkness. Drake is an extremist, turning the lights down until the phosphorescent instruments become their own illumination.

This is agreeable at the moment because the night is so sublime it must certainly depose a familiar apprehension. There is not a pilot flying the ocean who can altogether ignore the possibility of ditching. It is the one thing which cannot be practiced in any check flight—at least to its finality. Only those who have accomplished it know what it's like to land in the sea and they are the first to admit luck favored them as much as skill. The manuals say "the aircraft should be ditched on the back side of a swell." Ho, ho! Who is the maestro who can set ailing tons of machinery down on the back side of an ocean swell, which is itself moving at twenty or thirty miles an hour? Who can select such a convenient bosom from the night void below, slide cross wind with it, and survive to say it was skill?

Official directions for behavior during a ditching are wonderfully specific: the first officer does this, the second officer does that, and the cabin attendants are drilled to as near perfection as any frightened human being can be. But the most important item, which might presumably guarantee the landing of the airplane in one piece, is notably lacking in detail.

This we have all discussed endlessly, and most of us have secretly rehearsed our intended procedures until a measure of confidence has been found. Only one thing remains a certainty. Ditching can never be a matter of choice. Any measures, however unorthodox or absurd, are wise and worthy if they will keep a sick airplane up where it belongs.

I love such a night. I love entering its immensity in this way, enjoying the deception that there is as much below as above. We are suspended between the stars. The functions of our human conceit can expand without apparent folly here. The diminution in size and importance does not apply to night flight because from the darkened cockpit the stars are as close or as far away as anyone would please, and the light from the instruments is not sufficient to reveal a man's smug composure. Here it is possible to become one of the realm, and all the fixtures are comforting support to the fable of immortality. The night sky is a place for children, whose imaginations are equally limitless. Realists who would poison such a sky with platitudes on the actual distances to the stars should be exiled to the dungeons of sophistication. Away with you, realist Snow, and your forebodings! Yes, I see the Goddamned number one needle is jumping again and I do not approve of it any more than you do.

"Emergency rich on number one! Booster pump! Try some more alcohol! Drake, turn up the lights so we can see something!"

All of this is done almost instantly.

The airplane swerves to the left as number one engine gasps, loses all power, and finally responds to our treatment.

This moment of truce is shortened before it is honestly established.

All four engines quit simultaneously.

The relative silence is stunning until the juices of fear throb through our veins.

We start down toward the black sea.

Our thoughts are identical. The thing which was never going to happen to us is now going to happen to us.

I bank sharply back toward the Farallons. We might just stretch the glide and land close by—easier for the Coast Guard to find. Plus the yearning for land.

"Emergency rich on all four!"

"I've got 'em that way, Skipper!"

"All on main tanks!"

"So they be!" Bless you, realist Snow. Your voice has not a quaver in it.

"Booster pumps on high!"

"Right." *Click, click, click, click.*

"Vaclavick! On the horn! Send out a . . ."

Send out a May Day . . . the losing of hope?

But my order to Vaclavick is left unspoken, for hope has returned. The engines have caught, not with any integrity of power, but they are at least alive.

"Vaclavick! Hold it!"

"Aye!"

I remember La Guardia and the affair of the plugs. But that wasn't at night and there wasn't a roiling ocean below. And there were no passengers. Here once more every engine instrument has gone insane. How many times more?

We have lost two thousand feet and the altimeters are still unwinding. We must try everything. It is a wonderful show now that the juices are flowing. In spite of the crazy revolution outside we are all calm, efficient, and very ready for the worst. All of this is on the surface. We would now be quite willing to trade places with anyone but the surely condemned.

Hayes awaits the order to prepare the passengers for ditching.

Do wait, Hayes! Here is hope arrived and, although its shape is arbitrary, it is real. I have discovered that by shoving the propeller controls full forward and increasing the power almost to take-off requirements, the engines will run more or less continuously. I do not know why this is so. For the moment I am content to interrupt the awful silence.

"Vaclavick! Call Oakland control. Get a straight clearance in. All traffic to hell out of the way!"

"Roger."

We are suddenly over the Farallons again.

And we are faced with something very new in aviation, a madness, a preposterous combination that is writing its own rules. Moments before we were cursed with an airplane which would not stay up. To hoard altitude was our passion, our life, and instinct made us misers.

Now it appears we have an airplane which is going to prove a maverick before we can get it down. Anywhere.

Temporarily at least, we have found a way to keep all four engines running. But the bell rope is lifting the monk. The engines will only run at nearly full power and with the propellers in full low pitch. This sets up a terrible racket, as if we were in continuous take-off. By carefully controlling the engine cowl flaps we can probably avoid dangerous overheating, but our air speed is already out of all reason. The instant I start a descent our speed must become prohibitive. Even in straight and level flight we are much too fast.

It is plainly feast or famine. We fly full blast or not at all. We must yell now to hear anything.

"Try again!"

Snow carefully eases the throttles back. At once all four engines protest immediate starvation. Our hope dies with them.

"Shove them back up!"

They catch and hold beautifully. Our breathing becomes regular again.

The line of luminous fog marking the coast and San Francisco is only momentarily a line. Then all of the inviting coverlet is visible.

Our thousands of horses are racing for the stable. If we check, they lie down and expire. I have the stabilizer wheel rolled far forward to keep the ship from zooming into a climb.

Air traffic control has given us immediate co-operation. The whole sky over the bay area is ours. Because of the fog we cannot simply fly over Oakland Airport, cut our crazy engines, and try a barnstormer's landing as I had once managed to accomplish at Stevensville. We must make a standard instrument approach and unless something can be done about our speed it is going to be extremely interesting. Wisdom, experience, and practice have set the instrument approach speed at one hundred and forty miles per hour. I wondered how I would manage at two hundred and twenty.

There is no manual of instruction or convenient regulation to fall back upon for such a flying dilemma.

I wave my fist downward. "Gear down!"

"Skipper . . . the *speed?*"

I can see the small placard as well as Snow can. It prohibits lowering the landing gear at speeds in excess of one hundred and sixty miles an hour. The doors will probably be torn away. But I am not going to listen to that silence again if there is any choice. We must utilize the only brakes we have.

I repeat the order and Snow slams down the gear lever. There is an agonized groaning from the ship's vitals, a roaring, and then the gear is down. Three green lights on the instrument panel flash on to prove it. I have no idea if the doors are torn away. I am not even interested. Our speed slows to one hundred and ninety. Which is still much too fast.

"Give me the flaps a little at a time!"

The flaps are not to be lowered even partially at speeds in excess of one hundred and sixty. Otherwise they may also be torn from the ship. And that could throw us over on our back.

San Francisco is below. I try once more to ease off on the power. All is as before. The revolution begins again with familiar fireworks. This time I will not wait for the silence before shoving the throttles ahead again. Ten seconds of backfiring on all four engines is enough.

Now the co-ordination of a fine crew begins to count. Drake has turned one direction finder to San Francisco and the other to Oakland. He has properly set both our altimeters. He has made a complete cockpit check for both approach and landing. He reports our swift position changes to air traffic control and has obtained the wind and weather from the Oakland tower. Snow is constantly adjusting the engine cowl flaps, keeping the engine temperatures as low as he can. Hayes has opened the approach book to the chart of the Oakland range and placed it carefully on my lap. I know the procedure by heart, but only a fool trusts his memory.

All of this is done without any orders from me. I am busy enough trying to fly an airplane which is buffeting and shivering with ague and wants to run faster than I can think.

We are at five thousand feet. The problem, unless something blows up, is unchanged. How do we get down—at the right time and the right place? I dismiss a wild idea to feather one or even two of the engines. That would be true madness, particularly since any one of the working engines might break up under the strain.

"The tower wants to know if you are declaring an emergency." Drake's voice is raised slightly because of the noise, but his words are almost leisurely.

"No. Just make sure we're number one to land."

Most pilots are reluctant to declare an emergency. They feel, as I do now, that the word is overdramatic. It is a confession that something has occurred beyond the power of the pilot to conquer and this may be as disturbing as the situation itself.

And here, in truth, our problem is more perplexing than desperate. The airplane is holding together and so are the engines. Except for the thin coverlet of fog, the sky is clear, so the mental distractions of trying a complete and exact instrument approach are greatly minimized. We need not spend but thirty seconds in the actual overcast. And the clearance beneath is encouraging. Six hundred feet, with two miles of visibility.

Over the Oakland range station I force the airplane into a clumsy descent. With so much power and speed the controls are brick-hard. I try to ignore the buffeting. I try to pretend this is just another approach. Things are just going to happen a little faster.

"Try easing off a bit!" I nod at the throttles and sense, rather than see, Snow's hands cover them. My entire visual attention is on the flight instruments. Out the south leg of the range, procedure turn, but this very special time hold any attempt at descent until you're headed back toward the field. And hold an extra thousand feet until you're inbound.

There is no backfiring. The engines continue smoothly, though the power has been reduced.

"Ease off a little more."

The fuel meters flicker, but not as before. Enough. An approach at one eighty cannot be so bad.

We are headed back toward the field. The fog is thin enough so we can see the amber blobs of the runway lights. We are still much too high. Four thousand feet. I shove the nose down and hate the way the whole ship trembles.

"Try easing off some more."

Snow gradually decreases the power. There is not the slightest protest from the engines. All four are now running perfectly. None of us can believe our eyes or the even rhythm of sound.

"Try some more."

Snow eases the throttles back until the power is normal for descent in a final approach. There is the marker beacon a mile from the end of the runway.

We slip through the fog and emerge beneath. I take over the throttles, Drake snaps on the landing lights, and we swoop down for a perfectly normal landing.

We taxi to the passenger ramp in awkward silence.

Our total time in the air has been exactly fifty-four minutes.

The ramp attendants soothe our passengers and herd them into the waiting room. The businessmen aboard are sullen, the women passengers without babies are smiling thinly, and those with babies are not smiling at all. I do not envy the ramp agents who must now excuse the delay and invent various ambiguous reasons why certain things must be done before we start toward Honolulu again.

I wish they would invent some solidly comprehensible reasons for me.

Our welcoming committee is a group of mechanics in white overalls. They are unhappy. They want to know why we have returned and vague answers will not satisfy them. Since the engines ran so perfectly during the very last part of the flight, my own confidence is shaken. Was there something else we could have done? If it was only air, would it all have been blown out of the system in say another twenty seconds?

For the ignorant and puzzled, a defensive tack is the easiest, so my first reply is tinged with accusation.

"These engines don't choose to run."

"They sounded fine coming in here." These men can detect a sick engine as far as they can hear it.

"I know they sounded fine. But they don't sound so fine above four thousand feet."

"Just exactly what did they do?"

I leave the explanations to Snow. His parlance and idiom will better match the mechanics'. Their talk is of ignition harnesses, plugs, air, and fuel pumps—all of which is of but passing interest to most line pilots. As the discussion becomes increasingly esoteric we excuse ourselves and leave Snow to his troubles.

Later Snow stands before us. His heavy hands are now smudged with grease.

"There's nothing wrong with the engines, Skipper. We checked everything, then we took the ship down to the end of the ramp for a run-up. Perfect."

"Did you bleed all the air from the system?"

It is a silly question. Of course they have. But my rank calls for comment, however uninspired.

"There wasn't any air. I think we should make a test flight. It looks like just one of those things."

Just one of *what* things?

We are at the end of the runway again, exactly as we were some two hours previously. But there are no passengers. Even Vaclavick and Smith have been left behind since the test flight will be a local affair only. The chief mechanic stands observantly behind Snow as we again perform a most careful run-up of each engine.

"Well . . ." I sigh. It is late and I am already a little weary, and there is still a long flight to Honolulu to be flown. It is almost a certainty that the chief mechanic who waits to start down the runway with his precious engines must regard me with something less than admiration. It appears that I have brought a perfectly sound airplane back and left it in his lap. He is so sure of his conviction that he is quite willing to risk a test flight. Well, now, this is *my* world and we shall see.

The take-off is normal. We climb through fog and there are the stars again. We pass through three thousand feet. Turning in my seat, I can see the chief mechanic watching the engine instruments intently. Must he be so smug? Four thousand . . . five . . . on up to eight. We have flown in a wide circle and are over the Golden Gate again. I start leveling off.

"Okay. Set them up in cruise."

Snow starts to reduce the power. His action is barely begun before the whole show starts all over again. The foolish chorus of confusion outside the windows is repeated in every respect. But we are quicker to drop gear and flaps this time. Quicker to do everything—quicker to return.

The chief mechanic needs no further convincing. We are now his friends and he is very glad to be on the ground.

"Why should they run perfectly below three thousand?"

None of us have ever heard of such a thing happening before. And having twice known defeat, we are less than enthusiastic about further experiment. The ends of our nerves are frazzled and we are unreasonably suspicious of everything.

There is an unwritten airline law that if one pilot refuses to fly an airplane because of special mechanical ills, no other pilot will touch it. So I was not surprised when Sloniger scheduled us to make a third test flight in the morning.

There now began one of the strangest riddles in aviation history. It is related here only because it could have happened to any other airline captain and it is conceivable that his behavior would have been very nearly the same. All of us still had an enormous amount to learn about air transport whether we were on the ground or in the sky.

This was not a little postwar starvation airline trying desperately to keep a few woebegone ships in the air; nor could anyone even suggest that the staff was inexperienced or careless. The type of airplane was long familiar to all of us and our facilities for maintenance were of the very finest. Yet we could not, it seemed, keep this particular airplane in the air. It was a most inauspicious beginning for a steamship line bound to convince the government as well as the public that it should be granted a full franchise.

Sloniger and I made the test flight together in the morning. It lasted one hour and fifteen minutes. We tried everything. The results were exactly the same.

The mechanics were beside themselves. And none of us could explain how two round-trip flights had been made to Honolulu in the same airplane without incident. Every suspect part of the engines was changed again and again. All of the fuel was drained from the ship and analyzed. New fuel was put aboard in spite of a perfect report. Two days later we tried a fourth test flight. The same. Fortunately our two other airplanes carried out the schedule while this nervous experimentation continued.

All of the major components of modern airliners are brought together into one, but each is separately manufactured. The companies so engaged maintain staffs of experts who are, in fact, "trouble shooters." These men would not be human if they deliberately sought blame for their own creations. Thus, hydraulic experts are inclined to find fault with the oil, radio men question the generating system, propeller men suspect the engines.

After our failures, it seemed logical to call for expert help from the engine manufacturers. Three arrived with dispatch and we met in a hot and airless room adjacent to the hangars.

Schmidt, our operations manager, presided. Sloniger sat beside him. I was present as a mere witness since such highly technical conferences were rightly considered beyond my scope. So I only half-listened to the opening review of our failures. My thoughts were elsewhere and troubled with the whims of fortune. News had just come to me that Keim was through with flying forever. The insignificant bruise on his shaggy, ever-defiant head had led to a series of blackouts and so his physical disqualification. Now Keim, the old maestro who was really not old at all, was clipping the clearance papers of captains who were wetting diapers when he was long in the sky. Once he had been removed from flight status, his treasured seniority had become meaningless. Yet in losing so much Keim had kept his indomitable courage. He had accepted his fate without bitterness or the slightest complaint. He had simply shrugged his massive shoulders and found a way to live

with the only work available. This was a new and special variety
of bravery which few of us believed we could equal.

I could not be sure if it was the thoughts of Keim, or the vapid
heat of the room, or the sanctimonious voices of the engine experts which so depressed me. I was searching for a pretext to leave
when one of the leading experts threw out a challenge which I
could not ignore. He had a very high forehead which sloped rather
abruptly into a polished dome. His eyes were apparently all pupils,
an illusion which robbed them of life. But his eyes were of no
matter. His ears were inhumanly small and they wiggled when he
spoke. I could not watch anything else. Suddenly he turned upon
me with a patronizing smile.

"You were not commanding the previously successful flights in
this airplane, were you?"

"No."

"Have you ever flown Dash-13's before?"

"No." I was bewildered at the turn of things. An engine was an
engine. It ran or it did not run. I could not poke around their in-
teriors from where I sat in an airplane.

"Your previous experience was with our Dash-7 engines, wasn't
it?"

I glanced at Sloniger. He said nothing, but his broad wink was
reassuring. I knew he disliked this new turn of the investigation as
much as I did.

"It was. And in the same type airplane. What's that got to do
with our present problem?"

"Are you aware that we recommend operating in full rich mixture after you level off at cruising altitude?"

"Sure. It's standard practice. I think everyone does it."

"How long have you been waiting before going down to cruise
mixture?"

"Two or three minutes. I've never actually timed it."

"A half hour or even longer would be better."

"That would use up a lot of fuel we might need at the other
end."

The engineer toyed with his slide rule a moment, and I was

fascinated to discover that when he was thinking his ears remained perfectly still.

"Your reserve would easily take care of the slight extra consumption."

"I'm one of those people who never has too much fuel."

"We are only suggesting that if you operate correctly, the chances of air in the system will be eliminated."

It was easy enough to sense the trend of their thinking. The failures were my failures. And maybe they were right. I felt very alone in the room until I saw Sloniger's face and knew at once that his faith in me was unshaken.

"All right. Suppose we make another test flight? I will fly it exactly as on the first night with the passengers. But *you* operate the engines. I will do nothing but steer."

The experts agreed so promptly that I was entirely subdued as we left the room. Surely now my ignorance of machinery had at last caught up with me. My foolish decisions had cost this new airline reputation and considerable money. On the way to the airplane I told Sloniger that perhaps it would be much easier for him if he gave me a permanent leave of absence.

"Wait," said the wisest of pelicans.

There was not a cloud in the sky as we climbed above the Golden Gate and headed toward the glittering Pacific. I was careful to fly exactly the same course and duplicate the rate of climb. The leading expert sat in the jump seat where Snow had been, and the others stood solicitously behind him. Sloniger occupied Drake's seat.

We reached ten thousand feet and the Farallon Islands passed beneath the nose. I took the extra hundred feet, slid down to ten thousand again, and leveled off.

"Remember, I am only going to steer. You operate all engine controls. I want to learn."

My answer was an indulgent smile.

I confined my hands exclusively to the flight controls and when we were on the step gave the order to reduce power. Now? The expert slowly pulled back the throttle and propeller controls. We flew on course for Honolulu and the four engines sounded like a single healthy unit. Thoroughly humbled, I wished I had stayed on AM-21. My self-recrimination reached a peak when the engineer pushed the mixture controls down into cruise position and the power song continued without the slightest disturbance. No one spoke on the flight deck. We listened, watched, and waited.

I glanced over my shoulder and saw the coast line. It was already a thin and hazy separation between the sky and the sea. And I thought, We might as well turn back because most certainly the point has been firmly proven. I could not bear to look at the others. Their silence was overly polite, a gentle censure, but what do you do with a pilot who is frightened of shadows?

Then I saw it, and I was certain it was my private information because all the others were now so entirely relaxed. The number one fuel flow needle had developed a tic.

"You understand now, Captain?" the leading expert asked, in the same way he might reprimand a child.

"Yes. I understand."

"We're ready to go back any time you are."

His aplomb was marvelous and I wished there was some way to absorb it.

"Let's wait. A few minutes longer. . . ."

I did not want to stare at the fuel flow meters lest their attention be drawn to the number one needle. It was behaving exactly as it had done before—*tick . . . tick . . .*

I held my breath. Would it just please vindicate me ever so little? It was the only time in my career that I *wanted* an engine to misbehave.

I forced myself to look away from the fuel flow meters. Instead I concentrated on the sweep second hand of the instrument panel clock. In exactly one minute I would turn back.

Waiting the full time was unnecessary. For the engines very suddenly reached a unanimous decision.

All four quit in the most audibly spectacular manner I had ever witnessed. I most certainly had no desire for such a negative triumph, but now it had arrived a great mischief possessed me. I was able to indulge it with deceptively natural calm because I had been through this so many times before and knew the safe solution.

The engineers were unashamedly frightened out of their wits. Again we were headed down to the sea.

"Turn back, Captain!"

"Let's get to hell back over dry land!"

I deliberately held the ship on course for Honolulu. It was childish vengeance, but until now they had treated me like a child. They were frantically experimenting with the mixture controls, heat, booster pumps—everything we had done before. This time the engines were even sicker than I had seen them. No effort on the part of the experts had the slightest effect. We were losing about eight hundred feet per minute. Outside, the combustive insurrection was in full sway.

I saw the twisting of Sloniger's mouth and knew he shared my peculiar appreciation of these moments. Now I could make the little speech I had been secretly rehearsing ever since the first flick of the number one needle. Turning on the white-faced experts, I said, "The sea is calm and it's a beautiful day. We can see everything for ditching. Now how would you like to be up here at night with a full load of passengers plus a flock of babies?" The words soured in my mouth and I was instantly ashamed of such petty cruelty. These were not airmen. They were impractical under real stress. Even their mechanical theories had betrayed them. Seeing they were very close to terror, I turned the ship back toward the coast.

I tried very hard not to sound patronizing when I asked if our bargain was fulfilled and whether I could now operate the engines.

A grain of humor survived among the experts. One of them said, "You're welcome."

So I did exactly as we had done before, and after several nervous minutes of regurgitation the engines settled down. We had lost considerable altitude because of my fatuous delay so that our actual approach to the coast line was at three thousand feet. Here we found the engines functioned normally, even at reduced power. But an airplane which refuses to fly above three thousand feet is a useless collection of aluminum. So this one, our fanciest of airplanes, was grounded until the riddle was solved.

Fortunately the other ships of the line were equipped with the older-type engines. By constant juggling we managed to complete our required quota of flights back and forth to Honolulu. All of this was done without incident.

During this period Steen and Fox were killed trying a single-engine instrument approach at Moline. Then Campbell and Leatherman hit a ridge near Elko, Nevada. In both incidents the official verdict was "Pilot error," but since their passengers, who were innocent of the controls, also failed to survive, it seemed that fate was the hunter. As it had been and would be.

XVIII

TRAGEDY AND ESCAPE

THERE IS A DEGREE OF MERCY BEYOND WHICH ANY MAN IS RUDE TO INQUIRE

Now there came a time of great aeronautical confusion. The long-established airlines were fighting for position and the postwar ventures were striving for recognition. Surplus airplanes were cheap and could be converted to airline use with relative ease.

Thus, innumerable small airlines came into being. Some of these possessed only one heavily mortgaged airplane and it was not uncommon for the captain and co-pilot to be the entire board of directors. Economics soon eliminated most of these pitifully brave little outfits.

Many of the new airlines were irresponsible and actually dangerous. Yet, particularly in America, it was discouraging to witness the willful choking of free enterprise by the clammy hands of government. It was also prophetic. Aviation had grown up. Airline officials were no longer to be found in shirt sleeves, and a universal seeking for respectability drained much of the color from the scene. Yet the natural forces behind such a revolutionary means of human communication was so tremendous neither the governments, unions, the pettiness of newly cautious officials nor the international jealousy for power and prestige could restrain this era any longer.

The transformation amazed the eyes and the minds of those who had pioneered the skies so short a time before. It was already affecting the affairs of all mankind, from savages to the most polished sophisticates. And all of this, as if to match the intrinsic nature of the development, occurred in such a short span of time that the same men who had flown helmeted and goggled in primitive open-cockpit mail ships were still flying the most modern airliners. Since most of them had barely reached middle age there was no reason to believe anything but ill-luck could ground them for years.

One of these men was Sloniger. Now, in the establishment of a new airline, he was as eager and enthusiastic as in the days when he flew mail between St. Louis and Chicago. He seemed to be forever young although he was now burdened with the complicated responsibilities of many airplanes.

The governmental vacillations and consequent uncertainties created serious morale problems in all the new lines wherever they flew. Sloniger had also to explain our maverick airplane. It was understandable that our steamship sponsors should wonder why airplanes which looked exactly alike should perform so differently. The mystifying reluctance of our maverick led some of them to wish they had never heard of airplanes. Expensive and frustrating attempts to operate this airplane now had all of us tugging at our lower lips, and the mechanics were alternately snappish and inconsolable. The experts, long since humbled, were drinking their whisky in straight, desperate gulps. At last, after countless changes and outbursts of profanity, the airplane was considered safe to fly the two thousand four hundred odd miles to Honolulu.

It seemed that I had personally inherited this monster and I soon came to regard it with the same mistrust once reserved for C-87's. Here are actual comments from my logbook, each having been set down on a different flight and day.

". . . All engines cutting out for six hours. Very uncomfortable ride. Quit until they fix it!"

My determination was not very strong. Three days later:

"Test hop with Sloniger . . . ship no better."

Ten days later on a flight to Honolulu:

"Engines cutting out again . . . certain it is plugs."

Four days later:

"Engines not getting fuel."

Two days later:

"Ditto."

And there follows a series of ditto marks for seven more flights.

The additionally curious events on one of these flights were not set down in the logbook. I had neither space nor heart to record how one flight from Honolulu to Portland, Oregon, was flown at two thousand feet because the engines simply would not perform at any other altitude. Nor did I wish to record that one of the stewardesses became drunk at the approximate point of no return, and the labor pains of a lady passenger were occurring every five minutes.

I could no longer approach the maverick with anything but hatred. But I continued to fly it because it had taken on the quality of a living thing, a well-dressed dandy of a villain, and I intended to conquer it.

Before we killed each other, cooler heads came to a reluctant and extremely expensive conclusion. It was not the fault of the engines. It was not the fault of the airplane . . . or me. It was the combination of the DC-4A type ship and the Dash-13 engines.

The fundamental design of the fuel system simply would not continuously supply the new and hungrier engines with sufficient fuel—a circumstance aggravated by altitude. To correct the fault demanded the most elaborate alterations. So eighty thousand dollars' worth of beautiful new engines were removed and the older types set in place once again.

Thus equipped, the airplane flew quite happily ever after.

The visual aspects of the worlds aloft are as different as the corresponding areas below. And there are countless subtle variations for which there is no honest meteorological explanation. The mewling, drizzle-laden skies over the Bering Sea are not the same as the atmosphere to be encountered in the vicinity of Iceland, though the latitude of the observer may be nearly identical. The jungle skies of South America are lush and inviting and altogether lacking in the antagonism and elderly stink of skies over similar jungles in Africa. The skies of the Sudan are hostile and given to snarling phenomena, while the desert skies of Arizona and New Mexico seldom trouble an airplane. In many ways the North Atlantic skies suggest masculinity, while Pacific skies appear relatively feminine in character except over the Japanese archipelago. This is particularly true of the immense region from the West Coast of North America to the approximate longitude of the Philippines, where an occasional typhoon can destroy the illusion.

The steamship-airline proposed to operate all through these areas, which, in addition to the South Seas, had long been the domain of their surface ships. It was an enticing prospect, and with our earlier troubles defeated there was every reason to hope for growth and permanency. Month after month we flew the great triangle, gathering reputation and pride in the reliability as well as the luxury of the operation. We had no lack of passengers though the government had specifically warned against advertisement of any kind. Thus we were obliged to tiptoe around the increasingly concerned Pan American and rely on the praises of our passengers. Our flights were simply not supposed to be happening.

Another steamship-airline was similarly engaged over the Caribbean area and the operation was equally successful. It was inconceivable that any government agency could ever be persuaded to force such publicly convenient and well-founded organizations out of business.

During this time Abernathy and Holle were killed at Laramie, Wyoming, and later Anderson and Miner ended their brief careers at Richmond, Virginia. Both accidents occurred during attempts to land in bad weather. These were "hungry" airlines and unfortunately the airplanes had flown a great deal longer than the crews.

The same could not be said of Sprado and Weber, who soon afterward flew into Mt. Laguna, California. The official cause: "Let down below terrain without positive fix." The investigation carefully avoided any speculation on why two intelligent and experienced men should do such a thing.

It appeared that fate was on a rampage, taking the rich and highly skilled as well as those more hopeful than able. Now Tansey and Sparrow were killed at Shannon, Ireland. When the investigators discovered the cause, we found it harder than usual to shrug our shoulders. One of the finest and largest maintenance organizations in the world had made a tragic mistake and failed to discover it. They had somehow *reversed* the static pressure lines, which resulted in false altimeter readings. It was night. Circling the fog-shrouded airport, relying on his instruments as he should, Tansey flew into the ground.

Almost simultaneously Ham and Ring were lost at Michigan City, Indiana. The feeble technical explanation was "Probable carburetor ice." If Ham and Ring were amateurs, ill-schooled, and flying for an impoverished airline unable to maintain the equipment properly, this verdict might have been barely satisfying. But none of these shortcomings applied in their destruction. Whether they were many or few, occult or technical, there had to be other contributing factors to such an accident.

Fortune now also abandoned Haskew and Canepa, who flew into the Blue Ridge Mountains, Hearn and Day in a check flight, and Weeks and McKeirnan in another check flight. Cushing was lost in the most inexplicable of all appointments, a mid-air collision.

All of these men were gone in less than five months.

And there now occurred a combination of events which, if not so exactly proven by logbooks and records, would have been incredible. Afterward, I was at last thoroughly convinced that technical causes are only the active and recognizable instrument of a flying man's destiny. The fundamental cabal, the originating force of decision or postponement, remained exactly as it had been always—just an instant of distance beyond the reach of the human mind. But it was there, inscrutable, and only half hidden behind the comforting veil of our childish faiths. It did not linger for explanation, although it did allow the inquisitive to uncover the more obvious surface manipulations. It said to the boldest seekers, "Pry to the limits set for your intelligence but expect to retreat with bruises when you strike the veil. I am the final explanation. You could not long survive if you knew."

The date was the thirtieth of May.

Captain Coney and First Officer Willingham of Eastern Airlines were flying at four thousand feet in the vicinity of Bainbridge, Maryland. Forty-nine passengers attended by two stewardesses sat relaxed in the cabin. There was one infant aboard.

The weather was pleasant and routine radio reports were received from the flight by the various ground stations. Then suddenly the airplane went into a steep and uncontrollable dive. There was no call of distress. There was only silence. And the silence, except for the whimpering of metal fragments in the wind, continued forever because there were no survivors.

Again, the thirtieth of May.

Far to the west, over the Pacific, I was flying exactly the same type airplane bound from Honolulu to Burbank. The time was approximately the same, but since our fuel weight was greater, we carried only thirty-three passengers. This was the sole difference. Our weather was also most agreeable and the forecast for the California coast, plus unusually favorable winds, promised an easy arrival. All of this pleased me because I was due for my first vacation from the steamship-airline. It would commence when this flight was ended. I could not know how important the thought of this vacation would be to my continuing existence.

It had been my custom to leave the flight deck and visit the cabin after we had reached cruising altitude and were well established on course. As I had once schemed to preserve my captaincy, now I was determined to do all I could to help the steamship-airline stay in business. A lucky tour down the rows of seats could usually be managed in ten minutes of question-answering, and if it made future customers I was satisfied. Then I would stand in the galley, which was near the tail, and listen briefly to the woes or matrimonial progress of the stewardesses. Cardboard romance, culminating in official ritual, was an obsession with most of the girls who flew on any line, but Grimes was an unusually realistic young woman. She was petite, sparing of cosmetics, and forthright in manner. Now, as I reached the galley, she seemed to have been waiting for me.

"What's the matter with this airplane?"

"Nothing is the matter with it. Why?"

"Well, it sure shakes back here. It's a good thing I'm wearing a girdle."

I waited a moment. Here the sound of the engines was only a muted humming. It was not even loud enough to dominate the faint whisper of our slip stream along the fuselage. So we spoke softly, lest the passengers in the rear seats overhear us. I moved about the galley, touching at the bulkheads, listening, sensing the airplane as a man may question any unwillingness in a long-familiar love. But I could not detect the slightest quiver which might be thought unnatural. There was only the slight and regular yawing induced by the automatic pilot. The sensitivity control had only to be turned half an inch and the yawing would cease. I told Grimes that as soon as I returned to the flight deck I would ease off on the control and things would seem right again.

"No. That's not what I mean. It's a funny . . ."

"We passed through a little patch of choppy air about half an hour ago. Maybe that gave you ideas."

"I've flown long enough to know rough air when I feel it. This was something different. It sort of scared me."

"Relax. All airplanes shake a little back here."

I left Grimes with what I hoped was a reassuring smile and returned to the flight deck. There, everyone was busy about his duties. Drake and Hayes happily occupied both pilots' seats, and I was reluctant to pull rank. I asked them to reduce the sensitivity on the auto-pilot, then stood for a time between Smith, who was at his navigation table, and Vaclavick, who was, as usual, lost in a book. Snow occupied the jump seat, which cut down considerably on my forward line of vision. The view through the two small portholes alongside Smith's table and Vaclavick's radio gear was only of dappled clouds and splotches of sea between. What little I could see forward was exactly the same, interrupted at first by the less interesting side of human heads and the curving snout of the ship itself. Directly above me, the astrodome revealed a rather sour milk sky worthy of only a glance.

By now the normal characteristics of the route between the California coast and Honolulu were as familiar to me as the North Atlantic had once been and AM-21 had been in what already seemed the long ago. Here the seasons brought little variety. East of Honolulu and the Molokai passage, the small trade-wind clouds were almost a fixture and seldom rose above seven thousand feet. Then after a few hours' flying we would pass through a variable area which sometimes presented a weak front and, as often, clear skies. We were flying in this area now. Soon we would enter the almost dormant central area of the great Pacific "High" and it would hold for another two or three hundred miles. Then finally we would sight a very low layer of rumpled stratus which frequently extended as much as a thousand miles to the California coast. Except in the brief winter season this pattern was so regular that the slightest change called for comment. Even the forces and direction of the winds rarely surprised us. They appeared to blow or not to blow according to an eternal code.

I checked our progress and position with Smith and then went back to the crew compartment and sat down on the lower bunk because it was the only place available. I flipped through a magazine and thought more about my vacation, which was to be in a sailboat.

Anticipation of such pleasure lulled my senses and I had almost dozed off when Snow entered the crew compartment. He stood thoughtfully in the center of the small floor space with his head cocked toward one shoulder. I saw him do an about-face, but he remained in position. He bore the air of a man insulted, so I asked him of his trouble.

"I think we have a rough engine, but I can't figure out if it's number two or number three. Every time I make up my mind which one it is it seems to be the other."

Since we were directly in line with the four engines I thought it strange that I had failed to notice any roughness. Perhaps my thoughts were too much on sailing. I stood up beside Snow and listened. After a time he said, "It beats me. I can't notice anything back here, but up forward . . ."

The rumble of the engines was monotonously smooth, but I went forward and stood between Hayes and Drake.

"What's all this about rough engines?"

Drake spoke carefully. "Well, I *thought* I felt a little roughness a while ago, but nothing showed up on the instruments."

All three of us now instinctively looked back at the wings, although we knew very well the action was meaningless. Trouble would reveal itself first on the instrument panel. We checked the ignition on all four engines. Perfect.

Snow held the logbook open before me.

"Number three is about due for overhaul . . . might be a sticky valve. . . ."

We all now took turns at inspecting number three engine from the right window, and the repetitive dumb show struck me as sadly lacking in either originality or good sense. Since the engine was obviously as staunch and solid as anyone could wish, I was able to state my opinion with convincing nonchalance.

"Well, as long as it doesn't jump off the wing . . ."

Later in the afternoon I took over the flying, which at least gave me a comfortable place to sit down. The duties were almost embarrassing in their simplicity. With Hayes, I kept a casual lookout ahead. Otherwise my chief exertion was to reach forward every ten or fifteen minutes and turn a small knob on the auto-pilot to maintain exact course. Our altitude, varied only by the occasional movements of people in the cabin, could be corrected by a quarter turn of the stabilizer wheel. I performed this chore with mock delicacy, using the tip of my little finger.

The air was smooth and now the sun had descended enough to enliven the scenery ahead. There were great oblongs of brass upon the sea and the occasional bundles of clouds huddling along the southern horizon were also of brass. Far to the northeast I saw a lenticular cloud which was so unusual in this part of the Pacific we spent several minutes admiring its graceful, spooklike formation. Later, Smith reached in front of me and tore away the small slip of paper taped over the gyro compass. The figure 62° had been written on the paper—a reminder of our course for the zone in which we were flying. The figure 63° was written on the substitute paper which Smith now fixed in place. And there followed at once the usual badinage about who the hell did Smith think he was, the navigational genius of all time? And how could he fix our position so exactly that he dared change the course so little as one degree? We also made bitter comments on who he might think we were who could follow a course within one degree, and didn't he know that the compass was probably off more than one degree anyway? Then Vaclavick said that it was no wonder flight crews were so given to reading funny papers since their potential of concentration was constantly and thoughtlessly strained by existing in confined quarters with people who chattered like middle-aged ladies at a laundromat. And all of this exchange we found healthy and very pleasant and we had flown another hundred miles or so before we quieted again.

As the hours pass the subtleties of flying fatigue gradually reduce the mental alertness and physical smartness of any airline crew. Ties are pulled down and collars loosened; there is much stretching of limbs. It is at this point that some airmen become preoccupied with personal thoughts, their dreams transporting them over the horizons to more prosaic scenery. They create romantic visions of their homes in which their wives are continuously delightful, their children never cry, and all the bills are paid. Sometimes they become so sentimental they even trifle with thoughts of remaining permanently earth-bound. Only the cynics know this is next to impossible.

We had achieved this condition when Smith announced a more immediate fact. We had passed the point of no return.

All long-range flights are planned according to zones, so that as fuel is consumed and the weight of the aircraft correspondingly reduced, the most economical speed can be maintained. Thus we intended to reduce power at approximate intervals of three hours. There was such a change now due, and after Snow had consulted his power charts for our present weight and obtained my permission, he eased back on the throttles and propeller controls. I noticed at once that the engines seemed rougher. This was not unusual since one power setting may create quite different harmonics of vibration than another; yet this new note strangely annoyed my basic flying nerves. I saw the others were equally uncomfortable.

Again we twisted around so we could see the number three engine. Because I was seated on the opposite side of the ship I had to stand and lean across Hayes for a clear view. None of us knew what we expected to see. Our preconception that something was not altogether right with number three simply bade us stare at it.

We were still twisting and posturing when Grimes came forward and plucked at my sleeve. "We've got the shakes again. I was just starting to serve some drinks when—"

"I know. I know. There's a little roughness in the number three engine."

This was far from a confirmed truth because there was still no indication on the instrument panel that number three was not performing as well as the other engines.

"Is it going to quit?"

"No."

I spoke positively because I wanted to be positive.

The slight vibration passed through the ship in cycles. I had never felt anything exactly like it. It was nothing and yet it was something because certainly all of our imaginations could not create the same mischievous genie.

There . . . there was the cycle again. . . .

My mind explored the vitals of the airplane which I knew so well. Perhaps the entire ship was slightly out of rig? It could happen. It had happened. Yet the cycles of vibration denied any such fault.

I told Snow to set the power where it had been. He complied and all was serene once more. It seemed, then, that this was purely a mechanical matter. I thought that one of the propellers must be a hundredth of an ounce out of balance and the result was a vibrational harmonic at certain critical power settings. I told Snow to leave things as they were. We would forget power reduction for the rest of this flight. Because of the favorable winds en route and weather along the coast, there was no demand to hoard our fuel. So we are fat, I thought. If number three runs smoothly at this power setting why trouble it? An early arrival won't hurt anyone.

I sat back to think of sailing but found it impossible. My theory about unbalanced propellers was so weak I simply could not nurse it to probability. I knew well enough that the weight relation of the giant blades was actually measured to a hair's degree.

Damn Grimes! Her skittish complaints had started all this.

I brooded on our mysterious ailment until the evening sky held my favorite moments. A violet hue had already seeped upward from the eastern horizon and after a while I knew the limits of my sight would become washed with purple and magenta until finally, all of this fading, it would be night. Usually I could find infinite peace in the upper skies at this time, but now I could not.

"Snow?"

He looked up from the logbook where he had been noting the engine instrument readings and I saw in his eyes that he was also dissatisfied.

"Go back and stand around in the tail for a while. See if you can find out what's troubling Grimes."

Snow buttoned his collar, put on his coat and white cap, and went back to the cabin. I waited easily enough. There was no vibration. No . . . there. There it was again. Or was it? I looked at Hayes, who was preparing the weather report for the zone in which we were flying. He seemed unaware of anything unusual. I turned about to watch Smith. He was standing on his stool, his head projecting into the astrodome. I knew he would be waiting for the first stars of evening. Vaclavick? What about you? To see him, I had to half-rise in my seat, twisting my whole body around. Of course. His chin was cupped in his hands and his elbows sheltered a book as if it were a secret treasure. I rose still farther until I could see that the pages were mostly complex electrical diagrams. I could not imagine what Vaclavick could be studying since he already held the highest license obtainable. But from his absorption, it seemed certain he had not felt anything unusual.

Drake was resting back in the crew compartment. I could not see him.

I slumped unhappily in my seat and stretched my legs their full length. I placed my feet on the rudder pedals, a position of habit. I had long used the pedals as a convenient footrest when the airplane was on auto-pilot. Now very suddenly, as if the pedals had been waiting for me, the right one developed a tremor. There was no reason for this. When the auto-pilot was in operation the rudder pedals were practically locked in position. The trembling endured for several seconds and then was gone before I could be certain it bore any relation to our periods of vibration.

I disengaged the auto-pilot and flew manually for several minutes. It seemed the airplane had a tendency to yaw to the left. I adjusted the rudder trim tab, an incongruously large wheel below the magnetic compass. Why hadn't I checked this before? For a moment I thought the mystery was solved. The airplane was slightly out of trim, the auto-pilot tried to correct matters, and the consequent argument between two brainless entities set up a periodic vibration.

Snow returned. He pushed his cap far back on his head, blew out his cheeks, and took the pose of a farmer surveying a blighted crop.

"I'll be damned if I could feel anything back there."

Then he said that I knew how women were, which was assuming a great deal, and explained how he had even crawled into the tail cone. "It's colder than a whore's heart back in there."

"You didn't feel anything about five minutes ago?"

"Nary a thing. Smooth as silk all the time."

My theory on the auto-pilot was smashed. If it were fighting a directional correction the greatest force should be apparent in the tail.

I glanced out at the last of the evening. There would not be more than a few minutes even of this lilac light remaining.

"Take a look through the drift meter. See if there's anything hanging down."

I wondered if one of the various landing gear doors might have failed to close properly. It could be enough to create buffeting.

The drift meter was a periscopelike device fixed to the deck. It stood beside the navigation table. By adjusting and turning it properly we could examine the underside of the airplane.

Snow was bent over the device for several minutes. At last he straightened and shook his head. "Just fine. Everything sewed up tight."

There. Another spasm of vibration. It seemed to pass across the ship from one wing tip to the other and then it was gone. It was far from a violent reaction, yet it did seem to have more authority than any of the others. At least it was enough to bring Drake strolling from the crew compartment.

"Number three acting up again?"

We were back to thinking of number three. And I was momentarily ashamed because we were so like other men in blaming the understood, guilty or not. We had neither the courage nor the imagination to pry up the lid of anything unknown. We stared accusingly at the instruments, almost demanding they confirm our easy suspicions. But there was no signal.

"How about reducing power?"

Snow asked the question and with good reason. If there is something wrong with an airplane which cannot at once be detected, the specter of structural failure rises up, and it will not go away until the trouble is resolved. It just stands and stares . . . waiting. And it is axiomatic that the easiest way to postpone any such threat is to slow down.

But we all knew that cruising airplanes do not come apart in perfectly smooth skies, particularly after having been en route for several hours. A thunderstorm, a rough front, really excessive speed in a dive, there was always the remote possibility . . . but not under these conditions. It was something we not only had to believe but something supported by fact. So I spoke with conviction when I said that if number three was going to throw a master rod, or whatever it might conspire to do, the sooner we arrived over Burbank the better. Also, I thought without the slightest tinge of guilt, the sooner and better for sailing.

I asked Drake to take over the flying. Then I borrowed Snow's flashlight and went back to the cabin.

Grimes was in the buffet preparing to serve the passengers' dinner. She pointed to the glasses and dishes in the racks just above her head.

"Watch . . ."

As she continued with her work I studied the dishes and could find nothing wrong. I was about to turn away when the entire assembly came alive. The dishes clattered together and one glass which Grimes had placed upon the counter skittered across the metal surface until it came to rest against a low partition.

"How about that?" Grimes's manner was accusing, as if I had personally shaken the buffet. "See what I mean?"

I did. I sought through my whole aeronautical past for some logical explanation, needing it as much to reassure myself as Grimes. And I could find nothing. As she continued grimly about her work, I made several limping excuses. The airplane was perfectly all right, but it was far from new, of course. . . . I had noticed similar vibrations in other airplanes when the speed was just so. There was the number three engine to be considered . . . hem and haw. . . . Yes, it *had* to be number three engine and we would certainly give it a going over when we landed in Burbank. In the meantime Grimes should stop worrying about a very expensive airplane and try smiling. The passengers like it. "Think of your future. . . ."

"I am," she said.

I waited several minutes for another cycle of vibrations. The dishes remained still. So when Grimes went forward with a tray, I turned in the opposite direction and climbed through the small door leading to the tail cone. I closed the door after me and switched on the flashlight.

I directed the flashlight beam all around the circular compartment. Here, without benefit of heating or any upholstery, it was cold enough to see my breath. It was an eerie place, the relative silence somehow emphasized by the hushed murmur of the slip stream passing along the fuselage. There was no familiar sensation of flight because the area was windowless; it seemed rather that I stood in one end of a great projectile. We could be moving at fifteen miles an hour or fifteen thousand—the loneliness would have been the same. And it was difficult to remember that beyond such a thin skin there were only stars and ocean.

I straddled the harps of control wires which led through a multiple series of fiber sheaves. I plucked at several, not really expecting to find one loose, but more in curiosity because I had never been in this place before while the airplane was actually flying. In the flashlight beam I saw the various wires move ever so slightly, responding to corrections from the flight deck.

I waited patiently for any hint of vibration and at last decided that if I remained in the cold metallic cocoon any longer, the major shivering would be in myself. Before I returned to the cabin I examined every frame and all of the control wires. They appeared to be in perfect condition.

Grimes was waiting for me. I blew on my hands for warmth and told her that as far as I could determine the tail was still on the airplane.

"You're very funny."

I shrugged my shoulders. I did not like the look in Grimes's eyes because they were being far more honest than my own. She knew I was like a small boy whistling in a great and forbidding forest. If I ignored the goblins they might go away.

As I left her the dishes clattered again.

During the final four hours of the flight the vibration came unpredictably at intervals of five minutes or eight minutes or ten minutes and nothing we could do on the flight deck seemed to influence its arrival in any way. We called San Francisco on the radio and reported that we were experiencing unusual vibration.

"What is the nature of your vibration?"

"We don't know. It is not violent. One of our engines has been acting up."

"Are you going on three-engine operation?"

"Negative."

I wished we had never called in the first place. There was nothing anyone in San Francisco could do. We had, in the calling, instinctively sought assurance of our faith. We had succeeded only in raising eyebrows.

We were delayed a half hour in Burbank while Snow made a thorough inspection of the airplane. He joined with the regular ground mechanics and spent a long time atop a ladder examining the tail. Finally Snow came to operations office and I saw that he was much easier of mind. They had discovered only one very minor defect. An exhaust clamp on number two engine was broken. It had been replaced and was not worth further discussion since it could not possibly have caused any vibration.

Twenty-one of our passengers disembarked at Burbank. The twelve remaining would continue on to Oakland. I passed them at the boarding gate. They were clutching at their precious souvenir leis, and their midnight weariness seemed to have made a total conquest of their spirits. Even their palm-frond hats appeared to droop, so I told them the flight would be swift and they would soon be home in bed. It was a safe enough prediction. With so few aboard, the airplane would be very light and I intended to use the same power required for a full load.

The night was so benevolent and the air so tranquil I chose to fly the entire trip without surrendering the controls. For there was still a deep and sensuous joy in such personal dexterity, in selecting a star to guide upon and causing it to move up or down or slightly to either side at easy will. When we cared to look down there were the diadems of sleeping cities to invigorate our thoughts, and between them even the spaces of little habitation were enlivened by flashing airway beacons.

There was an unusual sensation of speed because the lights slid so quickly beneath, plus the magic awareness of flight, and none of us had ever seen the combination so rightly joined. Hence we were silent nearly all the way, each man wrapped in private counsel, and we found the visual environment subdued all sounds as other atmospheres had never done.

There was no vibration. Our notation in the logbook about a certain trembling now seemed baseless and even a little silly.

Grimes came forward for a cigarette and broke our silence momentarily. She said it was a heavenly night but, when she received no answer, said nothing more.

At eight o'clock in the morning the phone rang at my bedside. I answered with a yawn and at once a voice asked if I had been to church.

I said that I had been up most of the night and was trying to sleep . . . and furthermore I considered the joke ill-timed.

"Well, you'd better do some praying somewhere. Then come to the field."

I recognized the voice of our maintenance chief and protested a mistake. I was officially on vacation.

"It was almost permanent. The outboard hinge bolt of your left elevator was missing. Congratulations. See you shortly."

Because I resented losing even a few hours of a sailing vacation the journey to Oakland Airport seemed endless, and my grumpiness had overtones of self-pity by the time I arrived. I had some bitter things to say about time and tides as I joined the cluster of men now gathered near the tail of the airplane. They showed me the place where the hinge bolt should have been and was not, and it was easy enough to understand how anyone might have passed over its absence—particularly if the inspection occurred at night. I hoped that I had not been brought so far simply to look at the place where a metal pin of one-quarter-inch diameter was supposed to be, but since so many full-grown men affected concern about such a tiny object, I joined in the general head-shaking with all the enthusiasm of a social coward. Actually, the absence or the presence of one innocent little bolt failed to impress me. There were other bolts to keep the elevators where they belonged, and after having flown this same type airplane through all manner of violent turbulence and maneuvers, I was convinced its margin of strength was past my understanding.

When the head-shaking ceased and a written report was requested, I prepared one immediately as a sort of exit visa from the whole affair. Just before I left the airport I learned Coney and Willingham had crashed at Bainbridge. But the facts of the disaster were still few and on that morning it never occurred to any of us that there might be some relation between incident and accident.[15]

Released at last, vastly and happily preoccupied with more gentle elements, I went directly to sea. There I remained blessedly beyond any communication for three weeks.

At the end of this time I put into Los Angeles and there, by chance, joined with Howard at a Chinese restaurant. And he revealed certain surface workings combined with incident which persuaded me there was either marvelous order or sheer anarchy in the house of fate. Otherwise how could I be alive when Coney and Willingham were dead?

Howard might have been Sloniger's twin since both men were wiry, leather-complexioned, and notably sharp of feature. They were so hawklike it was easy to envision them wheeling over any terrain with effortless grace and it was true that both men seemed capable of levitation when confined to a room. Howard was also a very early bird and he affected a thin and dapper mustache in the tradition of the clan. He had lost one leg when the propeller came off his plane in a Bendix race, but he had never lost either his cour-age or enthusiasm for flight. Indeed, his career had greatly pros-pered and he became one of the most respected test pilots in his-tory. His flying skill was complemented by his engineering ability, and his combined talents were deeply involved in the design and proof of the fabulous DC-3 airplane. Later he went on to the DC-4 and was now wet-nursing the DC-6. Thus Howard was a unique figure in American aviation, and if he pronounced an airplane or any device of flight good or bad or indifferent, his views were re-garded most solemnly. Fortunately, there was nothing solemn about Howard.

He approached me slowly and his eyes were so filled with mis-chief I wondered if he had preceded all of us to the Chinese wine. A hand flew upward in a gesture which might have been made by Sloniger. The hand executed the beginning of a chandelle and landed lightly on my shoulder.

"Let me touch you," Howard said. "When we eat I'd like to sit at your side. Maybe some of your luck will drip on me."

He caressed my shoulder and then my arm as if I were some pagan statue and I was exceedingly embarrassed.

"Yes, you're the living proof that it doesn't pay to be overly smart."

My embarrassment turned to bewilderment. I didn't know How-ard well enough to exchange insults.

He led me to the table. "Please . . ." He pulled out a chair and bowed me into it.

Then he sat beside me and drew out a pencil. And while he talked, he made notations and diagrams on the tablecloth, each line and figure neatly set down after his hands had flown their interpretation. He began by saying that my written report on the suspected vibration had been a masterpiece of innocence. He stated flatly that if I had any training as an engineer I would never have had the opportunity to write it. It seemed that only a most remark-able series of causes and effects had kept us from duplicating the catastrophe of Bainbridge. The aura of fantasy was compounded when we considered both had occurred on the same day.

"Did you know we grounded every DC-4 in the world because of you?" he asked.

"I've been sailing. . . ."

"Never giving a thought to vibration, of course."

"No."

"Thank you for completing my picture of blessed ignorance." He frowned and his hands fluttered uncertainly. "But I will never understand your nonchalance. Listen to me very carefully. I've spent too much time on this investigation to miss the finale."

It soon became obvious that Howard's detective work had included my personal anticipations. Even what I had said to the crew and passengers had been remembered and considered.

"Although we can never be absolutely certain, we now believe the Eastern Airline crash at Bainbridge was caused by unporting. Do you know what that is?"

I confessed that I had never heard of it.

"Unporting is the balance destruction of the elevators by aerodynamic force. I won't confuse you with theory, but if enough separation between the fixed and the balance portion of your elevators occurs, your airplane will go into a vertical dive or even beyond the vertical, and no two men in the world are strong enough to bring it out. This can be caused by a missing hinge bolt."

He sighed heavily and drew wavelike lines on the table, then an airplane diving for the lines. He sketched another airplane more precisely and marked its approximate center of gravity. "Did you slow down when you first noticed the vibration? You did not because you had no fear of it. But if you *had* been the nervous type, if you *slowed* down, the center of gravity would have changed. That would have been quite enough to complete the process of unporting which had partially begun."

"The vibration really wasn't very bad."

"It doesn't take much. But let us assume another pilot would have reacted in the same way. It would only have postponed the inevitable. As soon as the time came for a normal power reduction and it was accomplished, unporting would begin. But not you. In the past you had lost all four engines so many times, the prospect of losing one gave you relatively little concern. So you sat there, fat, dumb, and happy, and you canceled all power reductions. This brilliant decision saved your life the *first* time that day."

I could think of nothing to say but a series of well . . . well's.

Howard held up one finger and then raised a second beside it.

"This was not enough," he said, and I saw that he was exasperated. "You landed at Burbank and disembarked twenty-one passengers. God alone knows why, but you took on just enough fuel to make up the difference in losing their weight. Even so your center of gravity would have been changed enough so that unporting was more likely than not. *But . . .*"

He moved a third finger up beside the others.

"You were in a hurry to reach Oakland so you could go about your silly sailing. As a result, and don't try to deny it because the figures are in the logbook, you used full gross weight cruising power all the way and your speed was correspondingly high. . . ." He paused, touched at his mustache, and stared at me incredulously. Then he spoke very slowly, clipping off each word as if he intended to impress them on my memory forever. "I would look at you quite differently if I thought you had planned what we eventually discovered. We had some long sessions with our slide rules and we found, my friend, that you had arranged the *only possible combination of power, speed, and weight* which would blockade the chances of unporting."

Later, when the wine had mellowed us both, I asked Howard if his slide rule could measure the fate of one man against another's.

✵

EPILOGUE

✵

Because of the rain, the wing looked and felt like an ice rink bent in the middle. Braced against the strong wind, I skated awkwardly along its expanse and thought that if I should slip and fall, and in the doing break my neck, then my end would constitute a fitting contrast to Howard's curious revelations. There was, I knew, a certain scheme of natural balances wherein a gift of fortune rarely arrives without setting the style for a subsequent penalty; and I believed that if this equation were not so, then certain people must be continuously and overwhelmingly happy until they lost their senses, while others would suffer such prolonged wretchedness that they must eventually reject both the living state and the will for reproduction. However, I had not been prepared for the balancing twist which had brought me to Wake Island in the middle of the Pacific Ocean. If some orthodox aerial disaster had befallen me, I fancied that my ability to accept the inevitable would have been much more at the ready.

The dire predictions made by Keim from his hospital cot were now fact, and I wondered if his own acquaintance with balances had somehow given him special clairvoyance. For the mighty steamship line had indeed lost great amounts of money striving to become air-borne. The effort crumbled rather than fell all at once, and now the logbooks were left to the moths.

In the last months, even Sloniger's spirit had been stabbed with repeated discouragements. Those departments of our government charged with all matters aeronautical were like children on a teeter-totter. While the CAA praised our technical record and attainments, the CAB at last murdered any hope for an approved franchise across the Pacific. There was nothing left except the back alleys of air transport, which inevitably brought us to the sorry business of flying Puerto Ricans to New York.

This occupation, so sordid and pitiful in every way, soon wrecked the last of our pride. There were repeated attempts by the avaricious agents, whoever they may have been, to load our airplanes far beyond legal limits. These agents absolutely controlled the politically inspired migration. They were paid by the head and were utterly indifferent to the safety or even the most primitive comfort of our hapless passengers. Since the average Puerto Rican is of slight physique two or even three were jammed into the same seat and a single safety belt held them firmly in place. Babies, and there were always many, were not even listed on the passenger manifest. The agents received their head payment all the same.

My last service to what was left of the steamship-airline began in a storm of argument before we ever left the ground. No accommodations whatever had been made for the flight crew, so we found what rest we could sprawling on the grass in a San Juan park. When we reported rumpled and unshaven for the return flight to New York, I found a total of fifty-six passengers crammed into the aircraft. The agent explained that their total weight was very little. And I explained with heat to match the morning's that the total number of life jackets aboard was forty-four and that in the event of an emergency I had no intention of sacrificing my own jacket to anyone, regardless of their weight or appeal. The agent said I was a cruel man. He could not possibly bring himself to remove passengers whose hearts were yearning for bountiful residence in New York. I gave my weary opinion of his sentiments in gutter Spanish. The resulting impasse prevailed for about an hour, after which the agent grudgingly complied.

It was not until we were three hundred miles out of San Juan that we discovered the agent had smuggled two extra souls in the lavatory.

All of this passed without the knowledge of Sloniger, who was far away in California trying desperately to hold the pieces of our tarnished airline together. His efforts were unavailing. The steamship-airline collapsed within weeks and for a time, it seemed, my career expired in sympathy. As Keim had foreseen, pilots who defy the numbers may well become hyenas.

It was no comfort to realize that my lonely howls were not the only ones to be heard. The great red-faced Carter, whose tattoos had so intrigued me in Lester's school, was also seeking an airplane to fly. Another contemporary had lost his license in a moment of sad folly. Strangely enough, a far less able airman, the irrepressible Dudley, had somehow managed to obtain one. We who had known his peculiar verbal magic considered this a grave mistake on the part of the authorities, and we had not long to wait before our fears were confirmed.[16]

My personal eclipse was but a tiny reflection of fate's general disfavor to our kind. In four months these unhappy events occurred:

Hart and McCoy lost one engine over the Syrian desert. Fire broke out when they lost a second engine and their attempt at a crash landing was unsuccessful. Hein and MacKinnon were lost at Melborne, Florida; Davidson and Zundel at La Guardia Field. Vaughan and Humes hit a mountain in Utah, as had so many others, and at Bryce Canyon, McMillan and Griesback failed by seconds to make a safe emergency landing after their DC-6 caught fire in mid-air. In an extraordinary display of courage, McMillan radioed reports until the last moment and his final words were "Looks like we might make it!" Eighteen days later Chatfield, of American Airlines, had exactly the same kind of fire aboard, but his luck was seconds better. He landed safely at Gallup, New Mexico. Finally, at Annette Island, Monsen and Foster perished in a terrible combination of ice, violent turbulence, and very high winds.

Now I stood on the wing, not brooding upon such things but considerably humbled by more immediate affairs. My uniform was second or third hand; I was not exactly sure. It had a peculiarly musty odor, as if the body emanations of former occupants had deliberately lingered to remind me of their similar fears and labors. Since it was the only uniform I could afford, I was grateful that it at least seemed to fit reasonably well. For I was once again a co-pilot, and a very lowly co-pilot with a number no one could envy. My thousands of hours of command, my more than a million miles of flight, helped me to get the job and no more. I might just as well have been back with Ross on AM-21. Better, perhaps. For in those eager times this wing-walking on a wild night would have seemed easier.

I had managed at last to join a new family and the numbers were once again in charge. But the family was not very high on the aeronautical social scale. We were in cold fact the equivalent of privateers, and our letters of marque were vague and most temporary. Our chieftain was Nelson, a true throwback to individual Yankee enterprise.

The circumstances which had defeated the lords of a powerful steamship line were only an additional challenge to a man like Nelson, who had deliberately forsaken a long and honorable career flying with United Airlines and started his own. By connivance, prayers, persuasion, and sheer determination, Nelson had managed to obtain airplanes as well as the men to fly and maintain them. He found cargo wherever he could—immigrants from Italy to Venezuela, Mohammedans to Mecca, displaced persons to Canada, soldiers to here or there, and fishermen to the Bering Sea.[17]

It was such a great and wonderful and continuous madness that the only surprise remaining was an on-time arrival of our pay checks. Pan American jeered at first, then complained to the government with practiced authority. The financing was so confused and unorthodox no one could understand how Nelson had the nerve to continue. It was freely said that his airline went out of existence once a week. In a very large and modern way, this airline operated exactly as the very first pioneering lines had done. The captains had absolute autonomy, carrying rolls of cash to buy fuel when credit was refused, personally arranging cargoes when they could, flying rugs from Persia or cane furniture from Manila—anything to meet the mortgage payments on the airplanes.

Nelson recruited his pilots from everywhere. It was natural that such an enterprise attracted the more individualistic type of men; some because there was no other opportunity, and others because they simply believed in Nelson. If a man could truly fly and was persistent in his applications, he stood a good chance of finding employment somewhere in Nelson's shaky empire. There was also a good chance of being furloughed the following week as one project or another expired.

Nelson suited his traditional Yankee-trader role in every old-time aspect. He stood well over six feet and was bold and quick of movement. The firmness of his jaw was emphasized by his thin lips, which compressed to a razor cut when he was angry. He had never touched tobacco and was a strict teetotaler. As a consequence his hard blue eyes would become merciless on discovering any dissipation among his flight crews. Yet a man's behavior had to be outrageous before Nelson would actually dismiss him. The results were often interesting, for his crews were anything but innocent and not given to penitence. Even so, their rancor was without malice and was reserved for members of the family. Nelson's

men swore by, as well as at, him, and outside commentators were
often fiercely advised to mind their own businesses.

Here on Wake Island, which was in truth only a lonely atoll of
coral and scrub bush, I had come to appreciate Nelson's quixotic
imagination, even though what I could see from my station on the
wing was limited by the driving rain.

Pan American had landed their first Pacific Clipper planes in
the lagoon at Wake and ever since had proclaimed the island as
their special domain. All invaders were actively discouraged unless
they paid high tribute. When Nelson discovered the Pan American
rights were unofficial he took over a collection of derelict shacks on
the western side of the island and squatted there. To Pan American's dismay he soon had an operating base, complete with all the
necessary impedimenta for quartering crews and serving his airplanes in transit. Thus the island was effectively divided into two
camps and the people of one rarely visited those in the other.

From Wake, Nelson's ships took out across the Pacific for
Tokyo, Hong Kong, Saigon, Manila, Guam, or Honolulu if they
were Orient-bound. There was no established schedule or routes.
If a cargo was destined for Saigon or Taiwan, Nelson's men took it
there, though they might never have seen the place before in their
flying lives. And the going was always without question.

Such erratic and unique operation demanded men of special
aeronautical virtues or else chaos would rule and disaster be inevitable. Nelson's airline was no place for the doctrinal pilot, nor
for those who, with the quick maturing of aviation, had already
bundled their spirits in the fat of security. Hence there were men
like Word, whose appearance and bustling manner would have
better suited a small-town hotel clerk—until it was possible to look
into the depths of his ever restless eyes and there apprehend, even
for a fleeting moment, a true slave of adventure. There was
Mathias, who was sometimes called "the magnificent" because of
his stature and physical beauty. Both of these men were to be
victimized by fate, perhaps in revenge for their constant teasing of
its power.

There was Rogers, a heavy, taciturn man who eventually became our chief pilot. There was always a certain inner sadness about Rogers and a way of shifting from the sternest demands upon his pilots to an air of remote indifference. It was as if he knew exactly how unavailing his personal skill and knowledge would be during those precious seconds when his end was determined.

There was Buckelew, whose formidable, rocklike appearance fulfilled every popular conception of an airline pilot, and Turner, whose easy jollity concealed a most astute technician. There was the wonderfully volatile Zottarelli, who frequently affected the roll of a bumbling clown chased by machinery quite beyond his control. Yet we knew Zottarelli's protests of inadequacy were but another form of humility and, knowing his true skill, applauded his histrionics.

There was Keating, whose face and bend of head was like that of a weary hound until he smiled, at which time the very pigment of his skin appeared to glow and his enthusiasm for everything that flew and all the world aloft became intoxicating.

There was Hennessy, known to some as "Three Star" and to others as "Cyrano," for his nose was a monument and it was inconceivable that he could see around it. Two thick and defiantly shaped hair hedges composed his eyebrows and below these his eyes glittered with some constant and often secret amusement. His speech was staccato, effervescent, and quite as quick as his wit. His heart was as full and warm and as sticky with sentiment as that of his literary nicknamesake.

I was very grateful that Hennessy was now my captain. He understood my predicament and made a great and hilarious business of treating me as if I were the rawest of co-pilots. It was the kindest thing he could possibly have done. Mocking his own rightful pride, he managed to rescue mine. "I have heard," he would say, "that every runway in the world has permanent dents from your landings. I have heard you are on the cement companies' payrolls. But I suppose you'll never learn unless you keep trying." Whereupon he would surrender his left-hand seat and allow me to be a pilot in command again.

Later, when my duties on the wing had been completed, I joined Hennessy in the cockpit. As we began the complex ritual of checking instruments and controls, our voices rose in a monotonous chant of command and acknowledgment. Our accompaniment was the snare-drum sound of the rain lashing at the thin metal surrounding us. Finally Hennessy pulled at his magnificent nose and said, "Well, here we go again." He spoke flatly, his voice devoid of either anticipation or reluctance. His words came as a mere formality, the accepted conclusion of our ceremony.

How easily he dismissed the vast ocean and sky in the night beyond. The rain was a triviality. All things were a triviality if we were not earth-bound. Even the wind would only hasten our casual departure.

Behind Hennessy's brief announcement there were many things left unsaid. Now here was work to be done—loved even though it no longer carried the trappings of conquest. This, which we were about to do, was also a thing of peculiar value, and our behavior in the few quick years of transformation had already become traditional. What little flavor of hazard remained was no more than a spicing of our now natural labors, an ingredient without which we should have been secretly discontent.

Now, as we started the engines, we did so as men might open an office or a factory. All errant thoughts were swept away by our professional absorption in this single endeavor. We knew of fate and how it might dispose our fortunes, but actual consideration of its influence would not come until later, if on a single flight it came at all. When we had climbed through the rain and found the stars, when comfortably on course at last, there would be relatively little to engage our thoughts. Then, perhaps, in the passing hours, Hennessy might touch upon the matter either directly or obtusely. He might massage his nose in a sly fashion and, eyes twinkling, confide in me. "All I want is another ten years of this—no more. Then I'm headed for a cabin in the mountains . . . permanent-like."

It would be a dream upon a dream, composed of all the same elements envisioned by so many other pilots. It was always a cabin in the mountains, a nice little chicken farm, a mushroom cave, or a fishing concession on some quiet lake. It was always something to keep a man firmly rooted in one place—always a project in which fate would seldom be a partner.

When we were almost halfway betwixt Wake Island and Honolulu, the same region in which Word would eventually meet his end, I went back to the crew compartment for a cup of coffee. The jug was on a shelf adjacent to the washbasin. Over the basin there was a mirror. Now, holding a paper cup to the coffee spigot, I could not avoid the specter in the mirror which I reluctantly recognized as my own face. It was too old a face for a co-pilot and it more than ever resembled the canvas flight bag now resting on the lower bunk. I turned to examine the bag and saw more clearly than ever before how punishment by weather from the arctic to the desert and the rotten air of the tropics had given it a look of utter resignation. The handle was calloused and limp, and the leather of its underside smudged black with the flesh oil of my hand. At one end of the handle the steel ring had cut halfway through the leather. I had been waiting for it to give way at my next hoist, but so far it had always held. There was a tear in the canvas where it rounded to form the bottom of the bag, and I knew this wound would never heal. And the strap which should hold the two containing halves together had vanished long ago. Both rumpled and dumpy faces of the bag were stained and spotted with the residue of a thousand floors, greasy airport ramps, conveyance trucks, and filthy flight decks. I was sorry about the bag, for I loved it. I was even sorrier we were beginning to look so much alike. And since I had never been able to develop any interest in an orange grove or a mushroom cave, I wondered how much longer such a sad bag would be my official residence.

But the bag held together for this flight with Hennessy, and then another and then another until there was recorded in my logbook almost ten thousand hours of flying time.

The numbers had become extremely capricious, so that I sometimes flew as co-pilot and on occasions as a captain. And there were many weeks when I could not fly at all because there was not enough work to accommodate my number. These periods were called furloughs. Pilots of low seniority on Nelson's airline were accustomed to such quick changes.

In these dismal times we sought comfort in the belief that unity among the wealthy and established lacks the strength of those still hungry. Most people in the established airlines regarded us as tramps with unwarranted pretensions, but in many ways this attitude became a tonic to our urge for survival. Even the rascals among us became dedicated and in time we earned a certain, if grudging, respect. We were allowed, as itinerant beggars, to trespass any sky we could afford although there was not a slim strip we could call our own.

So the economic alarm bell continued to ring constantly until the Korean War began.

Then the scene in the Pacific was again transformed, and Nelson's line above all others found its scattered and various services in much demand.

There was more bitterness than rejoicing. All of us recognized at least temporary survival, but the majority were depressed at the all too familiar nature of our salvation. We saw again the sticky, cosmolined instruments of national depravity loaded aboard the very airplanes we had hoped to fly in peace. And once again there were the leavings of combat carried aboard for the return trip from Japan. Our flights became a melancholy repetition of a certain nightmare in which all very young men used four-letter words continuously, and all very young men were of the same bewildered face, and all very young men wore some raveling of bandage or molding of plaster, and all very young men felt abused and cheated for reasons beyond their comprehension.

So we flew without exhilaration, regaining our spirit only when the fighting had ceased.

During this period, Warren and Irwin were lost near Fairbanks. A blizzard and seventy-below temperatures so hampered rescue operations that the wreckage was not found for a month. A flight from the Orient piloted by Pfaffinger and Kuhn terminated in the ice-cold waters of Hecate Strait. Then Reid and Indicello suddenly slipped off the radar screen while they were making a ground-controlled approach to Newark Airport. It should have been an easy approach. There was no satisfactory explanation for their failure. Three weeks later Foster and St. Clair were climbing out of the same airport. A propeller reversed. The ship went out of control. So ended. But there was no technical reason why the reversal occurred when thousands upon thousands of identical propellers had long operated to perfection.

Then Grossarth and Penn vanished near the same jungle region where Gillette and I had trouble but better fortune. It took weeks to find the wreckage and determine that the ship had disintegrated while still in the air. The basic reasons why number two engine separated from the wing and precipitated the disaster will never be known.

Now we were chiefly engaged in a six-thousand-mile shuttle service between California and Japan. The large majority of our cargoes were involved with the military although the smell of cosmoline and ether was gone. Instead, we carried dependents, and the atmosphere in the passenger cabin was expectant and gay. We carried thirty-four babies in one of my flights. Someone had thoughtfully provided the mothers with balloons and we had hardly reached cruising altitude before the cabin was in happy pandemonium.

These were pleasant days and nights, full of prospect and satisfaction. Nelson's eternal optimism was infectious. So we dared to hope for permanency and all fortune appeared to favor us. I even managed to maintain a tenuous hold on my captaincy, and there were very few distresses for anyone. My logbook recorded the occasional loss of an engine in flight, and twice there were hydraulic difficulties. But these were things to be expected. They occurred without special crisis and were no more prevalent than they might have been on any other line.

As if to balance such serenity, there was an occasion when Zottarelli turned over an airplane to me at Wake Island. It was loaded entirely with mailbags bound for Japan, and Zottarelli complained that it would not fly. In his volatile way he described how his crew had heaved the heavy mail sacks both forward and back, hoping a change in the center of gravity might improve the ship's performance. There had been no appreciable change.

Oliver, a dispatcher at Wake who had been with the R.A.F., leaned across the operations counter and said, "I told Orville Wright and I told Wilbur Wright the thing would never leave the ground. It's against the laws of nature."

And since this was a litany of the profession, and because Oliver's humor was noted for its acidity, we all laughed together. It was of no matter that we had heard such nonsense before. And Zottarelli said that some little old mother had mailed a birthday cake to her son in Japan and if we decided to toss the bags around we should be careful not to smash the cake. And we made several bad jokes about how he knew the mother was little and old and how miraculous it was that any cake could survive Zottarelli's greedy appetite.

I saw the cake placed carefully atop the mail sacks as I passed forward to the flight deck.

The take-off was a shock. The trade wind had expired and we stumbled off the very end of the runway. When the tenseness left me I thought of the Taj Mahal and a hot day in India. Once again I had instinctively tried to lift tons with my leg muscles.

We waddled up from the level of the sea and finally reached cruising altitude. I knew this particular ship had a reputation for sluggishness, but no one had ever reported its behavior as dangerous.

We slobbed along for hours and by using extra power eventually descended for Tokyo. The instant I eased off power for the final approach we sank like a gluttonous duck. We barely made the end of the runway. After we had left the ship I complained so bitterly of its performance that the army began an investigation. By the following morning we learned how a tragi-comedy of errors had occurred far back in California.

The ship had been loaded once, with its proper cargo of mail. Lunch hour came for the original loaders just as the job was completed. They went away. A second crew of loaders arrived with an equal batch of mail. Except for the numbers on the tail, one airplane looked exactly like another. The second crew was also impatient with hunger and, in their haste, neglected to check the numbers. So they loaded a second cargo upon the original and hastened away to fill their bellies.

The cake, only two days from some mother's oven, arrived in perfect condition. Its successful delivery was fated against an overload of twenty thousand pounds. And I thought of Ross's mother in the now so long ago.

On an October night, aloft once again between Honolulu and the mainland, my everlasting dispute with the numbers approached sheer fury. For beside me there sat a man victimized by the numbers, else he would never have been my co-pilot.

This man was Howe, whose name was nearly a legend. He was a contemporary of Sloniger's and there was in his logbook over seventeen thousand honest hours. Howe had barnstormed in Jennies, flown the mail with Lindbergh, and stayed faithfully with his devotion until at last, it seemed, he had saved enough to retire. But his business skill failed to match his flying ability. So now this veteran, returned to the only way of life in which he was a true master, was obliged to serve as my co-pilot. The most simple arithmetic argued against his flying captain again until he was a hundred years old.

Because Howe had been flying when I was in knee pants, our relationship was both difficult and embarrassing. It was like an upstart peasant commanding a prince of the realm and Howe's gratitude for my respect seemed only to make matters worse.

It was brilliant night and I had turned the cockpit light far down so that the luster of the moon would permeate the cockpit and for a little time, at least, relieve the hypnotic sensation of being stared at by the instruments. But my will to enjoy the night was divided when I discovered that Howe's face in the glow of the moon had taken on a statuelike quality, as if it had been forged and then pounded into final shape from a solid block of iron. There were intricate spheres and planes of cold light which seemed to daub his face with verdigris in the way of memorial masks long exposed to the elements. This strange luminosity combined with deep shadows and so chiseled each feature that his eyes appeared only as hollow and empty depths beneath the heavy corrugations of his brow. And his nose, which in daytime lacked any special character, now resembled the beak of an eagle. His lips were a hard black line, and a final trick of the moon set a highlight below the crevass of his chin so that it took on a pugnacious look.

All of this was a deception, I knew, because in daylight Howe's face suggested no such character. Actually he was the mildest of men, so shy and soft-spoken as to be almost self-effacing. If there was any remarkable quality about his face it was his eyes, which were extraordinarily compassionate and often suggested that he had suffered some great hurt. The wrinkles and crinkles of a lifetime aloft were all engraved in their proper places upon his face and they gave to Howe a look of virility unusual for his age. The effect would not bear study. It took only a little time to sense that Howe was weary deep within himself. It seemed the long contest of flying had consumed his energies and he had been left only with his love.

Yet now, in the moonlight, he seemed the symbol of the hard-bitten veteran. He was the true professional, challenging the greatest expanses of the atmosphere. He was helmet and goggles, fabric-covered wings, Wright Whirlwind engines, leather and oil. He was of cow-pasture landings and loops over Sunday crowds; he was of Curtis Condors, and the strumming of flying wires. There was now a special determination in the cant of his head, the fighting pose of a pilot in bad weather when instruments were new and help from the ground unavailing. He was distance and height and independence in a lonely sky—and he was uncertainty and sadness because too many of his comrades were lost to inexplicable fortune. He was wind and rain, thunder and terror, humility and pride. In this magically illuminated moment, Howe was all of these things, though only a trifle of his soul could be seen.

I waited for the image to fade, watching Howe's face while he flew on in silence. Suddenly, I knew that I was pitying him, and the realization disgusted me. How soon would some younger man regard me in the same light? Another five years perhaps—or even ten? Unless he was pressed, Howe was not the kind to speak of his own twistings away from fate. But I knew there had to be many, each subtracting a quantity from the balance of his luck. He would have had his Syracuse, his icing over Nashville, his Reykjaviks, his fires, his rebellious engines, his outlaws in the night, and possibly even his structural failures. He had known Watkins and Gay and Hunt and Charleton and Miller and a great many more so fated because his time was longer. He had known Keim, Hughen, O'Connor, Ross, and McCabe. He had known the indestructible Lester, the patchwork man who had first schooled me in airline flying. And what of Lester? Only recently he had driven his hunting dogs to a field trial. En route, he had collided with a truck. Not even the experts could put him together again.

Tell me now, Howe, since you are older and wiser, by what ends does a man ever partially control his fate? It is obvious from the special history of our kind that favorites are played, but if this is so, then how do you account for those who are ill-treated? The worship of pagan gods, which once answered all this, is no longer fashionable. Modern religions ignore the matter of fate. So we are left confused and without direction.

Let us admit, then, that the complete answer may only be revealed when it can no longer serve those most interested.

Perhaps we should hide in childlike visions of afterlife wherein those pronounced good may play upon harps and those pronounced evil, stoke fires. Or credit the devil, as the Dutchman preferred in Corumbá.

At least let us admit that the pattern of anyone's fate is only partly contrived by the individual. And let us now remember that a wealthy gambler once said the essence of his success was in knowing when to quit.

Ah, Howe, you of the iron face . . . when is when?

I turned up the lights and once again the instruments took up their staring and Howe became only Howe. There was the sadness, the weariness, the near-resignation. He turned to me and smiled.

"Nice night. . . ."

And from the special warmth in his eyes I thought he knew what I had been thinking. So I told him without elaboration that I had a silly notion which I intended to honor. For me, when was now.

And Howe seemed to understand.

Perhaps Howe understood better than I supposed my decision to set down the old flight bag for the last time. For fate allowed him only a little longer.

He lived aboard a small boat in Ala Wai Harbor, Honolulu. He rowed away in his dinghy one day, bound on some minor errand. The dinghy was found. Howe was not.

✿

NOTES

✿

1. Ross wore this cap in defiance of all authorities for several years. Polite pleas, attempts at ridicule, even threats of discharge, failed to make him exchange it. No one knows what finally caused him to surrender. It was a rather sad day when he eventually complied.
2. Not always. Captain Smith, of Delta Airlines, suffered this identical misfortune. Yet the take-off was accomplished, a climb made to safe altitude, and the flight continued to destination Atlanta some 370 miles distant. Arrival was seven minutes ahead of schedule.

There was no damage except to the propeller tips and, of course, to Smith's nerves and the passengers' serenity.

3. One testimony to the integral strength of airliners. A TWA ship inadvertently struck what is believed to have been a waterspout between the Azores and Newfoundland. The plane, a Douglas DC-4, was flipped over on its back and assumed a vertical power dive far in excess of its maximum allowable speed before control was regained. Although fuselage and wings were so twisted the plane had to be junked on arrival, it returned safely to the Azores. There are many other such proofs.

4. Printed lists had not yet been conceived. Too bad. The mind of man was not designed to remember everything in a modern cockpit. It was remarkable, and sometimes tragic, how many things *two* minds could forget—even such obvious matters as ascertaining whether the engines were drawing fuel from a full tank on take-off.

5. The Canadian Pacific. This was in a sense the true beginning of world flights by Canadian Pacific.

6. One of the strangest "crashes" in aviation history occurred on the icecap when the pilots of a PBY elected to fly across, relying entirely on their senses. Their first indication that anything was awry came through a lack of sound and air speed. With engines turning at full cruising speed, they literally flew on to the icecap, touching it so lightly at first that their speed was gradually reduced until they were at a standstill. Fortunately, they had slid upon a smooth area, and when they finally realized their predicament, they stepped out laughing into the snow. Their laughter was short-lived. They were very much alone with a useless flying machine and were a long time being rescued.

7. Now known as "Thule," a refueling place for present transpolar flights.

8. Although superficially the same, the C-87's described herein were *not* the same as the "Liberator" transports flown by the R.A.F. and a few fortunate American units. The true "Lib" had more powerful engine superchargers and consequently performed better in every way.

9. Years later we learned this was due to the tremendous mineral deposits in the region. The area near the Wynn Mountains was surveyed after the war by a magnitometer plane, which reported

similar findings. The site of the great new Canadian iron range not far from our actual course was one of the eventual consequences.

10. This report is in my aviation file and runs over two pages. Its essence is that the plugs were not much good for anything—which was hardly news to us. It was submitted without apology.

11. Captain Parmentier finally closed his impressive logbook forever. Returning to KLM service after the war, he crashed in Java.

Smirnoff flew twenty years between Amsterdam and Batavia mostly in Fokkers. He was shot down by a Japanese Zero off western Australia but survived.

Travers made the first commercial air crossing of the Indian Ocean.

Jones was a captain on Imperial Airways from its inception to his retirement in 1955. In 1951 he flew the Queen (then Princess Elizabeth) and the Duke of Edinburgh to Canada.

Kelly-Rogers commanded the first British transatlantic air-mail flight, the first transatlantic passenger service, and Churchill's three flights to America in 1942.

Captain Freng finally retired from active flying in 1957, at which time his total hours amounted to almost 28,000. On the occasion of his retirement an airplane was named in his honor.

Knight initiated the first transcontinental air mail using bonfires as beacons.

12. The lady was Ingrid Bergman.

13. The lady was Marlene Dietrich.

14. A TWA airplane on a training flight had a nearly identical fire in the baggage compartment. The pilots tried a quick crash landing. But the smoke blinded them. All were killed except Captain Brown, the instructor.

15. Coincidence seemed to be in full charge this thirtieth day of May. Most air disasters become especially difficult to solve since technically expert witnesses to the actual event are rarely available. Not so, this time. Some three miles behind the Eastern Airliner, in an ideal position for observation, there flew another airplane. It belonged to the *Civil Aeronautics Board!* The pilot and co-pilot were board personnel and witnessed the entire dive. As if this were not enough coincidence, the passengers aboard included the *Chief of the Safety Bureau's Accident Investigation Division.*

16. After Dudley obtained his license, his incredible persuasiveness

once more put him in command, this time of a regularly scheduled airliner. The inevitable happened when he was faced with a difficult weather approach and a landing on a rain-swept runway. Reverting to his former practice, he overshot, the plane skidded off the end of the runway and caught fire. Dudley escaped. But many of his passengers were lost. Guilt for the tragedy apparently haunted Dudley's already unstable mind, until at last he took his own life.

17. Some of his crews flew antiquated PBY's through the trust territories of the South Pacific, while others reactivated Japan Airlines. Others did the same for Philippine Airlines. Nelson built a bridge in California and bought a broom factory in Minnesota, although no one could discover how either of these projects had anything whatsoever to do with an airline that was literally staging a daily fight for its life.

Other Nelson projects at the time: a world-wide import-export business . . . an automobile agency on Okinawa . . . a restaurant operation at various airports . . . an instrument flight testing program at Arcata, California, one of the foggiest locations in America . . . a ground school at Oakland . . . and several et cetera's. Nelson's remarkably positive attitude toward all things whether on the ground or in the air was maintained with continuous aplomb in spite of the fact that many of these projects had a hard time surviving financially.